Financial Services Modernization

Gramm-Leach-Bliley Act of 1999

Law and Explanation

Kenneth R. Benson, J.D.
Katalina M. Bianco, J.D.
James Hamilton, J.D., LL.M.
John M. Pachkowski, J.D.
Richard A. Roth, J.D.
Andrew A. Turner, J.D.

CCH
CCH INCORPORATED
Chicago

This publication is designed to provide accurate and authoritative information in regard to the subject matter covered. It is sold with the understanding that the publisher is not engaged in rendering legal, accounting or other professional service. If legal advice or other expert assistance is required, the services of a competent professional person should be sought.

ISBN 0-8080-0449-2

4025 W. Peterson Ave.
Chicago, IL 60646-6085
1 800 248 3248
http://www.cch.com

FOREWORD

FINANCIAL SERVICES MODERNATION—GRAMM-LEACH-BLILEY ACT OF 1999 consists of three principal parts: (1) a comprehensive explanation of the legislation; (2) the text of the Act; and (3) the Conference Report embodying the final compromise before passage. In addition, a list of effective dates is at ¶ 1 and a table of statutes added or amended can be found at ¶ 2. The explanation begins with an overview of the Act at ¶ 51 and a chronology of banking reform at ¶ 75, followed by a detailed explanation of each of the seven titles in the Act.

To facilitate research, the explanations are back-referenced to the applicable law and Conference Report sections. Each section of the book is prefaced by a detailed table of contents. A topical index begins on page 283.

About the Act

Signed into law by President Clinton on November 12, 1999, the Gramm-Leach-Bliley Act represents the most sweeping reform of financial services regulation in over sixty years. The Act permits the creation of new financial services holding companies that can offer a full range of financial products under a strong regulatory regime based on the principle of functional regulation. The legislation eliminates legal barriers to affiliations among banks and securities firms, insurance companies, and other financial services companies. The Act provides financial organizations with flexibility in structuring these new financial affiliations through a holding company structure or a financial subsidiary, with appropriate safeguards.

The Act preserves the role of the Federal Reserve Board as the umbrella supervisor for holding companies while at the same time incorporating a system of functional regulation designed to utilize the strengths of the various federal and state regulators. It also sets up a mechanism for coordination between the Federal Reserve Board and the Secretary of the Treasury regarding the approval of new financial activities for both holding companies and national bank financial subsidiaries.

Gramm-Leach-Bliley also establishes, for the first time, a minimum federal standard of financial privacy. Financial institutions are required to have written privacy policies that must be disclosed to customers. The disclosure of a financial institution's privacy policy must take place at the time a customer relationship is established and not less than annually during the continuation of the relationship.

The Act also provides for the functional regulation of bank securities activities. The Act repeals the blanket exemption banks have enjoyed from the definition of "broker" and replaces it with a set of limited exemptions that allow the continuation of some traditional activities performed by banks. Similarly, the Act amends the Exchange Act to include banks within the general definition of dealer. The bank exclusion from the definition of investment adviser is also eliminated

It is expected that many complex new products will be developed with both banking and securities elements. The Act provides a procedure for handling new hybrid products sold by banks that have securities elements. The statute provides for a "jump ball" rulemaking and resolution process between the SEC and the Federal Reserve Board regarding new hybrid products, with a federal appeals court as final arbiter.

November 1999

CCH EDITORIAL STAFF

Explanations

Andrew A. Turner, J.D., Managing Editor

Kenneth R. Benson, J.D.

Katalina M. Bianco, J.D.

James Hamilton, J.D., LL.M.

John M. Pachkowski, J.D.

Richard A. Roth, J.D.

Production

Georgelen Kuhn

Karen Pavletich

Evelyn Reid

Edward M. Rubin

David Vanderway

Annette Wilk

TABLE OF CONTENTS

EFFECTIVE DATES

¶ 1

The chart shows the effective dates of the provisions in the Act in parenthesis following a description of the subject matter involved. The list also shows the Sections of the Gramm-Leach-Bliley Act containing the effective date provision and the paragraph number where the law text is located. Provisions become effective immediately unless otherwise specifically stated in the Act.

Sec.	Subject (Effective Date)	Law Text ¶
	Title I	
161	Facilitating affiliation among banks, securities firms, and insurance companies—other than Section 104 pertaining to operation of state law (3-11-00)	1161
	Title II, Subtitle A	
209	Functional regulation of brokers and dealers (5-12-01)	1209
	Title II, Subtitle B	
225	Functional regulation of bank investment company activities (5-12-01)	1225
	Title III, Subtitle B	
316	Redomestication of mutual insurers (11-12-99)	1316
	Title V, Subtitle A	
504(a)(3)	Final rulemaking concerning disclosure of personal information (5-12-00)	1504
506	Protection of the Fair Credit Reporting Act (11-12-99)	1506
510	Disclosure of nonpublic personal information—other than Sections 504 and 506 (6 months after rule adoptions)	1510
	Title VI (Selected Provisions)	
603	Federal Home Loan Bank membership (5-12-00)	1603
604(c)	Federal Home Loan Bank access (3 year waiting period)	1604
607(b)	Payments to the Resolution Funding Corporation (1-1-00)	1607
	Title VII (Selected Provision)	
736(b)	Elimination of SAIF and DIF special reserves (11-12-99)	1736

TABLE OF STATUTES ADDED OR AMENDED

¶ 2

The Gramm-Leach-Bliley Act of 1999 affected many existing federal banking and securities laws and provided many new provisions to accommodate new supervisory functions and responsibilities of federal banking and securities agencies. The chart below lists in alphabetical order the existing banking and securities laws affected by provisions of the Act. The list reflects the subject matter of each change and shows the paragraph number where the law text is located.

Sec.	Subject	Law Text ¶
	Act to Enable National Banking Associations to Increase Their Capital Stock and to Change Their Names or Locations	
2(d)	Converted federal savings association	1723
	Bank Holding Company Act of 1956	
2(a)(5)(E)(i)	Control of bankers' banks	1724
2(c)(2)(H)	Overdrafts of industrial loan companies	1107
2(n)	Incorporated definitions	1103
2(o)(1)(A)	Definition of insured depository institutions	1119
2(p)	Definition of financial holding company (new)	1103
2(q)	Definition of insurance company (new)	1103
3(f)	Savings bank subsidiaries of bank holding companies (repealed)	1118
3(g)(2)	Regulation of mutual bank holding companies	1105
4(c)(8)	Activity restrictions applicable to bank holding companies that are not financial holding companies	1102
4(f)(2)	Loss of the grandfather exemption	1107
4(f)(3)	Permissible overdrafts (new)	1107
4(f)(3)	Limitation on nonbank banks controlled by grandfathered companies (stricken)	1107
4(f)(4)	Divestiture in the case of loss of the grandfather exemption	1107
4(f)(14)	Foreign bank subsidiaries of limited purpose credit card banks	1107
4(j)	Notice procedures regarding engaging in activities with nonbanking organizations	1103
4(k)	Engaging in activities with nonbanking organizations that are financial in nature	1103
4(l)	Conditions for engaging in expanded financial activities with nonbanking organizations	1103
4(m)	Financial holding companies that fail to meet certain requirements	1103
4(n)	Authority to retain limited non-financial activities and affiliations	1103
4(o)	Regulation of certain financial holding companies	1103

Sec.	Subject	Law Text ¶
46	Safety and soundness firewalls applicable to financial subsidiaries of banks	1121
47	Insurance customer protections (new)	1305
48	Public disclosure of agreements made under Community Reinvestment Act of 1977 (new)	1711

Federal Home Loan Bank Act

Sec.	Subject	Law Text ¶
2, para. 1	Definitions of "Board" and "Finance Board"	1602
2, para. 3	Definition of "State"	1602
2, para. 13	Definition of "Community Finance Institution"	1602
2B(a)(5)	Powers and duties of Federal Housing Finance Board	1606
2B(a)(6)	Powers and duties of Federal Housing Finance Board	1606
2B(a)(7)	Powers and duties of Federal Housing Finance Board	1606
4(a)(2)(A)	Eligibility for Federal Home Loan Bank membership	1605
4(a)(4)	Limited exemption for community financial institutions	1605
6	Capital structure of Federal Home Loan banks	1608
7(a)	Board of directors	1606
7(d)	Term of directors' service	1606
7(g)	Election of chairman and vice-chairman (new)	1606
7(g)	Designation of chairman and vice-chairman (stricken)	1606
7(i)	Compensation of chairman and vice-chairman	1606
9	Eligibility to secure advances	1606
10(a)	Authorization to make secured advances	1604
10(c)	Authorization to make secured advances	1606
10(d)	Authorization to make secured advances	1606
10(e)	Qualified thrift lender status (stricken)	1604
12	Management of banks	1606
16(a)	Accumulation and maintenance of reserves	1606
18(b)(4)	Transition provision for assessments of administrative expenses (stricken)	1606
21B(f)(2)(C)	Payments by Federal Home Loan banks to the Resolution Funding Corporation	1607
22A	Eligibility for membership (stricken)	1606
27	Housing opportunity hotline program (stricken)	1606

Federal Power Act

Sec.	Subject	Law Text ¶
305(b)	Public utilities	1737

Federal Reserve Act

Sec.	Subject	Law Text ¶
9, para. 8 (last sentence)	Authorization to release reports	1727
9, para. 20	Dealing in investment securities	1121
11(m)	Stock loan limit (repealed)	1735
11B	Annual independent audits	1726
23A(b)(11)	Rebuttable presumption of control of portfolio companies	1121
23A(e)	Rules relating to banks with financial subsidiaries (new)	1121

Sec.	Subject	Law Text ¶

Public Law 93-495

111	Independence of financial regulatory agencies	1606

Revised Statutes (National Bank Act)

5136, para. 7	Authority of National Banks to underwrite municipal bonds	1151
5136A	Financial subsidiaries of national banks (new)	1121
5136B	Participation by national banks in lotteries and related activities (redesignated)	1121

Riegle Community Development and Regulatory Improvement Act of 1994

171	Provision of assistance to microenterprises (new)	1725
172	Definitions (new)	1725
173	Establishment of program (new)	1725
174	Uses of assistance (new)	1725
175	Qualified organizations (new)	1725
176	Allocation of assistance (new)	1725
177	Matching requirements (new)	1725
178	Applications for assistance (new)	1725
179	Recordkeeping requirements (new)	1725
180	Authorization of funds (new)	1725
181	Implementation (new)	1725

Riegle-Neal Interstate Banking and Branching Efficiency Act of 1994

109(e)(4)	Definition of out-of-state bank	1106

Right to Financial Privacy Act of 1978

1101(7)	Definition of "supervisory agency"	1727
1112(e)	Authorization of exchange of financial records or other information	1231
1112(e)	Authorization of exchange of financial records or other information	1727

Securities Act of 1933

3(a)(2)	Bank common trust funds	1221

Securities Exchange Act of 1934

3(a)(4)	Definition of "broker"	1201
3(a)(5)	Definition of "dealer"	1202
3(a)(12)(A)	Bank common trust funds	1221
3(a)(34)(H)	Definition of "appropriate regulatory agency"	1231
3(a)(42)	Definition of "Government Securities"	1208
3(a)(54)	Definition of "Qualified Investor"	1207
15(i)	Regulatory treatment of new hybrid products (new)	1205
15A(j)	Registration for sale of private offerings (new)	1203

Explanation—Table of Contents

FINANCIAL SERVICES MODERNIZATION

Explanation

Introduction

¶51 Overview of the Gramm-Leach-Bliley Act of 1999

More than 60 years after legislators first laid out a structure for banking in the United States, Congress finally took action to broaden the scope of financial services that banks are able to offer to consumers. Passage of financial services modernization legislation, known as the Gramm-Leach-Bliley Act, removes Depression-era barriers that had separated banks and securities firms. Enactment of the legislation makes it easier for affiliations between banks, securities firms and insurance companies to take place. The new financial "supermarket" is expected to give consumers the option of "one stop shopping" for bank accounts, insurance policies and securities transactions.

After decades of Congressional false starts and half-measures, Congress finally succeeded in repealing the barriers that had prevented affiliations between the banking, securities and insurance industries. The fundamental overhaul of the ground rules for banks, thrifts, brokerages, and insurance companies became reality when President Clinton signed the legislation on Nov. 12, 1999. The Act is divided into seven titles.

Financial Affiliations

Title I facilitates affiliations among banks, securities firms and insurance companies. Financial organizations are able to structure these new financial affiliations through a holding company structure, or a financial subsidiary (with limitations on activities and appropriate safeguards). A bank holding company can now qualify as a financial holding company and expand into a wide variety of services that are financial in nature, provided that its subsidiary depository institutions are well-managed, well-capitalized and have received a "satisfactory" rating on their last Community Reinvestment Act examination.

Functional Regulation

Title II sets forth changes related to the securities industry. Among these, the Act replaces the broad exemption banks had enjoyed from Securities and Exchange Commission regulation with more limited exemptions and directs the SEC and the Federal Reserve Board to work together to establish rules for future hybrid financial products. In addition, it will require banks that advise mutual funds to register with the SEC as investment advisers, and require banks selling mutual funds to clearly disclose that these funds are not federally insured. The Act also creates a new, voluntary investment bank holding company structure to be supervised by the SEC.

Insurance

Title III reaffirms that states are the regulators for the insurance activities of all persons, including acting as the functional regulator for the insurance activities of federally-chartered banks. However, states may not prevent depository institutions and their affiliates from conducting insurance activities. The Act also allows mutual insurance companies to redomesticate to another state and reorganize into a mutual holding company or stock company. In addition, the Act encourages the states to establish uniform or reciprocal requirements for the licensing of insurance agents.

Unitary Thrifts

Title IV closes the unitary thrift holding company loophole by outlawing the future acquisition or creation of new unitary thrifts by commercial enterprises.

Privacy

Title V provides consumers with new protections against the transfer and use of their nonpublic personal information by financial institutions. Privacy protection provisions enable customers of financial institutions to "opt-out" of having their personal financial information shared with unaffiliated third parties, subject to exceptions related largely to the processing of customer transactions. It also is made a federal crime, punishable by up to five years in prison, to obtain or attempt to obtain private customer financial information through fraudulent or deceptive means.

FHLB System Modernization

Title VI reforms the Federal Home Loan Bank system to provide small banks with greater access to funds for making loans to small businesses and small farmers, while establishing an improved capital structure for the system.

ATM Fee Reform

Title VII requires automated teller machine operators who impose a fee for use of an ATM by a noncustomer to disclose the surcharge both on a sign placed on the ATM and as part of the on-screen display before the transaction is made. Alternatively, the screen-posting requirement may be satisfied by a paper notice issued from the machine.

Community Reinvestment Act

Title VII also requires agreements between an insured depository institution or affiliate and a nongovernmental entity in connection with the Community Reinvestment Act to be disclosed to the public and to the federal banking agencies. Under the sunshine requirements, community groups who receive funds from banks in excess of defined thresholds now must disclose how those funds are used. For smaller institutions, the new law offers the possibility of regulatory relief in the form of a longer period between examinations.

Studies and Reports

The Gramm-Leach-Bliley Act calls for a variety of agency studies and reports to Congress. Topics and due dates are listed below, with the CCH explanation paragraph number in parenthesis:

Activities of financial holding companies—four years (¶ 103).

"Too big to fail" institutions and subordinated debt—18 months (¶ 108).

Small business and farm loans—five years (¶ 109).

Information sharing among financial affiliates—by Jan. 1, 2002 (¶ 509).

Pretext calling—18 months (¶ 514).

Enforcement actions for privacy violations—annual report (¶ 514).

ATM fee disclosure—6 months (¶ 704).

CRA lending—by March 15, 2000 (¶ 713).

Responsiveness to community needs for financial services—by March 15, 2000 (¶ 713).

Expanded small bank access to S corporation treatment—6 months (¶ 721).

Plain language requirement for banking agency rules—by March 1, 2001 (¶ 722).

Conflicts of interest faced by Federal Reserve—one year (¶ 728).

Online banking and lending—two years (¶ 729).

¶ 75 Chronology of Banking Reform

Glass-Steagall Act

When the Glass-Steagall Act was signed by President Roosevelt in 1933, he remarked that this was "the most important and far-reaching legislation ever enacted by the American Congress." And with his pen stroke, the barrier between banking and commerce was raised.

Insider Abuse

The Glass-Steagall Act was a response to the stock market crash of 1929, which in today's figures was equivalent to a more than 1,300 point one-day drop in the Dow Jones Industrial Average. Following the crash, the Senate Banking Committee convened a hearing headed by its chief counsel Ferdinand Pecora. The Pecora investigation provided detailed testimony on the self-dealing and other market abuses engaged in through securities affiliates by some officers of certain large money center banks.

Separate Rooms

The barrier between banking and commerce sought by the Glass-Steagall Act was intended to restore confidence in the country's financial system. By placing bankers and brokers in "separate rooms," it was thought that the insider abuses, which were felt to be the cause of the 1929 Crash, would be reduced. In addition, the separation acted as a safe harbor for ordinary Americans, under which they could deposit their money safely, protected by deposit insurance and shielded from the more speculative nature of stocks.

Removal of Barrier

Merely two years after the enactment of the Glass-Steagall Act, one of its primary sponsors, Senator Carter Glass, sought to soften the barriers during consideration of the Banking Act of 1935. He subsequently withdrew his efforts to revise the Glass-Steagall Act in deference to the wishes of President Roosevelt.

The Walls Come Tumblin' Down

For the next twenty years, the barrier between banking and commerce remained relatively intact. This changed with the passage of the Bank Holding Company Act of 1956 and the Bank Holding Company Act Amendments of 1970. These two Acts established a structure to regulate the permissible non-banking activities of companies that owned banks. Likewise, passage of the Savings and Loan Holding Company Act in 1967 was seen as another attack on the Glass-Steagall barriers. That legislation permitted any company to own a single savings and loan institution.

Agency Actions

Bank regulatory action also played a part in slowly dismantling the Glass-Steagall barriers.

Federal Reserve Board

For instance, the Federal Reserve Board in 1987 allowed banks to affiliate with companies engaged in the private placement of commercial paper. The Fed based its action on the rationale that Glass-Steagall's prohibition on banks' underwriting securities did not reach private placement activities. The Court of Appeals for the District of Columbia agreed with the Fed's decision [*see Securities Industry Association v. Board of Governors*, 807 F2d 1052 (DCCir 1987)].

Also in 1987, the Fed permitted subsidiaries of several of the largest bank holding companies to underwrite and deal in commercial paper, mortgage-backed securities, consumer-receivable related securities and municipal revenue bonds. These securities activities would have been prohibited if a bank directly engaged in them. Again the courts affirmed the Fed's action [*see Securities Industry Association v. Board of Governors*, 839 F2d 47 (DCCir 1987)].

Finally, in 1989, the Fed ruled that a bank affiliate which derived no more than 10 percent of its gross revenues from underwriting or dealing in securities that a bank may not underwrite or deal in directly was not "engaged principally" in underwriting or dealing securities. [The Fed expanded the percentage limitation in 1997 to 25 percent.]

Comptroller of the Currency

While the Fed allowed bank holding companies a greater participation in securities activities, the Office of the Comptroller of the Currency pursued a similar policy for national banks. In 1987, the OCC ruled that a national bank could underwrite securities backed by its own mortgage loans [*see* OCC *Interpretive Letter No.* 388 (1987), '88-'89 CCH FED. BANKING L. REP. ¶ 85,612]. The OCC reasoned that since the bank was merely selling its own assets, the Glass-Steagall Act was not implicated.

Legislative Initiatives

Since the Glass-Steagall Act was enacted, Congress has attempted on a number of occasions to repeal the measure.

Glass-Steagall Outlives Usefulness

In the 100th Congress, the Senate passed S. 1886, the "Proxmire Financial Modernization Act of 1988," which would have repealed the provisions of the Glass-Steagall Act that prohibit affiliations between commercial banks and investment banks. That same year the House Banking Committee reported out H.R. 5094, the "Depository Institutions Act of 1988."

Both houses of Congress sought repeal of the Glass-Steagall Act because it was deemed to have outlived its purpose. The Senate noted that there was a need to modernize the country's financial structure given the technological changes that had evolved at the time and the diminution of banks' traditional role in corporate finance. The Senate also cited a need for U.S. banks to be more competitive internationally.

The House of Representative agreed with the Senate, noting that "compartmentalization" of commercial banking and investment banking resulting from the Glass-Steagall Act was "out of step with the financial needs of consumers".

Nothing resulted from either legislative proposal.

. . . And What Did We Get? FDICIA!?!?

The next efforts at repealing the Glass-Steagall Act barriers began with a Treasury Department report entitled "Modernizing the Financial System: Recommendations for Safer, More Competitive Banks." The goal of the report, which was required by the Financial Institutions Reform, Recovery, and Enforcement Act of 1989 (FIRREA), was to develop practical proposals to reform and strengthen the federal deposit insurance system; modernize the country's financial system to make banks safer and more competitive, both domestically and internationally; and streamline the bank regulatory structure.

The report found that banks' competitiveness was undercut by the government's failure to adapt banking laws to the evolution of the financial markets. As with the 1988 initiatives, technological advances and development of innovative products by competitors were seen as reasons for a decline in bank competitiveness.

The report therefore concluded that the time had come for change. Laws needed to be adapted to permit banks to reclaim profit opportunities that they lost to changing markets.

Armed with the report's recommendations, the Senate passed S. 534, the "Comprehensive Deposit Insurance Reform and Taxpayer Protection Act of 1991." On the House side, the Banking Committee voted to favorably report H.R. 6, the "Financial Institutions Safety and Consumer Choice Act of 1991," which allowed banks to affiliate with securities firms, insurance companies and commercial entities under a diversified holding company structure. H.R. 6, however, was defeated on the House floor on Nov. 11, 1991, by a vote of 324-89.

What ultimately resulted from Congress' efforts was the Federal Deposit Insurance Corporation Improvement Act of 1991 (FDICIA), which a number of commentators called "draconian" at the time.

A Start in the Right Direction

Perhaps the enactment of the Riegle-Neal Interstate Banking and Branching Efficiency Act of 1994 signaled a new effort by Congress to remove impediments so that banks could reach new markets. This legislation allowed banking organizations to acquire banks in other states and to have the ability to branch into other states more easily. In effect, Congress had removed restrictions that were in place for more than 60 years.

¶75

Republican Revolution

With the Republican Party gaining control of both the House and Senate in 1994 elections, banking reform began anew.

The Clinton Administration issued financial services modernization recommendations, which became the basis of H.R. 1062, the "Financial Services Competitiveness Act of 1995." This bill would have allowed banks to affiliate with securities firms and engage in activities that are financial in nature. Later that year, as part of H.R. 1858, the "Financial Institutions Regulatory Relief Act of 1995," the House Banking Committee approved an amendment to the Bank Holding Company Act allowing banks to affiliate with insurance companies. Neither H.R. 1062 nor the Bank Holding Company Act amendment was considered by the full House in the 104th Congress.

Consensus Package

In 1997, the House Banking Committee again reported financial services modernization legislation as provided for in H.R. 10, the "Financial Services Competitiveness Act of 1997." For the first time since 1933, it appeared that legislation could become a reality. As part of the process, House Banking Committee Chairman James A. Leach, R-Iowa, led discussions with leading bank and insurance trade associations, which in turn helped the House Banking Committee develop a consensus package. This was crucial since, in most past endeavors, rivalries between the two industries doomed any initiatives. The full House passed H.R. 10 on May 13, 1998, by a one-vote margin.

The early fall of 1998 found the full Senate beginning its debate on financial legislation. A number of hurdles remained, with a few Senators vowing to stop the legislation. In addition, the White House threatened a veto. One major point of contention between Congress and the Administration centered on where new securities or insurance activity would be conducted. Both House and Senate bills called for conducting new activity in bank holding company affiliates, which are regulated by the Fed. The Administration supported allowing insurance and securities activity in a bank operating subsidiary (op-sub), which would be regulated, in the case of national banks, by the OCC.

The issue that ultimately doomed banking reform in the 105th Congress was Community Reinvestment Act regulation. Sens. Phil Gramm, R-Texas, and Richard Shelby, R-Ala., vowed to fight any expansion of CRA and threatened to offer amendments to prohibit financial institutions from providing any forms of payment to groups using CRA to challenge financial mergers.

At the close of the 105th Congress, House Banking Committee Chairman Jim Leach introduced a new financial modernization bill that would be the basis for a new initiative in the 106th Congress.

Déjà Vu All Over Again?

On Jan. 6, 1999, as the 106th Congress began its new session, Chairman Leach and other senior committee Republicans introduced H.R. 10, the "Financial Services Act of 1999." This legislation built on the regulatory framework developed during consideration of H.R. 10 in the 105th Congress.

The goal of Senate Banking Committee Chairman Phil Gramm was to report a financial services modernization bill out of committee by the end of February. Sen. Gramm said it was absolutely essential to seize the consensus on financial services reform that existed at the end of the 105th Congress.

However, some of the problems that existed before were still present. During the legislative process, there was still friction between the Treasury Department and the Federal Reserve Board regarding the affiliate/op-sub issue. Eventually, the Fed and the Treasury Department reached an agreement allowing each regulator to "veto" the other's decisions to grant new powers for the banking entities under their respective jurisdictions.

The summer of 1999 finally brought what the banking industry had sought for the past 65 years, legislation approved by both houses of Congress. All that was necessary was a reconciled bill and support from the Administration. However, Chairman Leach warned that final legislation was not a foregone conclusion. The Conference Committee was able to iron out most differences.

"Something Worthy of Being Remembered"

With most issues resolved, the legislation was almost doomed by the same issue that killed it in the 105th Conference—CRA. However, following a marathon late-night session, the House and Senate conferees reached a "credible resolution" in "good faith" over CRA. In addition, the White House found all aspects of the legislation acceptable.

In a statement announcing the agreement, Senate Banking Committe Chairman Phil Gramm stated that "tonight we have done something worthy of being remembered."

The End is Near

With consensus over the conference agreement reached, enactment of financial modernization was within sight.

Privacy

During debate on the Conference Report, privacy issues took center stage. In the House, Banking Committee Chairman James A. Leach noted that "American individuals are given powerful new rights to prevent financial institutions from transferring or selling information to third parties." Other members of the House, such as Marge Roukema, R-N.J., while echoing the Banking Committee Chairman's sentiments, noted that privacy will need to be looked at again in the future.

A Pause

On the Senate side, Sen. Gramm stated, "This is not the end of the process. I believe this is the most important banking bill in 60 years. But there will be another banking bill within 10 years, and it will deal with commerce. Banking and commerce is already a reality. This bill is a pause, and it is only a pause, and it is not going to last very long."

Fait Accompli

The end of the Glass-Steagall Act came on Nov. 12, 1999, when President Clinton signed the Gramm-Leach-Bliley Act into law. During the signing, the President noted the Act will benefit consumers and the economy alike. "Removal of barriers to competition will enhance the stability of our financial services system. Financial services firms will be able to diversify their product offerings and thus their sources of revenue. They will also be better equipped to compete in global financial markets," he stated.

The President also applauded the CRA provisions. In regards to privacy, the President noted that although "significant steps" were taken, he had directed the National Economic Council to work with the Treasury Department and the Office of Management and Budget on a privacy legislative proposal for the year 2000.

Title I—Facilitating Affiliation Among Banks, Securities Firms, and Insurance Companies

¶ 100 Introduction

Title I of the Gramm-Leach-Bliley Act makes some of the most far-reaching changes in the rules governing the financial services industry to date. It eliminates many of the restrictions placed on the activities of banks and bank holding companies 66 years ago by the Glass-Steagall Act. Through the use of two new structures—financial holding companies and financial subsidiaries—qualifying bank holding companies and banks will be allowed to provide a wide variety of financial services that have been reserved for insurance companies and securities firms. Affiliations with insurance and securities firms also are now permitted.

Subtitle A creates the financial holding company, a new type of bank holding company with powers greatly exceeding those of standard bank holding companies. These new powers include the authority to engage in merchant banking and insurance activities, including insurance portfolio investing (¶ 103).

Subtitle C creates the financial subsidiary, a subsidiary company that can be used by a national bank to engage in many of the same activities permitted for a financial holding company. However, several of these financial activities—including real estate and merchant banking—are reserved for financial holding companies (¶ 121). State banks are given authority comparable to that of national banks.

Subtitle B contains some of the Act's provisions establishing the concept of functional regulation. The intent is that various financial activities should be overseen by the regulator with the corresponding regulatory experience. Banking is to be supervised by banking regulators, securities activities by the Securities and Exchange Commission and state regulators, and insurance activities by state insurance regulators.

The remaining three subtitles maintain the antitrust authority of the Federal Trade Commission to participate in the examination of institution mergers, and govern the treatment of the financial activities of foreign banks that are financial holding companies.

Effective Date

Title I of the Act takes effect March 11, 2000, except that the provision in Section 104 establishing the parameters for the appropriate balance between federal and state regulation (pertaining mainly to state regulation of insurance) is effective immediately.

See Act Sec. 161 at ¶ 1161.

AFFILIATIONS

¶ 101 Repeal of Securities Activities Prohibitions

The Banking Act of 1933, better known as the Glass-Steagall Act, placed limits on the ability of banks to engage in many of their traditional financial activities. It was believed that bank involvement in these lines of business—particularly their involvement in securities activities—had contributed to the collapse of many financial institutions during the Great Depression. The most important of these restrictions are repealed by the Gramm-Leach-Bliley Act.

Under Sec. 20 of the Glass-Steagall Act (12 USC 377), banks have been prohibited from associating with any business organization "engaged principally in the issue, flotation, underwriting, public sale, or distribution" of securities. More recent rules of the Federal Reserve Board have allowed banks to participate to some degree in the securities industry through "Section 20 affiliates." These affiliates were not deemed to be "principally engaged" in prohibited activities as long as they derived no more than 25 percent of their income from securities activities that were prohibited for banks. Sec. 20 of the Glass-Steagall Act is repealed, lifting the prohibition on bank association with organizations in the securities industry. However, these activities are regulated by other parts of the Gramm-Leach-Bliley Act.

The Act also repeals Glass-Steagall Act Section 32 (12 USC 78), which prohibited management interlocks. An officer, director or employee of an organization that engaged principally in securities activities that were prohibited for banks was barred from being an officer, director or employee of a bank, as was any person who engaged in the prohibited activities on an individual basis. Such interlocks no longer are prohibited.

See Act Sec. 101 at ¶ 1101.

¶ 102 Restrictions on Bank Holding Company Activities

The Act establishes a new type of bank holding company known as a "financial holding company" (discussed in ¶ 103, below). Financial holding companies have powers that are not given to other bank holding companies. Sec. 4 of the Bank Holding Company Act (12 USC 1843) is amended to clarify that a bank holding company may hold shares of any company that the Federal Reserve Board determined, before the amendment, to be engaged in activities that were sufficiently closely related to banking.

Conforming amendments address proceedings before the Federal Reserve Board dealing with applications to engage in nonbanking activity and the locations where bank service companies may operate.

See Act Sec. 102 at ¶ 1102.

¶ 103 Identifying Financial Activities

Financial holding companies are granted the authority to engage in activities—referred to as "financial activities"—that are not permitted for other bank holding companies. They also are given the authority to affiliate with companies that are engaged in financial activities. New subsections are added to 12 USC 1843 to provide this power and to delineate what constitutes a financial activity.

A "financial activity" is an activity that is (1) financial in nature; (2) incidental to an activity that is financial in nature; or (3) complimentary to a financial activity and that does not pose a safety and soundness risk. The Federal Reserve Board, in coordination with the Secretary of the Treasury, is to determine which activities meet these criteria.

Determining if Activity is Financial

The question of whether an activity is financial in nature or incidental to a financial activity may arise before the Federal Reserve Board in two ways: it may be raised before the Fed, or it may be brought to the Fed by the Secretary of the Treasury. If the proposal is raised before the Fed, the Secretary of the Treasury is to be given a formal notice and the two regulatory agencies are to consult. The Secretary of the Treasury has the power to prevent the Fed from finding that a proposed activity is financial in nature or incidental to a financial activity by filing an objection within 30 days of the Fed's notice.

If the Secretary of the Treasury is the source of the proposal, the Fed has 30 days in which to give the Secretary notice of its decision either to initiate a public rulemaking or not to seek public comment. If the Fed decides not to go forward on the proposal, it must give its reasons.

Activities Financial in Nature

Certain activities are listed by the statute as being financial in nature. These include:

- Lending, investing or safeguarding money or securities;
- Underwriting insurance or annuities, or acting as an insurance or annuity principal, agent or broker;
- Providing financial or investment advice;
- Issuing or selling interests in pools of assets that a bank could hold;
- Underwriting, dealing in or making markets in securities;
- Engaging in any activity that the Federal Reserve Board found before the Act to be related closely to banking;
- Engaging within the United States in any activity that a bank holding company could engage in outside of the country, if the Federal Reserve Board determined before the Act that the activity was usual in connection with banking or other financial operations internationally;
- *Merchant banking*—acquiring or controlling ownership interests in an entity engaged in impermissible activities, if: the interests are not held by a depository institution; the interests are held by a securities affiliate or an investment advisory affiliate of an insurance company as part of underwriting, merchant or investment banking activity; the interests are held long enough to enable their sale in a manner consistent with the financial viability of such an activity; and the holding company

does not control the entity except to the extent necessary to obtain a reasonable return on the investment; or

- *Insurance portfolio investing*—acquiring or controlling ownership interests in an entity engaged in impermissible activities, if: the interests are not held by a depository institution; the interests are held by an insurance or annuity company; the interests represent investments made in the ordinary course of business in accordance with state law; and the holding company does not control the entity except to the extent necessary to obtain a reasonable return on the investment.

The Fed is instructed to adopt a regulation or order defining certain additional activities as financial in nature, to the extent they are consistent with the purposes of the Act. These are:

- Lending, exchanging, transferring, investing for others or safeguarding financial assets other than money or securities;

- Providing any method of transferring financial assets; and

- Arranging, effecting or facilitating financial transactions for third parties.

Other activities also may be decided by the Federal Reserve Board to be financial in nature or incidental to a financial activity if they meet specified criteria. The Fed is instructed to consider the purposes of the Act and the Bank Holding Company Act; changes in the market in which financial holding companies compete; changes in the technology used to deliver financial services; and whether the proposed activity is necessary or appropriate to allow a financial holding company and its affiliates to compete effectively, deliver services efficiently and offer services through the most advanced technological means available.

Under Subtitle C of the Gramm-Leach-Bliley Act, the Secretary of the Treasury has the same authority to deal with financial activities for national bank financial subsidiaries (see ¶ 121).

Required Notifications

As a general rule, a financial holding company that intends either to engage in a new financial activity or to acquire a company that already is engaged in such an activity is required to notify the Federal Reserve Board. The notice must be given no later than 30 calender days after the activity is commenced or the acquisition is consummated. If the activity involved is one specified by the Act as being financial in nature, or one that the Fed has determined by rule or regulation to be financial in nature or incidental to a financial activity, no prior approval is required. Otherwise, 60 days prior notice to, and the approval of, the Federal Reserve Board are required. Thus, prior notice and approval would be required for any activity that was deemed to be complementary to an activity that was financial in nature, according to the Conference Report (¶ 5002).

Merchant Banking

The Federal Reserve Board and the Secretary of the Treasury are authorized to adopt regulations dealing with merchant banking by financial holding companies, but they must act together to do so. The regulations may include limits on transactions between a holding company's subsidiary depository institutions and the companies that are controlled under the merchant banking authority.

The Fed and the Secretary of the Treasury have the authority to lift the ban on merchant banking by depository institution financial subsidiaries. However, they must wait five years after the Act is enacted before doing so.

Conditions for Engaging in Financial Activities

Not all bank holding companies may become financial holding companies and take up financial activities. There are three requirements. First, all of the bank holding company's depository institution subsidiaries must be well capitalized. Second, all of those depository institution subsidiaries must be well managed. Third, the bank holding company must file with the Federal Reserve Board a declaration of its intention to become a financial holding company, including a certification that its depository institution subsidiaries meet the first two requirements.

These requirements apply not only to the new financial activities authorized by the statute, but also to the continuation of some pre-existing nonfinancial activities and affiliations. Provisions are made to apply similar rules to foreign banks that are operating within the United States.

If a financial holding company engages in any of the described activities without fulfilling these general requirements, the Fed is to notify it of the violation. The holding company then has 45 days to sign an agreement with the Fed to bring itself into compliance. The Fed also has broad authority to place limits on the activities of the holding company or its affiliates until the problems described in the notice are corrected. If the problems are not corrected within 180 days, the Fed may require the holding company to divest itself either of any insured depository institutions or of any activities that are not permissible for bank holding companies.

Community Reinvestment Act

A financial holding company, bank, or insured depository institution subsidiary of either also must satisfy the Community Reinvestment Act in order to exercise the powers given by the Gramm-Leach-Bliley Act. If any insured depository institution, insured depository institution subsidiary or insured depository institution affiliate of a financial holding company did not receive a CRA rating of at least "satisfactory" at its most recent CRA examination, the regulatory agencies are directed to prevent the bank or holding company from exercising the new powers, either directly or through a subsidiary. Acquisitions under the merchant banking authority or by an insurance subsidiary under the investment portfolio authority are exempt from this prohibition, if the acquiring subsidiary previously was engaged in such activities.

The Community Reinvestment Act also is amended. A bank holding company's election to become a financial holding company will be "ineffective" if the Federal Reserve Board finds that not all of the holding company's insured depository institution subsidiaries received "satisfactory" or better CRA ratings at their last examinations. The Fed must notify the holding company of the finding within 30 days of the company's election.

The CRA ratings of a subsidiary acquired during the 12 months before the election may be disregarded for the 12 months following the acquisition, if the holding company has submitted to its primary federal regulatory agency a plan to improve the subsidiary's rating to at least "satisfactory" by the next examination, and the agency has accepted the plan.

Nonfinancial Activities and Affiliations

A company that is neither a bank holding company nor a foreign bank, and that becomes a financial holding company, may be able to continue to engage in nonfinancial activity. It also may be able to retain ownership interests in other companies that are engaged in nonfinancial activities. For the nonfinancial activities to continue, the holding company must either have been engaged in the activity or have held the shares on Sept. 30, 1999; the holding company must be engaged predominantly in financial activities; and the company engaged in the nonfinancial activities may not commence any additional nonfinancial activities.

To be predominantly engaged in financial activities means that at least 85 percent of the consolidated annual gross revenues of the holding company and its subsidiaries (other than depository institutions) must come from financial activities. The revenue limit is a continuing limit, not just a limit at the time the company elects to become a financial holding company.

Such a holding company may not acquire, in any way, the assets of any other company that engages in activities that have not been determined by the Federal Reserve Board to be financial. A limited exception for companies that own licensed broadcasting stations is specified.

The ability to continue nonfinancial activities or maintain ownership of a company that engages in nonfinancial activities ends 10 years after the enactment of the Gramm-Leach-Bliley Act. On application by the holding company, the Fed may grant one additional five year term.

Depository Institution/Affiliate Transactions

Depository institutions are limited in their ability to engage in cross-marketing with nonfinancial subsidiaries of the same holding company. If the nonfinancial subsidiary is owned by the holding company (a) under the grandfather authority of a holding company to retain nonfinancial activities or companies, (b) under the holding company's merchant banking authority or (c) by the holding company's insurance subsidiary under its investment portfolio authority, the bank and the subsidiary are prohibited from offering or marketing each other's products or services.

However, insurance products or services may be marketed by statement inserts or Internet websites if there is no illegal tying arrangement and the

Federal Reserve Board has given its approval. The Fed is to base its decision on the public interest, the separation of banking and commerce, and safety and soundness considerations.

Depository institutions also are prohibited from engaging in any "covered transactions" with nonfinancial affiliates owned by the same holding company. "Covered transactions" are: loans to the affiliate; investments in the affiliate's securities; most purchases of assets from the affiliate; acceptance of the affiliate's securities as collateral for any loan; and guaranteeing in any manner any extension of credit to the affiliate.

Commodities Trading

Commodities trading activities of financial holding companies that were neither bank holding companies nor foreign banks are grandfathered, to a limited degree. Such a financial holding company may continue activities it was legally conducting as of Sept. 30, 1997. If the commodities trading was carried out by a subsidiary, that subsidiary's assets may not total more than 5 percent of the total consolidated assets of the holding company (although the Federal Reserve Board has the authority to increase that percentage). The trading subsidiary is banned from any cross-marketing arrangements with any depository institution that is a subsidiary of the holding company.

Technical Amendments

In order to maintain consistency, the Bank Holding Company Act is changed to establish the meaning of "depository institution," and definitions of "financial holding company" and "insurance company" are added. A "financial holding company" is defined as "a bank holding company that meets the requirements of section 4(l)(1)." These requirements are that all of the holding company's depository institution subsidiaries are well capitalized and well managed, and that the company has filed an election to become a financial holding company, including a certification that its depository institution subsidiaries meet the specified criteria.

The provisions of the Bank Holding Company Act that specify the notice that must be given to the Fed before a holding company undertakes nonbanking activities also are changed to make them consistent with the remainder of the Act.

Report to Congress

The Federal Reserve Board and the Secretary of the Treasury are instructed, within four years of the enactment of the Act, to report jointly to Congress on the various activities being undertaken by financial holding companies. This report is to include a discussion of the regulators' actions dealing with activities that are incidental to those that are financial in nature or that are complementary to such financial activities; the safety and soundness risks posed by the commercial activities of financial holding companies; and the effect of mergers and acquisitions on market concentration in the financial services industry.

See Act Sec. 103 at ¶ 1103.

¶ 104 Operation of State Law

In order to fully implement the affiliated environment evisioned by the Gramm-Leach-Bliley Act, parameters were needed to establish the appropriate balance between federal and state regulation of the activities and affiliations undertaken by depository institutions, securities firms and insurance companies. Section 104 of the Act sets those parameters.

The bulk of the statute governs state regulation of insurance. State insurance laws and regulations are preempted if they "prevent or significantly interfere" with certain insurance activities of depository institutions, namely sales and affiliation activities. This topic is discussed in greater detail at ¶ 302–304.

State laws governing other financial activities, except securities and insurance activities, are not preempted as long as they do not discriminate against depository institutions.

A state securities commission's ability to investigate and enforce certain unlawful securities transactions or to require the licensure or registration of securities and securities brokers, dealers, and investment advisors and their associates are also unaffected by Section 104.

Finally, state actions of general corporate applicability applying to companies domiciled or incorporated in the state are also protected, as well as state laws similar to the antitrust laws, so long as the state actions are not inconsistent with the intent of the Gramm-Leach-Bliley Act to permit affiliations.

See Act Sec. 104(d)(4), (f), and (g) at ¶ 1104.

¶ 105 Mutual Bank Holding Companies

A bank holding company organized in a mutual form will be regulated in the same manner, and subject to the same limitations, as any other bank holding company. Put differently, there should be no difference between the regulation of mutual and stock bank holding companies.

The source of this section was H.R. 10, the House financial service reform proposal. According to the House Commerce Committee Report, the purpose of the section is to allow mutual insurance companies to adopt the financial holding company structure without forfeiting their mutual status.

See Act Sec. 105 at ¶ 1105.

¶ 106 Deposit Production Offices

Interstate banks have, since 1994, been prohibited from using branches in states other than their home states primarily for deposit production purposes. The intent is to ensure that these interstate branches serve the credit needs of their local communities. This prohibition is extended to include all branches of a bank owned by an out-of-state bank holding company.

See Act Sec. 106 at ¶ 1106.

¶ 107 Limited Purpose Banks

Gramm-Leach-Bliley Act Sec. 107 deals with the restrictions imposed on limited purpose banks, their holding companies and affiliates, principally by Bank Holding Company Act Sec. 4(f) (12 USC 1843(f)). Limited purpose banks—also known as CEBA banks, after the Competitive Equality Banking Act of 1987—are banks that either make commercial loans or accept demand deposits, but not both, and that are insured by the Federal Deposit Insurance Corp., according to the House Banking Committee Report. Such institutions were not considered to be banks until the Competitive Equality Banking Act was enacted, and companies that own them are not treated as bank holding companies as long as they comply with certain restrictions.

The prior complete prohibition on new activities by limited purpose banks has been removed, as has been the partial prohibition on marketing an affiliate's products or services. The limits on overdrafts by or for affiliates have been eased.

Limited purpose banks are restricted in the types of overdrafts they may allow by, or incur on behalf of, an affiliate with the Federal Reserve Bank. Until now, an overdraft was allowed only if it was (a) inadvertent or (b) on behalf of an affiliate that was supervised as a primary dealer by the Federal Reserve Bank of New York, and was properly secured. After the amendment, an overdraft also will be permitted if it is in connection with a financial activity and does not violate the prohibitions on transactions with affiliates that are established by Federal Reserve Act Sec. 23A and Sec. 23B (12 USC 371c and 12 USC 371c-1).

Limits designed to ensure that the banks remain limited purpose banks are imposed. A company will lose the exemption from being treated as a bank holding company if any of its bank subsidiaries accepts demand deposits and makes commercial loans, or if any bank subsidiary permits any prohibited overdraft by or on behalf of an affiliate. In such a case, the company must give up control of all banks it owns within 180 days of receiving a notice from the Fed that the company no longer qualifies for the exemption. However, the company may retain its subsidiary banks if, within the 180-day period, it (a) corrects the condition that caused it to lose the exemption or (b) submits to the Federal Reserve Board a plan to correct the problem within one year. The company also must adopt procedures to prevent any repetition of the problem.

A company that owns a limited purpose bank is allowed to own a foreign bank if the investment is permitted by the Federal Reserve Act, and if the foreign bank offers no products or services within the United States and engages only in permissible activities.

See Act Sec. 107 at ¶ 1107.

¶ 108 "Too Big to Fail" Institutions; Subordinated Debt

There is some apprehension that the failure of an unusually large depository institution or holding company could have adverse effects on deposit insurance funds, the financial system or even the economy as a whole. In order to begin addressing the possible damage that could arise from the failure of such a "too big to fail" institution, the Federal Reserve Board and the

Secretary of the Treasury are instructed to investigate the use of subordinated debt to bring market discipline into play.

"Subordinated debt" is defined as unsecured debt that bears an original weighted average maturity of at least five years; is subordinated to all other indebtedness of the institution (including deposits); is not supported by any type of credit enhancement; and is not held, to any degree, by any entity affiliated with the institution.

The regulators are to study the feasibility and appropriateness of the use of subordinated debt, determine the amount of capital that should be subordinated debt and the ways in which that debt could be incorporated into existing capital standards. Within 18 months of the enactment of the Act, they are to report to Congress on the study and include any legislative and administrative proposals that they might have developed.

See Act Sec. 108 at ¶ 1108.

¶ 109 Small Business and Farm Loans

The Secretary of the Treasury is instructed to consult with the federal banking regulators on the effect that the Act has on the availability of credit for small businesses and farms. A study is to be conducted and a report made to Congress within five years of the enactment of the Act. The Secretary of the Treasury's recommendations for legislative and administrative action are to be included in the report.

See Act Sec. 109 at ¶ 1109.

STREAMLINING SUPERVISION OF BANK HOLDING COMPANIES

¶ 111 Streamlining Bank Holding Company Supervision

The Gramm-Leach-Bliley Act establishes the concept of functional supervision. In the words of the Conference Report (¶ 5003), this means that "similar activities should be regulated by the same regulator." The Act spells out the authority of the bank regulatory agencies, Securities and Exchange Commission and state insurance regulators, in order to see that each type of activity is supervised by a regulator with corresponding expertise.

Reports to Federal Reserve Board

The Federal Reserve Board is intended to be an "umbrella supervisor." It is given the authority to require a bank holding company or bank holding company subsidiary to file reports on its financial condition, risk management systems, transactions with depository institution subsidiaries and affiliates, and compliance with any federal law that the Fed has the authority to enforce.

The Fed is instructed to rely on reports that have been filed with other regulatory agencies, publicly reported information and externally audited financial statements in fulfilling its supervisory role. If a functionally regulated subsidiary is requested to make a report that is not required routinely by its primary regulator, the Fed is first to ask the regulator to obtain the report rather than demanding it from the subsidiary directly. However, if the report is not furnished, the Fed may demand it directly, if it is needed to assess (1) a material risk to the holding company, (2) a material risk to any of the holding company's depository institution subsidiaries, (3) compliance with any federal law the Fed has the authority to enforce, or (4) compliance with the risk management systems.

Examinations by Federal Reserve Board

Examinations remain part of the Federal Reserve Board's regulatory arsenal. However, the agency's ability to examine functionally regulated bank holding company subsidiaries is limited. The Fed may examine a functionally regulated subsidiary only if it believes that: (1) the subsidiary is engaged in activities that pose a material risk to an affiliated depository institution; (2) an examination is needed to inform itself of the risk management systems; or (3) the subsidiary is not complying with a federal law that the Fed has the authority to enforce, and that a determination cannot be made by an examination of affiliated depository institutions or the holding company.

The focus and scope of bank holding company examinations are to be limited to the company itself and to any subsidiary that could have a materially adverse effect on the safety and soundness of an affiliated depository institution due to the subsidiary's size, its condition or activities, or the nature and size of transactions between the subsidiary and the affiliated depository institution.

Reports of examinations by other federal or state regulators are to be relied on by the Fed when it is possible to do so. The agency is instructed to, whenever possible, rely completely on a report: by the SEC of its examination of a registered broker or dealer; by the SEC or a state regulator of an examination of a registered investment adviser; or by a state regulator of its examination of a licensed insurance company. Also, the Fed is to rely completely on a report of examination of any other subsidiary that is comprehensively supervised by any federal or state regulator.

Capital Requirements

The ability of the Federal Reserve Board to impose capital requirements on holding company subsidiaries that are functionally regulated is greatly limited. If a subsidiary is not a depository institution and is in compliance with the capital requirements of its primary regulator, is a registered investment adviser, or is a licensed insurance agent, the Fed may not act. However, the Fed may impose capital requirements on registered investment adviser or licensed insurance agent subsidiaries with respect to other activities.

Indirect capital requirements also are restricted. In establishing the capitalization requirements for a bank holding company, the Fed may not consider the activities of the company's affiliated registered investment companies unless either the affiliate is itself a bank holding company or the owner holds more than 25 percent of the shares in the affiliate and those shares have a market value of more than $1,000,000.

Securities and Insurance Activities

Functional regulation is firmly established for securities and insurance activities of subsidiaries of depository institution. This applies to any company that is neither a bank holding company nor a depository institution, and that is a registered broker or dealer, a registered investment adviser (with respect to investment advisory activities), a registered investment company, an insurance company (with respect to its insurance activities) or an entity regulated by the Commodity Futures Trading Commission (with respect to the entity's commodities trading activities)—each of which is a "functionally regulated subsidiary" for the purposes of this provision.

The securities activities of a depository institution's functionally regulated subsidiary are to be regulated by the Securities and Exchange Commission or by state securities regulators, just as if the activities were conducted by a subsidiary of a company that was not a depository institution. In the same manner, the insurance agency activities, brokerage activities, and activities conducted as principal by a depository institution's functionally regulated subsidiary are to be regulated by state insurance authorities.

This subsection of the Gramm-Leach-Bliley Act thus displaces supervision by not only the Federal Reserve Board, but also by the Office of the Comptroller of the Currency and Office of Thrift Supervision.

See Act Sec. 111 at ¶ 1111.

¶ 112 Securities, Insurance Regulatory Authority

The Federal Reserve Board has long put forward the "source of strength" doctrine—the position that a bank holding company may be required to infuse capital into a depository institution subsidiary if doing so is necessary to the subsidiary's stability or solvency. The Gramm-Leach-Bliley Act restricts the Fed's ability to apply this rule to a bank holding company that is regulated by the Securities and Exchange Commission or a state insurance or securities regulator.

An order by the Fed that a bank holding company that is an insurance company, a registered broker or dealer, a registered investment company or a registered investment adviser provide funds or other assets to a depository institution subsidiary may be blocked by the company's regulator—the SEC or a state securities or insurance regulator—by a written determination that providing the assets would adversely effect the financial condition of the company. An order on a holding company subsidiary that falls into any of the same categories to provide assets to a depository institution affiliate is subject to the same process.

The Fed is not left powerless, however. If the SEC or state regulator blocks an order requiring a contribution to a depository institution subsidiary's capital, the Fed can require the bank holding company to divest the depository institution. The holding company must be given at least 180 days to complete the divestiture. In the interim, the Fed may impose conditions on the holding company's operation of the depository institution, including restricting or prohibiting transactions between the depository institution and any of its affiliates.

The Act also amends the Federal Deposit Insurance Act to clarify that the limits placed on the regulatory and examination powers of the Federal Reserve Board are also placed on the powers of the other federal banking agencies, under any other statute, to deal with functionally regulated affiliates of depository institutions. However, the Federal Deposit Insurance Corporation's authority to examine a depository institution's affiliate in order to determine the nature and effect of the relationship between the institution and the affiliate is retained. This is intended to protect deposit insurance funds, according to the Conference Report.

See Act Sec. 112 at ¶ 1112. See Conference Report at ¶ 5003.

¶ 113 Limits on Federal Reserve Board Authority

The Act seeks to place strict limits on the ability of the Federal Reserve Board to supervise or regulate bank holding company functionally regulated subsidiaries. Limits are imposed on the agency's ability to act either directly or indirectly.

The Fed is prohibited from regulating functionally regulated subsidiaries, or taking actions against a specific subsidiary, unless certain circumstances are present. It only may take actions that are necessary to prevent or correct an unsafe or unsound practice, or a breach of fiduciary duty, that poses a material risk to the safety, soundness or stability of an affiliated depository institution, or that poses a risk to the domestic or international payment system. As a further condition, the Fed also must find that it cannot address the risk by taking actions directed against the specific depository institution or against depository institutions in general.

The Fed also is prohibited from taking any measure that would require a bank holding company to cause a functionally regulated subsidiary to take or refrain from any action, unless the Fed could impose that measure on the subsidiary directly.

See Act Sec. 113 at ¶ 1113.

¶ 114 Affiliate Transactions and Prudential Safeguards

The federal banking agencies are permitted to issue prudential safeguards for banking organizations engaging in new financial activities.

National Banks

The Act gives the Office of the Comptroller of the Currency the authority to regulate transactions and relationships between national banks and their subsidiaries. The regulations must be those necessary to prevent significant risk to the safety and soundness of insured depository institutions or other adverse effects. Those other effects include undue concentration of resources, harm to unfair competition, conflicts of interest and unsound banking practices. The OCC is to review its regulations regularly.

Bank Holding Companies, State Member Banks, Foreign Branches

The Federal Reserve Board may impose regulations on relationships and transactions between bank holding company depository institution subsidiaries and their affiliates, and on relationships and transactions between state members banks and their subsidiaries. The regulations must be consistent with other laws, including the Gramm-Leach-Bliley Act. They also must be necessary to prevent an evasion of such laws, or to avoid risk to the safety and soundness of depository institutions, risk to federal deposit insurance funds, or risk of the other adverse consequences described in addressing the OCC's regulatory authority. The Fed also is to review its regulations regularly.

Additionally, the Fed has the authority to regulate relationships and transactions between a branch, agency or commercial lending company of a foreign bank in the United States and any U.S. affiliate of the foreign bank. These regulations must satisfy the same qualifications as the regulations on transactions between bank holding company depository institution subsidiaries and their affiliates.

State Nonmember Banks

The power to regulate relationships and transactions between state nonmember banks and their subsidiaries is vested in the Federal Deposit Insurance Corp. These regulations must be consistent with the Federal Deposit Insurance Act or other laws applicable to state nonmember banks, and must satisfy the same criteria as other transaction regulations. The FDIC also is instructed to review its regulations regularly.

See Act Sec. 114 at ¶ 1114.

¶ 115 Investment Company Examinations

As a general rule, no federal banking agency may examine a registered investment company unless the company is a bank holding company or a savings and loan holding company. The authority to perform these examinations is reserved for the Securities and Exchange Commission. The SEC is obligated to provide the banking agencies with any information they need to fulfill their regulatory responsibilities.

However, the Federal Deposit Insurance Corporation's authority to examine a depository institution's affiliate in order to determine the nature and effect of the relationship between the institution and the affiliate is retained.

See Act Sec. 115 at ¶ 1115.

¶ 116 Application and Registration

Under the Bank Holding Company Act, an entity that becomes a bank holding company must register with the Federal Reserve Board within 180 days. The Gramm-Leach-Bliley Act specifies that the filing of a declaration of an intent to become a financial holding company is sufficient and that no additional registration under the Bank Holding Company Act is needed. However, the declaration will not fulfill any requirement to apply for permission to acquire a bank.

See Act Sec. 116 at ¶ 1116.

¶ 117 Preserving Federal Deposit Insurance Resources

The Federal Deposit Insurance Act is amended to prevent deposit insurance from being used to pay claims by a failed depository institution's affiliates.

See Act Sec. 117 at ¶ 1117.

¶ 118 Savings Bank Powers

Sec. 3(f) of the Bank Holding Company Act (12 USC 1842(f)) previously granted savings bank subsidiaries of bank holding companies the ability to engage in some activities that were impermissible for banks. This included a "grandfather clause" relating to savings bank life insurance activities.

This entire subsection is repealed. The repeal is intended to make the regulation of savings bank life insurance consistent with the regulation of other bank insurance activities.

See Act Sec. 118 at ¶ 1118.

SUBSIDIARIES OF NATIONAL BANKS

¶ 121 National Bank Subsidiary Powers

The Gramm-Leach-Bliley Act gives national banks substantial, but not unlimited, authority to use "financial subsidiaries" to engage in financial activities. A financial subsidiary may be wholly owned by a single bank, or it may be owned by a number of different banks. However, all of the owners must be banks. Financial subsidiaries are created by a new Revised Statutes of the United States Sec. 5136A.

Other than saying that a financial subsidiary is a company controlled by one or more insured depository institutions, the Act gives a negative definition of the term—that is, the Act establishes what a financial subsidiary is by saying what it is not. It is a subsidiary: that does not engage only in activities that are permissible for national banks and that are conducted under the same rules that govern those activities when conducted by banks; and that cannot be owned or controlled by a national bank under any other section of federal law, including the Federal Reserve Act and the Bank Service Company Act. (In other words, it is a subsidiary that does something that a national bank cannot do, and that a national bank could not own if it were not for the Gramm-Leach-Bliley Act.)

Restrictions on Subsidiaries, Banks

A bank may own a financial subsidiary only if the subsidiary's activities are limited to those that are financial in nature or that a bank could engage in directly. A financial subsidiary may not, as a principal, underwrite insurance or annuities, engage in real estate development or investment, or engage in merchant banking or insurance portfolio investment activities.

There are qualifications for the bank as well as for the subsidiary. The bank and all of its depository institution affiliates must be well capitalized and well managed. There also is a size limitation. The aggregate consolidated total assets of all of a bank's financial subsidiaries may not exceed the lesser of 45 percent of the bank's consolidated total assets or $50,000,000,000 (to be indexed under a method set by the Secretary of the Treasury and the Federal Reserve Board). Also, the bank must have received the prior approval of the Comptroller of the Currency.

In addition, there are requirements aimed at ensuring the financial stability of large banks if they decide to invest in financial subsidiaries. If the bank is one of the 50 largest insured banks, it must have at least one issue of outstanding debt that is rated in one of the three highest investment grade rating categories by a nationally recognized rating organization. The debt issue must be unsecured long-term debt that is not supported by any credit enhancement, and that is not held in any significant part by any person or entity affiliated with the bank, acting for the bank, or using funds of the bank or any of its affiliates.

If the bank is one of the second 50 largest insured depository institutions, it must meet either the same criteria or any other comparable qualifications that are established jointly by the Secretary of the Treasury and the Fed.

These requirements do not apply to a bank's interest in a financial subsidiary that engages in financial activities only as an agent. There are no similar qualifications for a bank that is not one of the 100 largest insured depository institutions.

The Community Reinvestment Act comes into play as well. The bank and all of its financial institution subsidiaries must have received ratings of at least "satisfactory" at their last CRA examination.

Financial Activities

A financial activity for a national bank is essentially the same as a financial activity for a bank holding company. The activities that the amended Bank Holding Company Act lists as financial activities for bank holding companies (see ¶ 103) automatically are financial activities for national banks. Similarly, the Secretary of the Treasury is mandated to adopt regulations or rules establishing as financial activities the same activities that the Federal Reserve Board must accept. However, as noted above, financial subsidiaries may not be permitted to engage in four activities that are specifically allowed for financial holding companies—insurance or annuity underwriting, developing or investing in real estate, merchant banking and insurance portfolio investing.

The Secretary of the Treasury has the power to find that additional activities are financial in nature or incidental to a financial activity, in the same way the Fed may make such a finding for bank holding company. The process for considering such a proposal mirrors the process that the Fed is to follow. If the proposal is raised before the Secretary of the Treasury, the Fed must be notified. The activity may not be found to be financial if the Fed objects within 30 days.

If the Federal Reserve Board proposes to the Secretary of the Treasury that an activity should be found to be financial in nature or incidental to a financial activity, the Secretary of the Treasury must, within 30 days, decide whether to initiate a rulemaking. The Fed is to be notified of the Secretary of the Treasury's decision and, if the decision is not to proceed, the reasons must be given.

In deciding whether an activity is financial, the Secretary is to consider the following factors: the purposes of the statutes; changes in the markets in which banks compete; technological changes affecting the delivery of financial services; and whether the activity is needed to allow banks to compete effectively, deliver financial services efficiently and offer customers the most advanced technology that is available. Again, the same factors apply to a comparable decision by the Federal Reserve Board.

Capital Standards, Safety and Soundness

A bank's investment in a financial subsidiary affects the way in which the bank calculates its capital, for purposes of compliance with regulatory capital standards. The bank must deduct from its assets and tangible equity the total of its equity investments in all financial subsidiaries. A financial subsidiary's retained earnings are to be treated as part of the bank's investment. The assets and liabilities of the financial subsidiaries are not to be consolidated with those of the bank.

The bank's published financial statements must present the bank's financial information in two ways: (1) in accordance with generally accepted accounting principles and (2) separately, in a manner that reflects the segregation of the bank's investments in financial subsidiaries.

Separation is to be maintained between the bank and the financial subsidiary. The bank must be certain that its risk management procedures are adequate to protect it from financial and operational risks created both by itself and by any financial subsidiary. It also must have policies that will maintain the separate corporate identities of the bank and its subsidiary and that will prevent each from becoming liable for the obligations of the other.

Enforcement

In order to maintain an investment in a financial subsidiary, a bank must continue to comply with the safety and soundness rules—it, and its depository institution affiliates, must remain well managed and well capitalized and it must maintain risk management safeguards. If the bank fails to do so, the Office of the Comptroller is to notify the bank of the default.

Within 45 days of the OCC's notice, the bank must come to an agreement with the agency on how it will return to compliance. If the problem arises from one of the bank's affiliates, that affiliate must execute a comparable agreement with its federal regulator. The OCC has the authority to extend the 45-day time limit. Until the necessary agreements are reached, the OCC may place limits on operations of the bank and the subsidiary, and the affiliate's regulator has the same authority to limit the activities of the affiliate.

If the default is not cured within 180 days, the OCC has the authority to require the bank to divest the financial subsidiary.

A bank that is one of the 100 largest insured depository institutions also must continue to meet the long-term debt rating requirements. If it does not, the bank is prohibited from acquiring, directly or indirectly, any additional equity capital of any financial subsidiary until it returns to compliance. This includes acquiring any of a financial subsidiary's debt instruments if the instrument qualifies as capital of the subsidiary.

Exposure to Loss

In order to limit bank exposure to loss resulting from the activities of financial subsidiaries, a new subsection is added to the Federal Reserve Act rules on transaction with affiliates (12 USC 371c and 12 USC 371c-1). A financial subsidiary is to be treated as an affiliate for the purposes of these sections, with two exceptions. First, the rule limiting covered transactions between the bank and its affiliates to 10 percent of the bank's capital and surplus does not apply to transactions between the bank and any single financial subsidiary. Second, the retained earnings of a financial subsidiary are not to be considered part of the bank's investment, although they are part of the bank's investment for regulatory capital purposes.

Thus, transactions between a bank and its financial subsidiaries are subject to nearly all of the same limitations as transactions between the bank and its affiliates.

Under the new subsection, an investment in a financial subsidiary by a bank's affiliate is to be considered to be an investment by the bank. Also, the Federal Reserve Board has the authority to treat a loan by a bank's affiliate as a loan by the bank.

A bank's financial subsidiary or a bank holding company's subsidiary that holds more than 15 percent of the equity of a company under the merchant banking or insurance portfolio investment authority will be deemed to control that company. The presumption of control can be rebutted by providing sufficient information to the Fed.

The Federal Reserve Board is instructed to adopt rules governing credit exposure arising out of derivative transactions between member banks and their affiliates, and addressing intraday extensions of credit by member banks to their affiliates. The rules are to be adopted within 18 months of the enactment of the Gramm-Leach-Bliley Act, but the Fed may delay their effectiveness in order to allow banks enough time to comply.

Tying Arrangements

The prohibition on tying arrangements contained in the Bank Holding Company Act Amendments of 1970 (12 USC 1971) also is affected by Gramm-Leach-Bliley Act Sec. 121. The Act provides that, for purposes of that section, a bank financial subsidiary is to be deemed to be a subsidiary of a bank holding company, not a subsidiary of a bank.

The effect of the provision is to protect a consumer from a bank's attempt to tie the receipt of bank products services to the consumer's agreement to do business with the financial subsidiary or to refrain from doing business with the subsidiary's competitors.

Insured State Banks

Insured state banks also are given the ability to engage in financial activities through subsidiaries, by virtue of a new Federal Deposit Insurance Act Sec. 45. Under appropriate circumstances, an insured state bank may hold an interest in a subsidiary that is essentially equivalent to a national bank's financial subsidiary.

To begin with, the state bank and all of its insured depository institution affiliates must be well capitalized. The bank must comply with the same capital deduction and financial statement requirements and financial and operational safeguards that apply to national banks. In its transactions with the subsidiary, the bank must comply with the limits on transactions with affiliates.

State banks are not obligated to divest any interests in subsidiaries that they lawfully held when the Gramm-Leach-Bliley Act was enacted, and those subsidiaries are not required to change their activities. These activities are grandfathered by the Act.

State bank subsidiaries are subject to the Federal Deposit Insurance Corporation's examination authority to the same extent as any other state bank subsidiary. They also remain subject to the same securities-related rules that govern national banks, as long as those rules do not affect the state bank's interest in its equivalent of a financial subsidiary.

See Act Sec. 121 at ¶ 1121.

¶ 122 Financial Subsidiaries and Merchant Banking

The Gramm-Leach-Bliley Act as passed prohibits financial subsidiaries from engaging in merchant banking. Five years after the enactment of the Act, the Federal Reserve Board and the Secretary of the Treasury may jointly adopt rules lifting that prohibition.

See Act Sec. 122 at ¶ 1122.

PRESERVATION OF FEDERAL TRADE COMMISSION AUTHORITY

¶ 131 Notification and Post-Approval Waiting Period

Subtitle D of Title I helps the Federal Trade Commission coordinate with the Federal Reserve Board its review of nonbanking transactions under Section 4 of the Bank Holding Company Act, in cases involving a merger, acquisition, or change in control of a bank or bank holding company under BHCA Section 3 (12 USC 1842). An amendment to the Banking Holding Company Act requires the Fed to give notice to the FTC when the Fed approves a Section 3 transaction that also involves a Section 4 transaction.

See Act Sec. 131 at ¶ 1131.

¶ 132 Data Sharing in Antitrust Reviews

Except where otherwise prohibited, the banking regulators who review mergers or acquisitions must make available to the Justice Department and the Federal Trade Commission any information they possess that the antitrust agencies believe necessary for their lawful antitrust reviews. Any information that is shared is to be kept confidential, however.

In addition, before any information shared may be disclosed to a third party, the agency that shared it must first be notified in writing and given a chance to oppose or limit the disclosure. Also, any sharing does not waive or otherwise affect any claims of privilege with respect to the information. These provisions apply to any information or material obtained by one federal banking agency from another federal banking agency, and to any examination report or other confidential supervisory information obtained by any state agency or authority, or any other person, from a federal banking agency. According to the Conference report, interagency data sharing "simply allows all of the involved agencies to do their respective tasks in the most expeditious manner possible."

See Act Sec. 132 at ¶ 1132. See Conference Report at ¶ 5005.

¶ 133 Status of Subsidiaries and Affiliates

Subsidiaries or affiliates of banks or savings associations, which are not themselves banks or savings associations, are not to be treated as banks or savings associations by the Federal Trade Commission under the FTC Act. This is limited to laws that the FTC currently enforces and is not intended to provide any new enforcement authority. However, when banks or savings associations acquire other kinds of businesses against which the FTC can currently enforce the Act, such as securities firms, these businesses do not fall within the bank or savings association exemption to the Hart–Scott–Rodino Act by being owned by a banking entity.

When Financial Holding Companies acquire other FHCs, and either was involved in new activities under BHCA Section 4(k), the portion of the transaction involving those Section 4(k) activities will be subject to Hart–Scott–Rodino review. However, the remainder of the transaction will continue to be reviewed under the BHCA. This will allow the antitrust agencies to continue to review mergers between insurance companies, securities firms, and other businesses newly allowed to FHCs. It does not disturb existing law and precedents under which mergers involving complex corporate entities, some parts of which are in industries subject to merger review by specialized regulatory agencies and other parts of which are not, are considered according to agency jurisdiction over their respective parts, so that normal Hart–Scott–Rodino Act requirements apply to those parts that do not fall within the specialized agency's specific authority.

See Act Sec. 133 at ¶ 1133. See Conference Report at ¶ 5005.

NATIONAL TREATMENT

¶ 141 Foreign Bank Financial Holding Companies

An amendment to the International Banking Act of 1978 permits the termination of grandfathered authority granted to foreign banks to engage in certain financial activities. Foreign banks with grandfathered financial affiliates may retain these grandfathered companies under the same terms that apply to a domestic financial holding company. These activities also must comply with any prudential safeguards established under Section 114 of the Gramm-Leach Bliley Act. Prior Federal Reserve Board approval is required to establish representative offices that are foreign bank subsidiaries. The Fed is authorized to examine those offices if necessary to ensure compliance with federal banking laws.

See Act Sec. 141 at ¶ 1141 and Act Sec. 142 at ¶ 1142.

DIRECT ACTIVITIES OF BANKS

¶ 151 National Banks' Municipal Bond Authority

A provision is added to the end of 12 USC 24 Seventh, by Subtitle F, which authorizes well-capitalized national banks to deal in, underwrite, and purchase municipal bonds for their own investment accounts. Specifically included are: limited obligation bonds; revenue bonds; and obligations that satisfy Section 142(b)(1) of the Internal Revenue Code of 1986. The authorization applies the obligations of any state or political subdivision, including any municipal corporate instrumentality of 1 or more states, and any public agency or authority.

See Act Sec. 151 at ¶ 1151.

Title II—Functional Regulation

BROKERS AND DEALERS

¶ 201 Functional Regulation

Title II of the Act provides for the functional regulation of bank securities activities. The House-Senate conference retained some limited exemptions to facilitate activities in which banks have traditionally engaged. These exceptions relate to third-party networking arrangements, trust activities, traditional banking activities such as commercial paper and exempted securities, employee and shareholder benefit plans, sweep accounts, affiliate transactions, private placements, safekeeping, and custody services, asset-backed securities, and identified banking products.

Title II contains four specific subtitles. Subtitle A deals with bank brokerage activities. Subtitle B covers bank investment company and investment advisory activities. Subtitle C creates the new SEC-supervised investment bank holding company structure. Subtitle D, which essentially codifies an amendment offered in the House by Rep. Marge Roukema, deals with loan loss reserves. Subtitles A and B take effect on May 12, 2001. Subtitles C and D are effective immediately.

A dominant theme of the Act is functional regulation, which is a general principle positing that similar activities should be regulated by the same regulator. Senator Rod Grams, Chairman of the Senate Securities Subcommittee, stated that the Act establishes a system of functional regulation under which institutions will be overseen by experts in their areas. In other words, the securities operations will continue to be supervised by securities experts, banks by banking experts, and insurance by state insurance commissioners. (Cong. Record, Nov. 4, 1999, p.S13889.)

Congress has seen that meaningful oversight by the SEC of securities transactions by banks is critical to the economy and will help ensure confidence in the nation's financial system. (See colloquy between Senators Sarbanes and Levin, Cong. Record, Nov. 4, 1999, p.S13901.)

Noting that functional regulation was strengthened, Senate Banking Committee Chairman Phil Gramm emphasized that the general rule under the Act is that a bank in the securities business will be regulated by the SEC. (Cong. Record, Nov. 3, 1999, p.S13783.) House Commerce Committee Chairman Tom Bliley views functional regulation as meaning that everyone gets the same oversight, the same rules, with no special advantage towards any party. It also means that activities should be regulated with the same strong consumer protections and safeguards no matter where they take place. (Cong. Record, Nov. 4, 1999 p.H11533.)

In his signing statement of November 12, 1999, President Clinton remarked that the Act preserves financial regulation along functional lines, with activities overseen by those regulators who are most knowledgeable about a given financial activity, including the SEC for securities activities and state regulators for insurance activities. Given the broad new affiliations permitted under the Act, the President fully expects the regulators to work together to protect the integrity of the nation's financial system.

History of Bank Exclusion

Banks have historically been exempt from the definitions of "broker" and "dealer" under the Exchange Act and consequently have not had to register as broker-dealers with the SEC. These exemptions have been part of the Exchange Act since its inception. They were based on the assumption that the Glass Steagall Act, which became law one year before the Exchange Act, had prohibited most bank securities activities.

The bank exclusion was originally bestowed because Congress recognized that these institutions were already subject to a comprehensive scheme of federal regulation. In recent years, however, Congress has come to recognize that the banking regulators have allowed banks to expand their securities activities.

Plainly, the exemptions had become historic anomalies. With the approval of their regulators, banks have been offering an increasing array of securities outside the scope of the federal securities laws. Banks were competing directly with registered broker-dealers subject to full SEC oversight. Congress recognized that a complete exclusion from securities regulation was no longer appropriate for banks that engage in a greater universe of securities activity. Thus, the Act accommodates this trend within a functional regulation framework.

The question was not whether these affiliations should occur in the financial arena since they were occurring one way or another. The question facing Congress was whether the affiliations should take place on an orderly basis in the context of a responsible statutory framework or on an ad hoc basis as permitted by the regulators. (Cong. Record, Nov. 3, 1999, p.13787.)

¶ 202 Brokers

The Act repeals the blanket exemption banks have enjoyed from the definition of "broker" and replaces it with a set of limited exemptions that allow the continuation of some traditional activities performed by banks. Thus, a bank will be considered a "broker" under the Exchange Act and subject to the full panoply of SEC regulation if it engages in the business of effecting transactions in securities for the accounts of others. However, at the same time, the Act carves out a number of exemptions from the definition of broker.

These exemptions embrace a number of activities and transactions traditionally performed by banks and those involving identified excepted banking products. If a bank limits its brokerage activities to those described in the exceptions, the bank will not be subject to broker-dealer registration. But as a cautionary note, banks using the exceptions should be aware that they will be subject to other Exchange Act provisions that are not based on broker-dealer status, such as the antifraud provisions.

The exceptions are a recognition that it may not be necessary, under certain conditions, to require a bank to register as a broker-dealer. In particular, registration may not be required because the conditions imposed on the excepted activities are tailored to protect investors and ensure competitive fairness among different types of financial services providers.

What follows is a discussion of the exceptions.

Networking Arrangements

Currently, banks sell securities to bank customers in one of three ways. First, the bank contracts with registered broker-dealers. Secondly, the bank registers broker-dealer subsidiaries or affiliates. Third, the bank sells securities directly through bank employees who are neither registered as broker-dealers nor licensed as registered representatives of a broker-dealer. Banks have been able to sell securities directly to customers because, under prior law, banks had been specifically excluded from broker-dealer registration under the federal securities laws.

The Act exempts third party brokerage arrangements from the definition of "broker." The exception for these networking arrangements follows a long line of SEC no-action letters. Under this exception, a bank will not be considered a broker if it offers brokerage services pursuant to written contracts with a broker under which the broker offers brokerage services on or off the premises of a bank under a number of specified conditions.

The networking exception provides a bank with a flexible mechanism by which it can provide securities services to its customers, use its personnel, and obtain commission fee income from the brokerage firm, without full broker-dealer registration.

As a general matter, under the networking exception, the registered broker-dealer and its registered personnel will be conducting all significant securities activities for the customer, including establishing the account, making suitability determinations, taking and executing orders, and sending confirmations.

The conditions contained in the networking exception are designed to promote investor protection. They foster a degree of separation from the bank and restrict the securities activities of unregistered bank personnel to reduce sales practice concerns. Thus, the broker-dealer networking activities must be performed in a clearly marked area that is, to the extent practicable, physically separate from the routine taking of deposits.

In addition, advertising materials must clearly indicate that the brokerage is being performed by the firm and not the bank and the materials must be in compliance with the federal securities laws before distribution.

As part of networking, banks frequently designate employees who become licensed registered representatives under the supervision of a broker-dealer for purposes of conducting brokerage transactions. These dual employees are associated persons of a broker-dealer and receive incentive compensation that depends on the successful outcome of the transaction from the broker-dealer.

Bank employees who are not dual employees may perform only clerical or ministerial functions. Permissible clerical or ministerial functions may include the scheduling of appointments with an associated person of a broker-dealer. In addition, bank employees who routinely handle customer funds and securities as part of their banking function may also forward customer funds or securities to the broker-dealer.

Bank employees who are not registered representatives may not make general or specific investment recommendations regarding securities, qualify a customer as eligible to purchase securities, or accept orders for securities.

But they may generally describe the types of investments available from the bank. Similarly, bank employees may not receive incentive compensation for any brokerage transaction, except that they may be compensated for referral of customers if in the form of a nominal, fixed amount, one-time cash fee and payment is not contingent on whether the customers purchase the securities.

Another condition of the exemption is that the bank cannot carry a securities account of the brokerage customer except under the trust and custodial exceptions. According to the House Commerce Committee, requiring the broker-dealer that is part of a networking arrangement to carry the investor account was done to ensure that investors have SIPC protection for the securities they purchase.

Finally, the broker or dealer must be clearly identified as the person performing the brokerage services. The bank and the broker must inform each customer that the services are provided by the broker not the bank and that the securities are neither deposits guaranteed by the bank nor insured by the FDIC.

The conferees provided for an exception for networking arrangements between banks and brokers. Revisions to Rule 1060 recently approved by the NASD are in conflict with this provision. Consequently, the conferees said that revisions to the rule should be made to exempt banks and their employees from coverage under the provision.

Trust Activities

In recognition of the traditional role banks have played in executing securities transactions in a fiduciary capacity, the Act exempts bank transactions conducted in a trustee or fiduciary capacity. In general, Congress believes that bank trust and fiduciary activities in the securities area have arisen as an accommodation to bank customers and have not been promoted through public solicitation of bank brokerage services.

The exception, however, is subject to a number of conditions. The transactions must be effected in the bank's trust department or in another department that is regularly examined by bank examiners for compliance with fiduciary principles and standards. In addition, a bank acting as trustee or fiduciary is subject to limitations on the type of compensation it may receive.

The Act conditions the exemption on the bank being chiefly compensated for its trust and fiduciary activities on the basis of an administrative or annual fee, a percentage of assets under management, or a flat or capped per order processing fee equal to not more than the cost incurred in executing securities transactions for its trustee or fiduciary customers.

Charging such fees, or any combination of such fees, must also be consistent with fiduciary principles and standards. According to the House Commerce Committee, the SEC is expected to interpret this exception, and in particular the references to "chiefly" and "fiduciary principles and standards" contained in the exception so as to limit a bank's ability to receive incentive compensation or similar compensation that could foster what the Committee called a "salesman's stake" in promoting a securities transaction.

The Committee does not intend for a bank to conduct a full-scale securities brokerage operation in the trust department exempt from SEC regulation and the imposition of appropriate investor protections under the federal securities laws.

The Act defines "fiduciary capacity" to include banks that act in the capacity of trustee, executor, administrator, registrar of stocks and bonds, transfer agent, guardian, assignee, receiver, or custodian under a uniform gift to minors act, or as an investment adviser if the bank receives a fee for its investment advice, or in any capacity in which the bank possesses investment discretion on behalf of another. The definition also allows the SEC to interpret the term fiduciary activity to include a bank that acts in a "similar capacity" to the enumerated trust and fiduciary activities.

The Commerce Committee expects that the term "similar" will be read to mean strictly comparable without any diminution of fiduciary obligation. Any bank claiming to act in a "similar capacity" must be subject to a trust or fiduciary agreement with its customers, subject to federal and state trust and fiduciary requirements, and strictly regulated and examined for bank trust purposes, as contemplated by the exception. Also, the Committee believes that churning customer accounts and recommending investments without regard to suitability for the customer is not consistent with fiduciary obligations

A final condition on the exception for trust activities is that the bank cannot publicly solicit brokerage business, except in connection with advertising its other trust activities. The term "advertising" used in this context is not intended to permit general public solicitation, but to allow a bank to indicate briefly—in a more general announcement of all the services provided in its trust department—that securities execution services in connection with trust and fiduciary services are also provided.

The conferees noted that banks effecting transactions in a trustee or fiduciary capacity under some conditions will be exempt from registration under the federal securities laws if the bank is chiefly compensated by means of administration and other fees, including a combination of such fees, and does not publicly solicit brokerage business. Congress expects that the SEC will not disturb traditional bank trust activities under this provision.

Permissible Securities Transactions

The Act contains an exception for permissible securities transactions, which are transactions in specific types of securities and instruments that banks commonly engage in. In order to ease compliance for banks unfamiliar with the federal securities laws, the exceptions restate exceptions found elsewhere in the Exchange Act. A bank will not be considered a broker if it conducts brokerage transactions in commercial paper and bills or bankers acceptances. This exception mirrors the current exceptions found elsewhere in the Exchange Act, and Congress wants the exception construed in the same manner as the Exchange Act exceptions.

Similarly, a bank will not be considered a broker if it conducts brokerage transactions in exempted securities under the Exchange Act. Banks acting as government securities brokers are already subject to Section 15C of the Exchange Act in connection with their government securities business.

For purposes of this exception, municipal securities are not treated as exempted securities, but are covered by a separate exception. In addition, a bank will not be considered a broker if it effects transactions in qualified Canadian government obligations, securities of the North American Development Bank, or Brady bonds.

Stock Purchase Plans

Banks have traditionally handled employee and shareholder benefit plans involving securities. Another group of related exceptions contained in the Act allows banks to act as agents for companies that want to sell securities directly to employees and shareholders. Thus, the Act exempts transactions that the bank effects as part of its transfer agent activities in the securities of an issuer as part of any employee pension, retirement, profit-sharing, or bonus plan so long as the bank neither solicits the transactions nor provides investment advice in connection with the transactions.

Similarly, a bank will not be considered a broker if it conducts brokerage transactions as part of a company's dividend reinvestment plan or stock purchase plan. These exemptions are subject to two conditions. First, the bank cannot solicit investors or provide investment advice in connection with the transactions. Secondly, the bank cannot net shareholder buy and sell orders other than for programs for odd-lot holders or SEC-registered plans.

Sweep Accounts

The Act contains a limited exception for banks that sweep depositors' funds on an overnight basis into a money market account. The exception has the effect of allowing banks to continue investing deposit funds into money market funds. Also exempted are transactions for the account of any affiliate other than a brokerage firm or an affiliate engaged in merchant banking.

Private Securities Offerings

Private placement of securities is a traditional broker-dealer activity, requiring broker-dealer regulation. Because private placements are an agency activity, they pose little risk to the bank. Thus, the Act creates an exception for private securities offerings. If a bank is not affiliated with a broker or dealer, the bank would be limited in its private placement activities. Specifically, any one private placement offering in which the bank is involved could not exceed 25% of the bank's capital, although private placements of government and municipal securities would be exempted.

Safekeeping and Custody

Bank safekeeping and custodial services may involve effecting securities transactions for bank customers. The Act contains a limited exemption from broker-dealer registration for banks providing safekeeping or custodial services to their customers as part of their customary banking activities.

Many of the activities permitted under the safekeeping and custody exception are incidental to activities that banks currently perform, such as selling securities dividends on custody securities or satisfying a guarantee or investing cash that serves as collateral on a securities loan. Others technically may not even involve effecting transactions in securities, such as purchasing securities to cover shortfalls in an account or liquidating collateral for the bank's own account.

Banks traditionally engaged in such activities under the comfort of the blanket bank exemption from broker-dealer registration. The safekeeping and custody exception essentially allows banks to continue to engage in the limited and incidental activities they engage in today in conjunction with their clearing and depository activities.

However, according to the House Commerce Committee, for the exception to apply, banks that perform functions customarily performed by clearing agencies or transfer agents in connection with securities must register as clearing agencies or transfer agents as already required under the Exchange Act.

In addition, the Committee cautioned that the exception is not intended to allow banks to engage in broader securities activities. The exception also will not apply to a bank acting as a clearing broker in connection with securities transactions, except if the bank is acting in the United States as a clearing broker with regard to government securities.

Specifically, Section 201 provides that a bank will not be considered a broker if it engages in the following customary banking activities:

—providing safekeeping and custody services to its customers with regard to securities, including the exercise of warrants and other rights on behalf of bank customers;

—facilitating the transfer of funds or securities as a custodian or clearing agent in connection with the clearance and settlement of its customers' transactions in securities;

—facilitating lending or financing transactions or investing cash in connection with its safekeeping, custody, and securities transfer services;

—holding securities pledged by a customer to another person or securities subject to repurchase agreements involving a customer, or facilitating the pledging or transfer of such securities by book entry or as otherwise provided by law, provided that the bank maintains records separately identifying the securities and the customer;

—serving as a custodian or provider of other related administrative services to any individual retirement account, pension, retirement, profit sharing, bonus, thrift savings, incentive, or other similar benefit plan.

Municipal Securities

The Act grants an exception for a bank acting as a broker in municipal securities transactions. This preserves an exception for banks acting in a brokerage capacity that is found in the current regulatory scheme for bank municipal securities.

De Minimis Exception

In order to accommodate limited securities brokerage of small banks, the Act contains a de minimis exception for banks effecting up to 500 securities transactions a year, in addition to those within the excepted bank activities. A condition of this exception is that bank employees who are also brokerage firm employees (so called dual employees) may not claim the exception for any transactions that they effect.

Limitation on Exceptions

The Act provides for an additional limitation promoting best execution in connection with the new bank exceptions for trust and fiduciary activities, stock purchase plans, and safekeeping and custody services. Section 201 makes clear that these exceptions do not apply if the bank effects securities transactions that result in the trade in the United States of any security that is a publicly traded security in the U.S. unless the bank directs the trade to a registered broker or dealer, the trade is a cross-trade or substantially similar trade, or the trade is conducted in some other way permitted by the SEC.

Identified Banking Products

Finally, the Act contains an important exception for what the measure calls "identified banking products." These products generally involve products that have not traditionally been characterized as securities, such as savings accounts. The purpose of this provision is to provide for exceptions from the registration requirements of the federal securities laws for banks engaging in activities relating to specified products.

Under Section 206, an identified banking product includes a deposit account, a savings account, a certificate of deposit, a banker's acceptance, a letter of credit issued or a loan made by a bank, a debit account, or loan participations. Also within the definition are swap agreements, including all credit and equity swaps. The conferees indicated that the Act allows banks to continue to be active participants in the derivatives business for all credit and equity swaps, other than equity swaps to retail customers.

According to Rep. Patrick Toomey, a Banking Committee member, the Act reaffirms that swap contracts are legitimate bank products that can be executed and booked in banks and are adequately regulated by, and will continue to be regulated by, the banking supervisors. (Cong. Record, Nov. 4, 1999, p. H11521.) Rep. Larry Combest, Chairman of the House Agriculture Committee, indicated that a bank explicitly is not required to register as a broker-dealer for participating in "certain hybrid and swap" transactions. (Cong. Record, Nov. 4, 1999, p11550.)

The loan participation exception is qualified by the fact that it must be a participation in a loan which the bank or an affiliate, other than a broker or dealer, funds, participates in, or owns; and that is sold to qualified investors or to other persons that have the opportunity to review and assess any material information and, based on factors such as financial sophistication, net worth, and knowledge and experience in financial matters, are capable of evaluating the information available, as determined under generally applicable banking standards or guidelines.

With regard to loans and loan participations, the House Commerce Committee has pointed out that these two exceptions deserve special consideration. For example, legislative history indicates that the exception for loans may only be available for loans that are not securities under the Exchange Act. What constitutes a loan that is not a security should be determined by reference to the U.S. Supreme Court's 1990 ruling in *Reves v. Ernst & Young,* CCH FED. SEC. LAW REP. 1989-1990 Dec. ¶ 94,939, which sets out a family resemblance test for notes to determine if they are securities.

In *Reves,* a list of notes previously deemed not to be securities is recognized, including notes delivered in consumer financing, notes secured by a mortgage on a home, a short-term note secured by a lien on a small business or its assets, a short-term note secured by an assignment of accounts receivable, a note that simply formalizes an open-account debt incurred in the ordinary course of business, and notes evidencing loans by commercial banks for current operations.

For other instruments, the *Reves* Court presumes that every note is a security and then applies the family resemblance test to determine if the presumption is correct. The presumption is rebutted if a note bears a strong resemblance to any instrument on a list of notes that have previously been deemed not to be securities or, if upon applying the test, it is determined that the note should be added to the list.

The Court identifies four factors to consider in determining if a note should be added to the list: 1) the motivation that would prompt a reasonable buyer and seller to enter into the transaction; 2) the plan of distribution of the instrument; 3) the reasonable expectation of investors; and 4) whether some factor, such as the existence of another regulatory scheme, significantly reduces the risk of the instrument, thereby rendering application of the securities laws unnecessary.

In the view of the Commerce Committee, the loans included in the Act's exception do not include instruments that would be deemed to be securities under the *Reves* family resemblance test. In general, the *Reves* test does not include instruments that are purchased, delivered, or sold in connection with consumer or commercial financing transactions. In contrast, notes that have characteristics typically associated with an investment purpose would be deemed securities under the federal securities laws, and therefore outside the scope of the exception.

With regard to loan participations, the Commerce Committee expects that a similar analysis will be used to create the conditions for sale of loan participations by banks. It is also important to note that the requirement that purchasers of loan participations from banks have an opportunity to review and assess any material information, including information on the borrower's creditworthiness, comes from the opinion by the Second Circuit Court of Appeals in *Banco Espanol de Credito v. Security Pacific National Bank,* CCH FED. SEC. LAW REP. 1992 Dec. ¶ 96,819.

The appeals court ruled that loan participations sold by the bank were not securities. Under the facts, purchasers signed an agreement acknowledging that they had independently and without reliance on the bank, and based on such documents and information as the participants deemed appropriate, made their own credit analysis.

The court specifically noted that the plan of distribution limited eligible buyers to those with the capacity to acquire information about the debtor. It was determined that the offering was a limited solicitation to sophisticated financial or commercial institutions.

Later cases have distinguished the *Banco Espanol* decision when offerings are not restricted to sophisticated investors who have the capacity to acquire information about the debtor. In *Pollack v. Laidlaw Holdings, Inc.*, CCH FED. SEC. LAW REP. 1993-1994 Dec. ¶ 98,248, the Second Circuit ruled that the sale of mortgage interests to less sophisticated investors was a sale of securities.

Commodity Exchange Act

For purposes of the exception, Section 206 defines a "swap agreement" to be any individually negotiated contract, warrant, note, or option that is based on the value of, any interest in, or any quantitative measure or the occurrence of any event relating to, one or more commodities, securities, currencies, interest, or other rates, indices, or other assets.

Section 206 specifies that classification of a product as an identified banking product is not intended to imply that any such product is or is not a security, or an account, agreement, contract, or transaction for any purpose under the Commodity Exchange Act.

The conferees emphasized that the classification of a particular product as an identified banking product will not be construed as a finding or implication that the product is or is not a federal security, or is or is not a transaction for any purpose under the Commodity Exchange Act. The conferees did not intend to express an opinion in the Act or to address the issue of legal certainty for swap agreements under the securities and commodities laws.

This provision makes clear, in the view of House Agriculture Chairman Larry Combest, that, in the case of swaps and hybrids, the classification of a particular type of instrument for purposes of the Gramm-Leach-Bliley Act does not preclude that instrument or transaction from falling under CFTC jurisdiction under the Commodity Exchange Act. (Cong. Rec. Nov 4, 1999, p. H11550.)

See Act Sections 201 and 206 at ¶ 1201 and ¶ 1206. See Conference Report at ¶ 5008.

¶ 203 Dealers

The Exchange Act had excluded banks from the definition of "dealer." Section 202 of the Act amends the Exchange Act to include banks within the general definition of dealer. The Act defines "dealer" to mean any person engaged in the business of buying and selling securities for such person's own account through a broker or otherwise. Section 202 then creates specific exceptions from the definition for a number of bank activities.

Permissible Securities Transactions

An exception for permissible securities transactions—similar to the one for brokers—recognizes transactions in specific types of securities and instruments that banks commonly engage in. In some cases, in order to ease compliance for banks unfamiliar with the federal securities laws, these exceptions restate exceptions found elsewhere in the Exchange Act. Thus, a bank will be excepted from the definition of "dealer" if it buys or sells commercial paper, bankers acceptances, commercial bills, or exempted securities under the Exchange Act.

In addition, this exception extends to a bank if it buys or sells qualified Canadian government obligations under the regulatory framework applicable to U.S. government securities, securities of the North American Development Bank, or Brady bonds.

Investment, Trustee, and Fiduciary Transactions

Section 202 also excepts a bank from the definition of "dealer" when it buys or sells securities for investment purposes for the bank or for accounts for which the bank acts as trustee or fiduciary. This exception mirrors existing law distinguishing between investors and dealers, and is limited to the portfolio trading of the bank and accounts for which it makes investment decisions.

Asset-Backed Transactions

Banks increasingly engage in asset-backed securities transactions, which are designed to move assets off their balance sheets by selling them as securities to investors. Section 202 contains a limited exception for bank asset-backed securities transactions that is designed to foster investor protection while preserving the ability of banks to continue to provide services relating to asset-backed securities where the bank has a significant stake in the assets being securitized.

A bank will be excepted from the definition of "dealer" if it engages in the issuance or sale to qualified investors, through a grantor trust or other separate entity, of securities backed by or representing an interest in notes, drafts, acceptances, loans, leases, receivables, other obligations (other than securities of which the bank is not an issuer) or pools of any obligations predominantly originated by the bank, or an affiliate of the bank (other than a broker or dealer). Asset-backed transactions involving mortgage obligations or consumer-related receivables must be originated by a syndicate of banks of which the bank is a member.

For the exception to apply, the asset-backed securities must be placed in a grantor trust, or other separate entity, so that applicable Securities Act registration requirements apply. According to the House Commerce Committee, this separation requirement fosters the market practice of requiring rating agency scrutiny of the assets and appropriate collateralization. The Committee has emphasized that this exemption is intended to limit banks to the universe of asset-backed underwriting in which banks can engage.

Finally, similar to brokers, there is an exception for banks that buy or sell identified banking products. (For a discussion of identified banking products see ¶ 202.)

See Act Sec. 202 at ¶ 1202. See Conference Report at ¶ 5008.

¶ 204 Registration for Sales of Private Offerings

Section 203 creates a new limited qualification category of NASD registration for bank employees engaged in private securities offerings. In this context, Exchange Act provisions setting forth the requirements to be a registered securities association have been amended to direct a registered securities association to create a limited qualification category, without a testing requirement, for associated persons of members who effect private placement sales.

The registered securities association is further directed to deem qualified for such limited qualification category, without testing, those associated persons who have been bank employees engaged in private placement sales in the six months before enactment of the Gramm-Leach-Bliley Act.

See Act Sec. 203 at ¶ 1203.

¶ 205 Information Sharing

The Federal Deposit Insurance Act has been amended to require federal banking agencies, after consultation with the SEC and consideration of its views, to establish recordkeeping requirements for banks relying on the exceptions from the definitions of broker and dealer. These recordkeeping requirements must result in records that are sufficient to demonstrate compliance with the terms of the exceptions. The records kept must be made available by the appropriate federal banking agency upon the SEC's request.

Section 204 also provides that the SEC cannot be compelled to disclose any of this information. But the Commission is not authorized to withhold information from Congress. In addition, the SEC is not prevented from complying with a request for information from another federal agency or any self-regulatory organization, or complying with a federal court order in an action brought by the U.S. or the Commission.

See Act Sec. 204 at ¶ 1204.

¶ 206 New Hybrid Products

It is expected that many complex new products will be developed with both banking and securities elements. Section 205 provides a procedure for handling new hybrid products sold by banks that have securities elements. The statute provides for a "jump ball" rulemaking and resolution process between the SEC and the Federal Reserve Board regarding new hybrid products, with a federal appeals court as final arbiter.

For new hybrid products, the House-Senate conference codified in the securities laws a process requiring the SEC to act by rulemaking before seeking to regulate any bank sales of any such new product. This rulemaking process is designed to give notice to the banking industry in an area that could involve complex new products with many elements.

The process would work as follows. Before seeking to require a bank to register as a broker or dealer with regard to the sale of new hybrid products, the SEC will have to engage in rulemaking. Before commencing a rulemaking process, the SEC is required to consult with and seek the concurrence of the Federal Reserve Board concerning the imposition of broker and dealer registration requirements with regard to any new hybrid product.

Further, in developing and promulgating rules under this subsection, the SEC must consider the views of the Federal Reserve Board, including views with respect to the nature of the new hybrid product; the history, purpose, extent, and appropriateness of the regulation of the new product under the federal banking laws; and the impact of the proposed rule on the banking industry.

In its rulemaking, the SEC would need to find that the new product is a security. In addition, the SEC would have to determine that the product is a new hybrid product.

During the rulemaking process, the SEC is required to make a number of other findings. The SEC must also determine that imposing registration as a broker or dealer on a bank is necessary or appropriate in the public interest and for the protection of investors. The conferees noted that, when considering if such an action is in the public interest, the SEC must also consider if the action will promote efficiency, competition, and capital formation, as set forth in Section 3(f) of the Exchange Act. The conferees noted that the SEC's record in implementing Section 3(f) has failed to meet congressional intent. The conferees expect that the SEC will improve in this area.

In making determinations on whether the new hybrid product is a security and that imposing registration is in the public interest, the statute commands the Commission to consider the nature of the new product and the history, purpose, extent, and appropriateness of the regulation of the new product under the federal securities and banking laws.

The Act provides guidance to help the SEC in its analysis. Section 205 defines "new hybrid product" to carve out products that were already viewed as a security as of the enactment of the Gramm-Leach-Bliley Act. As a result, these traditional securities products do not require rulemaking, in the view of the House Commerce Committee, before bank compliance with broker-dealer registration requirements, even if these securities products are called by a different name. Traditional securities could include, for example, products that were regularly subject to securities registration statements or which have been viewed as a security in the context of SEC enforcement actions prior to enactment.

The definition also provides that a new hybrid product is not one of the products listed in the definition of identified banking product. Moreover, the conference indicated that including a product on the list of identified banking products should not be construed as a finding or implication that such product is or is not a security, but it would not be a new hybrid product. The conference codified the definition of identified banking product as a freestanding provision of law, neither in the securities laws nor in the banking laws.

If the Federal Reserve Board seeks review of any final regulation under this section, the review will serve as a stay on the rulemaking until final adjudication of the matter between the SEC and the Board.

In considering such an appeal, the U.S. Court of Appeals for the District of Columbia will determine to affirm and enforce or set aside an SEC regulation based on the determination of the court as to whether: 1) the subject product is a new hybrid product; 2) the subject product is a security; 3) imposing a requirement to register as a broker or dealer for banks engaging in transactions in such product is appropriate in light of the history, purpose, and extent of regulation under the federal securities laws and under the federal banking laws, giving deference neither to the views of the SEC nor to the Board.

See Act Sec. 205 at ¶ 1205. See Conference Report at ¶ 5008.

¶ 207 Qualified Investors

Section 207 adds a definition of "qualified investor" to the Exchange Act. A long list of entities are defined as qualified investors, including registered investment companies, banks, savings associations, brokers, dealers, insurance companies, and business development companies. Also included in the definition are state sponsored employee benefit plans, or any other employee benefit plan within the meaning of ERISA, other than an individual retirement account. Foreign banks as defined in the International Banking Act of 1978 and the governments of foreign countries are also qualified investors.

A company or individual investor that owns and invests at least $25 million on a discretionary basis is deemed a qualified investor. However, with regard to asset-backed securities and loan participations, the threshold is lowered to $10 million.

Finally, the SEC is authorized to define a "qualified investor" as any other person, taking into consideration such factors as the person's financial sophistication, net worth, and knowledge and experience in financial matters.

See Act Sec. 207 at ¶ 1207.

¶ 208 Government Securities

The Exchange Act was amended to include in the definition of "government securities" qualified Canadian government obligations. As a result of this change, banks engaging in activities in Canadian government obligations must comply with the government securities requirements with regard to these securities.

See Act Sec. 208 at ¶ 1208.

¶ 209 Commodity Exchange Act

Section 210 provides that nothing in the Act will supersede, effect, or otherwise limit the scope and applicability of the Commodity Exchange Act. Congress does not intend in any way to alter or affect the applicability of the Commodity Exchange Act to transactions covered by these provisions, to the extent that such Act might otherwise be applicable to such transactions.

The conference report emphasized that the CEA is not amended by the Act, and no transaction or person that is otherwise subject to the jurisdiction of the CFTC pursuant to the CEA is exempted from such jurisdiction because of the provisions of the modernization legislation.

In addition, Rep. Larry Combest stated that the CFTC's traditional authority is not affected by the Gramm-Leach-Bliley Act. The House Agriculture Chairman indicated that Section 210 recognizes that transactions which are futures contracts or commodity options under the CFTC's exclusive jurisdiction pursuant to the CEA do not receive an exemption from the CEA because of anything in the Act. No financial instrument described in the Act, be it a swap agreement, new hybrid product, or identified banking product, is exempted from CFTC jurisdiction solely by virtue of anything contained in the modernization measure. (Cong. Record, Nov 4. 1999, p.H11550.)

See Act Sec. 210 at ¶ 1210. See Conference Report at ¶ 5008.

¶ 210 Effective Date

The effective date of Subtitle A is 18 months from the date of enactment.

See Act Sec. 209 at ¶ 1209.

BANK INVESTMENT COMPANY ACTIVITIES

¶ 211 Bank Mutual Fund and Advisory Activities

The Gramm-Leach-Bliley Act addresses the concerns raised by the increased involvement of banks in the activities of investment companies, including mutual funds and unit investment trusts. Banks are now significant participants in the mutual fund industry. But it was not always so. In 1940, when the Investment Company Act was passed, bank involvement in funds was minimal.

Because of this, the 1940 Act does not address many of the concerns raised by the SEC and others when banks provide investment management and related services to funds. The Gramm-Leach-Bliley Act, however, recognizes these conflicts and seeks to address them. It applies the principle of functional regulation to bank investment company activities in much the same way as it applies that principle to bank brokerage activities.

¶ 212 Custodial Arrangements

The 1940 Act does not limit a bank's ability to serve as custodian of the assets of an affiliated management investment company. Although the Investment Company Act gives the SEC general rulemaking authority regarding investment company custodial arrangements, Section 211 confirms and clarifies that the SEC's rulemaking authority regarding mutual fund custodial arrangements extends to custodial arrangements involving affiliated banks.

The Act amends Section 17(f) of the Act to expressly authorize the SEC to adopt rules prescribing the conditions under which a bank or one of its affiliated persons may serve as the mutual fund's custodian.

Section 26(a)(1) of the Investment Company Act requires a unit investment trust to designate as trustee or custodian a bank meeting certain qualifications. The Act amends Section 26(a) to expressly authorize the SEC to adopt rules and issue orders prescribing the conditions under which a bank may serve as trustee or custodian of the trust.

Section 211 also mandates that any SEC rulemaking must be after consultation with the federal banking agencies and consideration of their views.

See Act Sec. 211 at ¶ 1211.

¶ 213 Affiliated Transactions

The 1940 Act governs transactions and relationships between mutual funds and their affiliates. Section 17(a) prohibits an affiliated person of a mutual fund from borrowing money or other property from the fund. The Act, however, does not clearly restrict a person's ability to make a loan to an affiliated mutual fund. Congress recognizes that loans to a mutual fund from an affiliate carry the potential for overreaching since the affiliate could, for example, charge the fund an above-market interest rate.

Addressing this potential for overreaching, the reform act makes it unlawful for any affiliated person of a mutual fund, or an affiliate of that person, to loan money or other property to the fund in contravention of any rules the SEC may issue. In issuing any rules, the SEC must consult with and take into consideration the views of the federal banking agencies.

See Act Sec. 212 at ¶ 1212.

¶ 214 Independent Directors

Under the 1940 Act, persons with a material relationship to a mutual fund or to a fund's adviser or principal underwriter are deemed interested persons of those entities. The Act limits the number of interested persons who may serve on a fund's board and generally uses the interested person concept to minimize conflicts of interest. For example, the Act requires a fund's investment advisory contract to be approved annually by a majority of directors who are not interested persons of the fund or the fund's adviser.

The 1940 Act's definition of interested person currently includes any registered broker or dealer or any affiliated person of the broker or dealer. The Gramm-Leach-Bliley Act amends the definition to include any person or its affiliate that, during the preceding six months, executed any portfolio transactions for the fund, engaged in any principal transactions with the fund, distributed shares for the fund, or lent money or property to the fund. Similar changes are made to the definition of interested person of an investment adviser or principal underwriter of an investment company.

In an effort to prevent interlocking relationships between mutual funds and banks, Section 10(c) of the 1940 Act prohibits a mutual fund from having a majority of its board of directors composed of individuals who are officers, directors, or employees of any one bank. The Act would extend this prohibition to any one bank, together with its affiliates and subsidiaries, or any one bank holding company, together with its affiliates and subsidiaries.

This extension is intended to strengthen the independence of a fund's board and eliminate the potential to circumvent the legislative intent of

Section 10(c) by a bank operating under a multiple bank holding structure. The rationale of Section 10(c) should apply whether or not a bank is affiliated with a holding company.

See Act Sec. 213 at ¶ 1213.

¶ 215 SEC Disclosure Authority

Concern has been expressed by the SEC and others that customers purchasing shares of a mutual fund sold through a bank may become confused and act on an implied belief that the investment is guaranteed by the bank or by the federal government. Because the federal government insures bank deposits, it is possible that some investors may mistakenly believe that a mutual fund advised by a bank or sold on bank premises is insured.

Section 214 of the Act addresses this concern by requiring persons issuing or selling shares in a mutual fund that is advised by or sold through a bank to prominently disclose that an investment in the mutual fund is not federally insured.

The SEC is authorized to adopt rules setting forth the manner in which such disclosure must be provided. In its rulemaking, the SEC must consult with and consider the views of the federal banking agencies. But even if the SEC has not adopted rules, legislative history indicates that bank advised mutual funds are still required to disclose that investments in their funds are not federally insured.

Legislative history also indicates that this disclosure obligation applies only to mutual funds sold through, or advised by, a bank and not to funds that are not sold through, or advised by, a bank

Section 214 also prohibits any person issuing or selling mutual fund shares from representing or implying that the fund or the shares are federally insured or are guaranteed by a bank.

See Act Sec. 214 at ¶ 1214.

¶ 216 Definition of Broker

Section 215 replaces the definition of "broker" in Section 2(a)(6) of the Investment Company Act with a reference to the definition of "broker" in the Exchange Act. The amended definition continues to exclude any person that would be deemed a broker solely because the person is an underwriter for one or more investment companies.

Similarly, Section 218 replaces the definition of "broker" in Section 202(a)(3) of the Investment Advisers Act with a reference to the definition of "broker" in the Exchange Act.

See Act Sections 215 and 218 at ¶ 1215 and ¶ 1218.

¶ 217 Definition of Dealer

Section 216 replaces the definition of "dealer" in Section 2(a)(11) of the Investment Company Act with a reference to the definition of "dealer" in the Exchange Act. The amended definition continues to exclude insurance companies and investment companies.

Similarly, Section 219 replaces the definition of "dealer" in Section 202(a)(7) of the Investment Advisers Act with a reference to the definition of "dealer" in the Exchange Act. The amended definition continues to exclude insurance companies and investment companies.

See Act Sections 216 and 219 at ¶ 1216 and ¶ 1219.

¶ 218 Bank Investment Advisers

The long-term exclusion of banks from regulation under the Investment Advisers Act of 1940 has come to an end. The Gramm-Leach-Bliley Act eliminates the bank exclusion from the definition of investment adviser. The bank exclusion had been under attack in Congress for some time. It was slated for repeal by similar provisions in the Proxmire Financial Modernization Act, which passed the Senate on March 30, 1988, in what was ultimately a failed attempt to achieve financial services reform.

The exclusion enjoyed by banks from the definition of investment adviser had allowed bank advisory activities to occur outside the SEC's securities oversight system and, therefore, outside the system of functional regulation. The Act would include within the definition of investment adviser under the Investment Advisers Act any bank or bank holding company serving as an investment adviser to a mutual fund.

The change is intended to make banks advising mutual funds subject to the same regulatory scheme as other mutual fund advisers. It is also designed to help the SEC more effectively protect the interests of shareholders in mutual funds advised by banks. This will be done by giving the SEC greater access to records and information necessary to ensure that bank advisers comply with the federal securities laws.

At present, when SEC staff examine an investment company advised by a bank not registered as an investment adviser, the staff does not have the authority to require the bank to produce trading records related to advisory customers other than registered mutual funds. This limitation makes it difficult to uncover practices that may violate the federal securities laws. For example, a bank advising a mutual fund could allocate more profitable trades to bank trust accounts and less profitable trades to the mutual fund.

Bank advisory personnel could also engage in front running the securities transactions of the mutual fund by trading the same securities for their personal accounts. By making banks that advise mutual funds subject to the Advisers Act, Congress believes that the SEC staff will have greater access to books and records that might reveal these abusive practices.

The removal of the exclusion would not mean that a bank is required to set up a separate subsidiary or affiliate in order to register as an investment adviser, although it would presumably be allowed to do so. Rather, the Act would give banks the option of conducting their advisory activities through what Congress calls a "separately identifiable department" or SID.

If a bank does that, only the SID and not the bank would be deemed an investment adviser subject to the full panoply of SEC regulation under the Advisers Act. The SEC would have the same authority over a SID as it would over any other investment adviser.

The Act defines a SID as a unit under the direct supervision of an officer designated by the bank's board of directors as responsible for the day-to-day conduct of the bank's investment advisory activities for one or more mutual funds, including the supervision of all bank employees engaged in the performance of such activities.

All records relating to investment advisory activities must be separately maintained in, or extractable from, the unit's own facilities or bank facilities so as to allow SEC examination and enforcement.

See Act Sec. 217 at ¶ 1217.

¶ 219 Interagency Consultations

In order to promote interagency consultations, the Act adds a new section 210A to the Advisers Act requiring federal banking regulators and the SEC to share the results of any examination, reports, records, or other information regarding the investment advisory activities of any bank, bank holding company, or separately identifiable department registered as an investment adviser. If a bank has a SID that is a registered investment adviser, the bill requires the bank regulator to share with the SEC the results of any examination, reports, records, or other information regarding the bank.

The statute does not in any way limit the authority of a banking agency to regulate the bank, bank holding company or SID. Rather, the new section is designed to assist the SEC and federal bank regulators in obtaining information from one another that may be helpful in carrying out their statutory duties. It is also intended to provide the SEC with access to information on a bank that, although not registered as an investment adviser itself, has a SID or subsidiary that is so registered.

The statute also provides that the SEC and the federal banking agencies cannot be compelled to disclose any information provided under it. However, the regulators are not authorized to withhold information from Congress and are not prevented from complying with a request for information from any other federal department or agency or any self-regulatory organization requesting the information for purposes within the scope of its jurisdiction, or complying with a federal court order in an action brought by the United States, the SEC, or the federal banking agencies.

See Act Sec. 220 at ¶ 1220.

¶ 220 Bank Common Trust Funds

Bank common trust funds currently enjoy an exemption from Securities Act registration and are excluded from the definition of investment company under the Investment Company Act. In addition, because interests in common trust funds are exempted securities under the Exchange Act, persons effecting transactions in these interests need not register as broker-dealers.

All three statutes limit the exception to a common trust fund or similar fund maintained by a bank exclusively for the collective investment or reinvestment of money contributed thereto by the bank in its capacity as a trustee, executor, administrator, or guardian.

The Act largely codifies a longstanding SEC position that the exception from the securities laws available to a bank common trust fund applies only when the underlying trust relationship is created for bona fide fiduciary purposes, and when the fund is operated for the administrative convenience of the bank in a manner incidental to the bank's traditional trust department activities and not as a vehicle for general investment by the public.

Gramm-Leach-Bliley also amends the exemption from the 1940 Act for bank common trust funds so that it applies to a common trust fund satisfying three conditions. Thus, a bank common trust fund is exempt from the 1940 Act only if it meets three conditions. First, the common trust fund must be employed solely as an aid to the administration of trusts, estates or other fiduciary accounts. Secondly, interests in the fund may not be advertised or offered for sale to the public except in connection with generic advertising of the bank's overall fiduciary services. Third, the common trust fund cannot charge fees in contravention of fiduciary principles established under applicable state or federal law.

See Act Sec. 221 at ¶ 1221.

¶ 221 Disqualification

In an effort to provide investors in bank-advised mutual funds with the same protection afforded to investors in other funds, the Act adds banks to a list of entities that are disqualified from acting as investment advisers because they have been convicted of a felony or misdemeanor or have been enjoined because of their conduct with regard to securities activities.

See Act Sec. 222 at ¶ 1222.

¶ 222 Change in Definition

Section 223 amends the definition of "bank" in Section 2(a)(5) of the Investment Company Act by deleting the reference to a banking institution organized under the laws of the United States and substituting a reference to a depository institution as defined in the Federal Deposit Insurance Act, or a branch or agency of a foreign bank, as those terms are defined in the International Banking Act of 1978. The Exchange Act continues to define banks by reference to organization under United States law.

See Act Sec. 223 at ¶ 1223.

¶ 223 Conforming Amendments

The Investment Advisers Act was amended to require that when the SEC, as part of a rulemaking, considers whether an action is necessary or appropriate in the public interest, it must also consider whether the action will promote efficiency, competition, and capital formation. This provision is intended to incorporate into the Advisers Act a standard for SEC rulemaking similar to those that were added to the Securities Act, the Exchange Act, and the Investment Company Act as part of the National Securities Markets Improvement Act of 1996.

See Act Sec. 224 at ¶ 1224.

¶ 224 Effective Date

It is provided in Section 225 of the Act that the effective date of Subtitle B is 18 months after the date of enactment.

See Act Sec. 225 at ¶ 1225.

¶ 225 Fair Treatment of Women by Advisers

Section 733 provides that it is the sense of Congress that individuals offering financial advice and products should offer such services and products in a non-discriminatory, non-gender specific manner. The genesis of this provision was an amendment to the House bill offered by Rep. Louise Slaughter that would have created a congressional finding that investment advisers and financial planners still use sales themes stereotyping women as uncomfortable handling money and needing protection from their own possible errors in judgment.

The probable goal of the provision, based on the legislative history of the amendment, is that the provision establishes the sense of the Congress that investment advisers and other financial consultants should eliminate examples in their materials portraying women as incapable and foolish.

According to Rep. Slaughter, her amendment was designed to encourage a rethinking of these financial practices. (Cong Record, July 1, 1999, H5293.) In remarks on the day the Act was passed, Rep. Slaughter remarked that Section 733 was based on her amendment and that its language was in response to estate documents that keep women from controlling their inherited financial assets. Some estate planning publications and sales literature for trusts use themes generally indicating that women should be relieved of the burden of managing money because they cannot learn.

Rep. Slaughter said it is past time that these outdated themes are addressed and discriminatory financial practices brought out in the open as "we move forward to modernize the rest of the financial services industry." (Cong. Record, Nov. 4, 1999, p.H11522.)

See Act Sec. 733 at ¶ 1773

SEC SUPERVISION OF INVESTMENT BANK HOLDING COMPANIES

¶ 226 Investment Bank Holding Companies

The most sweeping reform of financial services regulation in sixty years has created a new type of supervised entity that will engage primarily in securities-related activities. The new SEC-supervised entity is called an investment bank holding company. The creation of this new entity addresses concerns previously raised by the SEC that risk-oriented supervision is appropriate when an entity engages primarily in securities activities.

The SEC-supervised investment bank holding company is an alternative to a financial holding company. Under strictures spelled out in the Act, the SEC would assume a new role as a holding company supervisor. The concept embodies the principles of functional regulation and free association. Securities firms could freely elect to subject their holding company activities to consolidated SEC oversight and would also be free to withdraw from SEC supervision as holding companies.

The Act creates a voluntary supervisory structure for the investment bank holding company, which is defined as a person owning or controlling one or more brokers or dealers and any associated person of an investment bank holding company. A regime of voluntary SEC oversight is set forth for entities desiring consolidated holding company supervision, but that do not have affiliated banks or savings associations. This SEC supervision may be useful or necessary for firms seeking to engage in global financial activities.

In order to expand overseas, U.S. brokerage firms usually have to show foreign regulators that they are subject to comprehensive supervision on a worldwide basis. SEC Chairman Arthur Levitt has noted that a brokerage firm doing business in London may be affected as much by the activities of its New York or Singapore affiliates as by conditions in the U.S. markets. Thus, foreign regulators are concerned that the absence of a central authority overseeing the global activities of U.S. securities firms may put local investors at risk.

The vision offered by Gramm-Leach-Bliley is that, if brokerage firms elect to place themselves under the voluntary supervision offered by the investment bank holding company, the SEC will have the authority to oversee the entire entity, thus satisfying the expectations of foreign jurisdictions that the entity be subject to comprehensive supervision.

It is expected that the SEC's umbrella oversight will be based on a risk-supervision model that more appropriately reflects the pre-dominant risktaking activities of the consolidated entity. In turn, this option will be useful, or even necessary, for investment bank holding companies doing business in foreign jurisdictions requiring consolidated holding company supervision.

The Commission supports the establishment of investment bank holding companies. In testimony before the House Commerce Committee, Chairman Levitt emphasized the SEC's belief that holding companies with both securities and banking activities that are primarily engaged in securities activities should be overseen by the Commission.

The SEC also believes that, in addition to addressing the concerns of foreign regulators, a supervisory framework for holding companies that substantially engage in securities activities would allow securities firms the flexibility to innovate and keep pace with the rapid changes taking place in today's markets.

Reporting and Recordkeeping

If an investment bank holding company elects SEC supervision, the company and its affiliates become subject to SEC examinations and to SEC recordkeeping and reporting requirements. In its role as a holding company supervisor, the SEC can adopt rules needed to provide information about each supervised IBHC's activities, financial condition, policies, transactions and relationships between affiliated brokers or dealers, and any systems for monitoring and controlling financial and operational risks.

The Commission may also adopt rules it needs to ascertain the extent to which an IBHC is complying with the Exchange Act. In addition, the Commission may require IBHCs to keep records containing the information listed above and provide reports to the Commission. The reports may include financial statements, capital assessments, and reports by independent auditors regarding compliance with risk management and internal control.

In an effort to minimize regulatory burdens, the SEC is directed to use, to the fullest extent possible, any reports that an IBHC has provided to another regulator. Also, the IBHC must, when requested, give the SEC reports prepared for another regulator.

Examinations

The SEC would also be authorized to examine any supervised investment bank holding company and any affiliate to gather information about its operations and financial condition. The examination could include the risks within the company that may affect any affiliated brokerage firm, as well as any systems for monitoring that risk. The Commission must limit the scope of any examination to the company and any affiliate of the company that, because of its size or the nature of its transactions, could have a "materially adverse" effect on the broker-dealer's operational or financial condition.

To the fullest extent possible, the SEC must use examination reports prepared by other functional regulators, such as federal banking agencies and state insurance regulators. On the more general theme of functional regulation, the Act requires that, in exercising supervision over IBHCs, the SEC must defer to the appropriate banking or insurance regulator with regard to interpretations of banking and insurance law.

Withdrawal from SEC Supervision

Finally, a supervised investment bank holding company could voluntarily withdraw from SEC supervision, subject to any necessary conditions the Commission may see fit to impose. Similarly, the Commission may discontinue supervision of any investment bank holding company if, for example, it finds that the company no longer exists, is no longer an investment bank holding company or that supervision is no longer consistent with the federal securities laws.

Freedom of Information Act

The Act would also authorize the SEC to limit disclosure, pursuant to the Freedom of Information Act, of information required to be reported to it or information supplied to it by any domestic or foreign regulator that relates to the financial or operational condition of any associated person of a broker-dealer, investment bank holding company, or any affiliate of the IBHC. However, this subsection does not authorize the SEC to withhold information from Congress, or from another federal department or agency.

See Act Sec. 231 at ¶ 1231.

BANKS AND BANK HOLDING COMPANIES

¶ 227 Loan Loss Reserves

When banks make loans, they need loan loss reserves in order to have the padding to assure that they do not fail. (Cong. Record, July 1, 1999, p.H5295). Loan loss reserves are important to both bank safety and soundness and to transparent financial reporting. There has been an ongoing dialogue between the banking regulators and the SEC on providing guidance to financial institutions ensuring that the level of reserves is consistent with generally accepted accounting principles.

The Act directs the SEC to consult and coordinate with the federal banking agencies before taking any action or rendering any opinion with regard to the manner in which depository institutions report loan loss reserves in their financial statements. The conference report notes that the SEC's actions with regard to the reporting of loan loss reserves by certain insured depository institutions did not reflect adequate consultation with the federal banking agencies with regard to potential implications on the safety and soundness of the federal deposit insurance fund. The conferees expect that this provision will facilitate better coordination and decisionmaking by the SEC in this area.

This provision had its genesis as the Roukema amendment to H.R. 10, which was offered by Rep. Marge Roukema, Chair of the House Subcommittee on Financial Institutions. In explaining the intent of the amendment, Rep. Roukema said that the provision simply requires the regulators to communicate and coordinate before taking any action. It does not establish a different accounting system, nor does it eliminate the SEC's statutory authority to set accounting standards for these publicly-held companies. (Cong. Record, July 1, 1999, p.H5295.)

Echoing these sentiments, Rep. Bruce Vento said that the provision does not change the accounting rules or the standards, nor does it alter FASB interpretations. Rather, it simply says that when one is going to apply them one has to have coordination and regulatory discourse. Further, Rep. Vento emphasized that the provision does not eliminate SEC authority. But it will have, in his view, the positive impact of assuring that the SEC cannot act unilaterally to lower important loan loss reserves without consulting with the proper federal banking agency. Similarly, it should help ensure that FDIC insured institutions will not be caught "flat footed" when the business cycle turns downward. (Cong. Record, July 1, 1999 p. H5296).

In remarks on the day the bill passed Congress, Rep. Roukema emphasized that Congress expects the SEC to establish an informal process with the federal banking agencies for consultation and coordination on individual loan loss cases. She noted that the SEC has suggested that the consultation-coordination requirement will slow the review process and penalize banks.

It is not Congress' intent that the consultation and coordination process should delay SEC processing of securities filings. Rather, the process that the SEC establishes should be designed to expedite resolution of SEC staff questions. The informal process Congress envisions should involve telephone conferences, the faxing of relevant information between staffs, as well as other methods of communication that could expedite as quickly as possible the resolution of individual loan loss reserve cases. (Cong. Record, Nov. 4, 1999, p.H11516).

See Act Sec. 241 at ¶ 1241. See Conference Report at ¶ 5011.

Title III—Insurance

REGULATION OF INSURANCE

¶ 301 Introduction to Insurance Affiliations and Activities

Ever since the Great Depression and the enactment of Glass-Steagall barriers between banking and commerce, questions have been raised over the extent to which depository institutions should be allowed to participate in traditionally non-banking activities like insurance. Recent regulatory actions by the Office of the Comptroller of the Currency have greatly increased the controversy over appropriate insurance powers of depository institutions, especially national banks.

This controversy partially stems from the recognition of the differing goals of banking and insurance regulators. The primary goal of federal banking regulators is to protect the liquidity and solvency of the banking system. In contrast, insurance regulators are focused primarily on the conduct of agents, in terms of consumer protection and the long-term ability of underwriters to pay claims, in order to protect insurance consumers and state insurance guarantee funds.

With that in mind, the insurance provisions of the Gramm-Leach-Bliley Act seek to resolve the controversy over expanding depository institution insurance powers. Among other things, the Act:

- Sets forth the parameters of state regulation of activities and affiliations;
- Defines the types of activities that depository institutions can undertake;
- Establishes procedures to address the tensions between federal banking and state insurance regulators;
- Provides mutual insurance companies with a means to engage in affiliations envisioned under the Act; and
- Calls on the states to implement uniform requirements regarding licensing.

¶ 302 State Regulation of Insurance

Under the Gramm-Leach-Bliley Act, the states remain responsible for regulating the business of insurance. This is in keeping with the overall theme of functional regulation of financial services.

State regulation of the business of insurance has been formally recognized by Congress since 1945 when the McCarran-Ferguson Act was enacted. However, the regulation of insurance by the states can be traced back to the late 19th Century when the U.S. Supreme Court ruled in *Paul v. Virginia*, 75 US (8 Wall) 168 (1868), that insurance contracts were not in interstate commerce. As a result of that case, the states developed extensive insurance regulations. However, in 1944, the Supreme Court rejected the *Paul* decision in *United States v. South-Eastern Underwriters Ass'n*, 322 US 533, by holding that Congress could regulate insurance under its Commerce Clause powers. Congress passed the McCarran-Ferguson Act in response to that Supreme Court case.

By expressly stating that the states remain the primary regulator of the business of insurance, Congress also recognized the assertion of state insurance regulators that they are better equipped to regulate insurance.

See Act Sec. 104(a) at ¶ 1104.

¶ 303 Affiliations

Although the states remain the primary insurance regulators, the Gramm-Leach-Bliley Act sets up a "two-way street" regarding affiliations by depository institutions, their affiliates and insurance companies.

Affiliations by Depository Institutions

Under Section 104(c)(1) of the Act, the states cannot "prevent or restrict" depository institutions, and their affiliates, from affiliating with insurance companies as permitted under the Gramm-Leach-Bliley Act. Therefore states' "anti-affiliation" laws, such as the one in Florida prohibiting a Florida-licensed insurance agent from being associated with, owned or controlled by a financial institution, would be preempted.

There are a number of exceptions to this rule found in Section 104(c)(2) of the Act. These are intended to strike a balance between the preemption of "anti-affiliation" laws and state regulation of the business of insurance. These exceptions permit a state to review applications in order to ensure that an affiliation does not jeopardize the solvency of an insurance underwriter.

- First, states are free to collect information on any proposed affiliation. Under this information collection exception, an insurer's state of domicile—that is, the place the insurer is chartered or incorporated—may take any action on the affiliation, including approval or disapproval. There are two limitations placed on the state of domicile regulator: the action must be taken within 60 days of receiving notice of the affiliation; and the actions may not discriminate against the insurer based on an association with a depository institution.

- Second, an affiliating insurer's state of domicile may require capital restoration to the level required under state law, so long as the request is made within 60 days of notice of the affiliation.

- Third, any state may restrict changes in ownership of a demutualizing insurer—an insurance company that has changed from a mutual to stock form of ownership—so long as the restrictions are not "discriminatory." In other words, a state cannot prevent a depository institution from acquiring or changing the ownership of stock in newly demutualized insurance companies for reasons that would not apply to other persons.

NOTE: See ¶ 304 for a discussion on restrictions that would be deemed discriminatory under the Gramm-Leach-Bliley Act.

Affiliations by Insurance Companies

The parallel provision that removes the barriers to affiliations between depository institutions and insurance companies is found at Section 306 of the Act. Under that provision, state laws that prevent or restrict an insurance company or insurance affiliate from becoming a financial holding company (FHC) or acquiring control of a depository institution are preempted. Section 306 further preempts state laws that limit the amount of an insurer's assets that may be invested in a bank, except that the insurer's state of domicile may limit investments to 5 percent (or any higher threshold) of the insurer's admitted assets. If an insurance company is reorganizing from a mutual form into a stock company (including into a mutual holding company), then states other than the insurer's domicile may not prevent, restrict or require approval or formal review of such reorganization.

See Act Secs. 104(c) at ¶ 1104; and 306 at ¶ 1306.

¶ 304 Insurance Sales Activities

As with affiliations, certain state laws and regulations that place restrictions on a depository institution's insurance sales activities would be preempted. The manner in which the state law or regulation would be preempted depends upon when the state's restrictions were effective. Congress used a cutoff date of Sept. 3, 1998, to reflect that versions of the preemption test had been pending in Congress since that date.

Significant Interference

Any state law, regulation, or other action in effect before Sept. 3, 1998, that "prevents or significantly interferes" with a depository institution's insurance sales, solicitations, and cross-marketing activities is preempted. This preemption is in accordance with the U.S. Supreme Court decision in *Barnett Bank of Marion County N.A. v. Nelson* (1996), CCH FED. BANKING L. REP. 1995-1996 Dec. ¶ 100-028. In addition, a court reviewing these state laws or regulations is to apply traditional rules of judicial deference, which are the standards set forth in the U.S. Supreme Court decision in *Chevron, U.S.A., Inc. v. Natural Resources Defense Council,* 467 US 837 (1984). The *Chevron* standard sets forth a two-step process to guide judicial review of an agency's interpretation of a statute.

One type of state law that would be preempted is a requirement that all shareholders of an insurance agency be licensed by the state. This law would be preempted because it would "prevent or significantly interfere" with the ability of a depository institution to engage in insurance sales, since it is practically impossible for all shareholders of the agency to be licensed. Another example of a state law that would be preempted under the "prevent or significantly interferes" standard would be a statute that limits the volume or portion of insurance sales made by an insurance agent on the basis of whether the sales are made to customers of a depository institution or any affiliate of the agent. This statute would "prevent or significantly interfere" with the sale of insurance to an insured depository institution's customers.

Discriminatory Acts

State laws and regulations governing depository institution insurance sales activities that were enacted on or after Sept. 3, 1998 also are subject to the "prevents or significantly interferes" standard, found in the *Barnett* case and Section 104(d)(2)(A) of the Act. These laws and regulations also are subject to a nondiscrimination standard found in Section 104(e) of the Act. This nondiscrimination standard does not apply to state laws or regulations governing depository institution insurance sale activities in effect prior to Sept. 3, 1998.

The nondiscrimination standard would preempt any law or regulation that:

- Adversely distinguishes between depository institutions and other persons engaged in similar activity;
- If applied to a depository institution, would have a substantially more adverse impact as opposed to another person offering similar products or services;
- Effectively prevents a depository institution from exercising its powers under the Gramm-Leach-Bliley Act or federal law; or
- Conflicts with the intent of the Gramm-Leach-Bliley Act (i.e., providing a framework for the affiliation of banks, securities firms and insurance companies).

An example of a state law that would be preempted under the nondiscrimination standard would be a law prohibiting the sale of insurance within 100 yards of a teller window. Although the law would apply equally to all parties, the law's application would have a substantially more adverse impact on a depository institution since most other parties that sell insurance, such as insurance agents, do not have teller windows on their premises.

Safe Harbors

In light of the preemptive effect the Gramm-Leach-Bliley Act may have on state laws governing depository institutions' insurance sales, solicitation and cross-marketing activities, Congress created thirteen "safe harbors," which are based on the laws of Illinois and New York governing bank insurance sales. The safe harbors are intended to allow states some flexibility in regulating insurance sales and solicitation and cross-marketing activities without fear of preemption. The safe harbors will apply to state laws and regulations already in effect and any that may be enacted in the future.

The safe harbors deal with such items as:

- Tying of insurance to other products, such as loans;
- Misrepresenting the insured or guaranteed status of an insurance product in advertisements;
- Providing a written disclosure that an insurance product is not a bank deposit, not FDIC-insured and not guaranteed by the bank;
- Limiting commission payments to licensed insurance agents;

- Prohibiting referral fees to non-licensed individuals based on whether the referral results in a transaction;

- Prohibiting the release of insurance information to non-affiliated third parties to be used for soliciting or selling insurance;

- Prohibiting the use of health information obtained from insurancerecords without the express written consent of the customer.

- Prohibiting the use of forceplaced insurance in loan transactions; and

- Requiring the maintenance of separate insurance books and records that must be made available to state insurance regulators for inspection.

In order for a state law or regulation to fall within a safe harbor, it need not be identical to any of the categories, but it must be substantially the same as one of the safe harbors and must not be more burdensome or restrictive than the safe harbors. For example, a state law restricting a depository institution's use of promotional material would fall within the safe harbor if the law's intent was to avoid confusion by purchasers of insurance products about whether the insurance was guaranteed by a governmental agency. On the other hand, the state's advertising law would not fall within a safe harbor if it imposed a complex regulatory structure related to the review and approval of depository institution advertisements that was not applicable to other insurance providers.

Other Insurance Laws

There is another safe harbor for state insurance laws that do not regulate sales, solicitations or cross-marketing. This safe harbor will apply generally to various underwriting activities, such as claims processing and investment management of insurance premiums. State laws governing these underwriting activities will not be preempted as long as the state law: relates to the business of insurance in accordance with the McCarran-Ferguson Act; does not apply to depository institutions; does not relate to insurance sales activities; and is not discriminatory (see discussion above regarding "Discriminatory Acts"). Although this safe harbor generally does not apply to depository institutions, it will apply to any institution that provides savings bank life insurance as principal.

See Act Sec. 104(d) at ¶ 1104.

BANK INSURANCE ACTIVITIES

¶ 311 Overview of Bank Insurance Activities

Generally, Title III of the Gramm-Leach-Bliley Act governs the insurance activities of depository institutions. The specific provisions of Title III are broken down as follows:

- Subtitle A specifically provides that the states are functional regulators of insurance. This is in keeping with Section 104 of the Act, which expressly reaffirms that the McCarran-Ferguson Act remains the law of the land. Also, Subtitle A governs restrictions on underwriting and title insurance activities of national banks.

- Subtitle B allows for redomestication and reorganization of mutual insurance companies domiciled in states that do not have enabling reorganization laws or regulations for mutual holding companies.

- Subtitle C creates a voluntary licensing clearinghouse for insurance agents and brokers.

- Subtitle D establishes protections for insurance sales and solicitations made in connection with a short-term automobile rental or lease.

See Act Sec. 301 at ¶ 1301.

¶ 312 National Bank Underwriting Activities

National banks and their subsidiaries are prohibited from underwriting insurance under Section 302 of the Act. During Conference Committee deliberations, a "rule of construction" was added at Section 302(d). This provision closed a loophole allowing a bank to evade state insurance regulations. Section 302(d) provides that a foreign reinsurance subsidiary of a domestic bank, which offers insurance or reinsurance outside of the United States to indemnify an insurance product, will be considered to be providing insurance as principal in that state.

Authorized Products Excluded

The underwriting prohibition does not apply to "authorized products." A product is authorized if:

- The OCC had made a written determination, prior to Jan. 1, 1999, that national banks can provide the product or have lawfully provided the product as principal;

- The OCC's determination had survived any legal challenges; and

- The product is not title insurance or a taxable annuity contract.

Definition of Insurance

The Act further defines the term "insurance." This definition was deemed necessary to avoid regulatory arbitrage, that is, the ability of national banks to pick and choose the state or federal regulatory scheme in conducting their insurance activities. Regulatory arbitrage was a concern among some members of Congress, since actions of OCC are accorded deference over state regulators in court challenges. This, in effect, gives the OCC the upper hand in choosing which insurance powers it wants to give national banks.

The definition is based primarily on state insurance codes. A product is also deemed to be insurance if the Internal Revenue Code treats it as insurance for tax purposes. Core banking products, such as deposits, loans, letters of credits, trusts, derivatives, and guarantees would fall outside of the definition.

Any product developed in the future would be classified as insurance so long as the product insures against liability or loss. If a future product is a core banking product, it will be considered to be insurance if the Internal Revenue Code treats it as such. This test does not apply if the future product is a bank extension of credit, derivative or financial guaranty.

See Act Sec. 302 at ¶ 1302.

¶ 313 Title Insurance Activities

During the deliberations on the Gramm-Leach-Bliley Act in the House Commerce Committee, the propriety of allowing banks to underwrite and sell title insurance was questioned. On one side of the argument, concerns regarding conflicts of interest, consumer confusion and unfair competition were raised. The contrasting position was that allowing banks to underwrite and sell title insurance would increase competition, provide more availability for consumers, and create synergies between a bank's mortgage or loan functions and title insurance activities.

As a result of these conflicting positions, national banks are generally prohibited from underwriting and selling title insurance.

Parity Exception

A parity exception to the general prohibition for title insurance activities was created under Section 303(b)(1) of the Act. Under this exception, national banks may sell title insurance products in any state in which state-chartered banks are authorized sell title insurance.

For a national bank to avail itself of the parity exception, it must conduct its title insurance activities "in the same manner, to the same extent, and under the same restrictions" that apply to state-chartered banks. This means that if a state-chartered bank must comply with licensing, "title plant" data base requirements, financial responsibility, and (where relevant) practice of law requirements, national banks also must do so.

Wild Card Provisions

National banks cannot take advantage of the parity exception if a state-chartered bank's authority to sell title insurance is based upon any state "wild card" provision. A "wild card" provision generally authorizes state banks to exercise any power that national banks may exercise. Typically, state authority is based on such federal provisions as the "small towns" or "incidental to banking" powers found in 12 USC 92 and 12 USC 24(7), respectively.

Grandfathered Activities

If a national bank or a subsidiary was actively and lawfully engaged in title insurance activities before Nov. 12, 1999 (the date the Gramm-Leach-Bliley Act was signed into law), then the bank or subsidiary can continue to engage in the title insurance activities.

Although certain title insurance activities of national banks are grandfathered, national banks need to be mindful of their corporate structure to effectively take advantage of the grandfather provision. For instance, a national bank first must push out any title insurance underwriting activities to an insurance affiliate. If the bank does not have an insurance affiliate, then the bank must push out any title insurance underwriting activities into a subsidiary which underwrites insurance. The terms "affiliate" and "subsidiary" have the same meaning as found in Section 2 of the Bank Holding Company Act of 1956 (12 USC 1841).

Preservation of State Law

Finally, Section 303 of the Act provides protection to any state law prohibiting title insurance activities, which was effective on Nov. 12, 1999, from preemption by the Gramm-Leach-Bliley Act or other federal law, such as the national bank insurance powers codified at 12 USC 92.

See Act Sec. 303 at ¶ 1303.

¶ 314 Federal/State Dispute Resolution

In the event of a conflict between a state insurance regulator and a federal regulator as to whether a product is insurance or as to whether a state law or regulation regarding insurance sales or solicitation activity is preempted under federal law, Section 304 of the Act permits either regulator to seek expedited judicial review. Either regulator may file a petition for review in the U.S. Court of Appeals for the District of Columbia Circuit or in the U.S. Court of Appeals for the circuit in which the state is located.

This review process was included to address concerns that the insurance industry was placed at a competitive disadvantage versus national banks in terms of the regulatory tensions between federal banking and state insurance regulators. This regulatory tension can be best highlighted by the OCC's attempt to preempt a Rhode Island law governing bank insurance sales, which sets forth licensing and disclosure requirements, as well as limits on the sale of insurance by loan officers.

NOTE: The preemption of state laws and regulations governing insurance sales activities is discussed at ¶ 304.

Expedited Review

Once the case is filed, the U.S. Court of Appeals must complete all action, including rendering a judgment, within 60 days. The time period can be extended by agreement of all of the parties.

Once the U.S. Court of Appeals has issued its judgment, a request for certiorari to the U.S. Supreme Court must be filed as soon as practicable.

Statute of Limitations

Section 304(d) imposes a statute of limitations on when a challenge may be brought under the expedited review procedures. A challenge may be brought no later than 12 months after the agency's action was publicly announced in its final form or six months after the agency's action takes effect. It is likely that the statute of limitation was included to preclude a regulator from making a "first strike" challenge.

Unequal Deference

In resolving a conflict between a state and federal regulator regarding the classification of a product as insurance or a preemption of a state law or regulation governing an insurance sales activity, the Court of Appeals is directed to resolve the conflict based on the merits of all questions presented under state and federal law, including the nature of the product or activity and the history and purpose of its regulation under state and federal law, "without unequal deference." The phrase "without unequal deference" means that the court is not required to grant either party deference to resolve a particular question.

The "without unequal deference" standard is a departure from the traditional rules of judicial deference, which are the standards set forth in the U.S. Supreme Court decision in *Chevron, U.S.A., Inc. v. Natural Resources Defense Council*, 467 US 837 (1984). The unequal deference standard perhaps also was a response to Congressional concerns that a level playing field in the area of insurance regulation was needed in light of the OCC's regulatory action expanding the insurance powers of national banks.

See Act Sec. 304 at ¶ 1304.

¶ 315 Federal/State Cooperation

The Federal Reserve Board, acting as umbrella supervisor for financial holding companies (FHCs), and state insurance regulators have been directed to coordinate efforts to supervise companies that control both depository institutions and persons engaged in the business of insurance. Congress intended this coordinated effort to improve the efficiency and quality of the supervision of FHCs and their affiliated depository institutions and insurance companies.

Supervisory Information

In particular, the Fed and state regulators are to share supervisory information, including financial health and affiliate/business unit transactions. Other federal banking regulators are similarly directed to share supervisory information where appropriate.

The importance of the Fed/state information sharing requirement was emphasized in a Nov. 15, 1999, speech by Fed Chairman Alan Greenspan before the annual meeting of the American Council of Life Insurance. In his speech, Chairman Greenspan noted information generated by the Fed, in its umbrella supervisory role, will be beneficial to functional regulators because risks unfolding in one area of the organization could affect a unit for which the functional regulator is responsible.

Banking Agency Consultation

The banking agencies are also required to notify and consult with the appropriate state insurance regulator before making any determination relating to an affiliation between a depository institution or financial holding company and a company engaged in insurance activities.

Confidentiality and Privilege

All the information shared between the federal banking agencies and state insurance regulators is to be treated as confidential. A banking agency is not required to provide confidential information to a state insurance regulator unless the regulator agrees to keep the information in confidence and take all reasonable efforts to oppose disclosure of the information. Conversely, the federal banking agencies are directed to treat as confidential any information received from a state insurance regulator which is entitled to confidential treatment under state law, and to make similar reasonable efforts to oppose disclosure of the information.

See Act Sec. 309 at ¶ 1309.

¶ 316 Consumer Protection

During consideration of the Gramm-Leach-Bliley Act, the House Commerce Committee became concerned about the potential preemption of state consumer protection law by the federal regulators, especially the OCC. The Commerce Committee noted that a comment by the Comptroller of the Currency, that bank solvency was the most important factor in regards to insurance activities, left out the most important perspective—protecting the consumer. The Committee also cited the Comptroller's statement that any state consumer protection that infringes or burdens the ability of a bank to sell insurance may be preempted.

In response to these concerns, Section 305 of the Act requires the federal banking agencies—the OCC, Federal Reserve Board, and Federal Deposit Insurance Corp.—to jointly issue consumer protection regulations on the sale of insurance by depository institutions and their subsidiaries by Nov. 12, 2000. [The statutory basis for the new protection requirements is to be codified in a new Section 47 of the Federal Deposit Insurance Act.] The agencies are required to consult with state insurance regulators before issuing their regulations. Finally, the agencies' new rules cannot discriminate against any person engaged in insurance that is not affiliated with a depository institution.

The new protections are to address: sales practices; disclosure and advertising requirements; consumer grievance procedures; standards for the separation of banking and nonbanking activities; and nondiscrimination against domestic violence victims.

Sales Practices

Any sales practice that is considered to be coercive or that is dependent on tying arrangements would be prohibited under the new rules. Leading a consumer to believe that a bank's approval of a loan is conditioned on the purchase of insurance from the bank's insurance affiliate is prohibited. Likewise, telling a consumer that he or she would receive a quicker decision on a loan application if he or she uses a bank affiliated insurance agent violates the new consumer protection requirements.

Disclosure and Acknowledgement Requirements

The new consumer protection rules will also require oral and written disclosures to be made prior to the close of an insurance sale. It is not enough for a depository institution to tell the consumer that the disclosures are provided in printed material, such as a brochure. Once the depository institution makes the disclosures, it must to obtain a written acknowledgment, signed and dated by the consumer, that the consumer has received the disclosures.

In formulating the disclosure and acknowledgement rules, the banking agencies must take into account the various forms of consumer banking and make necessary adjustments for sales made in person, by telephone, or by electronic media (e.g., computer home banking), in order to provide for the most appropriate and complete form of disclosure and acknowledgment.

Required Disclosures

The new disclosures must state that the insurance product is not a deposit; is not insured by the FDIC; is not guaranteed by the financial institution or its subsidiaries or affiliates; and involves investment risk, including loss of principal. This last requirement is especially important if the bank sells variable annuity contracts.

Depository institutions that already sell investment products, such as mutual funds, will readily recognize these disclosures as being similar to those required by the "Interagency Statement on Retail Sale of Nondeposit Products" [reproduced at CCH FED. BANKING L. REP. ¶ 70-101].

If a consumer is seeking a loan, a bank must disclose to the consumer, at the time the loan application is made, that the loan's approval is not dependent upon the purchase of insurance products from a bank-affiliated insurance provider.

It should be noted that the disclosures are not required for a depository institution's general advertising materials listing the institution's products or services.

Disclosure Format

The new consumer protection requirements also require that the disclosures relating to uninsured status and investment risk be "conspicuous, simple, direct, and readily understandable." New FDIA Section 47(c)(1)(B) suggests the following format:

NOT FDIC–INSURED

NOT GUARANTEED BY THE BANK

MAY GO DOWN IN VALUE

NOT INSURED BY ANY GOVERNMENT AGENCY

Truthfulness of Promotional Materials

Any advertisements used by a depository institution to sell its insurance products cannot be misleading to the consumer. Specifically, the promotional material cannot cause a reasonable person to reach the wrong conclusions as to the insured or guaranteed status of an insurance product or the investment risks associated with a variable annuity contract.

Separating Banking and Insurance

As part of the consumer protection requirements, standards for the separation of banking and insurance activities, to "the extent practicable," must be established by the agencies. These standards must address delineating deposit-taking areas from insurance sales space, referrals and licensing.

Separate Settings

In segregating deposit-taking areas from insurance sales areas, Congress' qualifier "to the extent practicable" recognized the size constraints of some small bank offices or kiosks, located in retail establishments, that would make the separate space requirement unduly burdensome. Depository institutions that already sell mutual funds in their bank space have a fairly good grasp of how to separate deposit-taking areas from their nondeposit products sales areas.

Referral Fees

Another step in separating banking from insurance is limiting the referral fees paid to bank tellers for directing consumers to the insurance sales area. New FDIA Section 47(d)(2)(B) and the impending rules will limit referral fees to a one-time nominal fixed fee for each referral, which cannot be based upon a successful insurance sale.

Licensing

The final part of the bank/insurance separation will be a requirement that insurance sales on a depository institution's premise must be carried out by a person who is properly qualified and licensed under state law.

Domestic Violence Victims

The agencies' consumer protection requirements will also prohibit discrimination against victims of domestic abuse by preventing any history of domestic abuse from being considered as a criterion in any insurance activity conducted by or at a depository institution. This prohibition would not apply if state law requires affirmative discrimination. It should be noted that the National Association of Insurance Commissioners has a number of model laws which protect victims of domestic abuse from discriminatory insurance practices.

Grievance Process

The final component of the agencies' consumer protection rules would be a consumer grievance process to receive and investigate consumer complaints, inform consumers of their rights and address their concerns, and recover losses.

Effect on State Law and Regulation

Since the agencies' consumer protection requirements would provide additional protection to customers purchasing insurance from depository institutions, state consumer regulations that are more protective would still be effective. If the agencies make a joint determination that a state's consumer protection requirements are not more protective than the federal requirements, the state requirements are preempted. That state then will have an opportunity to override the preemption by enacting a law within three years of the preemption notice and establishing consumer protection requirements greater than the federal requirements.

See Act Sec. 305 at ¶ 1305.

REDOMESTICATION OF MUTUAL INSURERS

¶ 321 Introduction to Redomestication of Mutual Insurers

In order for all insurance companies to take advantage of the new affiliated environment permitted under the Gramm-Leach-Bliley Act, Title III of the Act provides a mechanism to allow mutual insurance companies to redomesticate to another state and reorganize into a stock or mutual holding company. Without this mechanism, mutual insurance companies' abilities to diversify would be limited.

As currently structured, a mutual insurance company, which is "owned" by its policyholders, can only own the stock of a downstream subsidiary and, since it does not have any shareholders, the mutual insurance company cannot be the subsidiary of an upstream holding company.

Demutualization

A mutual insurance company could "demutualize," that is, buy out the interests of the policyowners, become a stock company and take advantage of the Gramm-Leach-Bliley Act. However, the insurance industry has asserted that "demutualization" is an expensive and time-consuming process that requires valuing the interests of the policyowners and raising the capital necessary to buy out the policyowners. Also, a demutualized company could become vulnerable to takeover by another company.

Mutual Holding Companies

Another route a mutual insurance company can take is to reorganize under a mutual holding company statute. Several states, including California, the District of Columbia, Illinois, Iowa, Kentucky, Minnesota, Missouri, Pennsylvania, Rhode Island, and Vermont, have such a statutory scheme. By becoming a mutual holding company, the mutual insurance company obtains the organizational flexibility of a stock company while avoiding the expense and complexity of a demutualization.

Reorganization under a mutual holding company statute involves three simultaneous steps. First, the mutual insurance company becomes a stock insurance company. Second, a mutual holding company and at least one intermediate holding company are created. The mutual holding company owns the shares of the intermediate holding company, and the intermediate holding company, in turn, owns the shares of the former mutual insurance company. Third, the rights of the policyowners as owners of the former mutual insurance company are transferred to the mutual holding company. The rights of the policyowners as customers remain with the former mutual insurance company. Generally, mutual holding company statutes provide that the mutual holding company must own at least a majority of the shares of the intermediate holding company and that the intermediate holding company must own at least a majority of the shares of the former mutual insurance company.

¶ 322 Impact on State Law

The ability of a mutual insurance company to redomestice under Title III of the Gramm-Leach-Bliley Act only applies to those states which have not enacted a law which expressly establishes reasonable terms and conditions for allowing mutual insurance companies to reorganize into mutual holding companies. One such state is New York.

Laws Restricting Redomestication

Section 313 of the Act preempts or prohibits state laws that restrict redomestication or treat redomesticating insurers differently.

Transferor Domicile Laws

State laws of the "transferor domicile,"—the state from which the mutual insurance company is moving—are preempted if the laws impede the redomestication.

Discriminatory Treatment

State laws or regulations that treat a redomesticating or redomesticated insurer, or any affiliate, differently than an insurer operating in that state that is not a redomesticating or redomesticated insurer are prohibited.

Licensed State Law

If any "licensed state" takes adverse action against a redomesticated insurer immediately following redomestication, the redomesticating insurer is exempt from the laws of the licensed state affecting the operation of the redomesticated insurer. Actions that would trigger the compliance exemption would be a delay or failure by the licensed state to issue a certificate of authority, as well the revocation of an original certificate of authority.

The Act defines "licensed state" as a state in which the redomesticating insurer has a certificate of authority in effect immediately prior to the redomestication.

A licensed state's action would be saved from the exemption if the state shows that the action was consistent with its past practices regarding the issuance of certificates of authority to foreign insurers that are not redomesticating.

Although a redomesticated insurer may be exempt from laws affecting operations in the licensed state, the Gramm-Leach-Bliley Act does not apply to the licensed state's law pertaining to:

- Unfair claim settlement practices or nondiscriminatory premiums and taxes;
- Registration for service of legal documents and process;
- Financial examination of the redomestication company, if the insurance regulator of the new domicile has not scheduled such an examination to begin within a year of the redomestication;
- Delinquency proceedings and voluntary dissolution proceedings
- Deceptive or false or fraudulent acts or practices;
- Filing of petitions regarding financial impairment or hazardous condition of the redomesticating company;
- Participation in insurance insolvency guaranty associations or other state insurance guaranty funds; or
- Nondiscriminatory licensing requirements.

See Act Secs. 311 at ¶ 1311 and 313 at ¶ 1313.

¶ 323 Redomestication Process

When a mutual insurance company redomesticates to another state and reorganizes into a mutual holding company or stock company, all licenses of the insurer are preserved and all outstanding policies, contracts and forms remain in full force. A redomesticating company must also provide notice to the state insurance regulators of each state in which the company is licensed.

A redomesticating mutual insurance company also must be approved by its new insurance regulator. The state into which the mutual insurance redomesticates is known as the "transferee domicile." The insurance regulator of the transferee domicile may only approve the mutual insurance company's reorganization plan if certain criteria are met:

- The reorganization is approved by a majority of the company's board of directors and voting policyholders. The vote can be taken only after the policyholders have been notified of the reorganization and advised of its effects on their contractual rights. In addition, the policyholders must have a reasonable opportunity to vote. The insurance regulator of the transferee domicile must approve the notice and disclosure of the reorganiztion, as well as the voting procedures that were used.
- The policyholders have voting rights in the new mutual holding company that are equivalent to their voting rights in the original mutual insurer. In addition, any initial public offering of stock must comply with applicable securities laws and must be approved by the insurance regulator of the transferee domicile.

● No stock options or grants may be awarded to the new mutual holding company's elected officers or directors for six months after the initial public offering. This applies also to any officers or directors of the mutual holding company's reorganized stock insurance companies. An exception is created for stock grants or options awarded to policyholders, provided the stock grants or options are approved by the insurance regulator of the transferee domicile.

● The reorganization must preserve the contractual rights of the policyholders.

● The insurance regulator of the transferee domicile must determine that the reorganization is fair and equitable to the policyholders.

See Act Sec. 312 at ¶ 1312.

¶ 324 Judicial Review

If a dispute arises in regard to a redomestication under Title III of the Act, the U.S. District Courts are granted exclusive jurisdiction.

See Act Sec. 314(a) at ¶ 1314.

NATIONAL ASSOCIATION OF REGISTERED AGENTS AND BROKERS

¶ 331 Licensing

Two separate areas of the Gramm-Leach-Bliley Act govern some aspect of the licensing requirements for insurance agents and brokers. Also, there is a special rule regarding the licensing of car rental employees that offer insurance products.

State Licensing Requirements

Section 104(b) of the Act continues the theme of functional regulation by the states. Under that provision, each person engaged in the business of insurance must be licensed under state law. As part of the licensing process, states may not discriminate against any person based on an affiliation with a depository institution.

Uniformity and Reciprocity

Subtitle C of Title III of the Act sets forth a mechanism to encourage the states to provide a system of uniform or reciprocal laws for licensing persons engaged in insurance activities. Section 321(a) of the Act gives a majority of the states until Nov. 12, 2002, to establish uniform or reciprocal laws.

Uniformity

To meet the uniformity requirements found in Section 321(b) of the Act, a majority of the states must have:

● Criteria for licensed producers regarding integrity, personal qualifications, training, and experience, including suitability training requirements.

● Continuing education requirements.

● Ethics course requirements.

● Suitability requirements, including for annuity contracts that are regulated at least in part as insurance by the states.

● No other additional licensing requirement that limits a producer's activities based on residence or location of operations. However, the states may continue to impose counter-signature requirements.

Reciprocity

A majority of the states will meet the reciprocity requirements of Section 321(c) of the Act if they:

● Permit each other's resident licensed producers to conduct insurance activities to the same extent as allowed for resident producers.

● Impose no administrative licensing procedures on nonresident licensed "insurance producers" (e.g., agents, brokers, or any other person that offers services related to insurance) other than submitting: a request for licensure; a copy of the "home state" license application; proof of licensure and good standing in the "home state;" and payment of appropriate fees.

● Accept the completion by the non-resident producer of the producer's home state's continuing education requirements.

● Impose no limitations which discriminate against nonresidents (except for counter-signature laws).

Home State

An insurance producer's "home state" is the state where the producer maintains its principal place of business and is licensed to act as an insurance producer.

Effects on State Law

The provisions of the Act calling for uniformity or reciprocity do not require the states to adopt new or additional licensing requirements to achieve uniformity. Likewise, the states do not have to alter their laws or regulations governing such areas as unfair trade practices or consumer protection to satisfy the uniformity or reciprocity requirements, as long as the laws or regulations are inconsistent with the uniformity or reciprocity requirements found in Section 321(b) and (c) of the Act.

Rental Car Insurance

Section 341 of the Act (Subtitle D of Title III) establishes protections for insurance sales and solicitations made in connection with a short-term (90 days or less) automobile rental or lease. A three-year federal presumption is created which provides that a license is not required for car rental employees. The presumption only applies if the state has not spoken on the issue by statute, regulation, order, interpretation or other action. The presumption also does not apply after a court judgment has been rendered establishing a licensing requirement.

Congress provided this protection upon a finding that it was impractical in many instances for car rental employees to obtain comprehensive insurance licenses. It was noted that some states have worked out limited licenses required for either the rental companies or their employees while other states have chosen to not require an insurance license for *bona fide* short term car rental insurance sales. Congress also noted that Section 341 of the Act maintains the precedence of state law and limits the presumption to only the minimum amount of time necessary for the State legislatures to resolve the issue.

See Act Secs. 104(b) at ¶ 1104; 321(a)–(c), (f) and (g) at ¶ 1321; 336(1) at ¶ 1336; and 341 at ¶ 1341.

¶ 332 Establishment of NARAB

If the National Association of Insurance Commissioners (NAIC) determines that a majority of the states have not met the three-year deadline for uniformity or reciprocity, the NAIC is then required to establish a private, non-profit corporation to be known as the National Association of Registered Agents and Brokers (NARAB). The Gramm-Leach-Bliley Act gives the NAIC two years after the finding that there is no uniformity or reciprocity to establish NARAB.

Other Grounds for Establishment

The NAIC is also required to establish NARAB within two years if the NAIC finds that a majority of the states have failed to maintain uniformity and reciprocity unless, during that time period, a majority of the states reachieve the uniformity or reciprocity standards.

NAIC Supervision

The NAIC will be responsible for supervising NARAB. In its supervisory role, the NAIC may assess NARAB for any costs incurred. In addition, the NAIC is permitted to examine and inspect NARAB's records and to require NARAB to furnish it with any reports. NARAB must report to the NAIC annually on its activities.

Judicial Review

Exclusive jurisdiction over any challenge of an NAIC determination as to uniformity and reciprocity is given to the appropriate United States District Court. In addition, any dispute involving NARAB is to be brought in the appropriate U.S. District Court under federal law, after all administrative remedies through NARAB and the NAIC have been exhausted.

See Act Secs. 321(d) at ¶ 1321; 322 at 1322; 324 at 1324; 329(b) at ¶ 1329; 330 at ¶ 1330; and 335 at ¶ 1335.

¶ 333 NARAB's Responsibilities

NARAB's primary responsibility is to establish uniform licensing requirements and conditions that can be adopted and applied on a multistate basis.

Membership Criteria

NARAB will also be responsible for establishing criteria for membership in the organization. The criteria must bear a reasonable relationship to the purposes of establishing uniform or reciprocal licensing requirements and may not unfairly limit access of small insurance agencies to NARAB membership. In addition, NARAB may establish fees to fund its operations.

Office of Consumer Complaints

NARAB is also required to establish an Office of Consumer Complaints. This office will provide a toll-free phone number (and Internet website) to receive and investigate consumer complaints and recommend disciplinary actions. The office must also maintain records of any complaints, which will be made available to the NAIC and individual state insurance regulators. The officer also will refer complaints when appropriate to the state insurance regulators.

Disciplinary Actions

In a disciplinary action of one of its members, NARAB must provide notice to the member of the specific charges and provide a recorded opportunity for a defense. If a disciplinary action is ordered, NARAB must notify the NAIC, which may review and modify or overturn NARAB's action.

See Act Secs. 323 at ¶ 1323; 325(b) and (i) at 1325; 328(d) at ¶ 1328; and 329(a) at ¶ 1329.

¶ 334 Membership in NARAB

Membership in NARAB is voluntary and does not affect the rights of an insurance producer under an individual state license.

Membership Criteria

Any state-licensed insurance producer whose license has not been suspended or revoked is eligible to join NARAB. NARAB membership criteria is based on the highest levels of insurance producer qualification set by the states on standards such as integrity, personal qualification, education, training, and experience. Membership in NARAB must be renewed annually, and NARAB has the authority to revoke membership if an insurance producer fails to meet membership criteria or is subject to disciplinary action.

Continuing Compliance with State Laws

NARAB members will continue to pay the appropriate fees required by each state in which they are licensed.

Discriminatory Laws Preempted

On the other hand, state laws regulating insurance licensing that discriminate against NARAB members based on non-residency are preempted. Likewise, state laws and regulations which impose additional licensing requirements on non-resident NARAB members are preempted. State unfair trade practices and consumer protection laws are protected from preemption, including counter-signature requirements.

See Act Sec. 325(a), (d)–(f) and (h) at ¶ 1325; and 333 at ¶ 1333.

¶ 335 NARAB Management

The NAIC is responsible for appointing NARAB's seven member board of directors. At least four of the board members must have significant experience with the regulation of commercial insurance lines in the 20 states with the most commercial lines of business.

Alternative Board of Directors

If the NAIC fails to install an initial board of directors for NARAB within the two-year time period allotted for NARAB's creation, then the initial directors shall be the state insurance regulators of the seven states with the greatest amount of commercial lines of insurance.

The President of the United States, with the advice and consent of the Senate, also may appoint NARAB's board of directors if a majority of the states representing at least 50% of the total commercial lines of insurance premiums in the United States have not established uniform or reciprocal licensing regulations, and the NAIC has not approved NARAB's bylaws. Likewise, the President can replace the entire NARAB board if there is a determination that NARAB's board is not acting in the public interest. The President would receive a list of candidates recommended by the NAIC.

In a statement, made as part of the signing of the Gramm-Leach-Bliley Act, President Clinton raised a concern that the authority to appoint NARAB's board of directors may raise constitutional issues. It was postulated that since the board members would be exercising "significant federal governmental authority," the list of NAIC-recommended board candidates would not be binding on the President because the Appointments Clause of the Constitution does not permit any type of restrictions upon the President's power of appointment.

Bylaws

NARAB's bylaws are required to be filed with the NAIC, and take effect 30 days after filing unless they are disapproved by the NAIC as being contrary to the public interest or requiring a public hearing. The NAIC may require NARAB to adopt or repeal additional bylaws or rules if it determines that doing so is in the public interest.

See Act Secs. 326(a) and (c) at ¶ 1326; 328(a)–(c) at ¶ 1328; and 332(a) and (b) at ¶ 1332.

Title IV—Unitary Thrift Holding Company Provisions

¶ 401 Unitary Savings and Loan Holding Companies

Title IV of the Gramm-Leach-Bliley Act amends Section 10(c) of the Home Owners' Loan Act—12 USC 1467a(c)—to prohibit any new unitary savings and loan holding companies from engaging in nonfinancial activities or affiliating with nonfinancial organizations. The intention of the conferees on this issue is clear from the plain language of Section 401 (see remarks of Rep. James A. Leach, Cong. Record Nov. 4, 1999, p.E2371). This section contains a grandfather provision that permits a company that was a savings and loan holding company as of May 4, 1999, or had an application on file as of that date, to acquire and continue to control a thrift and engage in commercial activities. Any company that does acquire a thrift after May 4, 1999, cannot engage in any commercial activities. Under Section 401, a financial firm cannot acquire a grandfathered unitary thrift holding company engaged in commercial activities unless those activities are divested.

Corporate Reorganizations Permitted

Section 401 of the Act does permit corporate reorganizations. Specifically, it does not prevent transactions that:

- involve solely a company under common control with a savings and loan holding company from acquiring, directly or indirectly, control of the savings and loan holding company, or any savings association that is already a subsidiary of the savings and loan holding company; or

- involve solely a merger, consolidation or other type of business combination as a result of which a company that is under common control with the savings and loan holding company acquires, either directly or indirectly, control of that company or any savings association that is already a subsidiary of the holding company.

Authority to Prevent Evasions

The Director of the Office of Thrift Supervision may issue interpretations, regulations or orders that are necessary to administer and carry out the intent and prevent evasions of this paragraph. This would include a determination by the Director that despite the form of a transaction, the substantive result of the transaction would be a company acquiring control of a savings association.

See Act Sec. 401 at ¶ 1401. See Conference Report at ¶ 5017

Title V—Privacy

¶ 501 Introduction

As a result of the explosion of information available via electronic services, such as the Internet, as well as the expansion of financial institutions through affiliations and other means as they seek to provide more and better products to consumers, the privacy of data about personal financial information has become increasingly significant to consumers. And, according to Sen. John Edwards, privacy in financial services is an extremely complex issue because what one person may view as an invasion of privacy, another might appreciate as a timely and appropriate offering of a much-needed service. (Cong. Record, Nov. 4, 1999. p.S13884.)

The Gramm-Leach-Bliley Act would create new opportunities for financial supermarkets consisting of affiliated banking, securities, and insurance institutions. In turn, this will provide an environment that can benefit consumers by enhancing competition, expanding the array of available financial products, increasing the efficiency of institutions providing those products, and reducing costs to consumers.

At the same time, the use of personal customer information by these new financial conglomerates underscores the importance of providing consumers with the ability to prevent, if they choose, their personal financial information from being bartered to nonaffiliated third parties of a financial institution or otherwise used in ways unrelated to the purpose for which the consumer has provided the information.

Title V of the Act establishes a minimum federal standard of privacy. In this context, Subtitle A of Title V provides a mechanism to protect the confidentiality of a consumer's personal financial information and provides a power to choose how personal financial information may be used by financial institutions, without undermining the benefits that will result from enhanced affiliations and competition. Subtitle B establishes new penalties to prevent pretext calling, a practice President Clinton called a way in which unscrupulous persons use deceptive practices to determine the financial assets of consumers. (Signing statement of Nov. 12, 1999.)

The House-Senate conference recognized the need to foster technological innovation in the financial services and related industries. Congress believes that the development of new technologies that facilitate consumers' access to the broad range of products and services available through online media should be encouraged, provided that such technologies continue to incorporate safeguards for consumer privacy.

Echoing these sentiments, Senate Banking Committee Chairman Phil Gramm said that, with the privacy provisions, Congress tried to set a "rule of reason." He added that the Act is not the final word on privacy. "This is something we want to watch and follow and see where abuses are and, when they occur, try to fix them." (Cong. Record, Nov. 3, 1999, p.S13785.) In his signing statement of Nov. 12, 1999, President Clinton, while expressing his approval of the new privacy provisions, said that he would continue to press for even greater privacy protections, especially choice about whether personal financial information can be shared within a corporate family.

Under Title V, financial institutions would have to disclose their privacy policies to customers at the time a customer relationship is established and not less than annually during the continuation of the relationship. In addition, consumers can "opt out" of having private financial information shared with most third parties without their permission.

Federal and state regulators would be directed to establish comprehensive standards for ensuring the security and confidentiality of consumers' personal information. Pretext calling in which someone uses fraudulent or deceptive means to obtain private customer information would become a federal crime punishable by up to five years in prison. The new federal privacy protections would not supersede any stronger privacy protections provided under state law. Also, the regulators are given sufficient flexibility to prescribe necessary exceptions and clarifications to the prohibitions and requirements.

Generally, the privacy disclosure requirements will become effective six months after the required agency rulemaking action is taken (see ¶ 510). The provisions pertaining to pretext calling take effect immediately.

DISCLOSURE OF NONPUBLIC PERSONAL INFORMATION

¶ 502 Protection of Customer Information

In Section 501, Congress announces as policy that each financial institution has an affirmative and continuing duty to respect the privacy of its customers and protect the security and confidentiality of their nonpublic personal information.

To further this policy, in Section 501(b), Congress mandates that the regulators, including the Federal Reserve Board and the SEC, must establish appropriate standards for the financial institutions subject to their jurisdictions relating to administrative, technical, and physical safeguards in order to: 1) insure the security and confidentiality of customer records and information; 2) protect against any anticipated threats or hazards to the security or integrity of such records; and 3) protect against unauthorized access to or use of such records that could result in substantial harm or inconvenience to any customer.

Section 503 requires a financial institution to disclose to the consumer the policies that the institution maintains to protect the confidentiality and security of nonpublic personal information. Disclosure would occur at the time a customer relationship is established and not less than annually during the continuation of the relationship. (see ¶ 504.)

Congress has also provided specific enforcement provisions for violation of Section 501(b). See ¶ 506.

Nonpublic Personal Information

The Act, in Section 509, defines nonpublic personal information to mean personally identifiable financial information provided by a consumer to a financial institution or resulting from any transaction with the consumer or service performed for the consumer, or, as a catchall, information otherwise obtained by the financial institution. Nonpublic personal information does not include publicly available information as that term will be defined by the regulators.

Section 509 also states that nonpublic personal information includes any list, description, or other grouping of consumers (and publicly available information pertaining to them) that is derived using any nonpublic personal information other than publicly available information. The conferees clarified, and the statute provides, that the statutory definition of nonpublic personal information does not encompass any list, description, or other grouping of consumers (and publicly available information pertaining to them) that is derived without using any nonpublic personal information.

In a colloquy between Sens. Gramm and Allard, it was clarified that the term "nonpublic personal information" applies to information that describes an individual's financial condition obtained from one of the three sources set forth in the statutory definition, and by example would include experiences with the account established in the initial transaction or other private financial information. (Cong. Record, Nov. 4, 1999, p.S13902.)

Financial Institution

A "financial institution" is defined to mean any institution the business of which is engaging in financial activities as described in Section 4(k) of the Bank Holding Company Act of 1956. Section 4(k) contains a list of activities that are considered to be financial in nature. The list includes securities underwriting, dealing, and market making, as well as providing financial, investment, or economic advisory services, including advising an investment company.

There are a number of exceptions to the definition of "financial institution." Thus, the conferees excluded any person or entity that is subject to Commodity Futures Trading Commission jurisdiction under the Commodity Exchange Act, as well as the Federal Agricultural Mortgage Corporation or any entity chartered and operating under the Farm Credit Act of 1971. Also excluded are institutions chartered by Congress specifically to engage in securitization or secondary market transactions, so long as such institutions do not sell or transfer nonpublic personal information to non-affiliated third parties. The exception was granted based on the understanding that the covered entities do not market products directly to consumers.

See Act Sections 501 and 509 at ¶ 1501 and 1509. See Conference Report at ¶ 5018.

¶ 503 Disclosure of Personal Information

As a general matter, Section 502 sets out that a financial institution cannot disclose to a nonaffiliated third party any nonpublic personal information of its customers unless the institution provides a customer a notice that complies with Section 503 of the Act.

Also, a financial institution cannot disclose nonpublic information to a nonaffiliated third party unless it clearly and conspicuously discloses to the consumer that the information may be disclosed to a third party and gives the consumer the chance to direct that such information not be disclosed, along with an explanation of how the customer can exercise the non-disclosure option. This required disclosure can be in writing or in electronic format or other form permitted by regulation.

This gives customers the right to opt-out of information sharing with a nonaffiliated third party. It is the right to say no to the sharing or selling of personal information.

According to Senate Banking Committee Chairman Phil Gramm, the intent of Section 502 is to assure that consumers receive a clear and conspicuous notice of a financial institution's privacy policies and practices and to assure that consumers can direct that their nonpublic information not be disclosed to third parties. (Cong. Record, Nov. 4, 1999, p.S13902.)

The conferees agreed to provide that the disclosure of private personal information contained in a consumer report reported by a consumer reporting agency does not fall within Section 502's notice and opt-out requirements.

Sen. Mike Crapo sought to clarify that a financial institution's obligation to send an opt-out notice is satisfied when it has complied with notification requirements regarding privacy policies and practices under Section 503, and the consumer is further given the right to direct that his or her non-public personal information not be disclosed to non-affiliated third parties. A separate opt-out notice need not be provided for each third party disclosure so long as the consumer receives a prior clear and conspicuous opt-out opportunity covering third party disclosures generally.

Sen. Gramm agreed, noting that, so long as consumers receive a notice giving them a clear choice about whether or not that nonpublic personal information can be transferred to non-affiliated third parties, the opt-out choice need not be provided separately for each disclosure of such information. (Cong. Record, Nov. 4, 1999, p.S13901-13902.)

Joint Marketing Arrangements

The Act addresses a potential imbalance between the treatment of large financial services conglomerates and small banks by including an exception, subject to strict controls, for joint marketing arrangements between financial institutions.

Thus, a significant exception to the opt-out requirements is that a financial institution can provide nonpublic information to a nonaffiliated third party to perform services for or functions on behalf of the financial institution, including the marketing of the institution's own products and services, or financial products or services offered pursuant to joint agreements between two or more financial institutions that comply with prescribed regulations. A condition of the exception is that the financial institution fully disclose the providing of such information and enter into a contractual agreement with the third party requiring the third party to maintain the confidentiality of the information.

There are also limits on the reuse of the information. Thus, a nonaffiliated third party receiving nonpublic information from a financial institution cannot disclose the information to any other person that is a nonaffiliated third party of both the financial institution and the receiving third party, unless the disclosure would be permitted if made directly to the other person by the financial institution.

According to Senator Gramm, financial institutions will be allowed to partner with other financial services providers. This will give flexibility that Congress hopes will be implemented to allow, in particular, small banks to share information with their business partners in a manner so that they can compete with a larger company that does a variety of activities within the corporation or among its affiliates. (Cong. Record, Nov. 3, 1999, p.S13786.)

Thus, the joint marketing exception seeks to narrow the potentially unequal application of privacy restrictions between larger financial entities that operate through affiliates and smaller banks and credit unions that must contract with outside institutions to provide basic financial services such as credit cards or mortgages to customers.

It is important to note that the provision contains at least four levels of restrictions to limit its application. Thus, the joint marketing exception applies only to agreements under which one financial institution markets the products of another or markets financial products on the other institution's behalf. Permissible joint agreements and financial products would be limited by federal regulation. Moreover, any sharing of information must be clearly disclosed and subject to strict confidentiality contracts. (see remarks of Rep. John LaFalce, Cong. Record, Nov. 8, 1999, p.E2310.)

General Exceptions

Section 502 codifies a number of general exceptions to the prohibition on the disclosure of nonpublic personal information of customers. For example, disclosure can occur with the consent or at the discretion of the customer.

Similarly, there is an exception for disclosure necessary to effect, administer, or enforce a transaction requested or authorized by the consumer.

Other exceptions allow disclosure in connection with servicing or processing a financial product or service requested or authorized by the consumer, or maintaining or servicing the consumer's account with the financial institution, or with another entity as part of a private label credit card program.

The Act allows disclosure to protect the confidentiality or security of the financial institution's records pertaining to the customer or to protect against or prevent fraud, unauthorized transactions, claims, or other liability. A similar exception permits disclosure for required institutional risk control or for resolving customer disputes or inquiries.

There are exceptions for disclosure to persons holding a legal or beneficial interest relating to the consumer or to persons acting in a fiduciary or representative capacity on the consumer's behalf.

An exception allows disclosure to provide information to insurance rate advisory organizations, guaranty funds or agencies, rating agencies of the financial institution, persons assessing the institution's compliance with industry standards, and the institution's attorneys, accountants, and auditors. Disclosure is also permitted to the extent required or allowed under other provisions of law and in accordance with the Right to Financial Privacy Act, to law enforcement agencies, including the SEC and the Federal Reserve Board, self-regulatory organizations, or for an investigation related to public safety.

There can also be disclosure to a consumer reporting agency in accordance with the Fair Credit Reporting Act or from a consumer report reported by a consumer reporting agency. Another exception allows disclosure in connection with a sale, merger, transfer, or exchange of all or a portion of a business or operating unit so long as the disclosure of nonpublic personal information concerns only consumers of the business or unit.

An exception allows for disclosure needed to comply with federal, state, or local laws, or to comply with an authorized civil or criminal investigation or subpoena by federal, state or local authorities; or to respond to judicial process or government regulators with jurisdiction over the financial institution for examination, compliance, or other purposes as authorized by law.

Secondary Mortgage Market

There is also an exception for disclosure in connection with a proposed or actual securitization, secondary market sale, including sales of servicing rights, or similar transaction related to a customer transaction.

Companies chartered by Congress to operate in the secondary mortgage market are an example of entities whose daily business realities necessarily involve the disclosure of nonpublic personal information. Because these companies do not engage in mortgage transactions directly with the consumer, they are not in a position to provide the notices and disclosures mandated by Title V.

Moreover, sweeping them within Title V's purview would have created burdens and uncertainty without furthering the Title's consumer protection objectives. Thus, according to Rep. Spencer Bachus, these institutions are exempt from Title V's definition so long as they do not sell or transfer nonpublic personal information to nonaffiliated third parties.

The conferees intended to provide the FTC with regulatory and enforcement authority over secondary market institutions only to the extent that such institutions engage in activities outside the provisions of Section 502. Rep. Bachus clarified that the types of transfers that would pull these institutions back within Title V's scope are transfers other than those contemplated by Sections 502(b)(2) (the joint marketing exception) or 502(e) (general exceptions). For institutions covered by Title V, Congress recognizes that the use of nonpublic personal information that Sections 502(b)(2) or 502(e) contemplate are legitimate. This same standard applies to the secondary market institutions covered by Section 509(3)(D). To the extent that these companies go beyond these parameters, Rep. Bachus expects that they will be generally subject to Title V. (Cong. Record, Nov. 4, 1999, p.H11518-11519.)

Consumer Account Numbers

Under Section 502(d), a financial institution cannot disclose an account number or similar form of access number or access code for a credit card account, deposit account, or transaction account of a consumer to any nonaffiliated third party for use in telemarketing, direct mail marketing, or other marketing through electronic mail to the consumer. Consumer reporting agencies are statutorily excluded from the prohibition on disclosure.

The House-Senate conference noted that, in exercising their authority under Section 504(b) to grant exceptions, the agencies may consider it consistent with the purposes of this Subtitle to allow the disclosure of customer account numbers or similar forms of access numbers or access codes in an encrypted, scrambled, or similarly coded form, where the disclosure is expressly authorized by the customer and is necessary to service or process a transaction expressly requested or authorized by the customer.

Remarking on the conferees language, Sen. Charles Hagel said that the report language clarifies that when regulations are written to implement the Act they may exempt the sharing of encrypted credit card numbers and account numbers only when the financial institution has received express permission from the customer. He urged the regulators to exercise this exemption authority, adding that the conferees did not intend to hurt legitimate business practices that safeguard customer information. (Cong. Record, Nov. 4, 1999, p.S13876.)

In a colloquy with Sen. Gramm, Sen. Hagel determined that it is the intent of Congress that the third party be able to receive customer account numbers upon approval by the customer and that Sen. Gramm expects the regulators to use the broad exemptive authority bestowed on them by the Act to allow for the sharing of encrypted account numbers upon approval by the customer. Sen. Hagel, who is Vice-Chairman of the Financial Institutions Subcommittee, ended the discussion by noting that this is a "commonsense approach" consistent with consumer choice and customer privacy. (Cong. Record, Nov. 4, 1999, p.S13902.)

According to Rep. John LaFalce, Ranking Member of the House Banking Committee, the conference report makes clear that any exception the regulators may give to the strict prohibition against a customer's account number must be narrowly drawn and may be deemed consistent with the Act's purposes only when three factors are present: 1) the customer account number is encrypted, scrambled, or decoded; 2) the customer provides express consent to the financial institution to make such disclosure prior to the time of the disclosure, which essentially means that the customer opts-in to such disclosure; and 3) the disclosure is necessary to service or process a transaction that the customer expressly requests or authorizes. (Cong. Record, Nov. 4, 1999, p.E2310.)

Similarly, Rep. Bruce Vento indicated that the regulators should do nothing to further any sharing of account numbers or encrypted access codes that is not expressly conveyed through opt-in permission from consumers prior to any activity that would share such numbers. Moreover, the regulators should not make any exemptions that would make it possible for consumers to opt-in over the phone to a telemarketer regarding the sharing of their account number. Rep. Vento reasoned that condoning such a practice would reaffirm the status quo with regard to the bad actors who would take advantage of the practice and avoid the law's clear intent. (Cong. Record, Nov. 4, 1999, p.H11540.)

Necessary to Effect, Administer or Enforce the Transaction

The term "as necessary to effect, administer or enforce the transaction" is defined in Section 509 to mean the disclosure is required, or is a usual, appropriate, or acceptable method, to carry out the transaction or the product or service business of which the transaction is a part, and record or service or maintain the consumer's account in the ordinary course of providing the financial service or product, or to administer or service benefits or claims relating to the transaction or the product or service business of which it is a part, and includes: 1) providing the consumer or his or her agent or broker with a confirmation, statement, or other record of the transaction, or information on the status or value of the financial service or financial product; and 2) the accrual or recognition of incentives or bonuses associated with the transaction that are provided by the financial institution or any other party.

The term also means the disclosure is required, or is one of the methods, to enforce the rights of the financial institution or of other persons engaged in carrying out the financial transaction, or providing the product or service. Similarly, the term means the disclosure is required, or is a usual method, for insurance underwriting at the consumer's request or for reinsurance purposes, or for a number of specified purposes related to a consumer's insurance, including account administration and processing claims, and prevention of fraud.

Finally, the term means the disclosure is required in connection with: 1) the authorization, clearing, transferring, reconciling, or collection of amounts charged or debited using a debit or credit card; 2) the transfer of receivables, accounts, or interests therein; or 3) the audit or debit or credit information.

Consumer Defined

In Section 509, Congress defines "consumer" to mean an individual who obtains financial products or services from a financial institution that are to be used primarily for personal, family, or household purposes, and also means the legal representative of such an individual.

Joint Agreement Defined

Congress defines a joint agreement to be a formal written contract pursuant to which two or more financial institutions jointly offer, endorse, or sponsor a financial product or service, and as may be further defined in regulations.

Affiliate and Nonaffiliated Third Party

The term "affiliate" is defined in Section 509 to be any company that controls, is controlled by, or is under common control with another company. The term "nonaffiliated third party" means any entity that is not an affiliate of, or related by common ownership or affiliated by corporate control with, the financial institution, but does not include a joint employee of such institution.

See Act Secs. 502 and 509 at ¶ 1502 and ¶ 1509. See Conference Report at ¶ 5018.

¶ 504 Disclosure of Privacy Policy to Customers

At the time of establishing a customer relationship with a consumer, and at least annually during the relationship's continuance, a financial institution must provide the consumer with a clear and conspicuous disclosure of its policies and practices with regard to: 1) disclosing nonpublic personal information to affiliates and nonaffiliated third parties, including the categories of information that may be disclosed; 2) disclosing the nonpublic personal information of former customers; and 3) protecting the nonpublic personal information of consumers.

All of these disclosures must be in writing, or in electronic form, or other form permitted by regulation.

According to Sen. Gramm, the most important thing Congress did on privacy was the full disclosure requirement. It requires banks, when you open your account, to tell you precisely what their policy is. They must disclose if they share personal financial information within or outside the bank, and also whether they disclose nonpublic information once you are no longer a customer. They must tell consumers what they do to protect information. This is the ultimate privacy protection, he declared. (Cong. Record, Nov. 3, 1999, p.S13786.) Similarly, in the view of Sen. Wayne Allard, the required disclosure of the institution's privacy policy is an important tool for consumers to make an informed decision as to which financial institutions they wish to patronize. Just as some consumers select a bank based on the hours it is open or its branch locations, those for whom privacy is a key issue can make an informed decision based on a bank's privacy policies. (Cong. Record, Nov. 4, 1999, p.S13877.)

Generally, the disclosures will be made in accordance with regulations to be adopted by, among others, the federal banking agencies and the SEC. However, Section 503 specifically mandates four types of information that must be included in the required disclosure. First, the disclosure must contain the policies and practices of the financial institution with regard to disclosing nonpublic personal information to nonaffiliated third parties, other than agents of the institution, and including the categories of persons to whom the information is or may be disclosed and the policy for disclosure to former customers.

Secondly, the disclosure must include the categories of nonpublic personal information that are collected by the financial institution. Third, a financial institution must also disclose the policies that it maintains to protect the confidentiality and security of nonpublic personal information in accordance with Section 501. (see ¶ 502.) And fourth, it must include the disclosure required, if any, under Section 603(d)(2)(A)(iii) of the Fair Credit Reporting Act.

The conferees clarified that a financial institution's annual disclosure of its privacy policy to its customers must include a statement of the institution's policies and practices regarding the sharing of nonpublic personal information with affiliated entities, as well as with non-affiliated entities.

Time of Establishing Relationship

In Section 509, Congress generally provides that the phrase "time of establishing a customer relationship" will be defined by the regulators. But Congress specifically directs that, in the case of a financial institution engaged in extending credit directly to consumers to finance purchases of goods and services, the phrase must mean the time of establishing the credit relationship with the consumer.

Single-Event Transactions

A question arises concerning the required disclosure for single-event transactions with a financial institution, such as a customer's purchase of teller's checks, money orders, or remote bill payments at institutions that do not have an ongoing relationship with the customer. According to Rep. Michael Oxley, Chairman of the House Finance Subcommittee, in single-event transactions, financial institutions must disclose to the customer their privacy policies and practices at the time the transaction is entered into.

A customer relationship is created, but it is over in an extremely short amount of time. In these types of transactions, no continuing relationship between the financial institution and the customer is created. For this reason, the financial institution is not required to provide its privacy policies to such customers annually. House Banking Committee Chairman James Leach agreed with this interpretation. (Cong. Record, Nov. 4, 1999, p. H11535.)

See Act Sec. 503 at ¶ 1503. See Conference Report at ¶ 5018.

¶ 505 Rulemaking

A separate rulemaking process is set forth to carry out the purposes of the subtitle. Thus, Congress directs the federal banking agencies, the SEC, the FTC, the Treasury, and the National Credit Union Administration to prescribe, in consultation with state insurance authorities, any regulations that may be needed to carry out the purposes of the privacy subtitle with respect to the financial institutions subject to their jurisdiction. The regulations must be issued in final form within six months after enactment of the Gramm-Leach-Bliley Act. The House bill had called for joint rulemaking.

In its rulemaking, each agency is required to consult and coordinate with the other agencies so as to ensure, to the extent possible, that the regulations prescribed are consistent and comparable with those prescribed by the other agencies. The regulations may include additional exceptions to disclosure prohibitions as are deemed consistent with the purposes of the privacy subtitle. The conferees desire that state insurance authorities would implement regulations necessary to carry out the purposes of the privacy provisions and enforce such regulations as the Act provides.

The conferees wish to ensure that smaller financial institutions are not placed at a competitive disadvantage by a statutory regime that allows certain information to be shared freely within an affiliate structure while limiting the ability to share that same information with nonaffiliated third parties. Accordingly, in prescribing regulations pursuant to this subtitle, the agencies and authorities described in Section 504(a)(1) should take into consideration any adverse competitive effects on small commercial banks, thrifts, and credit unions. In issuing regulations under Section 503, which mandates disclosure of an institution's privacy policy, Congress wants the regulators to take into account the degree of consumer access to disclosure by electronic means.

In floor remarks, Rep. Bruce Vento urged regulators to look carefully at the clear statutory intent to limit exceptions as they begin to shape appropriate exceptions in regulation. Sharing with third parties outside the scope of these limited exceptions should not be allowed. He noted that the Act does try to provide some competitive equality to smaller institutions vis-a-vis larger affiliated structures without providing loopholes that would invade the financial privacy of consumers. Rep. Vento entreated the regulators not to provide exceptions merely to make something easier for financial institutions when it comes at the expense of the knowledge and benefit of consumers. (Comg. Record, Nov. 4, 1999, p.H11540.)

State Insurance Authority Defined

In Section 509, Congress defines a "state insurance authority" to mean, in the case of any person engaged in providing insurance, the state insurance authority of the state in which the person is domiciled.

See Act Secs. 504 and 509 at ¶ 1504 and ¶ 1509. See Conference Report at ¶ 5018.

¶ 506 Enforcement

The privacy provisions and the rules adopted under them will be enforced by the federal functional regulators, the state insurance authorities, and the FTC with regard to the financial institutions under their jurisdiction. Thus, for example, the SEC will conduct enforcement with regard to brokers, dealers, investment companies, and investment advisers. In order to address the concern that the House bill failed to provide an enforcement mechanism for enforcing the privacy provisions against non-financial institutions, the conferees clarified that the FTC's enforcement authority would extend to such entities.

In his signing statement of Nov. 12, 1999, President Clinton mentioned that the privacy restrictions "have teeth." For the first time, the Act allows privacy protections to be included in regular bank examinations. Also, the Act authorizes regulators to issue privacy rules and use the full range of their enforcement powers in case of violations.

The conferees agreed to modify Section 502(e)(5) to include the Secretary of the Treasury as a "law enforcement agency" for the purpose of the Bank Secrecy Act, to avoid unintended interference with the existing functions of the Treasury's anti-money laundering unit, the Financial Crimes Enforcement Network.

Section 505 provides that the agencies must implement the standards prescribed under Section 501(b) in the same manner, to the extent practicable, as standards prescribed pursuant to Section 39(a) of the Federal Deposit Insurance Act are implemented. An exception is that the SEC, the FTC, and the state insurance authorities must implement the standards by rule with regard to the financial institutions subject to their jurisdictions. It thus appears that, with regard to banks, violations could subject them to a wide range of possible sanctions, including termination of FDIC insurance and civil money penalties. (see remarks of House Banking Committee Chairman James Leach, Cong. Record, Nov. 4, 1999, p.H11528.)

State Insurance Authorities

If a state insurance authority fails to adopt regulations to carry out Subtitle A, Section 505(c) provides that the state will not be eligible to override the insurance customer protection regulations prescribed by a federal banking agency under Section 47 of the Federal Deposit Insurance Act.

In his signing statement of Nov. 12, 1999, President Clinton said that the Act raised constitutional issues with regard to the insurance privacy provisions. He said that the Act may be construed as contrary to Supreme Court decisions holding that Congress may not compel states to enact or administer a federal regulatory program. The President interprets Section 505(c), however, as providing states with a constitutionally permissible choice of whether to participate in such a program. States that choose to participate will gain the powers listed in Section 505(c), while states that decline will not.

The President believes that Congress, in giving states a choice in selecting Section 505(c) of whether to "adopt regulations to carry out this subtitle" intended to allow the states to accept or decline all of the rulemaking and enforcement obligations assigned to state authorities under Sections 501-505 of the Act. This interpretation is consistent with the explanation in the conference report that both the rulemaking and enforcement roles of state insurance authorities are voluntary not mandatory.

See Act Sec. 505 at ¶ 1505. See Conference Report at ¶ 5018.

¶ 507 Fair Credit Reporting Act

The conferees clarified the relation between the privacy provisions of Title V and other consumer protections already in law, by stating that nothing in Title V should be construed to modify, limit, or supersede the operation of the Fair Credit Reporting Act, and no inference is to be drawn on the basis of the provisions of the title regarding whether information is transaction or experience information under Section 603 of that Act.

Section 506 authorizes the federal banking agencies and the National Credit Union Administration to prescribe joint regulations governing the institutions under their jurisdiction with regard to the Fair Credit Reporting Act. The conferees agreed to an amendment giving the Federal Reserve Board the authority to set forth FCRA regulations governing bank holding companies and their affiliates.

In a colloquy between Sens. Gramm and Allard with regard to an amendment to the Fair Credit Reporting Act in Section 506(b) of Gramm-Leach-Bliley, it was determined that striking the FCRA's outright prohibition on various agencies drafting trade regulation rules or other regulations is intended to allow for these agencies to fulfill their mandate under the financial services modernization legislation to issue regulations. The deletion leaves the law silent on the issue of agencies issuing regulations outside of Gramm-Leach-Bliley, and it should not be construed to mean that an agency now has a mandate to issue any such regulations. (Cong. Record, Nov. 4, 1999, p.S13902-13903).

See Act Sec. 506 at ¶ 1506. See Conference Report at ¶ 5018.

¶ 508 State Laws

The Act preserves all existing and all future state privacy protections above and beyond the national floor established in the bill. (Sen. Rod Grams, Cong. Record, Nov. 4, 1999, S13890.) Thus, if any state law or regulation provides greater consumer privacy protections, it will remain in effect for that state. (Sen. Wayne Allard, Cong. Record, Nov. 4, 1999, p.S13877.)

Section 507 directs that the privacy provisions will not be construed to supersede or alter state law, except to the extent that state law is inconsistent with the provisions and then only to the extent of the inconsistency. It is further provided that state law will not be deemed inconsistent if the protections it affords are greater than the protection provided under the federal privacy provisions. The determination of whether state law does provide greater protection will be made by the FTC after consultation with the agency with jurisdiction of either the person that initiated the complaint or that is the subject of the complaint. Thus, if a broker initiated the complaint, the FTC would have to consult with the SEC. The FTC may act on its own motion or on the petition of any interested party.

In a colloquy with Sen. Connie Mack, Banking Committee Chairman Phil Gramm confirmed that Section 507 is intended to apply only to Subtitle A of Title V and is not to be construed to apply to any provision of law other than the provisions of the subtitle. Thus, Section 507 does not affect existing federal Fair Credit Reporting Act provisions on that statute's relationship to state laws. Sen. Mack had submitted that Section 507 did not supersede, alter, or affect the existing FCRA preemption of state laws with regard to the exchange of information among affiliated entities. (Cong. Record, Nov. 4, 1999, p.S13901.)

See Act Sec. 507 at ¶ 1507.

¶ 509 Study of Information Sharing

Congress directs the Treasury Secretary, in conjunction with the federal functional regulators and the FTC, to conduct a study of information sharing practices among financial institutions and their affiliates. The study must include the purposes for the sharing of confidential customer information with affiliates or with nonaffiliated third parties and the potential benefits for financial institutions and for customers of the sharing of information. Also required to be included is the extent and adequacy of security protections and the potential risks for customer privacy.

The study must also include the adequacy of existing laws to protect customer privacy and the adequacy of a financial institution's privacy policy and privacy rights disclosure under existing law. Finally, the congressionally-mandated study must discuss the feasibility of different approaches, including opt-in and opt-out, to allow customers to direct that confidential information not be shared with affiliates and nonaffiliated third parties, as well as the feasibility of restricting sharing of information for specific uses or of allowing customers to direct the uses for which information may be shared.

In conducting the study, the Treasury Secretary must consult with state insurance authorities, the financial services industry, consumer organizations, privacy groups, and other representatives of the general public.

The report must be submitted to Congress by Jan. 1, 2002 and contain the required findings and conclusions, together with appropriate recommendations for legislative or administrative action.

See Act Sec. 508 at ¶ 1508.

¶ 510 Effective Date

The privacy provisions of Subtitle A generally take effect six months after the date on which the rules to carry out the purposes of the provisions are required to be prescribed, which is six months after enactment of Gramm-Leach-Bliley. But a later effective date can be specified in the prescribed rules. Also, Section 504 (which authorizes the rulemaking) and Section 506 (dealing with the Fair Credit Reporting Act) take effect upon enactment.

See Act Sec. 510 at ¶ 1510.

FRAUDULENT ACCESS TO FINANCIAL INFORMATION

¶ 511 Pretext Calling

Subtitle B of Title V addresses the subject of pretexting, which is the obtaining of personal confidential information from financial institutions under false pretenses. Congress provides protection against pretexting violations by increasing the penalties for fraudulent information gathering, and enhancing the ability to prosecute such fraudulent activities.

Pretext calling has been described as blatant criminal activity in which an individual impersonates another in order to trick an institution into providing confidential information. (Cong. Record, Nov. 4, 1999, p.H11546.) According to Senate Banking Committee Chairman Phil Gramm, the provisions of Subtitle B basically have to do with people who willfully misrepresent themselves to get financial data. We came down on them "like a ton of bricks." (Cong. Record, Nov. 3, 1999, p. S13785). Sen. Rod Grams, Chairman of the Securities Subcommittee, said it criminalizes the actions of bad actors who use false pretenses or lie to obtain a customer's personal financial information. (Cong. Record, Nov. 4, 1999, p.S13890.)

Section 521 makes it unlawful for any person to obtain, attempt to obtain or cause to be disclosed to any person, customer information of a financial institution relating to another person by making false statements to an officer, employee, or agent of a financial institution or making a false statement to a customer of a financial institution, or providing any document to an officer, employee, or agent of a financial institution with knowledge that the document is forged, counterfeit, lost, or stolen or was fraudulently obtained, or contains a false statement. It is also unlawful to request a person to obtain customer information of a financial institution knowing that it was obtained through any of the three methods proscribed by the statute.

It is now a federal crime to obtain or attempt to obtain private customer financial information through fraudulent or deceptive means. According to House Banking Committee Chairman James Leach, such means could include misrepresenting the identity of the person requesting the information or otherwise tricking an institution or customer into making unwitting disclosures of such information. (Cong. Record, Nov. 4, 1999, p.H11528.)

Exceptions

The prohibitions set forth in Section 521 do not apply to any action by a law enforcement agency to obtain customer information of a financial institution in the performance of its official duties. According to the House Commerce Committee, the term law enforcement agency is intended to include federal, state, and local agencies, and encompasses those agencies responsible for enforcing child-support obligations. Similarly, Section 521 specifically provides that the prohibitions do not apply to prevent any state-licensed private investigator from obtaining customer information to the extent reasonably necessary to collect child support from a delinquent person.

The prohibitions do not apply when a financial institution obtains information about one of its customers in the course of testing the security procedures of the institution for maintaining the confidentiality of customer information or while investigating allegations of misconduct or negligence by an officer or employee of the institution, or in the course of recovering customer information that was obtained by another person in any manner described in the section.

For example, when a fraud prevention unit of a financial institution succeeds in retrieving information from an information broker that had been fraudulently obtained, the financial institution would not be in violation of the statute. This safe harbor should extend to any officer, employee, or agent retained by a financial institution to implement antifraud or self-testing programs.

Similarly, the prohibitions do not apply when an insurance company obtains information as part of an insurance investigation into criminal activity or fraud that is authorized for the company under state law. In addition, the statute does not apply to obtaining the customer information of a financial institution that is otherwise available as a public record filed under the federal securities laws.

In addition, the Commerce Committee does not intend that Subtitle B be construed as limiting, expanding, or otherwise interfering with the sharing of information among affiliates or subsidiaries within a financial services institution as permitted under any applicable law.

Criminal Penalties

Any person who knowingly and intentionally violates or attempts to violate these provisions is subject to criminal penalties for commission of a felony of up to five years in prison, plus fines of up to $250,000 for individuals and $500,000 for companies, with aggravated cases involving significant multiple offenses or a violation of multiple laws resulting in doubled penalties.

Administrative Enforcement

The conferees provided that authority for enforcing Subtitle B would be placed in the FTC, the federal banking agencies, and the National Credit Union Administration, for enforcement of these provisions with regard to compliance by depository institutions within their jurisdiction. Thus, Section 522 designates the Federal Trade Commission as the primary enforcer of the subtitle, in the same manner and with the same power and with authority under the Fair Debt Collection Practices Act. Other agencies are also given enforcement authority in certain cases. For example, compliance will be enforced under the Federal Deposit Insurance Act in the case of national banks and FDIC-insured banks and savings associations.

Definitions

For purposes of Subtitle B, Congress defined several terms. A "customer" is defined as any person to whom a financial institution provides a product or service, including that of acting as a fiduciary. The term "customer information of a financial institution" is defined as any information maintained by or for a financial institution that is derived from the relationship between the financial institution and its customer and is identified with the customer. "Document" is defined as any information in any form.

A "financial institution" is any institution engaged in the business of providing financial services to customers who maintain a credit, deposit, trust, or other financial account or relationship with the institution, including but not limited to depository institutions, brokers, and dealers, investment advisers, investment companies, insurance companies, loan or finance companies, credit card issuers, operators of credit card systems, and consumer reporting agencies. In addition, the FTC, after consultation with the SEC and the federal banking agencies, may further define the types of institutions to be treated as financial institutions under Subtitle B.

Congress, however, has specifically excluded from the term "financial institution" any person or entity with respect to any financial activity subject to CFTC jurisdiction.

See Act Secs. 521, 522, 523 and 527 at ¶ 1521, ¶ 1522, ¶ 1523, and ¶ 1527.

¶ 512 States Laws

Section 524 preempts state authority only to the extent that a state's laws are inconsistent with the Act. If state authority provides greater protection to any person, then that state authority remains controlling law.

See Act Sec. 524 at ¶ 1524.

¶ 513 Agency Guidance

The Act requires each federal banking agency, the National Credit Union Administration, and the SEC or self-regulatory organizations to review their rules and guidelines governing the protection of confidential consumer financial information for financial institutions under their respective jurisdictions. They must also make revisions necessary to ensure appropriate confidentiality safeguards. Those safeguards will include those policies, procedures, and controls as would reasonably be expected to prevent and detect, insofar as practicable, activities proscribed by the Act. The House Commerce Committee expects the appropriate examining authorities to include compliance with such guidelines and the adequacy of such internal controls in their examinations of these institutions.

See Act Sec. 525 at ¶ 1525.

¶ 514 Reports to Congress

The Comptroller General, in consultation with, among others, the SEC, federal banking agencies, and state insurance regulators. must report to Congress on the effectiveness and adequacy of the Act in preventing fraudulent attempts to obtain confidential consumer information, as well as on any recommendations for additional legislative or regulatory action that is appropriate. The report is due within 18 months of enactment.

Also, the Federal Trade Commission and the Attorney General must submit an annual report to Congress on their enforcement actions pursuant to Subtitle B.

See Act Sec. 526 at ¶ 1526.

Title VI—Federal Home Loan Bank System Modernization

¶ 601 Introduction

The Federal Home Loan Bank System Modernization Act of 1999 is embodied in Title VI of the Gramm-Leach-Bliley Act, revising a system which was established by the Federal Home Loan Bank Act of 1932 to provide a credit reserve system, similar to the Federal Reserve system, for thrift institutions engaged in long term home financing. Prior to the passage of the Financial Institutions Reform Recovery and Enforcement Act of 1989, the FHLBank System consisted of the Federal Home Loan Bank Board (FHLBB), twelve regional Federal Home Loan Banks, member institutions, and the Federal Savings and Loan Insurance Corporation (FSLIC). The Federal Savings and Loan Insurance Corporation was established as part of the National Housing Act in 1934. The FSLIC was established to insure accounts deposited with member banks and to regulate insured members.

The FHLBB was responsible for the administration and supervision of the FHLBank System. It was a three member Board, appointed to four year terms by the President, with the advice and consent of the Senate. However, the FHLBB was abolished with the enactment of FIRREA and the Federal Housing Finance Board was created to supervise the FHLBanks.

The 1999 Modernization Act reforms the FHLBank System in several critical ways. Mandatory FHLBank membership for federal savings associations is eliminated, thus making membership completely voluntary. Small bank members are granted expanded access to FHLBank advances. Governance of the FHLBanks is decentralized from the FHFB to the individual FHLBanks. In addition, the Resolution Funding Corporation obligation, stemming from the savings and loan crisis, is changed from a fixed dollar amount to a fixed percentage of annual net earnings.

¶ 602 Community Financial Institution Defined

The Modernization Act adds a definition of "community financial institution" to Section 2 of the Federal Home Loan Bank Act (12 USC 1422). In general, the term community financial institution is defined as a member that has deposits which are insured under the Federal Deposit Insurance Act and that has less than $500 million in average total assets at the time of the transaction at issue. This figure will be based on an average of total assets over the three years preceding that date. The $500 million limit will be adjusted annually by the Federal Housing Finance Board, based on an the annual percentage increase, if any, in the Consumer Price Index.

See Act Sec. 602 at ¶ 1602.

¶ 603 Savings Association Membership

Section 5(f) of the Home Owners' Loan Act (12 USC 1464(f)) is amended to provide that six months after the enactment of the Modernization Act, mandatory Federal Home Loan Bank membership for federal savings associations is eliminated in order to provide for a completely voluntary membership.

Should an association choose to become a member, it will qualify for membership under the current criteria of the Federal Home Loan Bank Act.

See Act Sec. 603 at ¶ 1603.

¶ 604 Advances to Members; Collateral

An amendment to Section 10(a) of the Federal Home Loan Bank Act (12 USC 1430(a)) authorizes long-term advances made for the purpose of providing funds to any FHLBank member for residential housing finance. In addition, it authorizes community financial institutions to obtain long-term advances for small businesses, small farms and small agri-businesses.

Eligible collateral for such long-term advances is expanded to include cash as well as deposits of an FHLBank. The Act also provides that eligible collateral for community financial institutions receiving any FHLBank advances could include secured loans for small business, agriculture or securities representing a whole interest in these loans.

Insufficient Eligible Collateral

The legislation specifically provides that if an advance existing on the date of enactment of FIRREA matures, and the member does not have sufficient eligible collateral to fully secure a renewal of the advance, an FHLBank has the authority to renew the advance secured by collateral it determines appropriate. Further, a member that has an advance secured by insufficient eligible collateral must reduce its level of outstanding advances promptly and prudently, in accordance with a schedule determined by the FHLBank. In the past, this authority rested with the FHFB as opposed to the individual bank.

The Act does, however, provide that the FHFB may review the collateral standards applicable to each FHLBank for the classes of collateral described in the section, and may, for purposes of safety and soundness, require an increase in the collateral standards for any or all classes of collateral.

Qualified Thrift Lender Status

The provisions of Section 10 that relate to qualified thrift lender (QTL) status are amended by elimination of the requirement that FHLBank members that are not QTLs when they receive their advances must make greater stock purchases than QTLs. Also eliminated is the requirement that such members only apply for advances for housing finance purposes. A priority for advances to members that are QTLS and a 30 percent limit on advances to non-QTLs are also removed by the amendment.

Restrictions on a non-QLT in obtaining new advances from any FHLBank are removed by the Act. Prior to the Act, savings associations that were non-QLTs also were required to repay advances after three years; this provision has been eliminated.

See Act Sec. 604 at ¶ 1604. See Conference Report at ¶ 5020.

¶ 605 Eligibility Criteria for FHLBank Membership

Section 4(a) of the Federal Home Loan Bank Act (12 USC 1424(a)) lists the eligibility criteria that institutions must meet to obtain FHLBank membership. A limited exemption for community financial institutions is added to this section by the Act. Section 4(a) specified that an insured depository institution that was not a member of an FHLBank by Jan. 1, 1989, could obtain membership only if:

- the insured depository institution had at least 10 percent of its total assets in residential mortgage loans;
- the financial condition of the institution would allow advances to be safely made to the institution; and
- the character of its management and its home financing policy were consistent with sound and economical home financing.

The new exemption for community financial institutions provides that, if an institution otherwise meets the requirements of Section 4(a), it may become a member without regard to the percentage of its total assets that is represented by residential mortgage loans.

See Act Sec. 605 at ¶ 1605.

¶ 606 Management of Federal Home Loan Banks

Residency Requirements

The provisions of the Federal Home Loan Bank Act governing the management of Federal Home Loan Banks (12 USC 1427(d)) have been amended. Whereas Section 7 of the FHLBank Act required directors of FHLBanks to be residents of the district in which the bank was located, the Act broadens this provision to allow FHLBank directors to reside outside the bank's district if they are an officer or director of a member institution located in the district.

Terms of Office—Procedures for Acting Chairperson

The Act sets the terms for both elected and appointed directors at three years, staggered with approximately one-third of the terms expiring each year. An FHLBank's board of directors is granted authority to elect by majority vote the board's Chairperson and Vice Chairperson from among the directors of the bank. The term of office for both Chairperson and Vice Chairperson is set at two years. The Vice Chairperson is granted the authority to act as Chairperson should there be a period of vacancy in the position of Chairperson of the board of directors, or during any absence or disability of a Chairperson. The board of each FHLBank must establish the specific procedures, outlined in the bylaws of the board, for designating an acting chairperson for any period during which the Chairperson and Vice Chairperson are unavailable to carry out the requirements of that position. Further, procedures for removing a Chairperson or Vice Chairperson from that position for good cause also must be established in the bylaws.

Compensation of FHLBank Directors

The annual salaries of FHLBank directors are established by the Act and may not exceed those specified amounts, plus reimbursement of expenses. The maximum amounts established by the Act are as follows:

- The Chairperson is allowed a maximum salary of $25,000.
- The Vice Chairperson's salary is set at a maximum of $20,000.
- All other directors are provided with a maximum salary of $15,000.

Effective on Jan. 1, 2001, each of these dollar amounts will be adjusted annually by the FHFB. The adjustments will be based on the annual percentage increase, if any, in the Consumer Price Index for all urban consumers, as published by the Department of Labor.

Decentralization of Authority

Governance of the FHLBanks is decentralized from the FHFB to the individual FHLBanks by the amendment to Section 12 of the Federal Home Loan Act (12 USC 1432). Specifically, authority is shifted from the FHFB to the FHLBanks in the circumstances described in Section 1432(a):

- The prior approval of the FHFB is no longer required when an FHLBank buys, builds or leases for a term of more than ten years a building intended for a bank.
- An FHLBank may select, employ and compensate officers, employees and agents necessary for the transaction of its business without the approval of the FHFB.
- An FHLBank's directors may prescribe, amend and repeal by-laws governing the administration of its affairs, as long as its actions are consistent with applicable laws and regulations, as administered by the FHFB.

The Act also amends Section 12 by providing that no officer, employee, attorney or agent of an FHLBank who receives compensation may be a member of its board of directors. Section 12 previously permitted the president of an FHLBank to be a director on its board.

Powers and Duties of FHFB

The general powers and duties of the FHFB, as described by Section 1422b(a) of the FHLB Act, are amended by the addition of provisions relating to the issuance of notices of violations. The FHFB is granted the authority to issue and serve a notice of charges on an FHLBank or any of its executive officers or directors, if the agency determines that the FHLBank or its officers or directors is about to engage in an unsafe or unsound practice while conducting bank business. This section further provides that these notices may be issued if the FHFB has a reasonable suspicion of such activities without actual knowledge.

The FHFB also may issue notices of violations if it reasonably believes any FHLBank, executive officer or director is about to engage in conduct that would violate any provisions of the Act or any law, order, rule, regulation or condition imposed in writing by the FHFB. In addition, this authority includes the authority to issue an order requiring affirmative action to correct any conditions that may result from the unpermitted conduct. The FHFB also may limit the activities of an FHLBank or any of its executive officers or directors if appropriate. In effect, the FHFB is granted the same enforcement authority over FHLBanks and their executive officers and directors as the federal banking agencies and the Office of Federal Housing Enterprise Oversight have under their statutes.

The Act also empowers the FHFB to address any capital insufficiencies that may occur as a result from the change to voluntary membership. Finally, the FHFB is permitted to act in its own name, and through its own attorneys: when enforcing any provision of the Act or any regulations that may stem from its enactment; or in any action, suit or proceeding in which the FHFB is a party and that involves the agency's regulation or supervision of any FHLBank.

Eligibility to Secure Advances

Section 9 of the FHLB Act (12 USC 1429) is amended by removing the requirement of FHFB approval when a member of an FHLBank applies in writing for advances. The applications must be in the form required by the FHLBank, and they do not require approval by the FHFB. An FHLBank also may use its discretion to deny or grant an application without obtaining FHFB approval.

Interest Rates Applied to Secured Advances

The Act amends Section 10 of the FHLB Act (12 USC 1430) by granting to the FHLBanks the authority to approve or determine the interest rate that is applied to secured advances made to members with sufficient collateral. The interest rate was determined by the FHFB prior to enactment of the Act.

Advances to Stock Ratio Limit—Obligations to Repay

Section 10 also established the 20:1 advances to stock ratio limit for an FHLBank member. This meant that the aggregate outstanding advances made by any FHLBank to any member could not exceed twenty times the amounts paid in by that member for the outstanding capital stock it held. The Act eliminates this ratio limit for FHLBank members.

The Act also eliminates the requirement of the FHLB Act that the terms and form of repayment of the advance by the member must be approved by the FHFB. The FHLBank has the authority to set the requirements for payment of the advance, but it will still remain a primary and unconditional obligation to pay off all advances, including interest and any unpaid costs and expenses in connection with the advance.

Reserves and Dividends

In its provision concerning FHLBank reserve accounts, Section 16(a) of the FHLB Act provided that no dividends could be paid except out of net earnings remaining after reductions for all reserves, charge-offs, purchases of capital certificates of the Financing Corporation, and payments relating to the

Funding Corporation under the FHLB Act have been made; this payment of dividends also was subject to approval of the FHFB. The Act revises this provision by allowing dividends to be paid out of previously retained earnings or net earnings. It also removes the requirement that payment be subject to approval by the FHFB.

Assessments for Administrative Expenses

Finally, the Modernization Act amends the FHLB Act's provisions relating to semiannual assessments imposed on the FHLBanks by the FHFB (12 USC 1438(b)). The Act eliminates the transition provision of this section, which permitted the FHFB to levy a one-time special assessment on the FHLBanks for the agency's estimated expenses for the transitional period following enactment of FIRREA in 1989. The assessment was permitted if it was made before the FHFB's first semiannual assessment. The Act does not substitute any provisions for the removal of this transition provision.

See Act Sec. 606 at ¶ 1606. See Conference Report at ¶ 5020.

¶ 607 Resolution Funding Corporation

Further amendments concern the Resolution Funding Corporation (REFCORP), established by Section 21B of the Federal Home Loan Bank Act. The purpose of the Resolution Funding Corporation is to provide funds to the Resolution Trust Company. The REFCORP obligation of the Federal Home Loan Banks, which stemmed from the savings and loan crisis, has been changed from a fixed dollar amount to a fixed percentage of annual net earnings.

The amendment specifically concerns the interest payments on obligations of REFCORP. Section 21B(f)(2)(C) of the FHLB Act provided that if the amounts available to REFCORP under this section are insufficient to cover the amount of those interest payments, each FHLBank must pay to REFCORP each calendar year: the aggregate amount of $300 million, minus the amounts required in that year for REFCORP principal payments; and the amounts required in that year by REFCORP for capitalization—12 USC 1441b(e).

The dollar amount specified in this paragraph is changed to 20 percent of the annual net earnings of each FHLBank, after deducting any allowable expenses, including operating expenses.

Annual Determination

The FHFB annually will determine the difference between the value of the aggregate amounts paid by the FHLBanks and the value of an annuity of $300 million per year that begins on the issuance date and ends on the final scheduled maturity date of the obligations. The agency will select appropriate value factors for making these determinations, in conjunction with the Secretary of the Treasury. This section further provides that the FHFB must extend or shorten the term of the payment obligations of an FHLBank to ensure that the value of all payments made by the FHLBanks is equivalent to the value of the annuity.

If the FHFB determines that it is necessary to extend the term of the payment obligations beyond the final scheduled maturity date, then each FHLBank will continue to pay 20 percent of its net earnings, minus the applicable deductions, to the U.S. Treasury until the value of the payments equals the value of the $300 million annuity. In the final year that the FHLBanks are required to make any payment to the Treasury, the FHFB will reduce their percentage pro rata if 20 percent of the FHLBanks' net earnings would exceed the amount of the remaining obligation.

This amendment will become effective on Jan. 1, 2000. Payments made before that date will be counted toward the total obligation of that FHLBank under Section 21.

See Act Sec. 607 at ¶ 1607.

¶ 608 Capital Structure of Federal Home Loan Banks

The Act establishes a new capital structure for Federal Home Loan Banks by amending Section 6 of the Federal Home Loan Bank Act (12 USC 1426). The FHFB will issue regulations prescribing uniform capital standards for each FHLBank by November 12, 2000.

Issuance of Stock

The regulations issued by the FHFB will permit each FHLBank to issue two classes of stock:

- Class A stock, which is redeemable in cash and at par with written notice six months prior to redemption; and
- Class B stock, which is redeemable in cash and at par five years after written notice of the intent to redeem.

The FHFB's regulations also will provide that the stock of an FHLBank may be issued to and held by only members of the bank, and that an FHLBank may not issue any stock other than the two classes authorized by this section. Further, the regulations to be issued will determine how the stock may be sold, transferred, redeemed, or repurchased, and how the outstanding stock held by a member that terminates its membership, or that provides notice of its intention to terminate, will be disposed.

Requirements of Regulations to be Issued by the FHFB

The regulations to be issued by the FHFB will require each bank to meet: a five percent leverage minimum that is based on the total assets of the bank; and a risk-based requirement that is tied to permanent capital. Each FHLBank will be required to maintain permanent capital in an amount that is sufficient to meet the bank'a credit risk and its market risk. Market risk will be based on a stress test established by the FHFB that tests for changes in certain market variables. In establishing the risk-based standard, the FHFB also will consider any risk-based capital test under Section 1361 of the Federal Housing Enterprises Financial Safety and Soundness Act of 1992 (12 USC 4611), modifying the test to be approproate for the needs of FHLBanks.

Permanent capital will include Class B stock and retained earnings. Total capital will include permanent capital plus Class A stock. In determining compliance with the five percent minimum leverage ratio, Class A stock will be counted at paid-in value, and Class B stock and retained earnings will be weighted at 1.5 times. However, the Act provides that an FHLBank's total capital, determined without taking into account any multiplier, will not be permitted to be less than four percent of the bank's total assets.

This weighting provision is intended to encourage FHLBanks to build more permanent, longer-term capital. Using the capital multiplier, the paid-in value of outstanding Class A stock plus 1.5 times the paid-in value of outstanding Class B stock and retained earnings must be at least five percent of an FHLBank'a total assets. Using no weighting factor, the total capital must be at least four percent of the bank's total assets.

Definitions of Capital

An FHLBank's permanent capital, which will be used to determine compliance with the risk-based requirement, will consist of the amounts paid by FHLBank members for Class B stock and the amount of the FHLBank's retained earnings. The amount of retained earnings that may be included in permanent capital will be determined in accordance with generally accepted accounting principles (GAAP). The amount of Class B stock that is to be included in permanent capital is the full amount paid by an FHLBank member to that bank for the purchase of Class B stock.

An FHLBank's total capital, used to measure compliance with the five percent leverage minimum, will consist of: permanent capital; the amounts paid by FHLBank members for Class A stock; any general allowance for losses that are consistent with GAAP and subject to FHFB regulation; and any other amounts from sources the FHFB determines to be available to absorb losses incurred by the FHLBank and appropriate for including as capital. The Modernization Act prohibits any loss reserve that is held or established against a specific asset of an FHLBank from being included in total capital.

Transition Period

The requirements relating to the purchase and retention of an FHLBank's capital stock by a member of the bank that were in effect on the day before the enactment of the Federal Home Loan Bank Modernization Act of 1999 will continue with respect to each FHLBank until the required regulations have become effective, and the capital structure plan outlined in this section has been approved by the FHFB and implemented by the FHLBank.

Capital Structure Plan

The board of directors of each FHLBank are required to submit a plan establishing and implementing a capital structure as described in this section for approval by the FHFB. This plan must be submitted no later than 270 days after the date of publication by the FHFB of any final regulations required by this section. Any modifications that an FHLBank proposes to make to an approved capital structure plan must also be submitted to the FHFB for approval.

See Act Sec. 608 at ¶ 1608. See Conference Report at ¶ 5020.

Title VII—Other Provisions

¶ 701 Introduction

Consumer protections in Title VII require banks to disclose bank surcharges on Automated Teller Machines before a transaction is made. A highly charged issue addressed in the final compromise before Congressional passage of the legislation was the Community Reinvestment Act, which requires financial institutions to make loans in the low-income and minority neighborhoods from which they also receive deposits. If defined thresholds are met, disclosure of CRA agreements to federal banking agencies and the public will be required. The legislation also provides regulatory relief to small banks by providing more of a gap between examinations.

The final portion of the Gramm-Leach Bliley Act contains an assortment of other regulatory improvements. Among these is the establishment of a new federal microenterprise program to provide grants for technical assistance for microenterprise lending organizations. In addition, a provision of the Federal Deposit Insurance Act relating to interstate bank mergers was amended by adding a subsection regulating applicable interest rates, finance charges and other similar charges.

ATM REFORM

¶ 702 Fee Disclosures at Automated Teller Machines

Automated teller machine operators are now required to disclose surcharge fees to cardholders who are not customers of the ATM operator. The ATM Fee Reform Act of 1999, which amends Section 904(d) of the Electronic Fund Transfer Act (15 USC 1693b), does not require disclosure of fees that the consumer's own bank may charge.

ATM operators assessing surcharges are required to (1) post a sign on the machine stating that a fee will be charged; and (2) post a notice on the screen that a fee will be charged and the amount of such fee, after the transaction is initiated and before the consumer is irrevocably committed to completing the transaction. The second disclosure may be made by a paper notice issued from the machine. No surcharge fee may be charged unless the required disclosures are made and the consumer elects to proceed with the transaction after receiving the notice.

A transaction that involves a balance inquiry initiated by a consumer in the same manner as an electronic fund transfer falls within the statutory requirements, whether or not the consumer initiates a transfer of funds in the course of the transaction.

Older ATMs that lack the technical capability to disclose the notice on the screen or to issue the alternative paper notice are exempt from that requirement until January 1, 2005.

ATM operators are exempt from liability if properly posted signs are subsequently removed, damaged, or altered by someone else.

See Act Secs. 702 and 705 at ¶ 1702 and ¶ 1705. See Conference Report at ¶ 5021.

¶ 703 Disclosure of Possible Fees

Banks, when issuing ATM cards, must notify customers that surcharges may be imposed by other parties for transactions initiated from ATMs not operated by the card issuer.

See Act Sec. 703 at ¶ 1703.

¶ 704 Feasibility Study

The Comptroller General is required to study the feasibility, costs, benefits to consumers, and competitive impact of requiring that ATM operators disclose not only any surcharge imposed by the machine in use, but also any fees imposed by the consumer's own bank, any network used to effect the transaction, and any other party involved in the transaction. The report must be submitted to Congress by May 12, 2000.

See Act Sec. 704 at ¶ 1704.

COMMUNITY REINVESTMENT

¶ 711 CRA Sunshine Requirements

Full disclosure is required of agreements between insured depository institutions or their affiliates and nongovernmental entities or persons made in connection with the "fulfillment" of Community Reinvestment Act requirements. The disclosure requirement contained in new Section 48 of the Federal Deposit Insurance Act is applicable to such agreements that involve funds or other resources of an insured depository institution or affiliate, if defined thresholds are exceeded. The parties will be required to disclose the full text of such agreements to both federal banking agencies and the public.

The CRA sunshine requirements apply to agreements providing for cash payments, grants, or other consideration with a value in excess of $10,000, or for loans exceeding $50,000, annually. To help define agreements subject to public disclosure, the appropriate federal banking agency is given the authority to identify a list of factors that have a material impact on the agency's decision to approve or disapprove an application for a deposit facility or to assign a rating in an examination under the CRA.

The disclosure requirement is not applicable to an individual mortgage loan. Also excluded is any other loan or extension of credit to an individual, business, farm, or other entity, if the funds are loaned at rates not substantially below market rates and the purpose of the transaction does not include any re-lending of borrowed funds to other parties.

The scope of the sunshine provision does not extend to an agreement entered into by an insured depository institution or affiliate with a nongovernmental entity or person who has not commented on, testified about, discussed with the institution, or otherwise contacted the institution, concerning the CRA. The Federal Reserve Board has the authority to prescribe regulations to prevent evasions of this requirement and to provide further exemptions consistent with the purposes of the Act.

Annual Reporting Requirement

Parties to a CRA agreement entered into after May 11, 2000 will be required to report at least once each year on the funds and resources provided pursuant to each agreement. It is anticipated that the annual activity report will require information relating to: (1) payments, fees, or loans made to or received from any party to the agreement, along with the terms and conditions; and (2) aggregate data on loans, investments, and services provided in the community pursuant to the agreement. A bank must file its report directly with its federal regulator.

A nongovernmental party is required to report an accounting of the use funds received under a CRA agreement with the appropriate federal banking supervisory agency for the insured depository institution that is a party to agreement. The report may be made either directly with the agency or via the insured depository institution, which would be required promptly to transmit the report to the federal banking agency. The required accounting of use of funds must include a detailed, itemized list of the uses to which the funds were made, including compensation, administrative expenses, travel, entertainment, consulting and professional fees paid.

Regulations

The federal banking agencies are directed to adopt regulations to ensure and monitor compliance with the CRA sunshine requirements. The statute calls for the agencies to take rulemaking action to establish the disclosure requirements for the annual CRA activity report by insured depository institutions. The agencies are expected to minimize the regulatory burden of reporting parties and to permit a nongovernmental entity or person who is a party to a large number of CRA agreements to file a single or consolidated report.

Violations

If a party to a CRA agreement who is not an insured depository institution or affiliate violates the disclosure requirement, the agreement will be unenforceable after the offending party has been given notice and a reasonable opportunity to comply. The federal banking agencies will assist in identifying a successor nongovernmental party to assume the responsibilities of an unenforceable agreement.

In cases where funds or resources received under a CRA agreement are diverted for personal financial gain, the federal banking agencies have authority to order disgorgement or to prohibit the offending individual from participating in a CRA agreement for up to 10 years. An inadvertent or de minimis error in a report does not subject the filing party to any penalty.

The statute does not confer any authority on the federal banking agencies to enforce the provisions a CRA agreement.

See Act Sec. 711 at ¶ 1711. See Conference Report at ¶ 5022.

¶ 712 Small Bank Regulatory Relief

Regulated financial institutions with aggregate assets of less than $250 million will be subject to routine examinations under the CRA no more than once every 5 years, if the institution received a rating of "outstanding record of meeting community credit needs" at its most recent examination. Routine examinations will be limited to not more than once every 4 years if the institution received a rating of "satisfactory record of meeting community credit needs," under newly added Section 809 of the Community Reinvestment Act.

The federal banking agencies may subject an institution to more frequent or less frequent examinations for reasonable cause. A regulated financial institution remains subject to CRA examination in connection with an application for a deposit facility.

It is explicitly stated that no provision of the Community Reinvestment Act has been repealed by the Gramm-Leach-Bliley Act.

See Act Secs. 712 and 714 at ¶ 1712 and ¶ 1714.

¶ 713 CRA Studies

The Federal Reserve Board must conduct a comprehensive study of the CRA focusing on default rates, delinquency rates, and the profitability of loans made in conformity with the Act. The study, to be conducted in consultation with the Chairman and Ranking members of the House and Senate Banking Committees, is to be submitted to those Congressional Committees by March 15, 2000.

Another study is designed to determine the extent to which adequate services are being provided as intended by the CRA, including services in low- and moderate-income neighborhoods and for persons of modest means, as a result of the Gramm-Leach-Bliley Act. The study of the Secretary of the Treasury, in consultation with the federal banking agencies, is to include any recommendations for administrative and legislative action pertinent to institutions covered under CRA.

The final report by the Treasury Secretary must be submitted to Congress within 2 years. A baseline report is due by March 15, 2000. The purpose of the baseline report is to give a set of data against which the Secretary will be able to measure change by the end of the two-year reporting period.

See Act Secs. 713 and 715 at ¶ 1713 and ¶ 1715. See Conference Report at ¶ 5022.

OTHER REGULATORY IMPROVEMENTS

¶ 721 Small Bank Access to S Corporation Treatment

A study of possible revisions to the rules governing S corporations and the potential impact on community banks will be conducted by the GAO. The report to Congress is due within six months.

Topics included within the scope of the S corporation study include: increasing the permissible number of shareholders; permitting shares to be held in individual retirement accounts; clarifying that interest on investments held for safety, soundness, and liquidity purposes should not be considered to be passive income; discontinuation of the treatment of stock held by bank directors as a disqualifying personal class of stock; and improving federal tax treatment of bad debt and interest deductions.

See Act Sec. 721 at ¶ 1721.

¶ 722 Plain Language Requirement for Agency Rules

The federal banking agencies are required to use plain language in all proposed and final rulemaking published in the Federal Register after January 1, 2000. Each federal banking agency must submit a report to Congress by March 1, 2001 describing how the agency has complied with the plain language requirement.

See Act Sec. 722 at ¶ 1722.

¶ 723 Converted Federal Savings Association

Federal savings associations that convert to national or state bank charters may keep the word "Federal" in their names. For example, if First Federal Savings Bank converts from a federal savings association to a state bank charter, it may retain its former name.

See Act Sec. 723 at ¶ 1723.

¶ 724 Control of Bankers' Banks

An amendment to the Bank Holding Company Act allows *one or more* thrift institutions to own a state-chartered bank or trust company, whose business is restricted to accepting (1) deposits from thrift institutions or savings banks; (2) deposits arising from the corporate business of the thrift institutions or savings banks that own the bank or trust company; (3) or deposits of public funds.

See Act Sect. 724 at ¶ 1724.

¶ 725 Technical Assistance to Microenterprises

The enactment of the "Program for Investment in Microentrepreneurs Act of 1999" (also referred to as the "PRIME Act") establishes a grant program to fund nonprofit microenterprise development organizations, programs, collaboratives, or intermediaries engaged in:

(1) providing training and technical assistance to low-income and disadvantaged entrepreneurs interested in starting or expanding their own businesses;

(2) building the capacity of organizations that serve low-income and disadvantaged entrepreneurs; and

(3) supporting research and development aimed at identifying and promoting training and technical assistance programs that effectively serve low-income and disadvantaged entrepreneurs.

A "microenterprise" consists of a sole proprietorship, partnership, or corporation that has fewer than 5 employees and generally lacks access to conventional loans, equity, or other banking services. A "microenterprise development organization or program" refers to a nonprofit entity, or a program administered by a nonprofit entity, that provides services to disadvantaged entrepreneurs. Training and technical assistance includes services and support to disadvantaged entrepreneurs to enhance business planning, marketing, management, financial management skills, and assistance in accessing financial services.

At least 50% of the grants are to be used to benefit very low income persons, including those residing on Indian reservations. Generally, not less than 50% of each dollar provided under the PRIME Act, must be matched with funds from sources other than the federal government.

The program will be administered by the Small Business Administration.

See Act. Sec. 725 at ¶ 1725. See Conference Report at ¶ 5023.

¶ 726 Federal Reserve Audits

The Federal Reserve Board is required to order an annual independent audit of the financial statements of each federal reserve bank and of the Board.

See Act Sec. 726 at ¶ 1726.

¶ 727 Authorization to Release Reports

At its discretion, the Federal Reserve Board is now authorized to furnish exam reports and other confidential supervisory information concerning state member banks or other entities it examines to any federal or state authorities with supervisory authority over the examined entity. The Board may also release the information to officers, directors, or receivers of the examined entity, or any other person deemed proper by the Board.

The Right to Financial Privacy Act has been amended to treat the Commodity Futures Trading Commission in a manner consistent with the other financial supervisory agencies.

See Act Sec. 727 at ¶ 1727.

¶ 728 Study of Conflicts of Interest

The conflict of interest faced by the Federal Reserve between its role as a primary regulator of the federal banking industry and its role as a vendor of services to the banking and financial services industry is the subject of a study to be conducted by the Comptroller General. Specifically, the study will look at the conflict of interest between the Federal Reserve's role as a regulator of the payment system and its role as a competitor with private sector providers of payments services, and how best to resolve that conflict. The report to Congress, along with any recommended legislative or administrative action, is due in one year.

See Act Sec. 728 at ¶ 1728.

¶ 729 Study of On-Line Banking and Lending

A mandated study by the federal banking agencies will examine banking regulations for the delivery of financial services, including those regulations that may assume that there will be person-to-person contact. Recommendations on adapting those existing requirements to online banking and lending, along with any other recommended legislative or regulatory action, must be submitted to Congress within two years.

See Act Sec. 729 at ¶ 1729.

¶ 730 Source of Strength Doctrine

The source of strength doctrine is enhanced by providing federal banking agencies protection from claims brought by the bankruptcy trustee of a depository institution or other person for the return of assets transferred to (or for the benefit of) an insured depository institution by an affiliate or controlling shareholder. A banking agency (including in its capacity as a conservator or receiver) is insulated from a claim for the return of assets, monetary damages or other legal or equitable relief if, at the time of the transfer, the depository institution was subject to a direction by a federal banking agency to increase its capital or was undercapitalized. Although the amendment to Section 18 of the Federal Deposit Insurance Act shields banking agencies from a cause of action to avoid preferential or fraudulent transfers or conveyances, any claim based on actual intent to hinder, delay or defraud is outside of the statutory protection.

See Act Sec. 730 at ¶ 1730.

¶ 731 Interest Rates and Charges at Interstate Branches

An amendment to Section 44 of the Federal Deposit Insurance Act (12 USC 1831u), which relates to interstate bank mergers, provides loans pricing parity among interstate banks. Specifically, if an interstate bank can charge a particular interest rate, then a local bank in the state into which the interstate bank has branched may charge a comparable rate. The rate and charge limitations contained in the statute are applicable only to states that have constitutional provisions that set a maximum lawful annual percentage rate of interest on any contract at not more than 5% above the discount rate for 90-day commercial paper in effect at the Federal Reserve Bank for the Federal Reserve District in which the state is located.

The amendment is not intended to affect banks whose home office and authorized branch offices are not located in a state subject to the statutory limitations. National banks with interstate offices continue to be authorized to export the interest rates of the state where their home office is located. National banks are also entitled to charge the rates of the host state of the interstate branch, under OCC interpretations, where there is some nexus between the host state and loan (Cong. Record Nov. 4, 1999, p. S13901).

See Act Sec. 731 at ¶ 1731.

¶ 732 Interstate Branches and Agencies of Foreign Banks

A foreign bank may upgrade an agency located in a state outside the foreign bank's home state into a federal or state branch with the approval of the appropriate chartering authority and the Federal Reserve Board. The amendment to Section 5(a)(7) of the International Banking Act of 1978 (12 USC 3103) also permits a foreign bank to establish and operate a federal branch or federal agency, or a state branch or state agency in any state outside the foreign bank's home state with the required approvals.

See Act Sec. 732 at ¶ 1732.

¶ 733 Fair Treatment of Women by Financial Advisers

The Act establishes the sense of the Congress that individuals offering financial advice and products should do so in a nondiscriminatory, non gender-specific manner (see ¶ 225).

See Act Sec. 733 at ¶ 1733

¶ 734 Membership of Loan Guarantee Boards

The membership requirements for the Emergency Steel Loan Guarantee Board and the Emergency Oil and Gas Loan Guarantee Board have been modified to allow the Chairmen of the Federal Reserve Board and the SEC to designate another member of the Board or another Commissioner to serve in their place.

See Act Sec. 734 at ¶ 1734.

¶ 735 Repeal of Stock Loan Limit

The restriction in Section 11(m) of the Federal Reserve Act (12 USC 248) on loans by Federal Reserve member banks secured by stock or bond collateral has been repealed. Limitations on loans to one borrower imposed pursuant to other statutory authorizations are not affected.

See Act Sec. 735 at ¶ 1735.

¶ 736 Elimination of SAIF AND DIF Special Reserves

The need for the establishment of special reserve for the Savings Association Insurance Fund, which the FDIC was required to create beginning in 1999, has been eliminated effective immediately.

See Act Sec. 736 at ¶ 1736.

¶ 737 Bank Officers and Directors—Public Utilities

An amendment to the Federal Power Act allows officers or directors of public utilities to serve as officers or directors of banks, trust companies, or securities firms if they comply with certain safeguards against conflicts of interest.

See Act Sec. 737 at ¶ 1737.

¶ 738 Approval for Purchases of Securities

A majority of the entire board of directors of a bank is authorized to vote on the purchase of securities from an affiliate, based on a determination that the purchase is a sound investment for the bank. Such a standard did not exist under prior law, which simply required the vote to be taken by a majority of independent directors.

See Act Sec. 738 at ¶ 1738.

¶ 739 Optional Conversion of Federal Savings Association

A federal savings association charted prior to November 12, 1999 is allowed to convert into one or more national or state banks, each of which may encompass one or more of the branches of the federal savings association in one or more states. The optional conversion is subject to the approval of the OCC or the appropriate state bank supervisor. Each resulting national or state bank must meet all applicable financial, management, and capital requirements.

See Act Sec. 739 at ¶ 1739.

¶ 740 Grand Jury Proceedings

U.S. attorneys may seek a court order granting permission to provide either federal or state financial regulatory agencies with access to grand jury material. The order may be sought during or after completion of a grand jury investigation into a banking law violation.

See Act Sec. 740 at ¶ 1740.

LAW TEXT—TABLE OF CONTENTS

Gramm-Leach-Bliley Act

TITLE I—FACILITATING AFFILIATION AMONG BANKS, SECURITIES FIRMS, AND INSURANCE COMPANIES

Subtitle A—Affiliations

Subtitle B—Streamlining Supervision of Bank Holding Companies

Subtitle C—Subsidiaries of National Banks

Subtitle D—Preservation of FTC Authority

Gramm-Leach-Bliley Act

Act of November 12, 1999, Public Law 106-102, 113 Stat. 1338

¶ 1001

SEC. 1. **SHORT TITLE; TABLE OF CONTENTS.**

(a) SHORT TITLE.—This Act may be cited as the "Gramm-Leach-Bliley Act".

(b) TABLE OF CONTENTS.—The table of contents for this Act is as follows: [see page 135 for table of contents to the Act.]

TITLE I—FACILITATING AFFILIATION AMONG BANKS, SECURITIES FIRMS, AND INSURANCE COMPANIES
Subtitle A—Affiliations

¶ 1101

SEC. 101. **GLASS-STEAGALL ACT REPEALS.**

(a) SECTION 20 REPEALED.—Section 20 of the Banking Act of 1933 (12 U.S.C. 377) (commonly referred to as the "Glass-Steagall Act") is repealed.

(b) SECTION 32 REPEALED.—Section 32 of the Banking Act of 1933 (12 U.S.C. 78) is repealed.

¶ 1102

SEC. 102. **ACTIVITY RESTRICTIONS APPLICABLE TO BANK HOLDING COMPANIES THAT ARE NOT FINANCIAL HOLDING COMPANIES.**

(a) IN GENERAL.—Section 4(c)(8) of the Bank Holding Company Act of 1956 (12 U.S.C. 1843(c)(8)) is amended to read as follows:

"(8) shares of any company the activities of which had been determined by the Board by regulation or order under this paragraph as of the day before the date of the enactment of the Gramm-Leach-Bliley Act, to be so closely related to banking as to be a proper incident thereto (subject to such terms and conditions contained in such regulation or order, unless modified by the Board);".

(b) CONFORMING CHANGES TO OTHER STATUTES.—

(1) AMENDMENT TO THE BANK HOLDING COMPANY ACT AMENDMENTS OF 1970.—Section 105 of the Bank Holding Company Act Amendments of 1970 (12 U.S.C. 1850) is amended by striking ", to engage directly or indirectly in a nonbanking activity pursuant to section 4 of such Act,".

(2) AMENDMENT TO THE BANK SERVICE COMPANY ACT.—Section 4(f) of the Bank Service Company Act (12 U.S.C. 1864(f)) is amended by inserting before the period at the end the following: "as of the day before the date of the enactment of the Gramm-Leach-Bliley Act".

¶ 1103

SEC. 103. **FINANCIAL ACTIVITIES.**

(a) IN GENERAL.—Section 4 of the Bank Holding Company Act of 1956 (12 U.S.C. 1843) is amended by adding at the end the following new subsections:

"Engaging in activities that are financial in nature

"(k)(1) IN GENERAL.—Notwithstanding subsection (a), a financial holding company may engage in any activity, and may acquire and retain the shares of any company engaged in any activity, that the Board, in accordance with paragraph (2), determines (by regulation or order)—

"(A) to be financial in nature or incidental to such financial activity; or

"(B) is complementary to a financial activity and does not pose a substantial risk to the safety or soundness of depository institutions or the financial system generally.

"(2) COORDINATION BETWEEN THE BOARD AND THE SECRETARY OF THE TREASURY.—

"(A) PROPOSALS RAISED BEFORE THE BOARD.—

"(i) CONSULTATION.—The Board shall notify the Secretary of the Treasury of, and consult with the Secretary of the Treasury concerning, any request, proposal, or application under this subsection for a determination of whether an activity is financial in nature or incidental to a financial activity.

"(ii) TREASURY VIEW.—The Board shall not determine that any activity is financial in nature or incidental to a financial activity under this subsection if the Secretary of the Treasury notifies the Board in writing, not later than 30 days after the date of receipt of the notice described in clause (i) (or such longer period as the Board determines to be appropriate under the circumstances) that the Secretary of the Treasury believes that the activity is not financial in nature or incidental to a financial activity or is not otherwise permissible under this section.

"(B) PROPOSALS RAISED BY THE TREASURY.—

"(i) TREASURY RECOMMENDATION.—The Secretary of the Treasury may, at any time, recommend in writing that the Board find an activity to be financial in nature or incidental to a financial activity.

"(ii) TIME PERIOD FOR BOARD ACTION.—Not later than 30 days after the date of receipt of a written recommendation from the Secretary of the Treasury under clause (i) (or such longer period as the Secretary of the Treasury and the Board determine to be appropriate under the circumstances), the Board shall determine whether to initiate a public rule-making proposing that the recommended activity be found to be financial in nature or incidental to a financial activity under this subsection, and shall notify the Secretary of the Treasury in writing of the determination of the Board and, if the Board determines not to seek public comment on the proposal, the reasons for that determination.

"(3) FACTORS TO BE CONSIDERED.—In determining whether an activity is financial in nature or incidental to a financial activity, the Board shall take into account—

"(A) the purposes of this Act and the Gramm-Leach-Bliley Act;

"(B) changes or reasonably expected changes in the marketplace in which financial holding companies compete;

"(C) changes or reasonably expected changes in the technology for delivering financial services; and

"(D) whether such activity is necessary or appropriate to allow a financial holding company and the affiliates of a financial holding company to—

"(i) compete effectively with any company seeking to provide financial services in the United States;

"(ii) efficiently deliver information and services that are financial in nature through the use of technological means, including any application necessary to protect the security or efficacy of systems for the transmission of data or financial transactions; and

"(iii) offer customers any available or emerging technological means for using financial services or for the document imaging of data.

"(4) ACTIVITIES THAT ARE FINANCIAL IN NATURE.—For purposes of this subsection, the following activities shall be considered to be financial in nature:

"(A) Lending, exchanging, transferring, investing for others, or safeguarding money or securities.

"(B) Insuring, guaranteeing, or indemnifying against loss, harm, damage, illness, disability, or death, or providing and issuing annuities, and acting as principal, agent, or broker for purposes of the foregoing, in any State.

"(C) Providing financial, investment, or economic advisory services, including advising an investment company (as defined in section 3 of the Investment Company Act of 1940).

"(D) Issuing or selling instruments representing interests in pools of assets permissible for a bank to hold directly.

"(E) Underwriting, dealing in, or making a market in securities.

"(F) Engaging in any activity that the Board has determined, by order or regulation that is in effect on the date of the enactment of the Gramm-Leach-Bliley Act, to be so closely related to banking or managing or controlling banks as to be a proper incident thereto (subject to the same terms and conditions contained in such order or regulation, unless modified by the Board).

"(G) Engaging, in the United States, in any activity that—

"(i) a bank holding company may engage in outside of the United States; and

"(ii) the Board has determined, under regulations prescribed or interpretations issued pursuant to subsection (c)(13) (as in effect on the day before the date of the enactment of the Gramm-Leach-Bliley Act) to be usual in connection with the transaction of banking or other financial operations abroad.

"(H) Directly or indirectly acquiring or controlling, whether as principal, on behalf of 1 or more entities (including entities, other than a depository institution or subsidiary of a depository institution, that the bank holding company controls), or otherwise, shares, assets, or ownership interests (including debt or equity securities, partnership interests, trust certificates, or other instruments representing ownership) of a company or other entity, whether or not constituting control of such company or entity, engaged in any activity not authorized pursuant to this section if—

"(i) the shares, assets, or ownership interests are not acquired or held by a depository institution or subsidiary of a depository institution;

"(ii) such shares, assets, or ownership interests are acquired and held by—

(I) a securities affiliate or an affiliate thereof; or

(II) an affiliate of an insurance company described in subparagraph (I)(ii) that provides investment advice to an insurance company and is registered pursuant to the Investment Advisers Act of 1940, or an affiliate of such investment adviser;

as part of a bona fide underwriting or merchant or investment banking activity, including investment activities engaged in for the purpose of appreciation and ultimate resale or disposition of the investment;

"(iii) such shares, assets, or ownership interests are held for a period of time to enable the sale or disposition thereof on a reasonable basis consistent with the financial viability of the activities described in clause (ii); and

"(iv) during the period such shares, assets, or ownership interests are held, the bank holding company does not routinely manage or operate such company or entity except as may be necessary or required to obtain a reasonable return on investment upon resale or disposition.

"(I) Directly or indirectly acquiring or controlling, whether as principal, on behalf of 1 or more entities (including entities, other than a depository institution or subsidiary of a depository institution, that the bank holding company controls) or otherwise, shares, assets, or ownership interests (including debt or equity securities, partnership interests, trust certificates or other instruments representing ownership) of a company or other entity, whether or not constituting control of such company or entity, engaged in any activity not authorized pursuant to this section if—

"(i) the shares, assets, or ownership interests are not acquired or held by a depository institution or a subsidiary of a depository institution;

"(ii) such shares, assets, or ownership interests are acquired and held by an insurance company that is predominantly engaged in underwriting life, accident and health, or property and casualty insurance (other than credit-related insurance) or providing and issuing annuities;

"(iii) such shares, assets, or ownership interests represent an investment made in the ordinary course of business of such insurance company in accordance with relevant State law governing such investments; and

"(iv) during the period such shares, assets, or ownership interests are held, the bank holding company does not routinely manage or operate such company except as may be necessary or required to obtain a reasonable return on investment.

"(5) ACTIONS REQUIRED.—

"(A) IN GENERAL.—The Board shall, by regulation or order, define, consistent with the purposes of this Act, the activities described in subparagraph (B) as financial in nature, and the extent to which such activities are financial in nature or incidental to a financial activity.

"(B) ACTIVITIES.—The activities described in this subparagraph are as follows:

"(i) Lending, exchanging, transferring, investing for others, or safeguarding financial assets other than money or securities.

"(ii) Providing any device or other instrumentality for transferring money or other financial assets.

"(iii) Arranging, effecting, or facilitating financial transactions for the account of third parties.

"(6) REQUIRED NOTIFICATION.—

"(A) IN GENERAL.—A financial holding company that acquires any company or commences any activity pursuant to this subsection shall provide written notice to the Board describing the activity commenced or conducted by the company acquired not later than 30 calendar days after commencing the activity or consummating the acquisition, as the case may be.

"(B) APPROVAL NOT REQUIRED FOR CERTAIN FINANCIAL ACTIVITIES.—Except as provided in subsection (j) with regard to the acquisition of a savings association, a financial holding company may commence any activity, or acquire any company, pursuant to paragraph (4) or any regulation prescribed or order issued under paragraph (5), without prior approval of the Board.

"(7) MERCHANT BANKING ACTIVITIES.—

"(A) JOINT REGULATIONS.—The Board and the Secretary of the Treasury may issue such regulations implementing paragraph (4)(H), including limitations on transactions between depository institutions and companies controlled pursuant to such paragraph, as the Board and the Secretary jointly deem appropriate to assure compliance with the purposes and prevent evasions of this Act and the Gramm-Leach-Bliley Act and to protect depository institutions.

"(B) SUNSET OF RESTRICTIONS ON MERCHANT BANKING ACTIVITIES OF FINANCIAL SUBSIDIARIES.—The restrictions contained in paragraph (4)(H) on the ownership and control of shares, assets, or ownership interests by or on behalf of a subsidiary of a depository institution shall not apply to a financial subsidiary (as defined in section 5136A of the Revised Statutes of the United States) of a bank, if the Board and the Secretary of the Treasury jointly authorize financial subsidiaries of banks to engage in merchant banking activities pursuant to section 122 of the Gramm-Leach-Bliley Act.

"Conditions for engaging in expanded financial activities

"(l)(1) IN GENERAL.—Notwithstanding subsection (k), (n), or (o), a bank holding company may not engage in any activity, or directly or indirectly acquire or retain shares of any company engaged in any activity, under subsection (k), (n), or (o), other than activities permissible for any bank holding company under subsection (c)(8), unless—

"(A) all of the depository institution subsidiaries of the bank holding company are well capitalized;

"(B) all of the depository institution subsidiaries of the bank holding company are well managed; and

"(C) the bank holding company has filed with the Board—

"(i) a declaration that the company elects to be a financial holding company to engage in activities or acquire and retain shares of a company that were not permissible for a bank holding company to engage in or acquire before the enactment of the Gramm-Leach-Bliley Act; and

"(ii) a certification that the company meets the requirements of subparagraphs (A) and (B).

"(2) CRA REQUIREMENT.—Notwithstanding subsection (k) or (n) of this section, section 5136A(a) of the Revised Statutes of the United States, or section 46(a) of the Federal Deposit Insurance Act, the appropriate Federal banking agency shall prohibit a financial holding company or any insured depository institution from—

"(A) commencing any new activity under subsection (k) or (n) of this section, section 5136A(a) of the Revised Statutes of the United States, or section 46(a) of the Federal Deposit Insurance Act; or

"(B) directly or indirectly acquiring control of a company engaged in any activity under subsection (k) or (n) of this section, section 5136A(a) of the Revised Statutes of the United States, or section 46(a) of the Federal Deposit Insurance Act (other than an investment made pursuant to subparagraph (H) or (I) of subsection (k)(4), or section 122 of the Gramm-Leach-Bliley Act, or under section 46(a) of the Federal Deposit Insurance Act by reason of such section 122, by an affiliate already engaged in activities under any such provision);

if any insured depository institution subsidiary of such financial holding company, or the insured depository institution or any of its insured depository institution affiliates, has received in its most recent examination under the Community Reinvestment Act of 1977, a rating of less than 'satisfactory record of meeting community credit needs'.

"(3) FOREIGN BANKS.—For purposes of paragraph (1), the Board shall apply comparable capital and management standards to a foreign bank that operates a branch or agency or owns or controls a commercial lending company in the United States, giving due regard to the principle of national treatment and equality of competitive opportunity.

"Provisions applicable to financial holding companies that fail to meet certain requirements

"(m)(1) IN GENERAL.—If the Board finds that—

"(A) a financial holding company is engaged, directly or indirectly, in any activity under subsection (k), (n), or (o), other than activities that are permissible for a bank holding company under subsection (c)(8); and

"(B) such financial holding company is not in compliance with the requirements of subsection (l)(1);

the Board shall give notice to the financial holding company to that effect, describing the conditions giving rise to the notice.

"(2) AGREEMENT TO CORRECT CONDITIONS REQUIRED.—Not later than 45 days after the date of receipt by a financial holding company of a notice given under paragraph (1) (or such additional period as the Board may permit), the financial holding company shall execute an agreement with the Board to comply with the requirements applicable to a financial holding company under subsection (l)(1).

"(3) BOARD MAY IMPOSE LIMITATIONS.—Until the conditions described in a notice to a financial holding company under paragraph (1) are corrected, the Board may impose such limitations on the conduct or activities of that financial holding company or any affiliate of that company as the Board determines to be appropriate under the circumstances and consistent with the purposes of this Act.

"(4) FAILURE TO CORRECT.—If the conditions described in a notice to a financial holding company under paragraph (1) are not corrected within 180 days after the date of receipt by the financial holding company of a notice under paragraph (1), the Board may require such financial holding company, under such terms and conditions as may be imposed by the Board and subject to such extension of time as may be granted in the discretion of the Board, either—

"(A) to divest control of any subsidiary depository institution; or

"(B) at the election of the financial holding company instead to cease to engage in any activity conducted by such financial holding company or its subsidiaries (other than a depository institution or a subsidiary of a depository institution) that is not an activity that is permissible for a bank holding company under subsection (c)(8).

"(5) CONSULTATION.—In taking any action under this subsection, the Board shall consult with all relevant Federal and State regulatory agencies and authorities.

"Authority to retain limited non-financial activities and affiliations

"(n)(1) IN GENERAL.—Notwithstanding subsection (a), a company that is not a bank holding company or a foreign bank (as defined in section 1(b)(7) of the International Banking Act of 1978) and becomes a financial holding company after the date of the enactment of the Gramm-Leach-Bliley Act may continue to engage in any activity and retain direct or indirect ownership or control of shares of a company engaged in any activity if—

"(A) the holding company lawfully was engaged in the activity or held the shares of such company on September 30, 1999;

"(B) the holding company is predominantly engaged in financial activities as defined in paragraph (2); and

"(C) the company engaged in such activity continues to engage only in the same activities that such company conducted on September 30, 1999, and other activities permissible under this Act.

"(2) PREDOMINANTLY FINANCIAL.—For purposes of this subsection, a company is predominantly engaged in financial activities if the annual gross revenues derived by the holding company and all subsidiaries of the holding company (excluding revenues derived from subsidiary depository institutions), on a consolidated basis, from engaging in activities that are financial in nature or are incidental to a financial activity under subsection (k) represent at least 85 percent of the consolidated annual gross revenues of the company.

"(3) NO EXPANSION OF GRANDFATHERED COMMERCIAL ACTIVITIES THROUGH MERGER OR CONSOLIDATION.—A financial holding company that engages in activities or holds shares pursuant to this subsection, or a subsidiary of such financial holding company, may not acquire, in any merger, consolidation, or other type of business combination, assets of any other company that is engaged in any activity that the Board has not determined to be financial in nature or incidental to a financial activity under subsection (k), except this paragraph shall not apply with respect to a company that owns a broadcasting station licensed under title III of the Communications Act of 1934 and the shares of which are under common control with an insurance company since January 1, 1998, unless such company is acquired by, or otherwise becomes an affiliate of, a bank holding company that, at the time such acquisition or affiliation is consummated, is 1 of the 5 largest domestic bank holding companies (as determined on the basis of the consolidated total assets of such companies).

"(4) CONTINUING REVENUE LIMITATION ON GRANDFATHERED COMMERCIAL ACTIVITIES.—Notwithstanding any other provision of this subsection, a financial holding company may continue to engage in activities or hold shares in companies pursuant to this subsection only to the extent that the aggregate annual gross revenues derived from all such activities and all such companies does not exceed 15 percent of the consolidated annual gross revenues of the financial holding company (excluding revenues derived from subsidiary depository institutions).

"(5) CROSS MARKETING RESTRICTIONS APPLICABLE TO COMMERCIAL ACTIVITIES.—

"(A) IN GENERAL.—A depository institution controlled by a financial holding company shall not—

"(i) offer or market, directly or through any arrangement, any product or service of a company whose activities are conducted or whose shares are owned or controlled by the financial holding company pursuant to this subsection or subparagraph (H) or (I) of subsection (k)(4); or

"(ii) permit any of its products or services to be offered or marketed, directly or through any arrangement, by or through any company described in clause (i).

"(B) RULE OF CONSTRUCTION.—Subparagraph (A) shall not be construed as prohibiting an arrangement between a depository institution and a company owned or controlled pursuant to subsection (k)(4)(I) for the marketing of products or services through statement inserts or Internet websites if—

"(i) such arrangement does not violate section 106 of the Bank Holding Company Act Amendments of 1970; and

"(ii) the Board determines that the arrangement is in the public interest, does not undermine the separation of banking and commerce, and is consistent with the safety and soundness of depository institutions.

"(6) TRANSACTIONS WITH NONFINANCIAL AFFILIATES.—A depository institution controlled by a financial holding company may not engage in a covered transaction (as defined in section 23A(b)(7) of the Federal Reserve Act) with any affiliate controlled by the company pursuant to this subsection.

"(7) SUNSET OF GRANDFATHER.—A financial holding company engaged in any activity, or retaining direct or indirect ownership or control of shares of a company, pursuant to this subsection, shall terminate such activity and divest ownership or control of the shares of such company before the end of the 10-year period beginning on the date of the enactment of the Gramm-Leach-Bliley Act. The Board may, upon application by a financial holding company, extend such 10-year period by a period not to exceed an additional 5 years if such extension would not be detrimental to the public interest.

"Regulation of certain financial holding companies

"(o) Notwithstanding subsection (a), a company that is not a bank holding company or a foreign bank (as defined in section 1(b)(7) of the International Banking Act of 1978) and becomes a financial holding company after the date of enactment of the Gramm-Leach-Bliley Act, may continue to engage in, or directly or indirectly own or control shares of a company engaged in, activities related to the trading, sale, or investment in commodities and underlying physical properties that were not permissible for bank holding companies to conduct in the United States as of September 30, 1997, if—

"(1) the holding company, or any subsidiary of the holding company, lawfully was engaged, directly or indirectly, in any of such activities as of September 30, 1997, in the United States;

"(2) the attributed aggregate consolidated assets of the company held by the holding company pursuant to this subsection, and not otherwise permitted to be held by a financial holding company, are equal to not more than 5 percent of the total consolidated assets of the bank holding company, except that the Board may increase that percentage by such amounts and under such circumstances as the Board considers appropriate, consistent with the purposes of this Act; and

"(3) the holding company does not permit—

"(A) any company, the shares of which it owns or controls pursuant to this subsection, to offer or market any product or service of an affiliated depository institution; or

"(B) any affiliated depository institution to offer or market any product or service of any company, the shares of which are owned or controlled by such holding company pursuant to this subsection.".

(b) COMMUNITY REINVESTMENT REQUIREMENT.—Section 804 of the Community Reinvestment Act of 1977 (12 U.S.C. 2903) is amended by adding at the end the following new subsection:

"Financial holding company requirement

"(c)(1) IN GENERAL.—An election by a bank holding company to become a financial holding company under section 4 of the Bank Holding Company Act of 1956 shall not be effective if—

"(A) the Board finds that, as of the date the declaration of such election and the certification is filed by such holding company under section 4(l)(1)(C) of the Bank Holding Company Act of 1956, not all of the subsidiary insured depository institutions of the bank holding company had achieved a rating of 'satisfactory record of meeting community credit needs', or better, at the most recent examination of each such institution; and

"(B) the Board notifies the company of such finding before the end of the 30-day period beginning on such date.

"(2) LIMITED EXCLUSIONS FOR NEWLY ACQUIRED INSURED DEPOSITORY INSTITUTIONS.—Any insured depository institution acquired by a bank holding company during the 12-month period preceding the date of the submission to the Board of the declaration and certification under section 4(l)(1)(C) of the Bank Holding Company Act of 1956 may be excluded for purposes of paragraph (1) during the 12-month period beginning on the date of such acquisition if—

"(A) the bank holding company has submitted an affirmative plan to the appropriate Federal financial supervisory agency to take such action as may be necessary in order for such institution to achieve a rating of 'satisfactory record of meeting community credit needs', or better, at the next examination of the institution; and

"(B) the plan has been accepted by such agency.

"(3) DEFINITIONS.—For purposes of this subsection, the following definitions shall apply:

"(A) BANK HOLDING COMPANY; FINANCIAL HOLDING COMPANY.—The terms 'bank holding company' and 'financial holding company' have the meanings given those terms in section 2 of the Bank Holding Company Act of 1956.

"(B) BOARD.—The term 'Board' means the Board of Governors of the Federal Reserve System.

"(C) INSURED DEPOSITORY INSTITUTION.—The term 'insured depository institution' has the meaning given the term in section 3(c) of the Federal Deposit Insurance Act.".

(c) TECHNICAL AND CONFORMING AMENDMENTS.—

(1) DEFINITIONS.—Section 2 of the Bank Holding Company Act of 1956 (12 U.S.C. 1841) is amended—

(A) in subsection (n), by inserting "depository institution'," after "the terms"; and

(B) by adding at the end the following new subsections:

"Financial holding company

"(p) For purposes of this Act, the term 'financial holding company' means a bank holding company that meets the requirements of section 4(l)(1).

"Insurance company

"(q) For purposes of sections 4 and 5, the term 'insurance company' includes any person engaged in the business of insurance to the extent of such activities.".

(2) NOTICE PROCEDURES.—Section 4(j) of the Bank Holding Company Act of 1956 (12 U.S.C. 1843(j)) is amended—

(A) in each of subparagraphs (A) and (E) of paragraph (1), by inserting "or in any complementary activity under subsection (k)(1)(B)" after "subsection (c)(8) or (a)(2)"; and

(B) in paragraph (3)—

(i) by inserting ", other than any complementary activity under subsection (k)(1)(B)," after "to engage in any activity"; and

(ii) by inserting "or a company engaged in any complementary activity under subsection (k)(1)(B)" after "insured depository institution".

(d) REPORT.—

(1) IN GENERAL.—By the end of the 4-year period beginning on the date of the enactment of this Act, the Board of Governors of the Federal Reserve System and the Secretary of the Treasury shall submit a joint report to the Congress containing a summary of new activities, including grandfathered commercial activities, in which any financial holding company is engaged pursuant to subsection (k)(1) or (n) of section 4 of the Bank Holding Company Act of 1956 (as added by subsection (a)).

(2) OTHER CONTENTS.—The report submitted to the Congress pursuant to paragraph (1) shall also contain the following:

(A) A discussion of actions by the Board of Governors of the Federal Reserve System and the Secretary of the Treasury, whether by regulation, order, interpretation, or guideline or by approval or disapproval of an application, with regard to activities of financial holding companies that are incidental to activities that are financial in nature or complementary to such financial activities.

(B) An analysis and discussion of the risks posed by commercial activities of financial holding companies to the safety and soundness of affiliate depository institutions.

(C) An analysis and discussion of the effect of mergers and acquisitions under section 4(k) of the Bank Holding Company Act of 1956 on market concentration in the financial services industry.

¶ 1104

SEC. 104. OPERATION OF STATE LAW.

(a) STATE REGULATION OF THE BUSINESS OF INSURANCE.—The Act entitled "An Act to express the intent of Congress with reference to the regulation of the business of insurance" and approved March 9, 1945 (15 U.S.C. 1011 et seq.) (commonly referred to as the "McCarran-Ferguson Act") remains the law of the United States.

(b) MANDATORY INSURANCE LICENSING REQUIREMENTS.—No person shall engage in the business of insurance in a State as principal or agent unless such person is licensed as required by the appropriate insurance regulator of such State in accordance with the relevant State insurance law, subject to subsections (c), (d), and (e).

(c) AFFILIATIONS.—

(1) IN GENERAL.—Except as provided in paragraph (2), no State may, by statute, regulation, order, interpretation, or other action, prevent or restrict a depository institution, or an affiliate thereof, from being affiliated directly or indirectly or associated with any person, as authorized or permitted by this Act or any other provision of Federal law.

(2) INSURANCE.—With respect to affiliations between depository institutions, or any affiliate thereof, and any insurer, paragraph (1) does not prohibit—

(A) any State from—

(i) collecting, reviewing, and taking actions (including approval and disapproval) on applications and other documents or reports concerning any proposed acquisition of, or a change or continuation of control of, an insurer domiciled in that State; and

(ii) exercising authority granted under applicable State law to collect information concerning any proposed acquisition of, or a change or continuation of control of, an insurer engaged in the business of insurance in, and regulated as an insurer by, such State;

during the 60-day period preceding the effective date of the acquisition or change or continuation of control, so long as the collecting, reviewing, taking actions, or exercising authority by the State does not have the effect of discriminating, intentionally or unintentionally, against a depository institution or an affiliate thereof, or against any other person based upon an association of such person with a depository institution;

(B) any State from requiring any person that is acquiring control of an insurer domiciled in that State to maintain or restore the capital requirements of that insurer to the level required under the capital regulations of general applicability in that State to avoid the requirement of preparing and filing with the insurance regulatory authority of that State a plan to increase the capital of the insurer, except that any determination by the State insurance regulatory authority with respect to such requirement shall be made not later than 60 days after the date of notification under subparagraph (A); or

(C) any State from restricting a change in the ownership of stock in an insurer, or a company formed for the purpose of controlling such insurer, after the conversion of the insurer from mutual to stock form so long as such restriction does not have the effect of discriminating, intentionally or unintentionally, against a depository institution or an affiliate thereof, or against any other person based upon an association of such person with a depository institution.

(d) ACTIVITIES.—

(1) IN GENERAL.—Except as provided in paragraph (3), and except with respect to insurance sales, solicitation, and cross marketing activities, which shall be governed by paragraph (2), no State may, by statute, regulation, order, interpretation, or other action, prevent or restrict a depository institution or an affiliate thereof from engaging directly or indirectly, either by itself or in conjunction with an affiliate, or any other person, in any activity authorized or permitted under this Act and the amendments made by this Act.

(2) INSURANCE SALES.—

(A) IN GENERAL.—In accordance with the legal standards for preemption set forth in the decision of the Supreme Court of the United States in Barnett Bank of Marion County N.A. v. Nelson, 517 U.S. 25 (1996), no State may, by statute, regulation, order, interpretation, or other action, prevent or significantly interfere with the ability of a depository institution, or an affiliate thereof, to engage, directly or indirectly, either by itself or in conjunction with an affiliate or any other person, in any insurance sales, solicitation, or cross-marketing activity.

(B) CERTAIN STATE LAWS PRESERVED.—Notwithstanding subparagraph (A), a State may impose any of the following restrictions, or restrictions that are substantially the same as but no more burdensome or restrictive than those in each of the following clauses:

(i) Restrictions prohibiting the rejection of an insurance policy by a depository institution or an affiliate of a depository institution, solely because the policy has been issued or underwritten by any person who is not associated with such depository institution or affiliate when the insurance is required in connection with a loan or extension of credit.

(ii) Restrictions prohibiting a requirement for any debtor, insurer, or insurance agent or broker to pay a separate charge in connection with the handling of insurance that is required in connection with a loan or other extension of credit or the provision of another traditional banking product by an depository institution, or any affiliate of a depository institution, unless such charge would be required when the depository institution or affiliate is the licensed insurance agent or broker providing the insurance.

(iii) Restrictions prohibiting the use of any advertisement or other insurance promotional material by a depository institution or any affiliate of a depository institution that would cause a reasonable person to believe mistakenly that—

(I) the Federal Government or a State is responsible for the insurance sales activities of, or stands behind the credit of, the institution or affiliate; or

(II) a State, or the Federal Government guarantees any returns on insurance products, or is a source of payment on any insurance obligation of or sold by the institution or affiliate;

(iv) Restrictions prohibiting the payment or receipt of any commission or brokerage fee or other valuable consideration for services as an insurance agent or broker to or by any person, unless such person holds a valid State license regarding the applicable class of insurance at the time at which the services are performed, except that, in this clause, the term "services as an insurance agent or broker" does not include a referral by an unlicensed person of a customer or potential customer to a licensed insurance agent or broker that does not include a discussion of specific insurance policy terms and conditions.

(v) Restrictions prohibiting any compensation paid to or received by any individual who is not licensed to sell insurance, for the referral of a customer that seeks to purchase, or seeks an opinion or advice on, any insurance product to a person that sells or provides opinions or advice on such product, based on the purchase of insurance by the customer.

(vi) Restrictions prohibiting the release of the insurance information of a customer (defined as information concerning the premiums, terms, and conditions of insurance coverage, including expiration dates and rates, and insurance claims of a customer contained in the records of the depository institution or an affiliate thereof) to any person other than an officer, director, employee, agent, or affiliate of a depository institution, for the purpose of soliciting or selling insurance, without the express consent of the customer, other than a provision that prohibits—

(I) a transfer of insurance information to an unaffiliated insurer in connection with transferring insurance in force on existing insureds of the depository institution or an affiliate thereof, or in connection with a merger with or acquisition of an unaffiliated insurer; or

(II) the release of information as otherwise authorized by State or Federal law.

(vii) Restrictions prohibiting the use of health information obtained from the insurance records of a customer for any purpose, other than for its activities as a licensed agent or broker, without the express consent of the customer.

(viii) Restrictions prohibiting the extension of credit or any product or service that is equivalent to an extension of credit, lease or sale of property of any kind, or furnishing of any services or fixing or varying the consideration for any of the foregoing, on the condition or requirement that the customer obtain insurance from a depository institution or an affiliate of a depository institution, or a particular insurer, agent, or broker, other than a prohibition that would prevent any such depository institution or affiliate—

(I) from engaging in any activity described in this clause that would not violate section 106 of the Bank Holding Company Act Amendments of 1970, as interpreted by the Board of Governors of the Federal Reserve System; or

(II) from informing a customer or prospective customer that insurance is required in order to obtain a loan or credit, that loan or credit approval is contingent upon the procurement by the customer of acceptable insurance, or that insurance is available from the depository institution or an affiliate of the depository institution.

(ix) Restrictions requiring, when an application by a consumer for a loan or other extension of credit from a depository institution is pending, and insurance is offered or sold to the consumer or is required in connection with the loan or extension of credit by the depository institution or any affiliate thereof, that a written disclosure be provided to the consumer or prospective customer indicating that the customer's choice of an insurance provider will not affect the credit decision or credit terms in any way, except that the depository institution may impose reasonable requirements concerning the creditworthiness of the insurer and scope of coverage chosen.

(x) Restrictions requiring clear and conspicuous disclosure, in writing, where practicable, to the customer prior to the sale of any insurance policy that such policy—

(I) is not a deposit;

(II) is not insured by the Federal Deposit Insurance Corporation;

(III) is not guaranteed by any depository institution or, if appropriate, an affiliate of any such institution or any person soliciting the purchase of or selling insurance on the premises thereof; and

(IV) where appropriate, involves investment risk, including potential loss of principal.

(xi) Restrictions requiring that, when a customer obtains insurance (other than credit insurance or flood insurance) and credit from a depository institution, or any affiliate of such institution, or any person soliciting the purchase of or selling insurance on the premises thereof, the credit and insurance transactions be completed through separate documents.

(xii) Restrictions prohibiting, when a customer obtains insurance (other than credit insurance or flood insurance) and credit from a depository institution or an affiliate of such institution, or any person soliciting the purchase of or selling insurance on the premises thereof, inclusion of the expense of insurance premiums in the primary credit transaction without the express written consent of the customer.

(xiii) Restrictions requiring maintenance of separate and distinct books and records relating to insurance transactions, including all files relating to and reflecting consumer complaints, and requiring that such insurance books and records be made available to the appropriate State insurance regulator for inspection upon reasonable notice.

(C) LIMITATIONS.—

(i) OCC DEFERENCE.—Section 304(e) does not apply with respect to any State statute, regulation, order, interpretation, or other action regarding insurance sales, solicitation, or cross marketing activities described in subparagraph (A) that was issued, adopted, or enacted before September 3, 1998, and that is not described in subparagraph (B).

(ii) NONDISCRIMINATION.—Subsection (e) does not apply with respect to any State statute, regulation, order, interpretation, or other action regarding insurance sales, solicitation, or cross marketing activities described in subparagraph (A) that was issued, adopted, or enacted before September 3, 1998, and that is not described in subparagraph (B).

(iii) CONSTRUCTION.—Nothing in this paragraph shall be construed—

(I) to limit the applicability of the decision of the Supreme Court in Barnett Bank of Marion County N.A. v. Nelson, 517 U.S. 25 (1996) with respect to any State statute, regulation, order, interpretation, or other action that is not referred to or described in subparagraph (B); or

(II) to create any inference with respect to any State statute, regulation, order, interpretation, or other action that is not described in this paragraph.

(3) INSURANCE ACTIVITIES OTHER THAN SALES.—State statutes, regulations, interpretations, orders, and other actions shall not be preempted under paragraph (1) to the extent that they—

(A) relate to, or are issued, adopted, or enacted for the purpose of regulating the business of insurance in accordance with the Act entitled "An Act to express the intent of Congress with reference to the regulation of the business of insurance" and approved March 9, 1945 (15 U.S.C. 1011 et seq.) (commonly referred to as the "McCarran-Ferguson Act");

(B) apply only to persons that are not depository institutions, but that are directly engaged in the business of insurance (except that they may apply to depository institutions engaged in providing savings bank life insurance as principal to the extent of regulating such insurance);

(C) do not relate to or directly or indirectly regulate insurance sales, solicitations, or cross marketing activities; and

(D) are not prohibited under subsection (e).

(4) FINANCIAL ACTIVITIES OTHER THAN INSURANCE.—No State statute, regulation, order, interpretation, or other action shall be preempted under paragraph (1) to the extent that—

(A) it does not relate to, and is not issued and adopted, or enacted for the purpose of regulating, directly or indirectly, insurance sales, solicitations, or cross marketing activities covered under paragraph (2);

(B) it does not relate to, and is not issued and adopted, or enacted for the purpose of regulating, directly or indirectly, the business of insurance activities other than sales, solicitations, or cross marketing activities, covered under paragraph (3);

(C) it does not relate to securities investigations or enforcement actions referred to in subsection (f); and

(D) it—

(i) does not distinguish by its terms between depository institutions, and affiliates thereof, engaged in the activity at issue and other persons engaged in the same activity in a manner that is in any way adverse with respect to the conduct of the activity by any such depository institution or affiliate engaged in the activity at issue;

(ii) as interpreted or applied, does not have, and will not have, an impact on depository institutions, or affiliates thereof, engaged in the activity at issue, or any person who has an association with any such depository institution or affiliate, that is substantially more adverse than its impact on other persons engaged in the same activity that are not depository institutions or affiliates thereof, or persons who do not have an association with any such depository institution or affiliate;

(iii) does not effectively prevent a depository institution or affiliate thereof from engaging in activities authorized or permitted by this Act or any other provision of Federal law; and

(iv) does not conflict with the intent of this Act generally to permit affiliations that are authorized or permitted by Federal law.

(e) NONDISCRIMINATION.—Except as provided in any restrictions described in subsection (d)(2)(B), no State may, by statute, regulation, order, interpretation, or other action, regulate the insurance activities authorized or permitted under this Act or any other provision of Federal law of a depository institution, or affiliate thereof, to the extent that such statute, regulation, order, interpretation, or other action—

(1) distinguishes by its terms between depository institutions, or affiliates thereof, and other persons engaged in such activities, in a manner that is in any way adverse to any such depository institution, or affiliate thereof;

(2) as interpreted or applied, has or will have an impact on depository institutions, or affiliates thereof, that is substantially more adverse than its impact on other persons providing the same products or services or engaged in the same activities that are not depository institutions, or affiliates thereof, or persons or entities affiliated therewith;

(3) effectively prevents a depository institution, or affiliate thereof, from engaging in insurance activities authorized or permitted by this Act or any other provision of Federal law; or

(4) conflicts with the intent of this Act generally to permit affiliations that are authorized or permitted by Federal law between depository institutions, or affiliates thereof, and persons engaged in the business of insurance.

(f) LIMITATION.—Subsections (c) and (d) shall not be construed to affect—

(1) the jurisdiction of the securities commission (or any agency or office performing like functions) of any State, under the laws of such State—

(A) to investigate and bring enforcement actions, consistent with section 18(c) of the Securities Act of 1933, with respect to fraud or deceit or unlawful conduct by any person, in connection with securities or securities transactions; or

(B) to require the registration of securities or the licensure or registration of brokers, dealers, or investment advisers (consistent with section 203A of the Investment Advisers Act of 1940), or the associated persons of a broker, dealer, or investment adviser (consistent with such section 203A); or

(2) State laws, regulations, orders, interpretations, or other actions of general applicability relating to the governance of corporations, partnerships, limited liability companies, or other business associations incorporated or formed under the laws of that State or domiciled in that State, or the applicability of the antitrust laws of any State or any State law that is similar to the antitrust laws if such laws, regulations, orders, interpretations, or other actions are not inconsistent with the purposes of this Act to authorize or permit certain affiliations and to remove barriers to such affiliations.

(g) DEFINITIONS.—For purposes of this section, the following definitions shall apply:

(1) AFFILIATE.—The term "affiliate" means any company that controls, is controlled by, or is under common control with another company.

(2) ANTITRUST LAWS.—The term "antitrust laws" has the meaning given the term in subsection (a) of the first section of the Clayton Act, and includes section 5 of the Federal Trade Commission Act (to the extent that such section 5 relates to unfair methods of competition).

(3) DEPOSITORY INSTITUTION.—The term "depository institution"—

(A) has the meaning given the term in section 3 of the Federal Deposit Insurance Act; and

(B) includes any foreign bank that maintains a branch, agency, or commercial lending company in the United States.

(4) INSURER.—The term "insurer" means any person engaged in the business of insurance.

(5) STATE.—The term "State" means any State of the United States, the District of Columbia, any territory of the United States, Puerto Rico, Guam, American Samoa, the Trust Territory of the Pacific Islands, the Virgin Islands, and the Northern Mariana Islands.

¶ 1105

SEC. 105. MUTUAL BANK HOLDING COMPANIES AUTHORIZED.

Section 3(g)(2) of the Bank Holding Company Act of 1956 (12 U.S.C. 1842(g)(2)) is amended to read as follows:

"(2) REGULATIONS.—A bank holding company organized as a mutual holding company shall be regulated on terms, and shall be subject to limitations, comparable to those applicable to any other bank holding company.".

¶ 1106

SEC. 106. PROHIBITION ON DEPOSIT PRODUCTION OFFICES.

Section 109(e)(4) of the Riegle-Neal Interstate Banking and Branching Efficiency Act of 1994 (12 U.S.C. 1835a(e)(4)) is amended by inserting "and any branch of a bank controlled by an out-of-State bank holding company (as defined in section 2(o)(7) of the Bank Holding Company Act of 1956)" before the period.

¶ 1107

SEC. 107. CROSS MARKETING RESTRICTION; LIMITED PURPOSE BANK RELIEF; DIVESTITURE.

(a) CROSS MARKETING RESTRICTION.—Section 4(f) of the Bank Holding Company Act of 1956 (12 U.S.C. 1843(f)) is amended by striking paragraph (3).

(b) DAYLIGHT OVERDRAFTS.—Section 4(f) of the Bank Holding Company Act of 1956 (12 U.S.C. 1843(f)) is amended by inserting after paragraph (2) the following new paragraph:

"(3) PERMISSIBLE OVERDRAFTS DESCRIBED.—For purposes of paragraph (2)(C), an overdraft is described in this paragraph if—

"(A) such overdraft results from an inadvertent computer or accounting error that is beyond the control of both the bank and the affiliate;

"(B) such overdraft—

"(i) is permitted or incurred on behalf of an affiliate that is monitored by, reports to, and is recognized as a primary dealer by the Federal Reserve Bank of New York; and

"(ii) is fully secured, as required by the Board, by bonds, notes, or other obligations that are direct obligations of the United States or on which the principal and interest are fully guaranteed by the United States or by securities and obligations eligible for settlement on the Federal Reserve book entry system; or

"(C) such overdraft—

"(i) is permitted or incurred by, or on behalf of, an affiliate in connection with an activity that is financial in nature or incidental to a financial activity; and

"(ii) does not cause the bank to violate any provision of section 23A or 23B of the Federal Reserve Act, either directly, in the case of a bank that is a member of the Federal Reserve System, or by virtue of section 18(j) of the Federal Deposit Insurance Act, in the case of a bank that is not a member of the Federal Reserve System.".

(c) INDUSTRIAL LOAN COMPANIES; AFFILIATE OVERDRAFTS.—Section 2(c)(2)(H) of the Bank Holding Company Act of 1956 (12 U.S.C. 1841(c)(2)(H)) is amended by inserting ", or that is otherwise permissible for a bank controlled by a company described in section 4(f)(1)" before the period at the end.

(d) ACTIVITIES LIMITATIONS.—Section 4(f)(2) of the Bank Holding Company Act of 1956 (12 U.S.C. 1843(f)(2)) is amended—

(1) by striking "Paragraph (1) shall cease to apply to any company described in such paragraph if—" and inserting "Subject to paragraph (3), a company described in paragraph (1) shall no longer qualify for the exemption provided under that paragraph if—";

(2) in subparagraph (A)—

(A) in clause (ii)(IX), by striking "and" at the end;

(B) in clause (ii)(X), by inserting "and" after the semicolon;

(C) in clause (ii), by inserting after subclause (X) the following new subclause:

"(XI) assets that are derived from, or incidental to, activities in which institutions described in subparagraph (F) or (H) of section 2(c)(2) are permitted to engage;"; and

(D) by striking "or" at the end; and

(3) by striking subparagraph (B) and inserting the following:

"(B) any bank subsidiary of such company—

"(i) accepts demand deposits or deposits that the depositor may withdraw by check or similar means for payment to third parties; and

"(ii) engages in the business of making commercial loans (except that, for purposes of this clause, loans made in the ordinary course of a credit card operation shall not be treated as commercial loans); or

"(C) after the date of the enactment of the Competitive Equality Amendments of 1987, any bank subsidiary of such company permits any overdraft (including any intraday overdraft), or incurs any such overdraft in the account of the bank at a Federal reserve bank, on behalf of an affiliate, other than an overdraft described in paragraph (3).".

(e) DIVESTITURE REQUIREMENT.—Section 4(f)(4) of the Bank Holding Company Act of 1956 (12 U.S.C. 1843(f)(4)) is amended to read as follows:

"(4) DIVESTITURE IN CASE OF LOSS OF EXEMPTION.—If any company described in paragraph (1) fails to qualify for the exemption provided under paragraph (1) by operation of paragraph (2), such exemption shall cease to apply to such company and such company shall divest control of each bank it controls before the end of the 180-day period beginning on the date on which the company receives notice from the Board that the company has failed to continue to qualify for such exemption, unless, before the end of such 180-day period, the company has—

"(A) either—

"(i) corrected the condition or ceased the activity that caused the company to fail to continue to qualify for the exemption; or

"(ii) submitted a plan to the Board for approval to cease the activity or correct the condition in a timely manner (which shall not exceed 1 year); and

"(B) implemented procedures that are reasonably adapted to avoid the reoccurrence of such condition or activity.".

(f) FOREIGN BANK SUBSIDIARIES OF LIMITED PURPOSE CREDIT CARD BANKS.—Section 4(f) of the Bank Holding Company Act of 1956 (12 U.S.C. 1843(f)) is amended by adding at the end the following new paragraph:

"(14) FOREIGN BANK SUBSIDIARIES OF LIMITED PURPOSE CREDIT CARD BANKS.—

"(A) IN GENERAL.—An institution described in section 2(c)(2)(F) may control a foreign bank if—

"(i) the investment of the institution in the foreign bank meets the requirements of section 25 or 25A of the Federal Reserve Act and the foreign bank qualifies under such sections;

"(ii) the foreign bank does not offer any products or services in the United States; and

"(iii) the activities of the foreign bank are permissible under otherwise applicable law.

"(B) OTHER LIMITATIONS INAPPLICABLE.—The limitations contained in any clause of section 2(c)(2)(F) shall not apply to a foreign bank described in subparagraph (A) that is controlled by an institution described in such section.".

¶ 1108

SEC. 108. USE OF SUBORDINATED DEBT TO PROTECT FINANCIAL SYSTEM AND DEPOSIT FUNDS FROM "TOO BIG TO FAIL" INSTITUTIONS.

(a) STUDY REQUIRED.—The Board of Governors of the Federal Reserve System and the Secretary of the Treasury shall conduct a study of—

(1) the feasibility and appropriateness of establishing a requirement that, with respect to large insured depository institutions and depository institution holding companies the failure of which could have serious adverse effects on economic conditions or financial stability, such institutions and holding companies maintain some portion of their capital in the form of subordinated debt in order to bring market forces and market discipline to bear on the operation of, and the assessment of the viability of, such institutions and companies and reduce the risk to economic conditions, financial stability, and any deposit insurance fund;

(2) if such requirement is feasible and appropriate, the appropriate amount or percentage of capital that should be subordinated debt consistent with such purposes; and

(3) the manner in which any such requirement could be incorporated into existing capital standards and other issues relating to the transition to such a requirement.

(b) REPORT.—Before the end of the 18-month period beginning on the date of the enactment of this Act, the Board of Governors of the Federal Reserve System and the Secretary of the Treasury shall submit a report to the Congress containing the findings and conclusions of the Board and the Secretary in connection with the study required under subsection (a), together with such legislative and administrative proposals as the Board and the Secretary may determine to be appropriate.

(c) DEFINITIONS.—For purposes of subsection (a), the following definitions shall apply:

(1) BANK HOLDING COMPANY.—The term "bank holding company" has the meaning given the term in section 2 of the Bank Holding Company Act of 1956.

(2) INSURED DEPOSITORY INSTITUTION.—The term "insured depository institution" has the meaning given the term in section 3(c) of the Federal Deposit Insurance Act.

(3) SUBORDINATED DEBT.—The term "subordinated debt" means unsecured debt that—

(A) has an original weighted average maturity of not less than 5 years;

(B) is subordinated as to payment of principal and interest to all other indebtedness of the bank, including deposits;

(C) is not supported by any form of credit enhancement, including a guarantee or standby letter of credit; and

(D) is not held in whole or in part by any affiliate or institution-affiliated party of the insured depository institution or bank holding company.

¶ 1109

SEC. 109. **STUDY OF FINANCIAL MODERNIZATION'S EFFECT ON THE ACCESSIBILITY OF SMALL BUSINESS AND FARM LOANS.**

(a) STUDY.—The Secretary of the Treasury, in consultation with the Federal banking agencies (as defined in section 3(z) of the Federal Deposit Insurance Act), shall conduct a study of the extent to which credit is being provided to and for small businesses and farms, as a result of this Act and the amendments made by this Act.

(b) REPORT.—Before the end of the 5-year period beginning on the date of the enactment of this Act, the Secretary, in consultation with the Federal banking agencies, shall submit a report to the Congress on the study conducted pursuant to subsection (a) and shall include such recommendations as the Secretary determines to be appropriate for administrative and legislative action.

Subtitle B—Streamlining Supervision of Bank Holding Companies

¶ 1111

SEC. 111. **STREAMLINING BANK HOLDING COMPANY SUPERVISION.**

Section 5(c) of the Bank Holding Company Act of 1956 (12 U.S.C. 1844(c)) is amended to read as follows:

"Reports and examinations

"(c)(1) REPORTS.—

"(A) IN GENERAL.—The Board, from time to time, may require a bank holding company and any subsidiary of such company to submit reports under oath to keep the Board informed as to—

"(i) its financial condition, systems for monitoring and controlling financial and operating risks, and transactions with depository institution subsidiaries of the bank holding company; and

"(ii) compliance by the company or subsidiary with applicable provisions of this Act or any other Federal law that the Board has specific jurisdiction to enforce against such company or subsidiary.

"(B) USE OF EXISTING REPORTS.—

"(i) IN GENERAL.—For purposes of compliance with this paragraph, the Board shall, to the fullest extent possible, accept—

"(I) reports that a bank holding company or any subsidiary of such company has provided or been required to provide to other Federal or State supervisors or to appropriate self-regulatory organizations;

"(II) information that is otherwise required to be reported publicly; and

"(III) externally audited financial statements.

"(ii) AVAILABILITY.—A bank holding company or a subsidiary of such company shall provide to the Board, at the request of the Board, a report referred to in clause (i).

"(iii) REPORTS FILED WITH OTHER AGENCIES.—

"(I) IN GENERAL.—In the event that the Board requires a report under this subsection from a functionally regulated subsidiary of a bank holding company of a kind that is not required by another Federal or State regulatory authority or an appropriate self-regulatory organization, the Board shall first request that the appropriate regulatory authority or self-regulatory organization obtain such report.

"(II) AVAILABILITY FROM OTHER SUBSIDIARY.—If the report is not made available to the Board, and the report is necessary to assess a material risk to the bank holding company or any of its depository institution subsidiaries or compliance with this Act or any other Federal law that the Board has specific jurisdiction to enforce against such company or subsidiary or the systems described in paragraph (2)(A)(ii)(II), the Board may require such functionally regulated subsidiary to provide such a report to the Board.

"(2) EXAMINATIONS.—

"(A) EXAMINATION AUTHORITY FOR BANK HOLDING COMPANIES AND SUBSIDIARIES.—Subject to subparagraph (B), the Board may make examinations of each bank holding company and each subsidiary of such holding company in order—

"(i) to inform the Board of the nature of the operations and financial condition of the holding company and such subsidiaries;

"(ii) to inform the Board of—

"(I) the financial and operational risks within the holding company system that may pose a threat to the safety and soundness of any depository institution subsidiary of such holding company; and

"(II) the systems for monitoring and controlling such risks; and

"(iii) to monitor compliance with the provisions of this Act or any other Federal law that the Board has specific jurisdiction to enforce against such company or subsidiary and those governing transactions and relationships between any depository institution subsidiary and its affiliates.

"(B) FUNCTIONALLY REGULATED SUBSIDIARIES.—Notwithstanding subparagraph (A), the Board may make examinations of a functionally regulated subsidiary of a bank holding company only if—

"(i) the Board has reasonable cause to believe that such subsidiary is engaged in activities that pose a material risk to an affiliated depository institution;

"(ii) the Board reasonably determines, after reviewing relevant reports, that examination of the subsidiary is necessary to adequately inform the Board of the systems described in subparagraph (A)(ii)(II); or

"(iii) based on reports and other available information, the Board has reasonable cause to believe that a subsidiary is not in compliance with this Act or any other Federal law that the Board has specific jurisdiction to enforce against such subsidiary, including provisions relating to transactions with an affiliated depository institution, and the Board cannot make such determination through examination of the affiliated depository institution or the bank holding company.

"(C) RESTRICTED FOCUS OF EXAMINATIONS.—The Board shall, to the fullest extent possible, limit the focus and scope of any examination of a bank holding company to—

"(i) the bank holding company; and

"(ii) any subsidiary of the bank holding company that could have a materially adverse effect on the safety and soundness of any depository institution subsidiary of the holding company due to—

"(I) the size, condition, or activities of the subsidiary; or

"(II) the nature or size of transactions between the subsidiary and any depository institution that is also a subsidiary of the bank holding company.

"(D) DEFERENCE TO BANK EXAMINATIONS.—The Board shall, to the fullest extent possible, for the purposes of this paragraph, use the reports of examinations of depository institutions made by the appropriate Federal and State depository institution supervisory authority.

"(E) DEFERENCE TO OTHER EXAMINATIONS.—The Board shall, to the fullest extent possible, forego an examination by the Board under this paragraph and instead review the reports of examination made of—

"(i) any registered broker or dealer by or on behalf of the Securities and Exchange Commission;

"(ii) any registered investment adviser properly registered by or on behalf of either the Securities and Exchange Commission or any State;

"(iii) any licensed insurance company by or on behalf of any State regulatory authority responsible for the supervision of insurance companies; and

"(iv) any other subsidiary that the Board finds to be comprehensively supervised by a Federal or State authority.

"(3) CAPITAL.—

"(A) IN GENERAL.—The Board may not, by regulation, guideline, order, or otherwise, prescribe or impose any capital or capital adequacy rules, guidelines, standards, or requirements on any functionally regulated subsidiary of a bank holding company that—

"(i) is not a depository institution; and

"(ii) is—

"(I) in compliance with the applicable capital requirements of its Federal regulatory authority (including the Securities and Exchange Commission) or State insurance authority;

"(II) properly registered as an investment adviser under the Investment Advisers Act of 1940, or with any State; or

"(III) is licensed as an insurance agent with the appropriate State insurance authority.

"(B) RULE OF CONSTRUCTION.—Subparagraph (A) shall not be construed as preventing the Board from imposing capital or capital adequacy rules, guidelines, standards, or requirements with respect to—

"(i) activities of a registered investment adviser other than with respect to investment advisory activities or activities incidental to investment advisory activities; or

"(ii) activities of a licensed insurance agent other than insurance agency activities or activities incidental to insurance agency activities.

"(C) LIMITATIONS ON INDIRECT ACTION.—In developing, establishing, or assessing bank holding company capital or capital adequacy rules, guidelines, standards, or requirements for purposes of this paragraph, the Board may not take into account the activities, operations, or investments of an affiliated investment company registered under the Investment Company Act of 1940, unless the investment company is—

"(i) a bank holding company; or

"(ii) controlled by a bank holding company by reason of ownership by the bank holding company (including through all of its affiliates) of 25 percent or more of the shares of the investment company, and the shares owned by the bank holding company have a market value equal to more than $1,000,000.

"(4) FUNCTIONAL REGULATION OF SECURITIES AND INSURANCE ACTIVITIES.—

"(A) SECURITIES ACTIVITIES.—Securities activities conducted in a functionally regulated subsidiary of a depository institution shall be subject to regulation by the Securities and Exchange Commission, and by relevant State securities authorities, as appropriate, subject to section 104 of the Gramm-Leach-Bliley Act, to the same extent as if they were conducted in a nondepository institution subsidiary of a bank holding company.

"(B) INSURANCE ACTIVITIES.—Subject to section 104 of the Gramm-Leach-Bliley Act, insurance agency and brokerage activities and activities as principal conducted in a functionally regulated subsidiary of a depository institution shall be subject to regulation by a State insurance authority to the same extent as if they were conducted in a nondepository institution subsidiary of a bank holding company.

"(5) DEFINITION.—For purposes of this subsection, the term 'functionally regulated subsidiary' means any company—

"(A) that is not a bank holding company or a depository institution; and

"(B) that is—

"(i) a broker or dealer that is registered under the Securities Exchange Act of 1934;

"(ii) a registered investment adviser, properly registered by or on behalf of either the Securities and Exchange Commission or any State, with respect to the investment advisory activities of such investment adviser and activities incidental to such investment advisory activities;

"(iii) an investment company that is registered under the Investment Company Act of 1940;

"(iv) an insurance company, with respect to insurance activities of the insurance company and activities incidental to such insurance activities, that is subject to supervision by a State insurance regulator; or

"(v) an entity that is subject to regulation by the Commodity Futures Trading Commission, with respect to the commodities activities of such entity and activities incidental to such commodities activities.".

¶ 1112

SEC. 112. **AUTHORITY OF STATE INSURANCE REGULATOR AND SECURITIES AND EXCHANGE COMMISSION.**

(a) BANK HOLDING COMPANIES.—Section 5 of the Bank Holding Company Act of 1956 (12 U.S.C. 1844) is amended by adding at the end the following new subsection:

"Authority of state insurance regulator and the securities and exchange commission

"(g)(1) IN GENERAL.—Notwithstanding any other provision of law, any regulation, order, or other action of the Board that requires a bank holding company to provide funds or other assets to a subsidiary depository institution shall not be effective nor enforceable with respect to an entity described in subparagraph (A) if—

"(A) such funds or assets are to be provided by—

"(i) a bank holding company that is an insurance company, a broker or dealer registered under the Securities Exchange Act of 1934, an investment company registered under the Investment Company Act of 1940, or an investment adviser registered by or on behalf of either the Securities and Exchange Commission or any State; or "(ii) an affiliate of the depository institution that is an insurance company or a broker or dealer registered under the Securities Exchange Act of 1934, an investment company registered under the Investment Company Act of 1940, or an investment adviser registered by or on behalf of either the Securities and Exchange Commission or any State; and

"(B) the State insurance authority for the insurance company or the Securities and Exchange Commission for the registered broker, dealer, investment adviser (solely with respect to investment advisory activities or activities incidental thereto), or investment company, as the case may be, determines in writing sent to the holding company and the Board that the holding company shall not provide such funds or assets because such action would have a material adverse effect on the financial condition of the insurance company or the broker, dealer, investment company, or investment adviser, as the case may be.

"(2) NOTICE TO STATE INSURANCE AUTHORITY OR SEC REQUIRED.—If the Board requires a bank holding company, or an affiliate of a bank holding company, that is an insurance company or a broker, dealer, investment company, or investment adviser described in paragraph (1)(A) to provide funds or assets to a depository institution subsidiary of the holding company pursuant to any regulation, order, or other action of the Board referred to in paragraph (1), the Board shall promptly notify the State insurance authority for the insurance company, the Securities and Exchange Commission, or State securities regulator, as the case may be, of such requirement.

"(3) DIVESTITURE IN LIEU OF OTHER ACTION.—If the Board receives a notice described in paragraph (1)(B) from a State insurance authority or the Securities and Exchange Commission with regard to a bank holding company or affiliate referred to in that paragraph, the Board may order the bank holding company to divest the depository institution not later than 180 days after receiving the notice, or such longer period as the Board determines consistent with the safe and sound operation of the depository institution.

"(4) CONDITIONS BEFORE DIVESTITURE.—During the period beginning on the date an order to divest is issued by the Board under paragraph (3) to a bank holding company and ending on the date the divestiture is completed, the Board may impose any conditions or restrictions on the holding company's ownership or operation of the depository institution, including restricting or prohibiting transactions between the depository institution and any affiliate of the institution, as are appropriate under the circumstances.

"(5) RULE OF CONSTRUCTION.—No provision of this subsection may be construed as limiting or otherwise affecting, except to the extent specifically provided in this subsection, the regulatory authority, including the scope of the authority, of any Federal agency or department with regard to any entity that is within the jurisdiction of such agency or department.".

(b) SUBSIDIARIES OF DEPOSITORY INSTITUTIONS.—The Federal Deposit Insurance Act (12 U.S.C. 1811 et seq.) is amended by adding at the end the following new section:

"SEC. 45. AUTHORITY OF STATE INSURANCE REGULATOR AND SECURITIES AND EXCHANGE COMMISSION.

"In general

"(a) Notwithstanding any other provision of law, the provisions of—

"(1) section 5(c) of the Bank Holding Company Act of 1956 that limit the authority of the Board of Governors of the Federal Reserve System to require reports from, to make examinations of, or to impose capital requirements on holding companies and their functionally regulated subsidiaries or that require deference to other regulators;

"(2) section 5(g) of the Bank Holding Company Act of 1956 that limit the authority of the Board to require a functionally regulated subsidiary of a holding company to provide capital or other funds or assets to a depository institution subsidiary of the holding company and to take certain actions including requiring divestiture of the depository institution; and

"(3) section 10A of the Bank Holding Company Act of 1956 that limit whatever authority the Board might otherwise have to take direct or indirect action with respect to holding companies and their functionally regulated subsidiaries;

shall also limit whatever authority that a Federal banking agency might otherwise have under any statute or regulation to require reports, make examinations, impose capital requirements, or take any other direct or indirect action with respect to any functionally regulated affiliate of a depository institution, subject to the same standards and requirements as are applicable to the Board under those provisions.

"Certain exemption authorized

"(b) No provision of this section shall be construed as preventing the Corporation, if the Corporation finds it necessary to determine the condition of a depository institution for insurance purposes, from examining an affiliate of any depository institution, pursuant to section 10(b)(4), as may be necessary to disclose fully the relationship between the depository institution and the affiliate, and the effect of such relationship on the depository institution.

"Definitions

"(c) For purposes of this section, the following definitions shall apply:

"(1) FUNCTIONALLY REGULATED SUBSIDIARY.—The term 'functionally regulated subsidiary' has the meaning given the term in section 5(c)(5) of the Bank Holding Company Act of 1956.

"(2) FUNCTIONALLY REGULATED AFFILIATE.—The term 'functionally regulated affiliate' means, with respect to any depository institution, any affiliate of such depository institution that is—

"(A) not a depository institution holding company; and

"(B) a company described in any clause of section 5(c)(5)(B) of the Bank Holding Company Act of 1956.".

¶1113

SEC. 113. ROLE OF THE BOARD OF GOVERNORS OF THE FEDERAL RESERVE SYSTEM.

The Bank Holding Company Act of 1956 (12 U.S.C. 1841 et seq.) is amended by inserting after section 10 the following new section:

"SEC. 10A. LIMITATION ON RULEMAKING, PRUDENTIAL, SUPERVISORY, AND ENFORCEMENT AUTHORITY OF THE BOARD.

"Limitation on direct action

"(a) The Board may not prescribe regulations, issue or seek entry of orders, impose restraints, restrictions, guidelines, requirements, safeguards, or standards, or otherwise take any action under or pursuant to any provision of this Act or section 8 of the Federal Deposit Insurance Act against or with respect to a functionally regulated subsidiary of a bank holding company unless—

"(1) the action is necessary to prevent or redress an unsafe or unsound practice or breach of fiduciary duty by such subsidiary that poses a material risk to—

"(A) the financial safety, soundness, or stability of an affiliated depository institution; or

"(B) the domestic or international payment system; and

"(2) the Board finds that it is not reasonably possible to protect effectively against the material risk at issue through action directed at or against the affiliated depository institution or against depository institutions generally.

"Limitation on indirect action

"(b) The Board may not prescribe regulations, issue or seek entry of orders, impose restraints, restrictions, guidelines, requirements, safeguards, or standards, or otherwise take any action under or pursuant to any provision of this Act or section 8 of the Federal Deposit Insurance Act against or with respect to a bank holding company that requires the bank holding company to require a functionally regulated subsidiary of the holding company to engage, or to refrain from engaging, in any conduct or activities unless the Board could take such action directly against or with respect to the functionally regulated subsidiary in accordance with subsection (a).

"Actions specifically authorized

"(c) Notwithstanding subsection (a) or (b), the Board may take action under this Act or section 8 of the Federal Deposit Insurance Act to enforce compliance by a functionally regulated subsidiary of a bank holding company with any Federal law that the Board has specific jurisdiction to enforce against such subsidiary.

"Functionally regulated subsidiary defined

"(d) For purposes of this section, the term 'functionally regulated subsidiary' has the meaning given the term in section 5(c)(5).".

¶ 1114

SEC. 114. **PRUDENTIAL SAFEGUARDS.**

(a) COMPTROLLER OF THE CURRENCY.—

(1) IN GENERAL.—The Comptroller of the Currency may, by regulation or order, impose restrictions or requirements on relationships or transactions between a national bank and a subsidiary of the national bank that the Comptroller finds are—

(A) consistent with the purposes of this Act, title LXII of the Revised Statutes of the United States, and other Federal law applicable to national banks; and

(B) appropriate to avoid any significant risk to the safety and soundness of insured depository institutions or any Federal deposit insurance fund or other adverse effects, such as undue concentration of resources, decreased or unfair competition, conflicts of interests, or unsound banking practices.

(2) REVIEW.—The Comptroller of the Currency shall regularly—

(A) review all restrictions or requirements established pursuant to paragraph (1) to determine whether there is a continuing need for any such restriction or requirement to carry out the purposes of the Act, including the avoidance of any adverse effect referred to in paragraph (1)(B); and

(B) modify or eliminate any such restriction or requirement the Comptroller finds is no longer required for such purposes.

(b) BOARD OF GOVERNORS OF THE FEDERAL RESERVE SYSTEM.—

(1) IN GENERAL.—The Board of Governors of the Federal Reserve System may, by regulation or order, impose restrictions or requirements on relationships or transactions—

(A) between a depository institution subsidiary of a bank holding company and any affiliate of such depository institution (other than a subsidiary of such institution); or

(B) between a State member bank and a subsidiary of such bank;

if the Board makes a finding described in paragraph (2) with respect to such restriction or requirement.

(2) FINDING.—The Board of Governors of the Federal Reserve System may exercise authority under paragraph (1) if the Board finds that the exercise of such authority is—

(A) consistent with the purposes of this Act, the Bank Holding Company Act of 1956, the Federal Reserve Act, and other Federal law applicable to depository institution subsidiaries of bank holding companies or State member banks, as the case may be; and

(B) appropriate to prevent an evasion of any provision of law referred to in subparagraph (A) or to avoid any significant risk to the safety and soundness of depository institutions or any Federal deposit insurance fund or other adverse effects, such as undue concentration of resources, decreased or unfair competition, conflicts of interests, or unsound banking practices.

(3) REVIEW.—The Board of Governors of the Federal Reserve System shall regularly—

(A) review all restrictions or requirements established pursuant to paragraph (1) or (4) to determine whether there is a continuing need for any such restriction or requirement to carry out the purposes of the Act, including the avoidance of any adverse effect referred to in paragraph (2)(B) or (4)(B); and

(B) modify or eliminate any such restriction or requirement the Board finds is no longer required for such purposes.

(4) FOREIGN BANKS.—The Board may, by regulation or order, impose restrictions or requirements on relationships or transactions between a branch, agency, or commercial lending company of a foreign bank in the United States and any affiliate in the United States of such foreign bank that the Board finds are—

(A) consistent with the purposes of this Act, the Bank Holding Company Act of 1956, the Federal Reserve Act, and other Federal law applicable to foreign banks and their affiliates in the United States; and

(B) appropriate to prevent an evasion of any provision of law referred to in subparagraph (A) or to avoid any significant risk to the safety and soundness of depository institutions or any Federal deposit insurance fund or other adverse effects, such as undue concentration of resources, decreased or unfair competition, conflicts of interests, or unsound banking practices.

(c) FEDERAL DEPOSIT INSURANCE CORPORATION.—

(1) IN GENERAL.—The Federal Deposit Insurance Corporation may, by regulation or order, impose restrictions or requirements on relationships or transactions between a State nonmember bank (as defined in section 3 of the Federal Deposit Insurance Act) and a subsidiary of the State nonmember bank that the Corporation finds are—

(A) consistent with the purposes of this Act, the Federal Deposit Insurance Act, or other Federal law applicable to State nonmember banks; and

(B) appropriate to avoid any significant risk to the safety and soundness of depository institutions or any Federal deposit insurance fund or other adverse effects, such as undue concentration of resources, decreased or unfair competition, conflicts of interests, or unsound banking practices.

(2) REVIEW.—The Federal Deposit Insurance Corporation shall regularly—

(A) review all restrictions or requirements established pursuant to paragraph (1) to determine whether there is a continuing need for any such restriction or requirement to carry out the purposes of the Act, including the avoidance of any adverse effect referred to in paragraph (1)(B); and

(B) modify or eliminate any such restriction or requirement the Corporation finds is no longer required for such purposes.

¶ 1115

SEC. 115. EXAMINATION OF INVESTMENT COMPANIES.

(a) EXCLUSIVE COMMISSION AUTHORITY.—Except as provided in subsection (c), a Federal banking agency may not inspect or examine any registered investment company that is not a bank holding company or a savings and loan holding company.

(b) EXAMINATION RESULTS AND OTHER INFORMATION.—The Commission shall provide to any Federal banking agency, upon request, the results of any examination, reports, records, or other information with respect to any registered investment company to the extent necessary for the agency to carry out its statutory responsibilities.

(c) CERTAIN EXAMINATIONS AUTHORIZED.—Nothing in this section shall prevent the Corporation, if the Corporation finds it necessary to determine the condition of an insured depository institution for insurance purposes, from examining an affiliate of any insured depository institution, pursuant to its authority under section 10(b)(4) of the Federal Deposit Insurance Act, as may be necessary to disclose fully the relationship between the insured depository institution and the affiliate, and the effect of such relationship on the insured depository institution.

(d) DEFINITIONS.—For purposes of this section, the following definitions shall apply:

(1) BANK HOLDING COMPANY.—The term "bank holding company" has the meaning given the term in section 2 of the Bank Holding Company Act of 1956.

(2) COMMISSION.—The term "Commission" means the Securities and Exchange Commission.

(3) Corporation.—The term "Corporation" means the Federal Deposit Insurance Corporation.

(4) FEDERAL BANKING AGENCY.—The term "Federal banking agency" has the meaning given the term in section 3(z) of the Federal Deposit Insurance Act.

(5) INSURED DEPOSITORY INSTITUTION.—The term "insured depository institution" has the meaning given the term in section 3(c) of the Federal Deposit Insurance Act.

(6) REGISTERED INVESTMENT COMPANY.—The term "registered investment company" means an investment company that is registered with the Commission under the Investment Company Act of 1940.

(7) SAVINGS AND LOAN HOLDING COMPANY.—The term "savings and loan holding company" has the meaning given the term in section 10(a)(1)(D) of the Home Owners' Loan Act.

¶ 1116

SEC. 116. **ELIMINATION OF APPLICATION REQUIREMENT FOR FINANCIAL HOLDING COMPANIES.**

(a) PREVENTION OF DUPLICATIVE FILINGS.—Section 5(a) of the Bank Holding Company Act of 1956 (12 U.S.C. 1844(a)) is amended by adding at the end the following new sentence: "A declaration filed in accordance with section 4(l)(1)(C) shall satisfy the requirements of this subsection with regard to the registration of a bank holding company but not any requirement to file an application to acquire a bank pursuant to section 3.".

(b) DIVESTITURE PROCEDURES.—Section 5(e)(1) of the Bank Holding Company Act of 1956 (12 U.S.C. 1844(e)(1)) is amended—

(1) by striking "Financial Institutions Supervisory Act of 1966, order" and inserting "Financial Institutions Supervisory Act of 1966, at the election of the bank holding company—

"(A) order"; and

(2) by striking "shareholders of the bank holding company. Such distribution" and inserting "shareholders of the bank holding company; or

"(B) order the bank holding company, after due notice and opportunity for hearing, and after consultation with the primary supervisor for the bank, which shall be the Comptroller of the Currency in the case of a national bank, and the Federal Deposit Insurance Corporation and the appropriate State supervisor in the case of an insured nonmember bank, to terminate (within 120 days or such longer period as the Board may direct) the ownership or control of any such bank by such company.

The distribution referred to in subparagraph (A)".

¶ 1117

SEC. 117. PRESERVING THE INTEGRITY OF FDIC RESOURCES.

Section 11(a)(4)(B) of the Federal Deposit Insurance Act (12 U.S.C. 1821(a)(4)(B)) is amended by striking "to benefit any shareholder of" and inserting "to benefit any shareholder or affiliate (other than an insured depository institution that receives assistance in accordance with the provisions of this Act) of".

¶ 1118

SEC. 118. REPEAL OF SAVINGS BANK PROVISIONS IN THE BANK HOLDING COMPANY ACT OF 1956.

Section 3(f) of the Bank Holding Company Act of 1956 (12 U.S.C. 1842(f)) is amended to read as follows:

"(f) [Repealed].".

¶ 1119

SEC. 119. TECHNICAL AMENDMENT.

Section 2(o)(1)(A) of the Bank Holding Company Act of 1956 (12 U.S.C. 1841(o)(1)(A)) is amended by striking "section 38(b)" and inserting "section 38".

Subtitle C—Subsidiaries of National Banks

¶ 1121

SEC. 121. SUBSIDIARIES OF NATIONAL BANKS.

(a) IN GENERAL.—Chapter one of title LXII of the Revised Statutes of the United States (12 U.S.C. 21 et seq.) is amended—

(1) by redesignating section 5136A as section 5136B; and

(2) by inserting after section 5136 (12 U.S.C. 24) the following new section:

"SEC. 5136A. FINANCIAL SUBSIDIARIES OF NATIONAL BANKS.

"Authorization to conduct in subsidiaries certain activities that are financial in nature

"(a)(1) IN GENERAL.—Subject to paragraph (2), a national bank may control a financial subsidiary, or hold an interest in a financial subsidiary.

"(2) CONDITIONS AND REQUIREMENTS.—A national bank may control a financial subsidiary, or hold an interest in a financial subsidiary, only if—

"(A) the financial subsidiary engages only in—

"(i) activities that are financial in nature or incidental to a financial activity pursuant to subsection (b); and

"(ii) activities that are permitted for national banks to engage in directly (subject to the same terms and conditions that govern the conduct of the activities by a national bank);

"(B) the activities engaged in by the financial subsidiary as a principal do not include—

"(i) insuring, guaranteeing, or indemnifying against loss, harm, damage, illness, disability, or death (except to the extent permitted under section 302 or 303(c) of the Gramm-Leach-Bliley Act) or providing or issuing annuities the income of which is subject to tax treatment under section 72 of the Internal Revenue Code of 1986;

"(ii) real estate development or real estate investment activities, unless otherwise expressly authorized by law; or "(iii) any activity permitted in subparagraph (H) or (I) of section 4(k)(4) of the Bank Holding Company Act of 1956, except activities described in section 4(k)(4)(H) that may be permitted in accordance with section 122 of the Gramm-Leach-Bliley Act;

"(C) the national bank and each depository institution affiliate of the national bank are well capitalized and well managed;

"(D) the aggregate consolidated total assets of all financial subsidiaries of the national bank do not exceed the lesser of—

"(i) 45 percent of the consolidated total assets of the parent bank; or

"(ii) $50,000,000,000;

"(E) except as provided in paragraph (4), the national bank meets any applicable rating or other requirement set forth in paragraph (3); and

"(F) the national bank has received the approval of the Comptroller of the Currency for the financial subsidiary to engage in such activities, which approval shall be based solely upon the factors set forth in this section.

"(3) RATING OR COMPARABLE REQUIREMENT.—

"(A) IN GENERAL.—A national bank meets the requirements of this paragraph if—

"(i) the bank is 1 of the 50 largest insured banks and has not fewer than 1 issue of outstanding eligible debt that is currently rated within the 3 highest investment grade rating categories by a nationally recognized statistical rating organization; or

"(ii) the bank is 1 of the second 50 largest insured banks and meets the criteria set forth in clause (i) or such other criteria as the Secretary of the Treasury and the Board of Governors of the Federal Reserve System may jointly establish by regulation and determine to be comparable to and consistent with the purposes of the rating required in clause (i).

"(B) CONSOLIDATED TOTAL ASSETS.—For purposes of this paragraph, the size of an insured bank shall be determined on the basis of the consolidated total assets of the bank as of the end of each calendar year.

"(4) FINANCIAL AGENCY SUBSIDIARY.—The requirement in paragraph (2)(E) shall not apply with respect to the ownership or control of a financial subsidiary that engages in activities described in subsection (b)(1) solely as agent and not directly or indirectly as principal.

"(5) REGULATIONS REQUIRED.—Before the end of the 270-day period beginning on the date of the enactment of the Gramm-Leach-Bliley Act, the Comptroller of the Currency shall, by regulation, prescribe procedures to implement this section.

"(6) INDEXED ASSET LIMIT.—The dollar amount contained in paragraph (2)(D) shall be adjusted according to an indexing mechanism jointly established by regulation by the Secretary of the Treasury and the Board of Governors of the Federal Reserve System.

"(7) COORDINATION WITH SECTION 4(1)(2) OF THE BANK HOLDING COMPANY ACT OF 1956.—Section 4(l)(2) of the Bank Holding Company Act of 1956 applies to a national bank that controls a financial subsidiary in the manner provided in that section.

"Activities that are financial in nature

"(b)(1) FINANCIAL ACTIVITIES.—

"(A) IN GENERAL.—An activity shall be financial in nature or incidental to such financial activity only if—

"(i) such activity has been defined to be financial in nature or incidental to a financial activity for bank holding companies pursuant to section 4(k)(4) of the Bank Holding Company Act of 1956; or

"(ii) the Secretary of the Treasury determines the activity is financial in nature or incidental to a financial activity in accordance with subparagraph (B).

"(B) COORDINATION BETWEEN THE BOARD AND THE SECRETARY OF THE TREASURY.—

"(i) PROPOSALS RAISED BEFORE THE SECRETARY OF THE TREASURY.—

"(I) CONSULTATION.—The Secretary of the Treasury shall notify the Board of, and consult with the Board concerning, any request, proposal, or application under this section for a determination of whether an activity is financial in nature or incidental to a financial activity.

"(II) BOARD VIEW.—The Secretary of the Treasury shall not determine that any activity is financial in nature or incidental to a financial activity under this section if the Board notifies the Secretary in writing, not later than 30 days after the date of receipt of the notice described in subclause (I) (or such longer period as the Secretary determines to be appropriate under the circumstances) that the Board believes that the activity is not financial in nature or incidental to a financial activity or is not otherwise permissible under this section.

"(ii) PROPOSALS RAISED BY THE BOARD.—

"(I) BOARD RECOMMENDATION.—The Board may, at any time, recommend in writing that the Secretary of the Treasury find an activity to be financial in nature or incidental to a financial activity for purposes of this section.

"(II) TIME PERIOD FOR SECRETARIAL ACTION.—Not later than 30 days after the date of receipt of a written recommendation from the Board under subclause (I) (or such longer period as the Secretary of the Treasury and the Board determine to be appropriate under the circumstances), the Secretary shall determine whether to initiate a public rulemaking proposing that the subject recommended activity be found to be financial in nature or incidental to a financial activity under this section, and shall notify the Board in writing of the determination of the Secretary and, in the event that the Secretary determines not to seek public comment on the proposal, the reasons for that determination.

"(2) FACTORS TO BE CONSIDERED.—In determining whether an activity is financial in nature or incidental to a financial activity, the Secretary shall take into account—

"(A) the purposes of this Act and the Gramm-Leach-Bliley Act;

"(B) changes or reasonably expected changes in the marketplace in which banks compete;

"(C) changes or reasonably expected changes in the technology for delivering financial services; and

"(D) whether such activity is necessary or appropriate to allow a bank and the subsidiaries of a bank to—

"(i) compete effectively with any company seeking to provide financial services in the United States;

"(ii) efficiently deliver information and services that are financial in nature through the use of technological means, including any application necessary to protect the security or efficacy of systems for the transmission of data or financial transactions; and

"(iii) offer customers any available or emerging technological means for using financial services or for the document imaging of data.

"(3) AUTHORIZATION OF NEW FINANCIAL ACTIVITIES.—The Secretary of the Treasury shall, by regulation or order and in accordance with paragraph (1)(B), define, consistent with the purposes of this Act and the Gramm-Leach-Bliley Act, the following activities as, and the extent to which such activities are, financial in nature or incidental to a financial activity:

"(A) Lending, exchanging, transferring, investing for others, or safeguarding financial assets other than money or securities.

"(B) Providing any device or other instrumentality for transferring money or other financial assets.

"(C) Arranging, effecting, or facilitating financial transactions for the account of third parties.

"**Capital deduction**

"(c)(1) CAPITAL DEDUCTION REQUIRED.—In determining compliance with applicable capital standards—

"(A) the aggregate amount of the outstanding equity investment, including retained earnings, of a national bank in all financial subsidiaries shall be deducted from the assets and tangible equity of the national bank; and

"(B) the assets and liabilities of the financial subsidiaries shall not be consolidated with those of the national bank.

"(2) FINANCIAL STATEMENT DISCLOSURE OF CAPITAL DEDUCTION.—Any published financial statement of a national bank that controls a financial subsidiary shall, in addition to providing information prepared in accordance with generally accepted accounting principles, separately present financial information for the bank in the manner provided in paragraph (1).

"**Safeguards for the bank**

"(d) A national bank that establishes or maintains a financial subsidiary shall assure that—

"(1) the procedures of the national bank for identifying and managing financial and operational risks within the national bank and the financial subsidiary adequately protect the national bank from such risks;

"(2) the national bank has, for the protection of the bank, reasonable policies and procedures to preserve the separate corporate identity and limited liability of the national bank and the financial subsidiaries of the national bank; and

"(3) the national bank is in compliance with this section.

"**Provisions applicable to national banks that fail to continue to meet certain requirements**

"(e)(1) IN GENERAL.—If a national bank or insured depository institution affiliate does not continue to meet the requirements of subsection (a)(2)(C) or subsection (d), the Comptroller of the Currency shall promptly give notice to the national bank to that effect describing the conditions giving rise to the notice.

"(2) AGREEMENT TO CORRECT CONDITIONS.—Not later than 45 days after the date of receipt by a national bank of a notice given under paragraph (1) (or such additional period as the Comptroller of the Currency may permit), the national bank shall execute an agreement with the Comptroller of the Currency and any relevant insured depository institution affiliate shall execute an agreement with its appropriate Federal banking agency to comply with the requirements of subsection (a)(2)(C) and subsection (d).

"(3) IMPOSITION OF CONDITIONS.—Until the conditions described in a notice under paragraph (1) are corrected—

"(A) the Comptroller of the Currency may impose such limitations on the conduct or activities of the national bank or any subsidiary of the national bank as the Comptroller of the Currency determines to be appropriate under the circumstances and consistent with the purposes of this section; and

"(B) the appropriate Federal banking agency may impose such limitations on the conduct or activities of any relevant insured depository institution affiliate or any subsidiary of the institution as such agency determines to be appropriate under the circumstances and consistent with the purposes of this section.

"(4) FAILURE TO CORRECT.—If the conditions described in a notice to a national bank under paragraph (1) are not corrected within 180 days after the date of receipt by the national bank of the notice, the Comptroller of the Currency may require the national bank, under such terms and conditions as may be imposed by the Comptroller and subject to such extension of time as may be granted in the discretion of the Comptroller, to divest control of any financial subsidiary.

"(5) CONSULTATION.—In taking any action under this subsection, the Comptroller shall consult with all relevant Federal and State regulatory agencies and authorities.

"Failure to maintain public rating or meet applicable criteria

"(f)(1) IN GENERAL.—A national bank that does not continue to meet any applicable rating or other requirement of subsection (a)(2)(E) after acquiring or establishing a financial subsidiary shall not, directly or through a subsidiary, purchase or acquire any additional equity capital of any financial subsidiary until the bank meets such requirements.

"(2) EQUITY CAPITAL.—For purposes of this subsection, the term 'equity capital' includes, in addition to any equity instrument, any debt instrument issued by a financial subsidiary, if the instrument qualifies as capital of the subsidiary under any Federal or State law, regulation, or interpretation applicable to the subsidiary.

"Definitions

"(g) For purposes of this section, the following definitions shall apply:

"(1) AFFILIATE, COMPANY, CONTROL, AND SUBSIDIARY.—The terms 'affiliate', 'company', 'control', and 'subsidiary' have the meanings given those terms in section 2 of the Bank Holding Company Act of 1956.

"(2) APPROPRIATE FEDERAL BANKING AGENCY, DEPOSITORY INSTITUTION,IMSURED BANK, AND INSURED DEPOSITORY INSTITUTION.—The terms 'appropriate Federal banking agency', 'depository institution', 'insured bank', and 'insured depository institution' have the meanings given those terms in section 3 of the Federal Deposit Insurance Act.

"(3) FINANCIAL SUBSIDIARY.—The term 'financial subsidiary' means any company that is controlled by 1 or more insured depository institutions other than a subsidiary that—

"(A) engages solely in activities that national banks are permitted to engage in directly and are conducted subject to the same terms and conditions that govern the conduct of such activities by national banks; or

"(B) a national bank is specifically authorized by the express terms of a Federal statute (other than this section), and not by implication or interpretation, to control, such as by section 25 or 25A of the Federal Reserve Act or the Bank Service Company Act.

"(4) ELIGIBLE DEBT.—The term 'eligible debt' means unsecured long-term debt that—

"(A) is not supported by any form of credit enhancement, including a guarantee or standby letter of credit; and

"(B) is not held in whole or in any significant part by any affiliate, officer, director, principal shareholder, or employee of the bank or any other person acting on behalf of or with funds from the bank or an affiliate of the bank.

"(5) WELL CAPITALIZED.—The term 'well capitalized' has the meaning given the term in section 38 of the Federal Deposit Insurance Act.

"(6) WELL MANAGED.—The term 'well managed' means—

"(A) in the case of a depository institution that has been examined, unless otherwise determined in writing by the appropriate Federal banking agency—

"(i) the achievement of a composite rating of 1 or 2 under the Uniform Financial Institutions Rating System (or an equivalent rating under an equivalent rating system) in connection with the most recent examination or subsequent review of the depository institution; and

"(ii) at least a rating of 2 for management, if such rating is given; or

"(B) in the case of any depository institution that has not been examined, the existence and use of managerial resources that the appropriate Federal banking agency determines are satisfactory.".

(b) SECTIONS 23A AND 23B OF THE FEDERAL RESERVE ACT.—

(1) LIMITING THE EXPOSURE OF A BANK TO A FINANCIAL SUBSIDIARY TO THE AMOUNT OF PERMISSIBLE EXPOSURE TO AN AFFILIATE.—Section 23A of the Federal Reserve Act (12 U.S.C. 371c) is amended—

(A) by redesignating subsection (e) as subsection (f); and

(B) by inserting after subsection (d), the following new subsection:

"Rules relating to banks with financial subsidiaries

"(e)(1) FINANCIAL SUBSIDIARY DEFINED.—For purposes of this section and section 23B, the term 'financial subsidiary' means any company that is a subsidiary of a bank that would be a financial subsidiary of a national bank under section 5136A of the Revised Statutes of the United States.

"(2) FINANCIAL SUBSIDIARY TREATED AS AN AFFILIATE.—For purposes of applying this section and section 23B, and notwithstanding subsection (b)(2) of this section or section 23B(d)(1), a financial subsidiary of a bank—

"(A) shall be deemed to be an affiliate of the bank; and

"(B) shall not be deemed to be a subsidiary of the bank.

"(3) EXCEPTIONS FOR TRANSACTIONS WITH FINANCIAL SUBSIDIARIES.—

"(A) EXCEPTION FROM LIMIT ON COVERED TRANSACTIONS WITH ANY INDIVIDUAL FINANCIAL SUBSIDIARY.—Notwithstanding paragraph (2), the restriction contained in subsection (a)(1)(A) shall not apply with respect to covered transactions between a bank and any individual financial subsidiary of the bank.

"(B) EXCEPTION FOR EARNINGS RETAINED BY FINANCIAL SUBSIDIARIES.—Notwithstanding paragraph (2) or subsection (b)(7), a bank's investment in a financial subsidiary of the bank shall not include retained earnings of the financial subsidiary.

"(4) ANTI-EVASION PROVISION.—For purposes of this section and section 23B—

"(A) any purchase of, or investment in, the securities of a financial subsidiary of a bank by an affiliate of the bank shall be considered to be a purchase of or investment in such securities by the bank; and

"(B) any extension of credit by an affiliate of a bank to a financial subsidiary of the bank shall be considered to be an extension of credit by the bank to the financial subsidiary if the Board determines that such treatment is necessary or appropriate to prevent evasions of this Act and the Gramm-Leach-Bliley Act.".

(2) REBUTTABLE PRESUMPTION OF CONTROL OF PORTFOLIO COMPANY.—Section 23A(b) of the Federal Reserve Act (12 U.S.C. 371c(b)) is amended by adding at the end the following new paragraph—

"(11) REBUTTABLE PRESUMPTION OF CONTROL OF PORTFOLIO COMPANIES.—In addition to paragraph (3), a company or shareholder shall be presumed to control any other company if the company or shareholder, directly or indirectly, or acting through 1 or more other persons, owns or controls 15 percent or more of the equity capital of the other company pursuant to subparagraph (H) or (I) of section 4(k)(4) of the Bank Holding Company Act of 1956 or rules adopted under section 122 of the Gramm-Leach-Bliley Act, if any, unless the company or shareholder provides information acceptable to the Board to rebut this presumption of control.".

(3) RULEMAKING REQUIRED CONCERNING DERIVATIVE TRANSACTIONS AND INTRADAY CREDIT.—Section 23A(f) of the Federal Reserve Act (12 U.S.C. 371c(f)) (as so redesignated by paragraph (1)(A) of this subsection) is amended by inserting at the end the following new paragraph:

"(3) RULEMAKING REQUIRED CONCERNING DERIVATIVE TRANSACTIONS AND INTRADAY CREDIT.—

"(A) IN GENERAL.—Not later than 18 months after the date of the enactment of the Gramm-Leach-Bliley Act, the Board shall adopt final rules under this section to address as covered transactions credit exposure arising out of derivative transactions between member banks and their affiliates and intraday extensions of credit by member banks to their affiliates.

"(B) EFFECTIVE DATE.—The effective date of any final rule adopted by the Board pursuant to subparagraph (A) shall be delayed for such period as the Board deems necessary or appropriate to permit banks to conform their activities to the requirements of the final rule without undue hardship.".

(c) ANTITYING.—Section 106(a) of the Bank Holding Company Act Amendments of 1970 (12 U.S.C. 1971) is amended by adding at the end the following: "For purposes of this section, a financial subsidiary of a national bank engaging in activities pursuant to section 5136A(a) of the Revised Statutes of the United States shall be deemed to be a subsidiary of a bank holding company, and not a subsidiary of a bank.".

(d) SAFETY AND SOUNDNESS FIREWALLS FOR STATE BANKS WITH FINANCIAL SUBSIDIARIES.—

(1) FEDERAL DEPOSIT INSURANCE ACT.—The Federal Deposit Insurance Act (12 U.S.C. 1811 et seq.) is amended by inserting after section 45 (as added by section 112(b) of this title) the following new section:

"SEC. 46. SAFETY AND SOUNDNESS FIREWALLS APPLICABLE TO FINANCIAL SUBSIDIARIES OF BANKS.

"In general

"(a) An insured State bank may control or hold an interest in a subsidiary that engages in activities as principal that would only be permissible for a national bank to conduct through a financial subsidiary if—

"(1) the State bank and each insured depository institution affiliate of the State bank are well capitalized (after the capital deduction required by paragraph (2));

"(2) the State bank complies with the capital deduction and financial statement disclosure requirements in section 5136A(c) of the Revised Statutes of the United States;

"(3) the State bank complies with the financial and operational safeguards required by section 5136A(d) of the Revised Statutes of the United States; and

"(4) the State bank complies with the amendments to sections 23A and 23B of the Federal Reserve Act made by section 121(b) of the Gramm-Leach-Bliley Act.

"Preservation of existing subsidiaries

"(b) Notwithstanding subsection (a), an insured State bank may retain control of a subsidiary, or retain an interest in a subsidiary, that the State bank lawfully controlled or acquired before the date of the enactment of the Gramm-Leach-Bliley Act, and conduct through such subsidiary any activities lawfully conducted in such subsidiary as of such date.

"Definitions

"(c) For purposes of this section, the following definitions shall apply:

"(1) SUBSIDIARY.—The term 'subsidiary' means any company that is a subsidiary (as defined in section 3(w)(4)) of 1 or more insured banks.

"(2) FINANCIAL SUBSIDIARY.—The term 'financial subsidiary' has the meaning given the term in section 5136A(g) of the Revised Statutes of the United States.

"Preservation of authority

"(d)(1) FEDERAL DEPOSIT INSURANCE ACT.—No provision of this section shall be construed as superseding the authority of the Federal Deposit Insurance Corporation to review subsidiary activities under section 24.

"(2) FEDERAL RESERVE ACT.—No provision of this section shall be construed as affecting the applicability of the 20th undesignated paragraph of section 9 of the Federal Reserve Act.".

(2) FEDERAL RESERVE ACT.—The 20th undesignated paragraph of section 9 of the Federal Reserve Act (12 U.S.C. 335) is amended by adding at the end the following: "This paragraph shall not apply to any interest held by a State member bank in accordance with section 5136A of the Revised Statutes of the United States and subject to the same conditions and limitations provided in such section.".

(e) CLERICAL AMENDMENT.—The table of sections for chapter one of title LXII of the Revised Statutes of the United States is amended—

(1) by redesignating the item relating to section 5136A as section 5136B; and

(2) by inserting after the item relating to section 5136 the following new item:

"5136A. Financial subsidiaries of national banks.".

¶ 1122

SEC. 122. **CONSIDERATION OF MERCHANT BANKING ACTIVITIES BY FINANCIAL SUBSIDIARIES.**

After the end of the 5-year period beginning on the date of the enactment of the Gramm-Leach-Bliley Act, the Board of Governors of the Federal Reserve System and the Secretary of the Treasury may, if appropriate, after considering—

(1) the experience with the effects of financial modernization under this Act and merchant banking activities of financial holding companies;

(2) the potential effects on depository institutions and the financial system of allowing merchant banking activities in financial subsidiaries; and

(3) other relevant facts;

jointly adopt rules that permit financial subsidiaries to engage in merchant banking activities described in section 4(k)(4)(H) of the Bank Holding Company Act of 1956, under such terms and conditions as the Board of Governors of the Federal Reserve System and the Secretary of the Treasury jointly determine to be appropriate.

Subtitle D—Preservation of FTC Authority

¶ 1131

SEC. 131. **AMENDMENT TO THE BANK HOLDING COMPANY ACT OF 1956 TO MODIFY NOTIFICATION AND POST-APPROVAL WAITING PERIOD FOR SECTION 3 TRANSACTIONS.**

Section 11(b)(1) of the Bank Holding Company Act of 1956 (12 U.S.C. 1849(b)(1)) is amended by inserting "and, if the transaction also involves an acquisition under section 4, the Board shall also notify the Federal Trade Commission of such approval" before the period at the end of the first sentence.

¶ 1132

SEC. 132. **INTERAGENCY DATA SHARING.**

(a) IN GENERAL.—To the extent not prohibited by other law, the Comptroller of the Currency, the Director of the Office of Thrift Supervision, the Federal Deposit Insurance Corporation, and the Board of Governors of the Federal Reserve System shall make available to the Attorney General and the Federal Trade Commission any data in the possession of any such banking agency that the antitrust agency deems necessary for antitrust review of any transaction requiring notice to any such antitrust agency or the approval of such agency under section 3 or 4 of the Bank Holding Company Act of 1956, section 18(c) of the Federal Deposit Insurance Act, the National Bank Consolidation and Merger Act, section 10 of the Home Owners' Loan Act, or the antitrust laws.

(b) CONFIDENTIALITY REQUIREMENTS.—

(1) IN GENERAL.—Any information or material obtained by any agency pursuant to subsection (a) shall be treated as confidential.

(2) PROCEDURES FOR DISCLOSURE.—If any information or material obtained by any agency pursuant to subsection (a) is proposed to be disclosed to a third party, written notice of such disclosure shall first be provided to the agency from which such information or material was obtained and an opportunity shall be given to such agency to oppose or limit the proposed disclosure.

(3) OTHER PRIVILEGES NOT WAIVED BY DISCLOSURE UNDER THIS SECTION.—The provision by any Federal agency of any information or material pursuant to subsection (a) to another agency shall not constitute a waiver, or otherwise affect, any privilege any agency or person may claim with respect to such information under Federal or State law.

(4) EXCEPTION.—No provision of this section shall be construed as preventing or limiting access to any information by any duly authorized committee of the Congress or the Comptroller General of the United States.

(c) BANKING AGENCY INFORMATION SHARING.—The provisions of subsection (b) shall apply to—

(1) any information or material obtained by any Federal banking agency (as defined in section 3(z) of the Federal Deposit Insurance Act) from any other Federal banking agency; and

(2) any report of examination or other confidential supervisory information obtained by any State agency or authority, or any other person, from a Federal banking agency.

¶ 1133

SEC. 133. CLARIFICATION OF STATUS OF SUBSIDIARIES AND AFFILIATES.

(a) CLARIFICATION OF FEDERAL TRADE COMMISSION JURISDICTION.—Any person that directly or indirectly controls, is controlled directly or indirectly by, or is directly or indirectly under common control with, any bank or savings association (as such terms are defined in section 3 of the Federal Deposit Insurance Act) and is not itself a bank or savings association shall not be deemed to be a bank or savings association for purposes of any provisions applied by the Federal Trade Commission under the Federal Trade Commission Act.

(b) SAVINGS PROVISION.—No provision of this section shall be construed as restricting the authority of any Federal banking agency (as defined in section 3 of the Federal Deposit Insurance Act) under any Federal banking law, including section 8 of the Federal Deposit Insurance Act.

(c) HART-SCOTT-RODINO AMENDMENTS.—

(1) BANKS.—Section 7A(c)(7) of the Clayton Act (15 U.S.C. 18a(c)(7)) is amended by inserting before the semicolon at the end the following: ", except that a portion of a transaction is not exempt under this paragraph if such portion of the transaction (A) is subject to section 4(k) of the Bank Holding Company Act of 1956; and (B) does not require agency approval under section 3 of the Bank Holding Company Act of 1956".

(2) BANK HOLDING COMPANIES.—Section 7A(c)(8) of the Clayton Act (15 U.S.C. 18a(c)(8)) is amended by inserting before the semicolon at the end the following: ",except that a portion of a transaction is not exempt under this paragraph if such portion of the transaction (A) is subject to section 4(k) of the Bank Holding Company Act of 1956; and (B) does not require agency approval under section 4 of the Bank Holding Company Act of 1956".

Subtitle E—National Treatment

¶ 1141

SEC. 141. **FOREIGN BANKS THAT ARE FINANCIAL HOLDING COMPANIES.**

Section 8(c) of the International Banking Act of 1978 (12 U.S.C. 3106(c)) is amended by adding at the end the following new paragraph:

"(3) TERMINATION OF GRANDFATHERED RIGHTS.—

"(A) IN GENERAL.—If any foreign bank or foreign company files a declaration under section 4(l)(1)(C) of the Bank Holding Company Act of 1956, any authority conferred by this subsection on any foreign bank or company to engage in any activity that the Board has determined to be permissible for financial holding companies under section 4(k) of such Act shall terminate immediately.

"(B) RESTRICTIONS AND REQUIREMENTS AUTHORIZED.—If a foreign bank or company that engages, directly or through an affiliate pursuant to paragraph (1), in an activity that the Board has determined to be permissible for financial holding companies under section 4(k) of the Bank Holding Company Act of 1956 has not filed a declaration with the Board of its status as a financial holding company under such section by the end of the 2-year period beginning on the date of the enactment of the Gramm-Leach-Bliley Act, the Board, giving due regard to the principle of national treatment and equality of competitive opportunity, may impose such restrictions and requirements on the conduct of such activities by such foreign bank or company as are comparable to those imposed on a financial holding company organized under the laws of the United States, including a requirement to conduct such activities in compliance with any prudential safeguards established under section 114 of the Gramm-Leach-Bliley Act.".

¶ 1142

SEC. 142. **REPRESENTATIVE OFFICES.**

(a) DEFINITION.—Section 1(b)(15) of the International Banking Act of 1978 (12 U.S.C. 3101(15)) is amended by striking "State agency, or subsidiary of a foreign bank" and inserting "or State agency".

(b) EXAMINATIONS.—Section 10(c) of the International Banking Act of 1978 (12 U.S.C. 3107(c)) is amended by adding at the end the following new sentence: "The Board may also make examinations of any affiliate of a foreign bank conducting business in any State if the Board deems it necessary to determine and enforce compliance with this Act, the Bank Holding Company Act of 1956, or other applicable Federal banking law.".

Subtitle F—Direct Activities of Banks

¶ 1151

SEC. 151. **AUTHORITY OF NATIONAL BANKS TO UNDERWRITE CERTAIN MUNICIPAL BONDS.**

The paragraph designated the Seventh of section 5136 of the Revised Statutes of the United States (12 U.S.C. 24(7)) is amended by adding at the end the following new sentence: "In addition to the provisions in this paragraph for dealing in, underwriting, or purchasing securities, the limitations and restrictions contained in this paragraph as to dealing in, underwriting, and purchasing investment securities for the national bank's own account shall not apply to obligations (including limited obligation bonds, revenue bonds, and obligations that satisfy the requirements of section 142(b)(1) of the Internal Revenue Code of 1986) issued by or on behalf of any State or political subdivision of a State, including any municipal corporate instrumentality of 1 or more States, or any public agency or authority of any State or political subdivision of a State, if the national bank is well capitalized (as defined in section 38 of the Federal Deposit Insurance Act).".

Subtitle G—Effective Date

¶ 1161

SEC. 161. **EFFECTIVE DATE.**

This title (other than section 104) and the amendments made by this title shall take effect 120 days after the date of the enactment of this Act.

TITLE II—FUNCTIONAL REGULATION

Subtitle A—Brokers and Dealers

¶ 1201

SEC. 201. **DEFINITION OF BROKER.**

Section 3(a)(4) of the Securities Exchange Act of 1934 (15 U.S.C. 78c(a)(4)) is amended to read as follows:

"(4) BROKER.—

"(A) IN GENERAL.—The term 'broker' means any person engaged in the business of effecting transactions in securities for the account of others.

"(B) EXCEPTION FOR CERTAIN BANK ACTIVITIES.—A bank shall not be considered to be a broker because the bank engages in any one or more of the following activities under the conditions described:

"(i) THIRD PARTY BROKERAGE ARRANGEMENTS.—The bank enters into a contractual or other written arrangement with a broker or dealer registered under this title under which the broker or dealer offers brokerage services on or off the premises of the bank if—

"(I) such broker or dealer is clearly identified as the person performing the brokerage services;

"(II) the broker or dealer performs brokerage services in an area that is clearly marked and, to the extent practicable, physically separate from the routine deposit-taking activities of the bank;

"(III) any materials used by the bank to advertise or promote generally the availability of brokerage services under the arrangement clearly indicate that the brokerage services are being provided by the broker or dealer and not by the bank;

"(IV) any materials used by the bank to advertise or promote generally the availability of brokerage services under the arrangement are in compliance with the Federal securities laws before distribution;

"(V) bank employees (other than associated persons of a broker or dealer who are qualified pursuant to the rules of a self-regulatory organization) perform only clerical or ministerial functions in connection with broker-age transactions including scheduling appointments with the associated persons of a broker or dealer, except that bank employees may forward customer funds or securities and may describe in general terms the types of investment vehicles available from the bank and the broker or dealer under the arrangement;

"(VI) bank employees do not receive incentive compensation for any brokerage transaction unless such employees are associated persons of a broker or dealer and are qualified pursuant to the rules of a self-regulatory organization, except that the bank employees may receive compensation for the referral of any customer if the compensation is a nominal one-time cash fee of a fixed dollar amount and the payment of the fee is not contingent on whether the referral results in a transaction;

"(VII) such services are provided by the broker or dealer on a basis in which all customers that receive any services are fully disclosed to the broker or dealer;

"(VIII) the bank does not carry a securities account of the customer except as permitted under clause (ii) or (viii) of this subparagraph; and

"(IX) the bank, broker, or dealer informs each customer that the brokerage services are provided by the broker or dealer and not by the bank and that the securities are not deposits or other obligations of the bank, are not guaranteed by the bank, and are not insured by the Federal Deposit Insurance Corporation.

"(ii) TRUST ACTIVITIES.—The bank effects transactions in a trustee capacity, or effects transactions in a fiduciary capacity in its trust department or other department that is regularly examined by bank examiners for compliance with fiduciary principles and standards, and—

"(I) is chiefly compensated for such transactions, consistent with fiduciary principles and standards, on the basis of an administration or annual fee (payable on a monthly, quarterly, or other basis), a percentage of assets under management, or a flat or capped per order processing fee equal to not more than the cost incurred by the bank in connection with executing securities transactions for trustee and fiduciary customers, or any combination of such fees; and

"(II) does not publicly solicit brokerage business, other than by advertising that it effects transactions in securities in conjunction with advertising its other trust activities.

"(iii) PERMISSIBLE SECURITIES TRANSACTIONS.—The bank effects transactions in—

"(I) commercial paper, bankers acceptances, or commercial bills;

"(II) exempted securities;

"(III) qualified Canadian government obligations as defined in section 5136 of the Revised Statutes, in conformity with section 15C of this title and the rules and regulations thereunder, or obligations of the North American Development Bank; or

"(IV) any standardized, credit enhanced debt security issued by a foreign government pursuant to the March 1989 plan of then Secretary of the Treasury Brady, used by such foreign government to retire outstanding commercial bank loans.

"(iv) CERTAIN STOCK PURCHASE PLANS.—

"(I) EMPLOYEE BENEFIT PLANS.—The bank effects transactions, as part of its transfer agency activities, in the securities of an issuer as part of any pension, retirement, profit-sharing, bonus, thrift, savings, incentive, or other similar benefit plan for the employees of that issuer or its affiliates (as defined in section 2 of the Bank Holding Company Act of 1956), if the bank does not solicit transactions or provide investment advice with respect to the purchase or sale of securities in connection with the plan.

"(II) DIVIDEND REINVESTMENT PLANS.—The bank effects transactions, as part of its transfer agency activities, in the securities of an issuer as part of that issuer's dividend reinvestment plan, if—

"(aa) the bank does not solicit transactions or provide investment advice with respect to the purchase or sale of securities in connection with the plan; and

"(bb) the bank does not net shareholders' buy and sell orders, other than for programs for odd-lot holders or plans registered with the Commission.

"(III) ISSUER PLANS.—The bank effects transactions, as part of its transfer agency activities, in the securities of an issuer as part of a plan or program for the purchase or sale of that issuer's shares, if—

"(aa) the bank does not solicit transactions or provide investment advice with respect to the purchase or sale of securities in connection with the plan or program; and

"(bb) the bank does not net shareholders' buy and sell orders, other than for programs for odd-lot holders or plans registered with the Commission.

"(IV) PERMISSIBLE DELIVERY OF MATERIALS.—The exception to being considered a broker for a bank engaged in activities described in subclauses (I), (II), and (III) will not be affected by delivery of written or electronic plan materials by a bank to employees of the issuer, shareholders of the issuer, or members of affinity groups of the issuer, so long as such materials are—

"(aa) comparable in scope or nature to that permitted by the Commission as of the date of the enactment of the Gramm-LeachBliley Act; or

"(bb) otherwise permitted by the Commission.

"(v) SWEEP ACCOUNTS.—The bank effects transactions as part of a program for the investment or reinvestment of deposit funds into any no-load, open-end management investment company registered under the Investment Company Act of 1940 that holds itself out as a money market fund.

"(vi) AFFILIATE TRANSACTIONS.—The bank effects transactions for the account of any affiliate of the bank (as defined in section 2 of the Bank Holding Company Act of 1956) other than—

"(I) a registered broker or dealer; or

"(II) an affiliate that is engaged in merchant banking, as described in section 4(k)(4)(H) of the Bank Holding Company Act of 1956.

"(vii) PRIVATE SECURITIES OFFERINGS.—The bank—

"(I) effects sales as part of a primary offering of securities not involving a public offering, pursuant to section 3(b), 4(2), or 4(6) of the Securities Act of 1933 or the rules and regulations issued thereunder;

"(II) at any time after the date that is 1 year after the date of the enactment of the Gramm-Leach-Bliley Act, is not affiliated with a broker or dealer that has been registered for more than 1 year in accordance with this Act, and engages in dealing, market making, or underwriting activities, other than with respect to exempted securities; and

"(III) if the bank is not affiliated with a broker or dealer, does not effect any primary offering described in subclause (I) the aggregate amount of which exceeds 25 percent of the capital of the bank, except that the limitation of this subclause shall not apply with respect to any sale of government securities or municipal securities.

"(viii) SAFEKEEPING AND CUSTODY ACTIVITIES.—

"(I) IN GENERAL.—The bank, as part of customary banking activities—

"(aa) provides safekeeping or custody services with respect to securities, including the exercise of warrants and other rights on behalf of customers;

"(bb) facilitates the transfer of funds or securities, as a custodian or a clearing agency, in connection with the clearance and settlement of its customers' transactions in securities;

"(cc) effects securities lending or borrowing transactions with or on behalf of customers as part of services provided to customers pursuant to division (aa) or (bb) or invests cash collateral pledged in connection with such transactions;

"(dd) holds securities pledged by a customer to another person or securities subject to purchase or resale agreements involving a customer, or facilitates the pledging or transfer of such securities by book entry or as otherwise provided under applicable law, if the bank maintains records separately identifying the securities and the customer; or

"(ee) serves as a custodian or provider of other related administrative services to any individual retirement account, pension, retirement, profit sharing, bonus, thrift savings, incentive, or other similar benefit plan.

"(II) EXCEPTION FOR CARRYING BROKER ACTIVITIES.—The exception to being considered a broker for a bank engaged in activities described in subclause (I) shall not apply if the bank, in connection with such activities, acts in the United States as a carrying broker (as such term, and different formulations thereof, are used in section 15(c)(3) of this title and the rules and regulations thereunder) for any broker or dealer, unless such carrying broker activities are engaged in with respect to government securities (as defined in paragraph (42) of this subsection).

"(ix) IDENTIFIED BANKING PRODUCTS.—The bank effects transactions in identified banking products as defined in section 206 of the Gramm-Leach-Bliley Act.

"(x) MUNICIPAL SECURITIES.—The bank effects transactions in municipal securities.

"(xi) DE MINIMIS EXCEPTION.—The bank effects, other than in transactions referred to in clauses (i) through (x), not more than 500 transactions in securities in any calendar year, and such transactions are not effected by an employee of the bank who is also an employee of a broker or dealer.

"(C) EXECUTION BY BROKER OR DEALER.—The exception to being considered a broker for a bank engaged in activities described in clauses (ii), (iv), and (viii) of subparagraph (B) shall not apply if the activities described in such provisions result in the trade in the United States of any security that is a publicly traded security in the United States, unless—

"(i) the bank directs such trade to a registered broker or dealer for execution;

"(ii) the trade is a cross trade or other substantially similar trade of a security that—

"(I) is made by the bank or between the bank and an affiliated fiduciary; and

"(II) is not in contravention of fiduciary principles established under applicable Federal or State law; or

"(iii) the trade is conducted in some other manner permitted under rules, regulations, or orders as the Commission may prescribe or issue.

"(D) FIDUCIARY CAPACITY.—For purposes of subparagraph (B)(ii), the term 'fiduciary capacity' means—

"(i) in the capacity as trustee, executor, administrator, registrar of stocks and bonds, transfer agent, guardian, assignee, receiver, or custodian under a uniform gift to minor act, or as an investment adviser if the bank receives a fee for its investment advice;

"(ii) in any capacity in which the bank possesses investment discretion on behalf of another; or

"(iii) in any other similar capacity.

"(E) EXCEPTION FOR ENTITIES SUBJECT TO SECTION 15(e).—The term 'broker' does not include a bank that—

"(i) was, on the day before the date of enactment of the Gramm-Leach-Bliley Act, subject to section 15(e); and

"(ii) is subject to such restrictions and requirements as the Commission considers appropriate.".

¶ 1202

SEC. 202. **DEFINITION OF DEALER.**

Section 3(a)(5) of the Securities Exchange Act of 1934 (15 U.S.C. 78c(a)(5)) is amended to read as follows:

"(5) DEALER.—

"(A) IN GENERAL.—The term 'dealer' means any person engaged in the business of buying and selling securities for such person's own account through a broker or otherwise.

"(B) EXCEPTION FOR PERSON NOT ENGAGED IN THE BUSINESS OF DEALING.—The term 'dealer' does not include a person that buys or sells securities for such person's own account, either individually or in a fiduciary capacity, but not as a part of a regular business.

"(C) EXCEPTION FOR CERTAIN BANK ACTIVITIES.—A bank shall not be considered to be a dealer because the bank engages in any of the following activities under the conditions described:

"(i) PERMISSIBLE SECURITIES TRANSACTIONS.—The bank buys or sells—

"(I) commercial paper, bankers acceptances, or commercial bills;

"(II) exempted securities;

"(III) qualified Canadian government obligations as defined in section 5136 of the Revised Statutes of the United States, in conformity with section 15C of this title and the rules and regulations thereunder, or obligations of the North American Development Bank; or

"(IV) any standardized, credit enhanced debt security issued by a foreign government pursuant to the March 1989 plan of then Secretary of the Treasury Brady, used by such foreign government to retire outstanding commercial bank loans.

"(ii) INVESTMENT, TRUSTEE, AND FIDUCIARY TRANSACTIONS.—The bank buys or sells securities for investment purposes—

"(I) for the bank; or

"(II) for accounts for which the bank acts as a trustee or fiduciary.

"(iii) ASSET-BACKED TRANSACTIONS.—The bank engages in the issuance or sale to qualified investors, through a grantor trust or other separate entity, of securities backed by or representing an interest in notes, drafts, acceptances, loans, leases, receivables, other obligations (other than securities of which the bank is not the issuer), or pools of any such obligations predominantly originated by—

"(I) the bank;

"(II) an affiliate of any such bank other than a broker or dealer; or

"(III) a syndicate of banks of which the bank is a member, if the obligations or pool of obligations consists of mortgage obligations or consumer-related receivables.

"(iv) IDENTIFIED BANKING PRODUCTS.—The bank buys or sells identified banking products, as defined in section 206 of the Gramm-Leach-Bliley Act.".

¶ 1203

SEC. 203. REGISTRATION FOR SALES OF PRIVATE SECURITIES OFFERINGS.

Section 15A of the Securities Exchange Act of 1934 (15 U.S.C. 78o-3) is amended by inserting after subsection (i) the following new subsection:

"Registration for sales of private securities offerings

"(j) A registered securities association shall create a limited qualification category for any associated person of a member who effects sales as part of a primary offering of securities not involving a public offering, pursuant to section 3(b), 4(2), or 4(6) of the Securities Act of 1933 and the rules and regulations thereunder, and shall deem qualified in such limited qualification category, without testing, any bank employee who, in the six month period preceding the date of the enactment of the Gramm-Leach-Bliley Act, engaged in effecting such sales.".

¶ 1204

SEC. 204. INFORMATION SHARING.

Section 18 of the Federal Deposit Insurance Act is amended by adding at the end the following new subsection:

"Recordkeeping requirements

"(t)(1) REQUIREMENTS.—Each appropriate Federal banking agency, after consultation with and consideration of the views of the Commission, shall establish recordkeeping requirements for banks relying on exceptions contained in paragraphs (4) and (5) of section 3(a) of the Securities Exchange Act of 1934. Such recordkeeping requirements shall be sufficient to demonstrate compliance with the terms of such exceptions and be designed to facilitate compliance with such exceptions.

"(2) AVAILABILITY TO COMMISSION; CONFIDENTIALITY.—Each appropriate Federal banking agency shall make any information required under paragraph (1) available to the Commission upon request. Notwithstanding any other provision of law, the Commission shall not be compelled to disclose any such information. Nothing in this paragraph shall authorize the Commission to withhold information from Congress, or prevent the Commission from complying with a request for information from any other Federal department or agency or any self-regulatory organization requesting the information for purposes within the scope of its jurisdiction, or complying with an order of a court of the United States in an action brought by the United States or the Commission. For purposes of section 552 of title 5, United States Code, this paragraph shall be considered a statute described in subsection (b)(3)(B) of such section 552.

"(3) DEFINITIONS.—As used in this subsection the term 'Commission' means the Securities and Exchange Commission.".

¶ 1205

SEC. 205. **TREATMENT OF NEW HYBRID PRODUCTS.**

Section 15 of the Securities Exchange Act of 1934 (15 U.S.C. 78o) is amended by adding at the end the following new subsection:

"Rulemaking to extend requirements to new hybrid products

"(i)(1) CONSULTATION.—Prior to commencing a rulemaking under this subsection, the Commission shall consult with and seek the concurrence of the Board concerning the imposition of broker or dealer registration requirements with respect any new hybrid product. In developing and promulgating rules under this subsection, the Commission shall consider the views of the Board, including views with respect to the nature of the new hybrid product; the history, purpose, extent, and appropriateness of the regulation of the new product under the Federal banking laws; and the impact of the proposed rule on the banking industry.

"(2) LIMITATION.—The Commission shall not—

"(A) require a bank to register as a broker or dealer under this section because the bank engages in any transaction in, or buys or sells, a new hybrid product; or

"(B) bring an action against a bank for a failure to comply with a requirement described in subparagraph (A),

unless the Commission has imposed such requirement by rule or regulation issued in accordance with this section.

"(3) CRITERIA FOR RULEMAKING.—The Commission shall not impose a requirement under paragraph (2) of this subsection with respect to any new hybrid product unless the Commission determines that—

"(A) the new hybrid product is a security; and

"(B) imposing such requirement is necessary and appropriate in the public interest and for the protection of investors.

"(4) CONSIDERATIONS.—In making a determination under paragraph (3), the Commission shall consider—

"(A) the nature of the new hybrid product; and

"(B) the history, purpose, extent, and appropriateness of the regulation of the new hybrid product under the Federal securities laws and under the Federal banking laws.

"(5) OBJECTION TO COMMISSION REGULATION.—

"(A) FILING OF PETITION FOR REVIEW.—The Board may obtain review of any final regulation described in paragraph (2) in the United States Court of Appeals for the District of Columbia Circuit by filing in such court, not later than 60 days after the date of publication of the final regulation, a written petition requesting that the regulation be set aside. Any proceeding to challenge any such rule shall be expedited by the Court of Appeals.

"(B) TRANSMITTAL OF PETITION AND RECORD.—A copy of a petition described in subparagraph (A) shall be transmitted as soon as possible by the Clerk of the Court to an officer or employee of the Commission designated for that purpose. Upon receipt of the petition, the Commission shall file with the court the regulation under review and any documents referred to therein, and any other relevant materials prescribed by the court.

"(C) EXCLUSIVE JURISDICTION.—On the date of the filing of the petition under subparagraph (A), the court has jurisdiction, which becomes exclusive on the filing of the materials set forth in subparagraph (B), to affirm and enforce or to set aside the regulation at issue.

"(D) STANDARD OF REVIEW.—The court shall determine to affirm and enforce or set aside a regulation of the Commission under this subsection, based on the determination of the court as to whether—

"(i) the subject product is a new hybrid product, as defined in this subsection;

"(ii) the subject product is a security; and

"(iii) imposing a requirement to register as a broker or dealer for banks engaging in transactions in such product is appropriate in light of the history, purpose, and extent of regulation under the Federal securities laws and under the Federal banking laws, giving deference neither to the views of the Commission nor the Board.

"(E) JUDICIAL STAY.—The filing of a petition by the Board pursuant to subparagraph (A) shall operate as a judicial stay, until the date on which the determination of the court is final (including any appeal of such determination).

"(F) OTHER AUTHORITY TO CHALLENGE.—Any aggrieved party may seek judicial review of the Commission's rulemaking under this subsection pursuant to section 25 of this title.

"(6) DEFINITIONS.—For purposes of this subsection:

"(A) NEW HYBRID PRODUCT.—The term 'new hybrid product' means a product that—

"(i) was not subjected to regulation by the Commission as a security prior to the date of the enactment of the GrammLeach-Bliley Act;

"(ii) is not an identified banking product as such term is defined in section 206 of such Act; and

"(iii) is not an equity swap within the meaning of section 206(a)(6) of such Act.

"(B) BOARD.—The term 'Board' means the Board of Governors of the Federal Reserve System.".

¶ 1206

SEC. 206. DEFINITION OF IDENTIFIED BANKING PRODUCT.

(a) DEFINITION OF IDENTIFIED BANKING PRODUCT.—For purposes of paragraphs (4) and (5) of section 3(a) of the Securities Exchange Act of 1934 (15 U.S.C. 78c(a) (4), (5)), the term "identified banking product" means—

(1) a deposit account, savings account, certificate of deposit, or other deposit instrument issued by a bank;

(2) a banker's acceptance;

(3) a letter of credit issued or loan made by a bank;

(4) a debit account at a bank arising from a credit card or similar arrangement;

(5) a participation in a loan which the bank or an affiliate of the bank (other than a broker or dealer) funds, participates in, or owns that is sold—

(A) to qualified investors; or

(B) to other persons that—

(i) have the opportunity to review and assess any material information, including information regarding the borrower's creditworthiness; and

(ii) based on such factors as financial sophistication, net worth, and knowledge and experience in financial matters, have the capability to evaluate the information available, as determined under generally applicable banking standards or guidelines; or

(6) any swap agreement, including credit and equity swaps, except that an equity swap that is sold directly to any person other than a qualified investor (as defined in section 3(a)(54) of the Securities Act of 1934) shall not be treated as an identified banking product.

(b) DEFINITION OF SWAP AGREEMENT.—For purposes of subsection (a)(6), the term "swap agreement" means any individually negotiated contract, agreement, warrant, note, or option that is based, in whole or in part, on the value of, any interest in, or any quantitative measure or the occurrence of any event relating to, one or more commodities, securities, currencies, interest or other rates, indices, or other assets, but does not include any other identified banking product, as defined in paragraphs (1) through (5) of subsection (a).

(c) CLASSIFICATION LIMITED.—Classification of a particular product as an identified banking product pursuant to this section shall not be construed as finding or implying that such product is or is not a security for any purpose under the securities laws, or is or is not an account, agreement, contract, or transaction for any purpose under the Commodity Exchange Act.

(d) INCORPORATED DEFINITIONS.—For purposes of this section, the terms "bank" and "qualified investor" have the same meanings as given in section 3(a) of the Securities Exchange Act of 1934, as amended by this Act.

¶ 1207

SEC. 207. **ADDITIONAL DEFINITIONS.**

Section 3(a) of the Securities Exchange Act of 1934 is amended by adding at the end the following new paragraph:

"(54) QUALIFIED INVESTOR.—

"(A) DEFINITION.—Except as provided in subparagraph (B), for purposes of this title, the term 'qualified investor' means—

"(i) any investment company registered with the Commission under section 8 of the Investment Company Act of 1940;

"(ii) any issuer eligible for an exclusion from the definition of investment company pursuant to section 3(c)(7) of the Investment Company Act of 1940;

"(iii) any bank (as defined in paragraph (6) of this subsection), savings association (as defined in section 3(b) of the Federal Deposit Insurance Act), broker, dealer, insurance company (as defined in section 2(a)(13) of the Securities Act of 1933), or business development company (as defined in section 2(a)(48) of the Investment Company Act of 1940);

"(iv) any small business investment company licensed by the United States Small Business Administration under section 301(c) or (d) of the Small Business Investment Act of 1958;

"(v) any State sponsored employee benefit plan, or any other employee benefit plan, within the meaning of the Employee Retirement Income Security Act of 1974, other than an individual retirement account, if the investment decisions are made by a plan fiduciary, as defined in section 3(21) of that Act, which is either a bank, savings and loan association, insurance company, or registered investment adviser;

"(vi) any trust whose purchases of securities are directed by a person described in clauses (i) through (v) of this subparagraph;

"(vii) any market intermediary exempt under section 3(c)(2) of the Investment Company Act of 1940;

"(viii) any associated person of a broker or dealer other than a natural person;

"(ix) any foreign bank (as defined in section 1(b)(7) of the International Banking Act of 1978);

"(x) the government of any foreign country;

"(xi) any corporation, company, or partnership that owns and invests on a discretionary basis, not less than $25,000,000 in investments;

"(xii) any natural person who owns and invests on a discretionary basis, not less than $25,000,000 in investments;

"(xiii) any government or political subdivision, agency, or instrumentality of a government who owns and invests on a discretionary basis not less than $50,000,000 in investments; or

"(xiv) any multinational or supranational entity or any agency or instrumentality thereof.

"(B) ALTERED THRESHOLDS FOR ASSETBACK SECURITIES AND LOAN PARTICIPATIONS.—For purposes sections 3(a)(5)(C)(iii) of this title and section 206(a)(5) of the GrammLeach-Bliley Act, the term 'qualified investor' has the meaning given such term by subparagraph (A) of this paragraph except that clauses (xi) and (xii) shall be applied by substituting '$10,000,000' for '$25,000,000'.

"(C) ADDITIONAL AUTHORITY.—The Commission may, by rule or order, define a 'qualified investor' as any other person, taking into consideration such factors as the financial sophistication of the person, net worth, and knowledge and experience in financial matters.".

¶ 1208

SEC. 208. **GOVERNMENT SECURITIES DEFINED.**

Section 3(a)(42) of the Securities Exchange Act of 1934 (15 U.S.C. 78c(a)(42)) is amended—

(1) by striking "or" at the end of subparagraph (C);

(2) by striking the period at the end of subparagraph (D) and inserting "; or"; and

(3) by adding at the end the following new subparagraph:

"(E) for purposes of sections 15, 15C, and 17A as applied to a bank, a qualified Canadian government obligation as defined in section 5136 of the Revised Statutes of the United States.".

¶ 1209

SEC. 209. **EFFECTIVE DATE.**

This subtitle shall take effect at the end of the 18-month period beginning on the date of the enactment of this Act.

¶ 1210

SEC. 210. **RULE OF CONSTRUCTION.**

Nothing in this Act shall supersede, affect, or otherwise limit the scope and applicability of the Commodity Exchange Act (7 U.S.C. 1 et seq.).

Subtitle B—Bank Investment Company Activities

¶ 1211

SEC. 211. **CUSTODY OF INVESTMENT COMPANY ASSETS BY AFFILIATED BANK.**

(a) MANAGEMENT COMPANIES.—Section 17(f) of the Investment Company Act of 1940 (15 U.S.C. 80a-17(f)) is amended—

(1) by redesignating paragraphs (1), (2), and (3) as subparagraphs (A), (B), and (C), respectively;

(2) by striking "(f) Every registered" and inserting the following:

"Custody of securities

"(f)(1) Every registered";

(3) by redesignating the second, third, fourth, and fifth sentences of such subsection as paragraphs (2) through (5), respectively, and indenting the left margin of such paragraphs appropriately; and

(4) by adding at the end the following new paragraph:

"(6) The Commission may, after consultation with and taking into consideration the views of the Federal banking agencies (as defined in section 3 of the Federal Deposit Insurance Act), adopt rules and regulations, and issue orders, consistent with the protection of investors, prescribing the conditions under which a bank, or an affiliated person of a bank, either of which is an affiliated person, promoter, organizer, or sponsor of, or principal underwriter for, a registered management company may serve as custodian of that registered management company.".

(b) UNIT INVESTMENT TRUSTS.—Section 26 of the Investment Company Act of 1940 (15 U.S.C. 80a-26) is amended—

(1) by redesignating subsections (b) through (e) as subsections (c) through (f), respectively; and

(2) by inserting after subsection (a) the following new subsection:

"(b) The Commission may, after consultation with and taking into consideration the views of the Federal banking agencies (as defined in section 3 of the Federal Deposit Insurance Act), adopt rules and regulations, and issue orders, consistent with the protection of investors, prescribing the conditions under which a bank, or an affiliated person of a bank, either of which is an affiliated person of a principal underwriter for, or depositor of, a registered unit investment trust, may serve as trustee or custodian under subsection (a)(1).".

¶ 1212

SEC. 212. **LENDING TO AN AFFILIATED INVESTMENT COMPANY.**

Section 17(a) of the Investment Company Act of 1940 (15 U.S.C. 80a-17(a)) is amended—

(1) by striking "or" at the end of paragraph (2);

(2) by striking the period at the end of paragraph (3) and inserting "; or"; and

(3) by adding at the end the following new paragraph:

"(4) to loan money or other property to such registered company, or to any company controlled by such registered company, in contravention of such rules, regulations, or orders as the Commission may, after consultation with and taking into consideration the views of the Federal banking agencies (as defined in section 3 of the Federal Deposit Insurance Act), prescribe or issue consistent with the protection of investors.".

¶ 1213

SEC. 213. INDEPENDENT DIRECTORS.

(a) IN GENERAL.—Section 2(a)(19)(A) of the Investment Company Act of 1940 (15 U.S.C. 80a-2(a)(19)(A)) is amended—

(1) by striking clause (v) and inserting the following new clause:

"(v) any person or any affiliated person of a person (other than a registered investment company) that, at any time during the 6-month period preceding the date of the determination of whether that person or affiliated person is an interested person, has executed any portfolio transactions for, engaged in any principal transactions with, or distributed shares for—

"(I) the investment company;

"(II) any other investment company having the same investment adviser as such investment company or holding itself out to investors as a related company for purposes of investment or investor services; or

"(III) any account over which the investment company's investment adviser has brokerage placement discretion,";

(2) by redesignating clause (vi) as clause (vii); and

(3) by inserting after clause (v) the following new clause:

"(vi) any person or any affiliated person of a person (other than a registered investment company) that, at any time during the 6-month period preceding the date of the determination of whether that person or affiliated person is an interested person, has loaned money or other property to—

"(I) the investment company;

"(II) any other investment company having the same investment adviser as such investment company or holding itself out to investors as a related company for purposes of investment or investor services; or

"(III) any account for which the investment company's investment adviser has borrowing authority,".

(b) CONFORMING AMENDMENT.—Section 2(a)(19)(B) of the Investment Company Act of 1940 (15 U.S.C. 80a-2(a)(19)(B)) is amended—

(1) by striking clause (v) and inserting the following new clause:

"(v) any person or any affiliated person of a person (other than a registered investment company) that, at any time during the 6-month period preceding the date of the determination of whether that person or affiliated person is an interested person, has executed any portfolio transactions for, engaged in any principal transactions with, or distributed shares for—

"(I) any investment company for which the investment adviser or principal underwriter serves as such;

"(II) any investment company holding itself out to investors, for purposes of investment or investor services, as a company related to any investment company for which the investment adviser or principal underwriter serves as such; or

"(III) any account over which the investment adviser has brokerage placement discretion,";

(2) by redesignating clause (vi) as clause (vii); and

(3) by inserting after clause (v) the following new clause:

"(vi) any person or any affiliated person of a person (other than a registered investment company) that, at any time during the 6-month period preceding the date of the determination of whether that person or affiliated person is an interested person, has loaned money or other property to—

"(I) any investment company for which the investment adviser or principal underwriter serves as such;

"(II) any investment company holding itself out to investors, for purposes of investment or investor services, as a company related to any investment company for which the investment adviser or principal underwriter serves as such; or

"(III) any account for which the investment adviser has borrowing authority,".

(c) AFFILIATION OF DIRECTORS.—Section 10(c) of the Investment Company Act of 1940 (15 U.S.C. 80a-10(c)) is amended by striking "bank, except" and inserting "bank (together with its affiliates and subsidiaries) or any one bank holding company (together with its affiliates and subsidiaries) (as such terms are defined in section 2 of the Bank Holding Company Act of 1956), except".

¶ 1214

SEC. 214. ADDITIONAL SEC DISCLOSURE AUTHORITY.

Section 35(a) of the Investment Company Act of 1940 (15 U.S.C. 80a-34(a)) is amended to read as follows:

"Misrepresentation of guarantees

"(a)(1) IN GENERAL.—It shall be unlawful for any person, issuing or selling any security of which a registered investment company is the issuer, to represent or imply in any manner whatsoever that such security or company—

"(A) has been guaranteed, sponsored, recommended, or approved by the United States, or any agency, instrumentality or officer of the United States;

"(B) has been insured by the Federal Deposit Insurance Corporation; or

"(C) is guaranteed by or is otherwise an obligation of any bank or insured depository institution.

"(2) DISCLOSURES.—Any person issuing or selling the securities of a registered investment company that is advised by, or sold through, a bank shall prominently disclose that an investment in the company is not insured by the Federal Deposit Insurance Corporation or any other government agency. The Commission may, after consultation with and taking into consideration the views of the Federal banking agencies (as defined in section 3 of the Federal Deposit Insurance Act), adopt rules and regulations, and issue orders, consistent with the protection of investors, prescribing the manner in which the disclosure under this paragraph shall be provided.

"(3) DEFINITIONS.—The terms 'insured depository institution' and 'appropriate Federal banking agency' have the same meanings as given in section 3 of the Federal Deposit Insurance Act.".

¶ 1215

SEC. 215. DEFINITION OF BROKER UNDER THE INVESTMENT COMPANY ACT OF 1940.

Section 2(a)(6) of the Investment Company Act of 1940 (15 U.S.C. 80a-2(a)(6)) is amended to read as follows:

"(6) The term 'broker' has the same meaning as given in section 3 of the Securities Exchange Act of 1934, except that such term does not include any person solely by reason of the fact that such person is an underwriter for one or more investment companies.".

¶ 1216

SEC. 216. DEFINITION OF DEALER UNDER THE INVESTMENT COMPANY ACT OF 1940.

Section 2(a)(11) of the Investment Company Act of 1940 (15 U.S.C. 80a-2(a)(11)) is amended to read as follows:

"(11) The term 'dealer' has the same meaning as given in the Securities Exchange Act of 1934, but does not include an insurance company or investment company.".

¶ 1217

SEC. 217. REMOVAL OF THE EXCLUSION FROM THE DEFINITION OF INVESTMENT ADVISER FOR BANKS THAT ADVISE INVESTMENT COMPANIES.

(a) INVESTMENT ADVISER.—Section 202(a)(11)(A) of the Investment Advisers Act of 1940 (15 U.S.C. 80b-2(a)(11)(A)) is amended by striking "investment company" and inserting "investment company, except that the term 'investment adviser' includes any bank or bank holding company to the extent that such bank or bank holding company serves or acts as an investment adviser to a registered investment company, but if, in the case of a bank, such services or actions are performed through a separately identifiable department or division, the department or division, and not the bank itself, shall be deemed to be the investment adviser".

(b) SEPARATELY IDENTIFIABLE DEPARTMENT OR DIVISION.—Section 202(a) of the Investment Advisers Act of 1940 (15 U.S.C. 80b-2(a)) is amended by adding at the end the following:

"(26) The term 'separately identifiable department or division' of a bank means a unit—

"(A) that is under the direct supervision of an officer or officers designated by the board of directors of the bank as responsible for the day-to-day conduct of the bank's investment adviser activities for one or more investment companies, including the supervision of all bank employees engaged in the performance of such activities; and

"(B) for which all of the records relating to its investment adviser activities are separately maintained in or extractable from such unit's own facilities or the facilities of the bank, and such records are so maintained or otherwise accessible as to permit independent examination and enforcement by the Commission of this Act or the Investment Company Act of 1940 and rules and regulations promulgated under this Act or the Investment Company Act of 1940.".

¶ 1218

SEC. 218. DEFINITION OF BROKER UNDER THE INVESTMENT ADVISERS ACT OF 1940.

Section 202(a)(3) of the Investment Advisers Act of 1940 (15 U.S.C. 80b-2(a)(3)) is amended to read as follows:

"(3) The term 'broker' has the same meaning as given in section 3 of the Securities Exchange Act of 1934.".

¶ 1219

SEC. 219. DEFINITION OF DEALER UNDER THE INVESTMENT ADVISERS ACT OF 1940.

Section 202(a)(7) of the Investment Advisers Act of 1940 (15 U.S.C. 80b-2(a)(7)) is amended to read as follows:

"(7) The term 'dealer' has the same meaning as given in section 3 of the Securities Exchange Act of 1934, but does not include an insurance company or investment company.".

¶ 1220

Sec. 220. INTERAGENCY CONSULTATION.

The Investment Advisers Act of 1940 (15 U.S.C. 80b-1 et seq.) is amended by inserting after section 210 the following new section:

"SEC. 210A. CONSULTATION.

"Examination results and other information

"(a)(1) The appropriate Federal banking agency shall provide the Commission upon request the results of any examination, reports, records, or other information to which such agency may have access—

"(A) with respect to the investment advisory activities of any—

"(i) bank holding company;

"(ii) bank; or

"(iii) separately identifiable department or division of a bank, that is registered under section 203 of this title; and

"(B) in the case of a bank holding company or bank that has a subsidiary or a separately identifiable department or division registered under that section, with respect to the investment advisory activities of such bank or bank holding company.

"(2) The Commission shall provide to the appropriate Federal banking agency upon request the results of any examination, reports, records, or other information with respect to the investment advisory activities of any bank holding company, bank, or separately identifiable department or division of a bank, which is registered under section 203 of this title.

"(3) Notwithstanding any other provision of law, the Commission and the appropriate Federal banking agencies shall not be compelled to disclose any information provided under paragraph (1) or (2). Nothing in this paragraph shall authorize the Commission or such agencies to withhold information from Congress, or prevent the Commission or such agencies from complying with a request for information from any other Federal department or agency or any self-regulatory organization requesting the information for purposes within the scope of its jurisdiction, or complying with an order of a court of the United States in an action brought by the United States, the Commission, or such agencies. For purposes of section 552 of title 5, United States Code, this paragraph shall be considered a statute described in subsection (b)(3)(B) of such section 552.

"Effect on other authority

"(b) Nothing in this section shall limit in any respect the authority of the appropriate Federal banking agency with respect to such bank holding company (or affiliates or subsidiaries thereof), bank, or subsidiary, department, or division or a bank under any other provision of law.

"Definition

"(c) For purposes of this section, the term 'appropriate Federal banking agency' shall have the same meaning as given in section 3 of the Federal Deposit Insurance Act.".

¶1221

SEC. 221. TREATMENT OF BANK COMMON TRUST FUNDS.

(a) SECURITIES ACT OF 1933.—Section 3(a)(2) of the Securities Act of 1933 (15 U.S.C. 77c(a)(2)) is amended by striking "or any interest or participation in any common trust fund or similar fund maintained by a bank exclusively for the collective investment and reinvestment of assets contributed thereto by such bank in its capacity as trustee, executor, administrator, or guardian" and inserting "or any interest or participation in any common trust fund or similar fund that is excluded from the definition of the term 'investment company' under section 3(c)(3) of the Investment Company Act of 1940".

(b) SECURITIES EXCHANGE ACT OF 1934.—Section 3(a)(12)(A)(iii) of the Securities Exchange Act of 1934 (15 U.S.C. 78c(a)(12)(A)(iii)) is amended to read as follows:

"(iii) any interest or participation in any common trust fund or similar fund that is excluded from the definition of the term 'investment company' under section 3(c)(3) of the Investment Company Act of 1940;".

(c) INVESTMENT COMPANY ACT OF 1940.—Section 3(c)(3) of the Investment Company Act of 1940 (15 U.S.C. 80a-3(c)(3)) is amended by inserting before the period the following: ", if—

"(A) such fund is employed by the bank solely as an aid to the administration of trusts, estates, or other accounts created and maintained for a fiduciary purpose;

"(B) except in connection with the ordinary advertising of the bank's fiduciary services, interests in such fund are not—

"(i) advertised; or

"(ii) offered for sale to the general public; and

"(C) fees and expenses charged by such fund are not in contravention of fiduciary principles established under applicable Federal or State law".

¶1222

SEC. 222. STATUTORY DISQUALIFICATION FOR BANK WRONGDOING.

Section 9(a) of the Investment Company Act of 1940 (15 U.S.C. 80a-9(a)) is amended in paragraphs (1) and (2) by striking "securities dealer, transfer agent," and inserting "securities dealer, bank, transfer agent,".

¶1223

SEC. 223. CONFORMING CHANGE IN DEFINITION.

Section 2(a)(5) of the Investment Company Act of 1940 (15 U.S.C. 80a-2(a)(5)) is amended by striking "(A) a banking institution organized under the laws of the United States" and inserting "(A) a depository institution (as defined in section 3 of the Federal Deposit Insurance Act) or a branch or agency of a foreign bank (as such terms are defined in section 1(b) of the International Banking Act of 1978)".

¶1224

SEC. 224. CONFORMING AMENDMENT.

Section 202 of the Investment Advisers Act of 1940 (15 U.S.C. 80b-2) is amended by adding at the end the following new subsection:

"Consideration of promotion of efficiency, competition, and capital formation

"(c) Whenever pursuant to this title the Commission is engaged in rulemaking and is required to consider or determine whether an action is necessary or appropriate in the public interest, the Commission shall also consider, in addition to the protection of investors, whether the action will promote efficiency, competition, and capital formation.".

¶ 1225

SEC. 225. **EFFECTIVE DATE.**

This subtitle shall take effect 18 months after the date of the enactment of this Act.

Subtitle C—Securities and Exchange Commission Supervision of Investment Bank Holding Companies

¶ 1231

SEC. 231. **SUPERVISION OF INVESTMENT BANK HOLDING COMPANIES BY THE SECURITIES AND EXCHANGE COMMISSION.**

(a) AMENDMENT.—Section 17 of the Securities Exchange Act of 1934 (15 U.S.C. 78q) is amended—

(1) by redesignating subsection (i) as subsection (k); and

(2) by inserting after subsection (h) the following new subsections:

"Investment bank holding companies

"(i)(1) ELECTIVE SUPERVISION OF AN INVESTMENT BANK HOLDING COMPANY NOT HAVING A BANK OR SAVINGS ASSOCIATION AFFILIATE.—

"(A) IN GENERAL.—An investment bank holding company that is not—

"(i) an affiliate of an insured bank (other than an institution described in subparagraph (D), (F), or (G) of section 2(c)(2), or held under section 4(f), of the Bank Holding Company Act of 1956), or a savings association;

"(ii) a foreign bank, foreign company, or company that is described in section 8(a) of the International Banking Act of 1978; or

"(iii) a foreign bank that controls, directly or indirectly, a corporation chartered under section 25A of the Federal Reserve Act,

may elect to become supervised by filing with the Commission a notice of intention to become supervised, pursuant to subparagraph (B) of this paragraph. Any investment bank holding company filing such a notice shall be supervised in accordance with this section and comply with the rules promulgated by the Commission applicable to supervised investment bank holding companies.

"(B) NOTIFICATION OF STATUS AS A SUPERVISED INVESTMENT BANK HOLDING COMPANY.—An investment bank holding company that elects under subparagraph (A) to become supervised by the Commission shall file with the Commission a written notice of intention to become supervised by the Commission in such form and containing such information and documents concerning such investment bank holding company as the Commission, by rule, may prescribe as necessary or appropriate in furtherance of the purposes of this section. Unless the Commission finds that such supervision is not necessary or appropriate in furtherance of the purposes of this section, such supervision shall become effective 45 days after the date of receipt of such written notice by the Commission or within such shorter time period as the Commission, by rule or order, may determine.

"(2) ELECTION NOT TO BE SUPERVISED BY THE COMMISSION AS AN INVESTMENT BANK HOLDING COMPANY.—

"(A) VOLUNTARY WITHDRAWAL.—A supervised investment bank holding company that is supervised pursuant to paragraph (1) may, upon such terms and conditions as the Commission deems necessary or appropriate, elect not to be supervised by the Commission by filing a written notice of withdrawal from Commission supervision. Such notice shall not become effective until 1 year after receipt by the Commission, or such shorter or longer period as the Commission deems necessary or appropriate to ensure effective supervision of the material risks to the supervised investment bank holding company and to the affiliated broker or dealer, or to prevent evasion of the purposes of this section.

"(B) DISCONTINUATION OF COMMISSION SUPERVISION.—If the Commission finds that any supervised investment bank holding company that is supervised pursuant to paragraph (1) is no longer in existence or has ceased to be an investment bank holding company, or if the Commission finds that continued supervision of such a supervised investment bank holding company is not consistent with the purposes of this section, the Commission may discontinue the supervision pursuant to a rule or order, if any, promulgated by the Commission under this section.

"(3) SUPERVISION OF INVESTMENT BANK HOLDING COMPANIES.—

"(A) RECORDKEEPING AND REPORTING.—

"(i) IN GENERAL.—Every supervised investment bank holding company and each affiliate thereof shall make and keep for prescribed periods such records, furnish copies thereof, and make such reports, as the Commission may require by rule, in order to keep the Commission informed as to—

"(I) the company's or affiliate's activities, financial condition, policies, systems for monitoring and controlling financial and operational risks, and transactions and relationships between any broker or dealer affiliate of the supervised investment bank holding company; and

"(II) the extent to which the company or affiliate has complied with the provisions of this Act and regulations prescribed and orders issued under this Act.

"(ii) FORM AND CONTENTS.—Such records and reports shall be prepared in such form and according to such specifications (including certification by an independent public accountant), as the Commission may require and shall be provided promptly at any time upon request by the Commission. Such records and reports may include—

"(I) a balance sheet and income statement;

"(II) an assessment of the consolidated capital of the supervised investment bank holding company;

"(III) an independent auditor's report attesting to the supervised investment bank holding company's compliance with its internal risk management and internal control objectives; and

"(IV) reports concerning the extent to which the company or affiliate has complied with the provisions of this title and any regulations prescribed and orders issued under this title.

"(B) USE OF EXISTING REPORTS.—

"(i) IN GENERAL.—The Commission shall, to the fullest extent possible, accept reports in fulfillment of the requirements under this paragraph that the supervised investment bank holding company or its affiliates have been required to provide to another appropriate regulatory agency or self-regulatory organization.

"(ii) AVAILABILITY.—A supervised investment bank holding company or an affiliate of such company shall provide to the Commission, at the request of the Commission, any report referred to in clause (i).

"(C) EXAMINATION AUTHORITY.—

"(i) FOCUS OF EXAMINATION AUTHORITY.—The Commission may make examinations of any supervised investment bank holding company and any affiliate of such company in order to—

"(I) inform the Commission regarding—

"(aa) the nature of the operations and financial condition of the supervised investment bank holding company and its affiliates;

"(bb) the financial and operational risks within the supervised investment bank holding company that may affect any broker or dealer controlled by such supervised investment bank holding company; and

"(cc) the systems of the supervised investment bank holding company and its affiliates for monitoring and controlling those risks; and

"(II) monitor compliance with the provisions of this subsection, provisions governing transactions and relationships between any broker or dealer affiliated with the supervised investment bank holding company and any of the company's other affiliates, and applicable provisions of subchapter II of chapter 53, title 31, United States Code (commonly referred to as the 'Bank Secrecy Act') and regulations thereunder.

"(ii) RESTRICTED FOCUS OF EXAMINATIONS.—The Commission shall limit the focus and scope of any examination of a supervised investment bank holding company to—

"(I) the company; and

"(II) any affiliate of the company that, because of its size, condition, or activities, the nature or size of the transactions between such affiliate and any affiliated broker or dealer, or the centralization of functions within the holding company system, could, in the discretion of the Commission, have a materially adverse effect on the operational or financial condition of the broker or dealer.

"(iii) DEFERENCE TO OTHER EXAMINATIONS.—For purposes of this subparagraph, the Commission shall, to the fullest extent possible, use the reports of examination of an institution described in subparagraph (D), (F), or (G) of section 2(c)(2), or held under section 4(f), of the Bank Holding Company Act of 1956 made by the appropriate regulatory agency, or of a licensed insurance company made by the appropriate State insurance regulator.

"(4) FUNCTIONAL REGULATION OF BANKING AND INSURANCE ACTIVITIES OF SUPERVISED INVESTMENT BANK HOLDING COMPANIES.—The Commission shall defer to—

"(A) the appropriate regulatory agency with regard to all interpretations of, and the enforcement of, applicable banking laws relating to the activities, conduct, ownership, and operations of banks, and institutions described in subparagraph (D), (F), and (G) of section 2(c)(2), or held under section 4(f), of the Bank Holding Company Act of 1956; and

"(B) the appropriate State insurance regulators with regard to all interpretations of, and the enforcement of, applicable State insurance laws relating to the activities, conduct, and operations of insurance companies and insurance agents.

"(5) DEFINITIONS.—For purposes of this subsection:

"(A) The term 'investment bank holding company' means—

"(i) any person other than a natural person that owns or controls one or more brokers or dealers; and

"(ii) the associated persons of the investment bank holding company.

"(B) The term 'supervised investment bank holding company' means any investment bank holding company that is supervised by the Commission pursuant to this subsection.

"(C) The terms 'affiliate', 'bank', 'bank holding company', 'company', 'control', and 'savings association' have the same meanings as given in section 2 of the Bank Holding Company Act of 1956 (12 U.S.C. 1841).

"(D) The term 'insured bank' has the same meaning as given in section 3 of the Federal Deposit Insurance Act.

"(E) The term 'foreign bank' has the same meaning as given in section 1(b)(7) of the International Banking Act of 1978.

"(F) The terms 'person associated with an investment bank holding company' and 'associated person of an investment bank holding company' mean any person directly or indirectly controlling, controlled by, or under common control with, an investment bank holding company.

"Authority to limit disclosure of information

"(j) Notwithstanding any other provision of law, the Commission shall not be compelled to disclose any information required to be reported under subsection (h) or (i) or any information supplied to the Commission by any domestic or foreign regulatory agency that relates to the financial or operational condition of any associated person of a broker or dealer, investment bank holding company, or any affiliate of an investment bank holding company. Nothing in this subsection shall authorize the Commission to withhold information from Congress, or prevent the Commission from complying with a request for information from any other Federal department or agency or any self-regulatory organization requesting the information for purposes within the scope of its jurisdiction, or complying with an order of a court of the United States in an action brought by the United States or the Commission. For purposes of section 552 of title 5, United States Code, this subsection shall be considered a statute described in subsection (b)(3)(B) of such section 552. In prescribing regulations to carry out the requirements of this subsection, the Commission shall designate information described in or obtained pursuant to subparagraphs (A), (B), and (C) of subsection (i)(5) as confidential information for purposes of section 24(b)(2) of this title.".

(b) CONFORMING AMENDMENTS.—

(1) Section 3(a)(34) of the Securities Exchange Act of 1934 (15 U.S.C. 78c(a)(34)) is amended by adding at the end the following new subparagraph:

"(H) When used with respect to an institution described in subparagraph (D), (F), or (G) of section 2(c)(2), or held under section 4(f), of the Bank Holding Company Act of 1956—

"(i) the Comptroller of the Currency, in the case of a national bank or a bank in the District of Columbia examined by the Comptroller of the Currency;

"(ii) the Board of Governors of the Federal Reserve System, in the case of a State member bank of the Federal Reserve System or any corporation chartered under section 25A of the Federal Reserve Act;

"(iii) the Federal Deposit Insurance Corporation, in the case of any other bank the deposits of which are insured in accordance with the Federal Deposit Insurance Act; or

"(iv) the Commission in the case of all other such institutions.".

(2) Section 1112(e) of the Right to Financial Privacy Act of 1978 (12 U.S.C. 3412(e)) is amended—

(A) by striking "this title" and inserting "law"; and

(B) by inserting ", examination reports" after "financial records".

Subtitle D—Banks and Bank Holding Companies

¶ 1241

SEC. 241. CONSULTATION.

(a) IN GENERAL.—The Securities and Exchange Commission shall consult and coordinate comments with the appropriate Federal banking agency before taking any action or rendering any opinion with respect to the manner in which any insured depository institution or depository institution holding company reports loan loss reserves in its financial statement, including the amount of any such loan loss reserve.

(b) DEFINITIONS.—For purposes of subsection (a), the terms "insured depository institution", "depository institution holding company", and "appropriate Federal banking agency" have the same meaning as given in section 3 of the Federal Deposit Insurance Act.

TITLE III—INSURANCE

Subtitle A—State Regulation of Insurance

¶ 1301

SEC. 301. FUNCTIONAL REGULATION OF INSURANCE.

The insurance activities of any person (including a national bank exercising its power to act as agent under the eleventh undesignated paragraph of section 13 of the Federal Reserve Act) shall be functionally regulated by the States, subject to section 104.

¶ 1302

SEC. 302. INSURANCE UNDERWRITING IN NATIONAL BANKS.

(a) IN GENERAL.—Except as provided in section 303, a national bank and the subsidiaries of a national bank may not provide insurance in a State as principal except that this prohibition shall not apply to authorized products.

(b) AUTHORIZED PRODUCTS.—For the purposes of this section, a product is authorized if—

(1) as of January 1, 1999, the Comptroller of the Currency had determined in writing that national banks may provide such product as principal, or national banks were in fact lawfully providing such product as principal;

(2) no court of relevant jurisdiction had, by final judgment, overturned a determination of the Comptroller of the Currency that national banks may provide such product as principal; and

(3) the product is not title insurance, or an annuity contract the income of which is subject to tax treatment under section 72 of the Internal Revenue Code of 1986.

(c) DEFINITION.—For purposes of this section, the term "insurance" means—

(1) any product regulated as insurance as of January 1, 1999, in accordance with the relevant State insurance law, in the State in which the product is provided;

(2) any product first offered after January 1, 1999, which—

(A) a State insurance regulator determines shall be regulated as insurance in the State in which the product is provided because the product insures, guarantees, or indemnifies against liability, loss of life, loss of health, or loss through damage to or destruction of property, including, but not limited to, surety bonds, life insurance, health insurance, title insurance, and property and casualty insurance (such as private passenger or commercial automobile, homeowners, mortgage, commercial multiperil, general liability, professional liability, workers' compensation, fire and allied lines, farm owners multiperil, aircraft, fidelity, surety, medical malpractice, ocean marine, inland marine, and boiler and machinery insurance); and

(B) is not a product or service of a bank that is—

(i) a deposit product;

(ii) a loan, discount, letter of credit, or other extension of credit;

(iii) a trust or other fiduciary service;

(iv) a qualified financial contract (as defined in or determined pursuant to section 11(e)(8)(D)(i) of the Federal Deposit Insurance Act); or

(v) a financial guaranty, except that this subparagraph (B) shall not apply to a product that includes an insurance component such that if the product is offered or proposed to be offered by the bank as principal—

(I) it would be treated as a life insurance contract under section 7702 of the Internal Revenue Code of 1986; or

(II) in the event that the product is not a letter of credit or other similar extension of credit, a qualified financial contract, or a financial guaranty, it would qualify for treatment for losses incurred with respect to such product under section 832(b)(5) of the Internal

Revenue Code of 1986, if the bank were subject to tax as an insurance company under section 831 of that Code; or

(3) any annuity contract, the income on which is subject to tax treatment under section 72 of the Internal Revenue Code of 1986.

(d) RULE OF CONSTRUCTION.—For purposes of this section, providing insurance (including reinsurance) outside the United States that insures, guarantees, or indemnifies insurance products provided in a State, or that indemnifies an insurance company with regard to insurance products provided in a State, shall be considered to be providing insurance as principal in that State.

¶ 1303

SEC. 303. TITLE INSURANCE ACTIVITIES OF NATIONAL BANKS AND THEIR AFFILIATES.

(a) GENERAL PROHIBITION.—No national bank may engage in any activity involving the underwriting or sale of title insurance.

(b) NONDISCRIMINATION PARITY EXCEPTION.—

(1) IN GENERAL.—Notwithstanding any other provision of law (including section 104 of this Act), in the case of any State in which banks organized under the laws of such State are authorized to sell title insurance as agent, a national bank may sell title insurance as agent in such State, but only in the same manner, to the same extent, and under the same restrictions as such State banks are authorized to sell title insurance as agent in such State.

(2) COORDINATION WITH "WILDCARD" PROVISION.—A State law which authorizes State banks to engage in any activities in such State in which a national bank may engage shall not be treated as a statute which authorizes State banks to sell title insurance as agent, for purposes of paragraph (1).

(c) GRANDFATHERING WITH CONSISTENT REGULATION.—

(1) IN GENERAL.—Except as provided in paragraphs (2) and (3) and notwithstanding subsections (a) and (b), a national bank, and a subsidiary of a national bank, may conduct title insurance activities which such national bank or subsidiary was actively and lawfully conducting before the date of the enactment of this Act.

(2) INSURANCE AFFILIATE.—In the case of a national bank which has an affiliate which provides insurance as principal and is not a subsidiary of the bank, the national bank and any subsidiary of the national bank may not engage in the underwriting of title insurance pursuant to paragraph (1).

(3) INSURANCE SUBSIDIARY.—In the case of a national bank which has a subsidiary which provides insurance as principal and has no affiliate other than a subsidiary which provides insurance as principal, the national bank may not directly engage in any activity involving the underwriting of title insurance.

(d) "AFFILIATE" AND "SUBSIDIARY" DEFINED.—For purposes of this section, the terms "affiliate" and "subsidiary" have the same meanings as in section 2 of the Bank Holding Company Act of 1956.

(e) RULE OF CONSTRUCTION.—No provision of this Act or any other Federal law shall be construed as superseding or affecting a State law which was in effect before the date of the enactment of this Act and which prohibits title insurance from being offered, provided, or sold in such State, or from being underwritten with respect to real property in such State, by any person whatsoever.

¶ 1304

SEC. 304. **EXPEDITED AND EQUALIZED DISPUTE RESOLUTION FOR FEDERAL REGULATORS.**

(a) FILING IN COURT OF APPEALS.—In the case of a regulatory conflict between a State insurance regulator and a Federal regulator regarding insurance issues, including whether a State law, rule, regulation, order, or interpretation regarding any insurance sales or solicitation activity is properly treated as preempted under Federal law, the Federal or State regulator may seek expedited judicial review of such determination by the United States Court of Appeals for the circuit in which the State is located or in the United States Court of Appeals for the District of Columbia Circuit by filing a petition for review in such court.

(b) EXPEDITED REVIEW.—The United States Court of Appeals in which a petition for review is filed in accordance with subsection (a) shall complete all action on such petition, including rendering a judgment, before the end of the 60-day period beginning on the date on which such petition is filed, unless all parties to such proceeding agree to any extension of such period.

(c) SUPREME COURT REVIEW.—Any request for certiorari to the Supreme Court of the United States of any judgment of a United States Court of Appeals with respect to a petition for review under this section shall be filed with the Supreme Court of the United States as soon as practicable after such judgment is issued.

(d) STATUTE OF LIMITATION.—No petition may be filed under this section challenging an order, ruling, determination, or other action of a Federal regulator or State insurance regulator after the later of—

(1) the end of the 12-month period beginning on the date on which the first public notice is made of such order, ruling, determination or other action in its final form; or

(2) the end of the 6-month period beginning on the date on which such order, ruling, determination, or other action takes effect.

(e) STANDARD OF REVIEW.—The court shall decide a petition filed under this section based on its review on the merits of all questions presented under State and Federal law, including the nature of the product or activity and the history and purpose of its regulation under State and Federal law, without unequal deference.

¶ 1305

SEC. 305. **INSURANCE CUSTOMER PROTECTIONS.**

The Federal Deposit Insurance Act (12 U.S.C. 1811 et seq.) is amended by inserting after section 46, as added by section 121(d) of this Act, the following new section:

"SEC. 47. INSURANCE CUSTOMER PROTECTIONS.

"Regulations required

"(a)(1) IN GENERAL.—The Federal banking agencies shall prescribe and publish in final form, before the end of the 1-year period beginning on the date of the enactment of the Gramm-Leach-Bliley Act, customer protection regulations (which the agencies jointly determine to be appropriate) that—

"(A) apply to retail sales practices, solicitations, advertising, or offers of any insurance product by any depository institution or any person that is engaged in such activities at an office of the institution or on behalf of the institution; and

"(B) are consistent with the requirements of this Act and provide such additional protections for customers to whom such sales, solicitations, advertising, or offers are directed.

"(2) APPLICABILITY TO SUBSIDIARIES.—The regulations prescribed pursuant to paragraph (1) shall extend such protections to any subsidiary of a depository institution, as deemed appropriate by the regulators referred to in paragraph (3), where such extension is determined to be necessary to ensure the consumer protections provided by this section.

"(3) CONSULTATION AND JOINT REGULATIONS.—The Federal banking agencies shall consult with each other and prescribe joint regulations pursuant to paragraph (1), after consultation with the State insurance regulators, as appropriate.

"Sales practices

"(b) The regulations prescribed pursuant to subsection (a) shall include antitying and anticoercion rules applicable to the sale of insurance products that prohibit a depository institution from engaging in any practice that would lead a customer to believe an extension of credit, in violation of section 106(b) of the Bank Holding Company Act Amendments of 1970, is conditional upon—

"(1) the purchase of an insurance product from the institution or any of its affiliates; or

"(2) an agreement by the consumer not to obtain, or a prohibition on the consumer from obtaining, an insurance product from an unaffiliated entity.

"Disclosures and advertising

"(c) The regulations prescribed pursuant to subsection (a) shall include the following provisions relating to disclosures and advertising in connection with the initial purchase of an insurance product:

"(1) DISCLOSURES.—

"(A) IN GENERAL.—Requirements that the following disclosures be made orally and in writing before the completion of the initial sale and, in the case of clause (iii), at the time of application for an extension of credit:

"(i) UNINSURED STATUS.—As appropriate, the product is not insured by the Federal Deposit Insurance Corporation, the United States Government, or the depository institution.

"(ii) INVESTMENT RISK.—In the case of a variable annuity or other insurance product which involves an investment risk, that there is an investment risk associated with the product, including possible loss of value.

"(iii) COERCION.—The approval of an extension of credit may not be conditioned on—

"(I) the purchase of an insurance product from the institution in which the application for credit is pending or any of affiliate of the institution; or

"(II) an agreement by the consumer not to obtain, or a prohibition on the consumer from obtaining, an insurance product from an unaffiliated entity.

"(B) MAKING DISCLOSURE READILY UNDERSTANDABLE.—Regulations prescribed under subparagraph (A) shall encourage the use of disclosure that is conspicuous, simple, direct, and readily understandable, such as the following:

"(i) 'NOT FDIC—INSURED'.

"(ii) 'NOT GUARANTEED BY THE BANK'.

"(iii) 'MAY GO DOWN IN VALUE'.

"(iv) 'NOT INSURED BY ANY GOVERNMENT AGENCY'.

"(C) LIMITATION.—Nothing in this paragraph requires the inclusion of the foregoing disclosures in advertisements of a general nature describing or listing the services or products offered by an institution.

"(D) MEANINGFUL DISCLOSURES.—Disclosures shall not be considered to be meaningfully provided under this paragraph if the institution or its representative states that disclosures required by this subsection were available to the customer in printed material available for distribution, where such printed material is not provided and such information is not orally disclosed to the customer.

"(E) ADJUSTMENTS FOR ALTERNATIVE METHODS OF PURCHASE.—In prescribing the requirements under subparagraphs (A) and (F), necessary adjustments shall be made for purchase in person, by telephone, or by electronic media to provide for the most appropriate and complete form of disclosure and acknowledgments.

"(F) CONSUMER ACKNOWLEDGMENT.—A requirement that a depository institution shall require any person selling an insurance product at any office of, or on behalf of, the institution to obtain, at the time a consumer receives the disclosures required under this paragraph or at the time of the initial purchase by the consumer of such product, an acknowledgment by such consumer of the receipt of the disclosure required under this subsection with respect to such product.

"(2) PROHIBITION ON MISREPRESENTATIONS.—A prohibition on any practice, or any advertising, at any office of, or on behalf of, the depository institution, or any subsidiary, as appropriate, that could mislead any person or otherwise cause a reasonable person to reach an erroneous belief with respect to—

"(A) the uninsured nature of any insurance product sold, or offered for sale, by the institution or any subsidiary of the institution;

"(B) in the case of a variable annuity or insurance product that involves an investment risk, the investment risk associated with any such product; or

"(C) in the case of an institution or subsidiary at which insurance products are sold or offered for sale, the fact that—

"(i) the approval of an extension of credit to a customer by the institution or subsidiary may not be conditioned on the purchase of an insurance product by such customer from the institution or subsidiary; and

"(ii) the customer is free to purchase the insurance product from another source.

"Separation of banking and nonbanking activities

"(d)(1) REGULATIONS REQUIRED.—The regulations prescribed pursuant to subsection (a) shall include such provisions as the Federal banking agencies consider appropriate to ensure that the routine acceptance of deposits is kept, to the extent practicable, physically segregated from insurance product activity.

"(2) REQUIREMENTS.—Regulations prescribed pursuant to paragraph (1) shall include the following requirements:

"(A) SEPARATE SETTING.—A clear delineation of the setting in which, and the circumstances under which, transactions involving insurance products should be conducted in a location physically segregated from an area where retail deposits are routinely accepted.

"(B) REFERRALS.—Standards that permit any person accepting deposits from the public in an area where such transactions are routinely conducted in a depository institution to refer a customer who seeks to purchase any insurance product to a qualified person who sells such product, only if the person making the referral receives no more than a one-time nominal fee of a fixed dollar amount for each referral that does not depend on whether the referral results in a transaction.

"(C) QUALIFICATION AND LICENSING REQUIREMENTS.—Standards prohibiting any depository institution from permitting any person to sell or offer for sale any insurance product in any part of any office of the institution, or on behalf of the institution, unless such person is appropriately qualified and licensed.

"Domestic violence discrimination prohibition

"(e)(1) IN GENERAL.—In the case of an applicant for, or an insured under, any insurance product described in paragraph (2), the status of the applicant or insured as a victim of domestic violence, or as a provider of services to victims of domestic violence, shall not be considered as a criterion in any decision with regard to insurance underwriting, pricing, renewal, or scope of coverage of insurance policies, or payment of insurance claims, except as required or expressly permitted under State law.

"(2) SCOPE OF APPLICATION.—The prohibition contained in paragraph (1) shall apply to any life or health insurance product which is sold or offered for sale, as principal, agent, or broker, by any depository institution or any person who is engaged in such activities at an office of the institution or on behalf of the institution.

"(3) DOMESTIC VIOLENCE DEFINED.—For purposes of this subsection, the term 'domestic violence' means the occurrence of one or more of the following acts by a current or former family member, household member, intimate partner, or caretaker:

"(A) Attempting to cause or causing or threatening another person physical harm, severe emotional distress, psychological trauma, rape, or sexual assault.

"(B) Engaging in a course of conduct or repeatedly committing acts toward another person, including following the person without proper authority, under circumstances that place the person in reasonable fear of bodily injury or physical harm.

"(C) Subjecting another person to false imprisonment.

"(D) Attempting to cause or cause damage to property so as to intimidate or attempt to control the behavior of another person.

"Consumer grievance process

"(f) The Federal banking agencies shall jointly establish a consumer complaint mechanism, for receiving and expeditiously addressing consumer complaints alleging a violation of regulations issued under the section, which shall—

"(1) establish a group within each regulatory agency to receive such complaints;

"(2) develop procedures for investigating such complaints;

"(3) develop procedures for informing consumers of rights they may have in connection with such complaints; and

"(4) develop procedures for addressing concerns raised by such complaints, as appropriate, including procedures for the recovery of losses to the extent appropriate.

"Effect on other authority

"(g)(1) IN GENERAL.—No provision of this section shall be construed as granting, limiting, or otherwise affecting—

"(A) any authority of the Securities and Exchange Commission, any self-regulatory organization, the Municipal Securities Rulemaking Board, or the Secretary of the Treasury under any Federal securities law; or

"(B) except as provided in paragraph (2), any authority of any State insurance commission (or any agency or office performing like functions), or of any State securities commission (or any agency or office performing like functions), or other State authority under any State law.

"(2) COORDINATION WITH STATE LAW.—

"(A) IN GENERAL.—Except as provided in subparagraph (B), insurance customer protection regulations prescribed by a Federal banking agency under this section shall not apply to retail sales, solicitations, advertising, or offers of any insurance product by any depository institution or to any person who is engaged in such activities at an office of such institution or on behalf of the institution, in a State where the State has in effect statutes, regulations, orders, or interpretations, that are inconsistent with or contrary to the regulations prescribed by the Federal banking agencies.

"(B) PREEMPTION.—

"(i) IN GENERAL.—If, with respect to any provision of the regulations prescribed under this section, the Board of Governors of the Federal Reserve System, the Comptroller of the Currency, and the Board of Directors of the Corporation determine jointly that the protection afforded by such provision for customers is greater than the protection provided by a comparable provision of the statutes, regulations, orders, or interpretations referred to in subparagraph (A) of any State, the appropriate State regulatory authority shall be notified of such determination in writing.

"(ii) CONSIDERATIONS.—Before making a final determination under clause (i), the Federal agencies referred to in clause (i) shall give appropriate consideration to comments submitted by the appropriate State regulatory authorities relating to the level of protection afforded to consumers under State law.

"(iii) FEDERAL PREEMPTION AND ABILITY OF STATES TO OVERRIDE FEDERAL PREEMPTION.—If the Federal agencies referred to in clause (i) jointly determine that any provision of the regulations prescribed under this section affords greater protections than a comparable State law, rule, regulation, order, or interpretation, those agencies shall send a written preemption notice to the appropriate State regulatory authority to notify the State that the Federal provision will preempt the State provision and will become applicable unless, not later than 3 years after the date of such notice, the State adopts legislation to override such preemption.

"Non-discrimination against non-affiliated agents

"(h) The Federal banking agencies shall ensure that the regulations prescribed pursuant to subsection (a) shall not have the effect of discriminating, either intentionally or unintentionally, against any person engaged in insurance sales or solicitations that is not affiliated with a depository institution.".

¶ 1306

SEC. 306. **CERTAIN STATE AFFILIATION LAWS PREEMPTED FOR INSURANCE COMPANIES AND AFFILIATES.**

Except as provided in section 104(c)(2), no State may, by law, regulation, order, interpretation, or otherwise—

(1) prevent or significantly interfere with the ability of any insurer, or any affiliate of an insurer (whether such affiliate is organized as a stock company, mutual holding company, or otherwise), to become a financial holding company or to acquire control of a depository institution;

(2) limit the amount of an insurer's assets that may be invested in the voting securities of a depository institution (or any company which controls such institution), except that the laws of an insurer's State of domicile may limit the amount of such investment to an amount that is not less than 5 percent of the insurer's admitted assets; or

(3) prevent, significantly interfere with, or have the authority to review, approve, or disapprove a plan of reorganization by which an insurer proposes to reorganize from mutual form to become a stock insurer (whether as a direct or indirect subsidiary of a mutual holding company or otherwise) unless such State is the State of domicile of the insurer.

¶ 1307

SEC. 307. **INTERAGENCY CONSULTATION.**

(a) PURPOSE.—It is the intention of the Congress that the Board of Governors of the Federal Reserve System, as the umbrella supervisor for financial holding companies, and the State insurance regulators, as the functional regulators of companies engaged in insurance activities, coordinate efforts to supervise companies that control both a depository institution and a company engaged in insurance activities regulated under State law. In particular, Congress believes that the Board and the State insurance regulators should share, on a confidential basis, information relevant to the supervision of companies that control both a depository institution and a company engaged in insurance activities, including information regarding the financial health of the consolidated organization and information regarding transactions and relationships between insurance companies and affiliated depository institutions. The appropriate Federal banking agencies for depository institutions should also share, on a confidential basis, information with the relevant State insurance regulators regarding transactions and relationships between depository institutions and affiliated companies engaged in insurance activities. The purpose of this section is to encourage this coordination and confidential sharing of information, and to thereby improve both the efficiency and the quality of the supervision of financial holding companies and their affiliated depository institutions and companies engaged in insurance activities.

(b) EXAMINATION RESULTS AND OTHER INFORMATION.—

(1) INFORMATION OF THE BOARD.—Upon the request of the appropriate insurance regulator of any State, the Board may provide any information of the Board regarding the financial condition, risk management policies, and operations of any financial holding company that controls a company that is engaged in insurance activities and is regulated by such State insurance regulator, and regarding any transaction or relationship between such an insurance company and any affiliated depository institution. The Board may provide any other information to the appropriate State insurance regulator that the Board believes is necessary or appropriate to permit the State insurance regulator to administer and enforce applicable State insurance laws.

(2) BANKING AGENCY INFORMATION.—Upon the request of the appropriate insurance regulator of any State, the appropriate Federal banking agency may provide any information of the agency regarding any transaction or relationship between a depository institution supervised by such Federal banking agency and any affiliated company that is engaged in insurance activities regulated by such State insurance regulator. The appropriate Federal banking agency may provide any other information to the appropriate State insurance regulator that the agency believes is necessary or appropriate to permit the State insurance regulator to administer and enforce applicable State insurance laws.

(3) STATE INSURANCE REGULATOR INFORMATION.—Upon the request of the Board or the appropriate Federal banking agency, a State insurance regulator may provide any examination or other reports, records, or other information to which such insurance regulator may have access with respect to a company which—

(A) is engaged in insurance activities and regulated by such insurance regulator; and

(B) is an affiliate of a depository institution or financial holding company.

(c) CONSULTATION.—Before making any determination relating to the initial affiliation of, or the continuing affiliation of, a depository institution or financial holding company with a company engaged in insurance activities, the appropriate Federal banking agency shall consult with the appropriate State insurance regulator of such company and take the views of such insurance regulator into account in making such determination.

(d) EFFECT ON OTHER AUTHORITY.—Nothing in this section shall limit in any respect the authority of the appropriate Federal banking agency with respect to a depository institution or bank holding company or any affiliate thereof under any provision of law.

(e) CONFIDENTIALITY AND PRIVILEGE.—

(1) CONFIDENTIALITY.—The appropriate Federal banking agency shall not provide any information or material that is entitled to confidential treatment under applicable Federal banking agency regulations, or other applicable law, to a State insurance regulator unless such regulator agrees to maintain the information or material in confidence and to take all reasonable steps to oppose any effort to secure disclosure of the information or material by the regulator. The appropriate Federal banking agency shall treat as confidential any information or material obtained from a State insurance regulator that is entitled to confidential treatment under applicable State regulations, or other applicable law, and take all reasonable steps to oppose any effort to secure disclosure of the information or material by the Federal banking agency.

(2) PRIVILEGE.—The provision pursuant to this section of information or material by a Federal banking agency or State insurance regulator shall not constitute a waiver of, or otherwise affect, any privilege to which the information or material is otherwise subject.

(f) DEFINITIONS.—For purposes of this section, the following definitions shall apply:

(1) APPROPRIATE FEDERAL BANKING AGENCY; DEPOSITORY INSTITUTION.—The terms "appropriate Federal banking agency" and "depository institution" have the same meanings as in section 3 of the Federal Deposit Insurance Act.

(2) BOARD AND FINANCIAL HOLDING COMPANY.—The terms "Board" and "financial holding company" have the same meanings as in section 2 of the Bank Holding Company Act of 1956.

¶ 1308

SEC. 308. **DEFINITION OF STATE.**

For purposes of this subtitle, the term "State" means any State of the United States, the District of Columbia, any territory of the United States, Puerto Rico, Guam, American Samoa, the Trust Territory of the Pacific Islands, the Virgin Islands, and the Northern Mariana Islands.

Subtitle B—Redomestication of Mutual Insurers

¶ 1311

SEC. 311. **GENERAL APPLICATION.**

This subtitle shall only apply to a mutual insurance company in a State which has not enacted a law which expressly establishes reasonable terms and conditions for a mutual insurance company domiciled in such State to reorganize into a mutual holding company.

¶ 1312

SEC. 312. **REDOMESTICATION OF MUTUAL INSURERS.**

(a) REDOMESTICATION.—A mutual insurer organized under the laws of any State may transfer its domicile to a transferee domicile as a step in a reorganization in which, pursuant to the laws of the transferee domicile and consistent with the standards in subsection (f), the mutual insurer becomes a stock insurer that is a direct or indirect subsidiary of a mutual holding company.

(b) RESULTING DOMICILE.—Upon complying with the applicable law of the transferee domicile governing transfers of domicile and completion of a transfer pursuant to this section, the mutual insurer shall cease to be a domestic insurer in the transferor domicile and, as a continuation of its corporate existence, shall be a domestic insurer of the transferee domicile.

(c) LICENSES PRESERVED.—The certificate of authority, agents' appointments and licenses, rates, approvals and other items that a licensed State allows and that are in existence immediately prior to the date that a redomesticating insurer transfers its domicile pursuant to this subtitle shall continue in full force and effect upon transfer, if the insurer remains duly qualified to transact the business of insurance in such licensed State.

(d) EFFECTIVENESS OF OUTSTANDING POLICIES AND CONTRACTS.—

(1) IN GENERAL.—All outstanding insurance policies and annuities contracts of a redomesticating insurer shall remain in full force and effect and need not be endorsed as to the new domicile of the insurer, unless so ordered by the State insurance regulator of a licensed State, and then only in the case of outstanding policies and contracts whose owners reside in such licensed State.

(2) FORMS.—

(A) Applicable State law may require a redomesticating insurer to file new policy forms with the State insurance regulator of a licensed State on or before the effective date of the transfer.

(B) Notwithstanding subparagraph (A), a redomesticating insurer may use existing policy forms with appropriate endorsements to reflect the new domicile of the redomesticating insurer until the new policy forms are approved for use by the State insurance regulator of such licensed State.

(e) NOTICE.—A redomesticating insurer shall give notice of the proposed transfer to the State insurance regulator of each licensed State and shall file promptly any resulting amendments to corporate documents required to be filed by a foreign licensed mutual insurer with the insurance regulator of each such licensed State.

(f) PROCEDURAL REQUIREMENTS.—No mutual insurer may redomesticate to another State and reorganize into a mutual holding company pursuant to this section unless the State insurance regulator of the transferee domicile determines that the plan of reorganization of the insurer includes the following requirements:

(1) APPROVAL BY BOARD OF DIRECTORS AND POLICYHOLDERS.—The reorganization is approved by at least a majority of the board of directors of the mutual insurer and at least a majority of the policyholders who vote after notice, disclosure of the reorganization and the effects of the transaction on policyholder contractual rights, and reasonable opportunity to vote, in accordance with such notice, disclosure, and voting procedures as are approved by the State insurance regulator of the transferee domicile.

(2) CONTINUED VOTING CONTROL BY POLICYHOLDERS; REVIEW OF PUBLIC STOCK OFFERING.—After the consummation of a reorganization, the policyholders of the reorganized insurer shall have the same voting rights with respect to the mutual holding company as they had before the reorganization with respect to the mutual insurer. With respect to an initial public offering of stock, the offering shall be conducted in compliance with applicable securities laws and in a manner approved by the State insurance regulator of the transferee domicile.

(3) AWARD OF STOCK OR GRANT OF OPTIONS TO OFFICERS AND DIRECTORS.—During the applicable period provided for under the State law of the transferee domicile following completion of an initial public offering, or for a period of six months if no such applicable period is provided, neither a stock holding company nor the converted insurer shall award any stock options or stock grants to persons who are elected officers or directors of the mutual holding company, the stock holding company, or the converted insurer, except with respect to any such awards or options to which a person is entitled as a policyholder and as approved by the State insurance regulator of the transferee domicile.

(4) POLICYHOLDER RIGHTS.—Upon reorganization into a mutual holding company, the contractual rights of the policyholders are preserved.

(5) FAIR AND EQUITABLE TREATMENT OF POLICYHOLDERS.—The reorganization is approved as fair and equitable to the policyholders by the insurance regulator of the transferee domicile.

¶ 1313

SEC. 313. EFFECT ON STATE LAWS RESTRICTING REDOMESTICATION.

(a) IN GENERAL.—Unless otherwise permitted by this subtitle, State laws of any transferor domicile that conflict with the purposes and intent of this subtitle are preempted, including but not limited to—

(1) any law that has the purpose or effect of impeding the activities of, taking any action against, or applying any provision of law or regulation to, any insurer or an affiliate of such insurer because that insurer or any affiliate plans to redomesticate, or has redomesticated, pursuant to this subtitle;

(2) any law that has the purpose or effect of impeding the activities of, taking action against, or applying any provision of law or regulation to, any insured or any insurance licensee or other intermediary because such person has procured insurance from or placed insurance with any insurer or affiliate of such insurer that plans to redomesticate, or has redomesticated, pursuant to this subtitle, but only to the extent that such law would treat such insured licensee or other intermediary differently than if the person procured insurance from, or placed insurance with, an insured licensee or other intermediary which had not redomesticated; and

(3) any law that has the purpose or effect of terminating, because of the redomestication of a mutual insurer pursuant to this subtitle, any certificate of authority, agent appointment or license, rate approval, or other approval, of any State insurance regulator or other State authority in existence immediately prior to the redomestication in any State other than the transferee domicile.

(b) DIFFERENTIAL TREATMENT PROHIBITED.—No State law, regulation, interpretation, or functional equivalent thereof, of a State other than a transferee domicile may treat a redomesticating or redomesticated insurer or any affiliate thereof any differently than an insurer operating in that State that is not a redomesticating or redomesticated insurer.

(c) LAWS PROHIBITING OPERATIONS.—If any licensed State fails to issue, delays the issuance of, or seeks to revoke an original or renewal certificate of authority of a redomesticated insurer promptly following redomestication, except on grounds and in a manner consistent with its past practices regarding the issuance of certificates of authority to foreign insurers that are not redomesticating, then the redomesticating insurer shall be exempt from any State law of the licensed State to the extent that such State law or the operation of such State law would make unlawful, or regulate, directly or indirectly, the operation of the redomesticated insurer, except that such licensed State may require the redomesticated insurer to—

(1) comply with the unfair claim settlement practices law of the licensed State;

(2) pay, on a nondiscriminatory basis, applicable premium and other taxes which are levied on licensed insurers or policyholders under the laws of the licensed State;

(3) register with and designate the State insurance regulator as its agent solely for the purpose of receiving service of legal documents or process;

(4) submit to an examination by the State insurance regulator in any licensed State in which the redomesticated insurer is doing business to determine the insurer's financial condition, if—

(A) the State insurance regulator of the transferee domicile has not begun an examination of the redomesticated insurer and has not scheduled such an examination to begin before the end of the 1-year period beginning on the date of the redomestication; and

(B) any such examination is coordinated to avoid unjustified duplication and repetition;
(5) comply with a lawful order issued in—

(A) a delinquency proceeding commenced by the State insurance regulator of any licensed State if there has been a judicial finding of financial impairment under paragraph (7); or

(B) a voluntary dissolution proceeding;

(6) comply with any State law regarding deceptive, false, or fraudulent acts or practices, except that if the licensed State seeks an injunction regarding the conduct described in this paragraph, such injunction must be obtained from a court of competent jurisdiction as provided in section 314(a);

(7) comply with an injunction issued by a court of competent jurisdiction, upon a petition by the State insurance regulator alleging that the redomesticating insurer is in hazardous financial condition or is financially impaired;

(8) participate in any insurance insolvency guaranty association on the same basis as any other insurer licensed in the licensed State; and

(9) require a person acting, or offering to act, as an insurance licensee for a redomesticated insurer in the licensed State to obtain a license from that State, except that such State may not impose any qualification or requirement that discriminates against a nonresident insurance licensee.

¶ 1314

SEC. 314. OTHER PROVISIONS.

(a) JUDICIAL REVIEW.—The appropriate United States district court shall have exclusive jurisdiction over litigation arising under this section involving any redomesticating or redomesticated insurer.

(b) SEVERABILITY.—If any provision of this section, or the application thereof to any person or circumstances, is held invalid, the remainder of the section, and the application of such provision to other persons or circumstances, shall not be affected thereby.

¶ 1315

SEC. 315. DEFINITIONS.

For purposes of this subtitle, the following definitions shall apply:

(1) COURT OF COMPETENT JURISDICTION.—The term "court of competent jurisdiction" means a court authorized pursuant to section 314(a) to adjudicate litigation arising under this subtitle.

(2) DOMICILE.—The term "domicile" means the State in which an insurer is incorporated, chartered, or organized.

(3) INSURANCE LICENSEE.—The term "insurance licensee" means any person holding a license under State law to act as insurance agent, subagent, broker, or consultant.

(4) INSTITUTION.—The term "institution" means a corporation, joint stock company, limited liability company, limited liability partnership, association, trust, partnership, or any similar entity.

(5) LICENSED STATE.—The term "licensed State" means any State, the District of Columbia, any territory of the United States, Puerto Rico, Guam, American Samoa, the Trust Territory of the Pacific Islands, the Virgin Islands, and the Northern Mariana Islands in which the redomesticating insurer has a certificate of authority in effect immediately prior to the redomestication.

(6) MUTUAL INSURER.—The term "mutual insurer" means a mutual insurer organized under the laws of any State.

(7) PERSON.—The term "person" means an individual, institution, government or governmental agency, State or political subdivision of a State, public corporation, board, association, estate, trustee, or fiduciary, or other similar entity.

(8) POLICYHOLDER.—The term "policyholder" means the owner of a policy issued by a mutual insurer, except that, with respect to voting rights, the term means a member of a mutual insurer or mutual holding company granted the right to vote, as determined under applicable State law.

(9) REDOMESTICATED INSURER.—The term "redomesticated insurer" means a mutual insurer that has redomesticated pursuant to this subtitle.

(10) REDOMESTICATING INSURER.—The term "redomesticating insurer" means a mutual insurer that is redomesticating pursuant to this subtitle.

(11) REDOMESTICATION OR TRANSFER.—The term "redomestication" or "transfer" means the transfer of the domicile of a mutual insurer from one State to another State pursuant to this subtitle.

(12) STATE INSURANCE REGULATOR.—The term "State insurance regulator" means the principal insurance regulatory authority of a State, the District of Columbia, any territory of the United States, Puerto Rico, Guam, American Samoa, the Trust Territory of the Pacific Islands, the Virgin Islands, and the Northern Mariana Islands.

(13) STATE LAW.—The term "State law" means the statutes of any State, the District of Columbia, any territory of the United States, Puerto Rico, Guam, American Samoa, the Trust Territory of the Pacific Islands, the Virgin Islands, and the Northern Mariana Islands and any regulation, order, or requirement prescribed pursuant to any such statute.

(14) TRANSFEREE DOMICILE.—The term "transferee domicile" means the State to which a mutual insurer is redomesticating pursuant to this subtitle.

(15) TRANSFEROR DOMICILE.—The term "transferor domicile" means the State from which a mutual insurer is redomesticating pursuant to this subtitle.

¶ 1316

SEC. 316. **EFFECTIVE DATE.**

This subtitle shall take effect on the date of the enactment of this Act.

Subtitle C—National Association of Registered Agents and Brokers

¶ 1321

SEC. 321. **STATE FLEXIBILITY IN MULTISTATE LICENSING REFORMS.**

(a) IN GENERAL.—The provisions of this subtitle shall take effect unless, not later than 3 years after the date of the enactment of this Act, at least a majority of the States—

(1) have enacted uniform laws and regulations governing the licensure of individuals and entities authorized to sell and solicit the purchase of insurance within the State; or

(2) have enacted reciprocity laws and regulations governing the licensure of nonresident individuals and entities authorized to sell and solicit insurance within those States.

(b) UNIFORMITY REQUIRED.—States shall be deemed to have established the uniformity necessary to satisfy subsection (a)(1) if the States—

(1) establish uniform criteria regarding the integrity, personal qualifications, education, training, and experience of licensed insurance producers, including the qualification and training of sales personnel in ascertaining the appropriateness of a particular insurance product for a prospective customer;

(2) establish uniform continuing education requirements for licensed insurance producers;

(3) establish uniform ethics course requirements for licensed insurance producers in conjunction with the continuing education requirements under paragraph (2);

(4) establish uniform criteria to ensure that an insurance product, including any annuity contract, sold to a consumer is suitable and appropriate for the consumer based on financial information disclosed by the consumer; and

(5) do not impose any requirement upon any insurance producer to be licensed or otherwise qualified to do business as a nonresident that has the effect of limiting or conditioning that producer's activities because of its residence or place of operations, except that counter-signature requirements imposed on nonresident producers shall not be deemed to have the effect of limiting or conditioning a producer's activities because of its residence or place of operations under this section.

(c) RECIPROCITY REQUIRED.—States shall be deemed to have established the reciprocity required to satisfy subsection (a)(2) if the following conditions are met:

(1) ADMINISTRATIVE LICENSING PROCEDURES.—At least a majority of the States permit a producer that has a resident license for selling or soliciting the purchase of insurance in its home State to receive a license to sell or solicit the purchase of insurance in such majority of States as a nonresident to the same extent that such producer is permitted to sell or solicit the purchase of insurance in its State, if the producer's home State also awards such licenses on such a reciprocal basis, without satisfying any additional requirements other than submitting—

(A) a request for licensure;

(B) the application for licensure that the producer submitted to its home State;

(C) proof that the producer is licensed and in good standing in its home State; and

(D) the payment of any requisite fee to the appropriate authority.

(2) CONTINUING EDUCATION REQUIREMENTS.—A majority of the States accept an insurance producer's satisfaction of its home State's continuing education require-

ments for licensed insurance producers to satisfy the States' own continuing education requirements if the producer's home State also recognizes the satisfaction of continuing education requirements on such a reciprocal basis.

(3) NO LIMITING NONRESIDENT REQUIREMENTS.—A majority of the States do not impose any requirement upon any insurance producer to be licensed or otherwise qualified to do business as a nonresident that has the effect of limiting or conditioning that producer's activities because of its residence or place of operations, except that countersignature requirements imposed on nonresident producers shall not be deemed to have the effect of limiting or conditioning a producer's activities because of its residence or place of operations under this section.

(4) RECIPROCAL RECIPROCITY.—Each of the States that satisfies paragraphs (1), (2), and (3) grants reciprocity to residents of all of the other States that satisfy such paragraphs.

(d) DETERMINATION.—

(1) NAIC DETERMINATION.—At the end of the 3-year period beginning on the date of the enactment of this Act, the National Association of Insurance Commissioners (hereafter in this subtitle referred to as the "NAIC") shall determine, in consultation with the insurance commissioners or chief insurance regulatory officials of the States, whether the uniformity or reciprocity required by subsections (b) and (c) has been achieved.

(2) JUDICIAL REVIEW.—The appropriate United States district court shall have exclusive jurisdiction over any challenge to the NAIC's determination under this section and such court shall apply the standards set forth in section 706 of title 5, United States Code, when reviewing any such challenge.

(e) CONTINUED APPLICATION.—If, at any time, the uniformity or reciprocity required by subsections (b) and (c) no longer exists, the provisions of this subtitle shall take effect 2 years after the date on which such uniformity or reciprocity ceases to exist, unless the uniformity or reciprocity required by those provisions is satisfied before the expiration of that 2-year period.

(f) SAVINGS PROVISION.—No provision of this section shall be construed as requiring that any law, regulation, provision, or action of any State which purports to regulate insurance producers, including any such law, regulation, provision, or action which purports to regulate unfair trade practices or establish consumer protections, including countersignature laws, be altered or amended in order to satisfy the uniformity or reciprocity required by subsections (b) and (c), unless any such law, regulation, provision, or action is inconsistent with a specific requirement of any such subsection and then only to the extent of such inconsistency.

(g) UNIFORM LICENSING.—Nothing in this section shall be construed to require any State to adopt new or additional licensing requirements to achieve the uniformity necessary to satisfy subsection (a)(1).

¶ 1322

SEC. 322. **NATIONAL ASSOCIATION OF REGISTERED AGENTS AND BROKERS.**

(a) ESTABLISHMENT.—There is established the National Association of Registered Agents and Brokers (hereafter in this subtitle referred to as the "Association").

(b) STATUS.—The Association shall—

(1) be a nonprofit corporation;

(2) have succession until dissolved by an Act of Congress;

(3) not be an agent or instrumentality of the United States Government; and

(4) except as otherwise provided in this Act, be subject to, and have all the powers conferred upon a nonprofit corporation by the District of Columbia Nonprofit Corporation Act (D.C. Code, sec. 29y-1001 et seq.).

¶ 1323

SEC. 323. **PURPOSE.**

The purpose of the Association shall be to provide a mechanism through which uniform licensing, appointment, continuing education, and other insurance producer sales qualification requirements and conditions can be adopted and applied on a multistate basis, while preserving the right of States to license, supervise, and discipline insurance producers and to prescribe and enforce laws and regulations with regard to insurance-related consumer protection and unfair trade practices.

¶ 1324

SEC. 324. **RELATIONSHIP TO THE FEDERAL GOVERNMENT.**

The Association shall be subject to the supervision and oversight of the NAIC.

¶ 1325

SEC. 325. **MEMBERSHIP.**

(a) ELIGIBILITY.—

(1) IN GENERAL.—Any State-licensed insurance producer shall be eligible to become a member in the Association.

(2) INELIGIBILITY FOR SUSPENSION OR REVOCATION OF LICENSE.—Notwithstanding paragraph (1), a State-licensed insurance producer shall not be eligible to become a member if a State insurance regulator has suspended or revoked such producer's license in that State during the 3-year period preceding the date on which such producer applies for membership.

(3) RESUMPTION OF ELIGIBILITY.—Paragraph (2) shall cease to apply to any insurance producer if—

(A) the State insurance regulator renews the license of such producer in the State in which the license was suspended or revoked; or

(B) the suspension or revocation is subsequently overturned.

(b) AUTHORITY TO ESTABLISH MEMBERSHIP CRITERIA.—The Association shall have the authority to establish membership criteria that—

(1) bear a reasonable relationship to the purposes for which the Association was established; and

(2) do not unfairly limit the access of smaller agencies to the Association membership.

(c) ESTABLISHMENT OF CLASSES AND CATEGORIES.—

(1) CLASSES OF MEMBERSHIP.—The Association may establish separate classes of membership, with separate criteria, if the Association reasonably determines that performance of different duties requires different levels of education, training, or experience.

(2) CATEGORIES.—The Association may establish separate categories of membership for individuals and for other persons. The establishment of any such categories of membership shall be based either on the types of licensing categories that exist under State laws or on the aggregate amount of business handled by an insurance producer. No special categories of membership, and no distinct membership criteria, shall be established for members which are depository institutions or for their employees, agents, or affiliates.

(d) MEMBERSHIP CRITERIA.—

(1) IN GENERAL.—The Association may establish criteria for membership which shall include standards for integrity, personal qualifications, education, training, and experience.

(2) MINIMUM STANDARD.—In establishing criteria under paragraph (1), the Association shall consider the highest levels of insurance producer qualifications established under the licensing laws of the States.

(e) EFFECT OF MEMBERSHIP.—Membership in the Association shall entitle the member to licensure in each State for which the member pays the requisite fees, including licensing fees and, where applicable, bonding requirements, set by such State.

(f) ANNUAL RENEWAL.—Membership in the Association shall be renewed on an annual basis.

(g) CONTINUING EDUCATION.—The Association shall establish, as a condition of membership, continuing education requirements which shall be comparable to or greater than the continuing education requirements under the licensing laws of a majority of the States.

(h) SUSPENSION AND REVOCATION.—The Association may—

(1) inspect and examine the records and offices of the members of the Association to determine compliance with the criteria for membership established by the Association; and

(2) suspend or revoke the membership of an insurance producer if—

(A) the producer fails to meet the applicable membership criteria of the Association; or

(B) the producer has been subject to disciplinary action pursuant to a final adjudicatory proceeding under the jurisdiction of a State insurance regulator, and the Association concludes that retention of membership in the Association would not be in the public interest.

(i) OFFICE OF CONSUMER COMPLAINTS.—

(1) IN GENERAL.—The Association shall establish an office of consumer complaints that shall—

(A) receive and investigate complaints from both consumers and State insurance regulators related to members of the Association; and

(B) recommend to the Association any disciplinary actions that the office considers appropriate, to the extent that any such recommendation is not inconsistent with State law.

(2) RECORDS AND REFERRALS.—The office of consumer complaints of the Association shall—

(A) maintain records of all complaints received in accordance with paragraph (1) and make such records available to the NAIC and to each State insurance regulator for the State of residence of the consumer who filed the complaint; and

(B) refer, when appropriate, any such complaint to any appropriate State insurance regulator.

(3) TELEPHONE AND OTHER ACCESS.—The office of consumer complaints shall maintain a toll-free telephone number for the purpose of this subsection and, as practicable, other alternative means of communication with consumers, such as an Internet home page.

¶ 1326

SEC. 326. **BOARD OF DIRECTORS.**

(a) ESTABLISHMENT.—There is established the board of directors of the Association (hereafter in this subtitle referred to as the "Board") for the purpose of governing and supervising the activities of the Association and the members of the Association.

(b) POWERS.—The Board shall have such powers and authority as may be specified in the bylaws of the Association.

(c) COMPOSITION.—

(1) MEMBERS.—The Board shall be composed of 7 members appointed by the NAIC.

(2) REQUIREMENT.—At least 4 of the members of the Board shall each have significant experience with the regulation of commercial lines of insurance in at least 1 of the 20 States in which the greatest total dollar amount of commercial-lines insurance is placed in the United States.

(3) INITIAL BOARD MEMBERSHIP.—

(A) IN GENERAL.—If, by the end of the 2-year period beginning on the date of the enactment of this Act, the NAIC has not appointed the initial 7 members of the Board of the Association, the initial Board shall consist of the 7 State insurance regulators of the 7 States with the greatest total dollar amount of commercial-lines insurance in place as of the end of such period.

(B) ALTERNATE COMPOSITION.—If any of the State insurance regulators described in subparagraph (A) declines to serve on the Board, the State insurance regulator with the next greatest total dollar amount of commercial-lines insurance in place, as determined by the NAIC as of the end of such period, shall serve as a member of the Board.

(C) INOPERABILITY.—If fewer than 7 State insurance regulators accept appointment to the Board, the Association shall be established without NAIC oversight pursuant to section 332.

(d) TERMS.—The term of each director shall, after the initial appointment of the members of the Board, be for 3 years, with one-third of the directors to be appointed each year.

(e) BOARD VACANCIES.—A vacancy on the Board shall be filled in the same manner as the original appointment of the initial Board for the remainder of the term of the vacating member.

(f) MEETINGS.—The Board shall meet at the call of the chairperson, or as otherwise provided by the bylaws of the Association.

¶ 1327

SEC. 327. OFFICERS.

(a) IN GENERAL.—

(1) POSITIONS.—The officers of the Association shall consist of a chairperson and a vice chairperson of the Board, a president, secretary, and treasurer of the Association, and such other officers and assistant officers as may be deemed necessary.

(2) MANNER OF SELECTION.—Each officer of the Board and the Association shall be elected or appointed at such time and in such manner and for such terms not exceeding 3 years as may be prescribed in the bylaws of the Association.

(b) CRITERIA FOR CHAIRPERSON.—Only individuals who are members of the NAIC shall be eligible to serve as the chairperson of the board of directors.

¶ 1328

SEC. 328. BYLAWS, RULES, AND DISCIPLINARY ACTION.

(a) ADOPTION AND AMENDMENT OF BYLAWS.—

(1) COPY REQUIRED TO BE FILED WITH THE NAIC.—The board of directors of the Association shall file with the NAIC a copy of the proposed by-laws or any proposed amendment to the bylaws, accompanied by a concise general statement of the basis and purpose of such proposal.

(2) EFFECTIVE DATE.—Except as provided in paragraph (3), any proposed bylaw or proposed amendment shall take effect—

(A) 30 days after the date of the filing of a copy with the NAIC;

(B) upon such later date as the Association may designate; or

(C) upon such earlier date as the NAIC may determine.

(3) DISAPPROVAL BY THE NAIC.—Notwithstanding paragraph (2), a proposed bylaw or amendment shall not take effect if, after public notice and opportunity to participate in a public hearing—

(A) the NAIC disapproves such proposal as being contrary to the public interest or contrary to the purposes of this subtitle and provides notice to the Association setting forth the reasons for such disapproval; or

(B) the NAIC finds that such proposal involves a matter of such significant public interest that public comment should be obtained, in which case it may, after notifying the Association in writing of such finding, require that the procedures set forth in subsection (b) be followed with respect to such proposal, in the same manner as if such proposed bylaw change were a proposed rule change within the meaning of such subsection.

(b) ADOPTION AND AMENDMENT OF RULES.—

(1) FILING PROPOSED REGULATIONS WITH THE NAIC.—

(A) IN GENERAL.—The board of directors of the Association shall file with the NAIC a copy of any proposed rule or any proposed amendment to a rule of the Association which shall be accompanied by a concise general statement of the basis and purpose of such proposal.

(B) OTHER RULES AND AMENDMENTS INEFFECTIVE.—No proposed rule or amendment shall take effect unless approved by the NAIC or otherwise permitted in accordance with this paragraph.

(2) INITIAL CONSIDERATION BY THE NAIC.—Not later than 35 days after the date of publication of notice of filing of a proposal, or before the end of such longer period not to exceed 90 days as the NAIC may designate after such date, if the NAIC finds such longer period to be appropriate and sets forth its reasons for so finding, or as to which the Association consents, the NAIC shall—

(A) by order approve such proposed rule or amendment; or

(B) institute proceedings to determine whether such proposed rule or amendment should be modified or disapproved.

(3) NAIC PROCEEDINGS.—

(A) IN GENERAL.—Proceedings instituted by the NAIC with respect to a proposed rule or amendment pursuant to paragraph (2) shall—

(i) include notice of the grounds for disapproval under consideration;

(ii) provide opportunity for hearing; and

(iii) be concluded not later than 180 days after the date of the Association's filing of such proposed rule or amendment.

(B) DISPOSITION OF PROPOSAL.—At the conclusion of any proceeding under subparagraph (A), the NAIC shall, by order, approve or disapprove the proposed rule or amendment.

(C) EXTENSION OF TIME FOR CONSIDERATION.—The NAIC may extend the time for concluding any proceeding under subparagraph (A) for—

(i) not more than 60 days if the NAIC finds good cause for such extension and sets forth its reasons for so finding; or

(ii) such longer period as to which the Association consents.

(4) STANDARDS FOR REVIEW.—

(A) GROUNDS FOR APPROVAL.—The NAIC shall approve a proposed rule or amendment if the NAIC finds that the rule or amendment is in the public interest and is consistent with the purposes of this Act.

(B) APPROVAL BEFORE END OF NOTICE PERIOD.—The NAIC shall not approve any proposed rule before the end of the 30-day period beginning on the date on which the Association files proposed rules or amendments in accordance with paragraph (1), unless the NAIC finds good cause for so doing and sets forth the reasons for so finding.

(5) ALTERNATE PROCEDURE.—

(A) IN GENERAL.—Notwithstanding any provision of this subsection other than subparagraph (B), a proposed rule or amendment relating to the administration or organization of the Association shall take effect—

(i) upon the date of filing with the NAIC, if such proposed rule or amendment is designated by the Association as relating solely to matters which the NAIC, consistent with the public interest and the purposes of this subsection, determines by rule do not require the procedures set forth in this paragraph; or

(ii) upon such date as the NAIC shall for good cause determine.

(B) ABROGATION BY THE NAIC.—

(i) IN GENERAL.—At any time within 60 days after the date of filing of any proposed rule or amendment under subparagraph (A)(i) or clause (ii) of this subparagraph, the NAIC may repeal such rule or amendment and require that the rule or amendment be refiled and reviewed in accordance with this paragraph, if the NAIC finds that such action is necessary or appropriate in the public interest, for the protection of insurance producers or policyholders, or otherwise in furtherance of the purposes of this subtitle.

(ii) EFFECT OF RECONSIDERATION BY THE NAIC.—Any action of the NAIC pursuant to clause (i) shall—

(I) not affect the validity or force of a rule change during the period such rule or amendment was in effect; and

(II) not be considered to be a final action.

(c) ACTION REQUIRED BY THE NAIC.—The NAIC may, in accordance with such rules as the NAIC determines to be necessary or appropriate to the public interest or to carry out the purposes of this subtitle, require the Association to adopt, amend, or repeal any bylaw, rule, or amendment of the Association, whenever adopted.

(d) DISCIPLINARY ACTION BY THE ASSOCIATION.—

(1) SPECIFICATION OF CHARGES.—In any proceeding to determine whether membership shall be denied, suspended, revoked, or not renewed (hereafter in this section referred to as a "disciplinary action"), the Association shall bring specific charges, notify such member of such charges, give the member an opportunity to defend against the charges, and keep a record.

(2) SUPPORTING STATEMENT.—A determination to take disciplinary action shall be supported by a statement setting forth—

(A) any act or practice in which such member has been found to have been engaged;

(B) the specific provision of this subtitle, the rules or regulations under this subtitle, or the rules of the Association which any such act or practice is deemed to violate; and

(C) the sanction imposed and the reason for such sanction.

(e) NAIC REVIEW OF DISCIPLINARY ACTION.—

(1) NOTICE TO THE NAIC.—If the Association orders any disciplinary action, the Association shall promptly notify the NAIC of such action.

(2) REVIEW BY THE NAIC.—Any disciplinary action taken by the Association shall be subject to review by the NAIC—

(A) on the NAIC's own motion; or

(B) upon application by any person aggrieved by such action if such application is filed with the NAIC not more than 30 days after the later of—

(i) the date the notice was filed with the NAIC pursuant to paragraph (1); or

(ii) the date the notice of the disciplinary action was received by such aggrieved person.

(f) EFFECT OF REVIEW.—The filing of an application to the NAIC for review of a disciplinary action, or the institution of review by the NAIC on the NAIC's own motion, shall not operate as a stay of disciplinary action unless the NAIC otherwise orders.

(g) SCOPE OF REVIEW.—

(1) IN GENERAL.—In any proceeding to review such action, after notice and the opportunity for hearing, the NAIC shall—

(A) determine whether the action should be taken;

(B) affirm, modify, or rescind the disciplinary sanction; or

(C) remand to the Association for further proceedings.

(2) DISMISSAL OF REVIEW.—The NAIC may dismiss a proceeding to review disciplinary action if the NAIC finds that—

(A) the specific grounds on which the action is based exist in fact;

(B) the action is in accordance with applicable rules and regulations; and

(C) such rules and regulations are, and were, applied in a manner consistent with the purposes of this subtitle.

¶ 1329

SEC. 329. **ASSESSMENTS.**

(a) INSURANCE PRODUCERS SUBJECT TO ASSESSMENT.—The Association may establish such application and membership fees as the Association finds necessary to cover the costs of its operations, including fees made reimbursable to the NAIC under subsection (b), except that, in setting such fees, the Association may not discriminate against smaller insurance producers.

(b) NAIC ASSESSMENTS.—The NAIC may assess the Association for any costs that the NAIC incurs under this subtitle.

¶ 1330

SEC. 330. **FUNCTIONS OF THE NAIC.**

(a) ADMINISTRATIVE PROCEDURE.—Determinations of the NAIC, for purposes of making rules pursuant to section 328, shall be made after appropriate notice and opportunity for a hearing and for submission of views of interested persons.

(b) EXAMINATIONS AND REPORTS.—

(1) EXAMINATIONS.—The NAIC may make such examinations and inspections of the Association and require the Association to furnish to the NAIC such reports and records or copies thereof as the NAIC may consider necessary or appropriate in the public interest or to effectuate the purposes of this subtitle.

(2) REPORT BY ASSOCIATION.—As soon as practicable after the close of each fiscal year, the Association shall submit to the NAIC a written report regarding the conduct of its business, and the exercise of the other rights and powers granted by this subtitle, during such

fiscal year. Such report shall include financial statements setting forth the financial position of the Association at the end of such fiscal year and the results of its operations (including the source and application of its funds) for such fiscal year. The NAIC shall transmit such report to the President and the Congress with such comment thereon as the NAIC determines to be appropriate.

¶ 1331

SEC. 331. **LIABILITY OF THE ASSOCIATION AND THE DIRECTORS, OFFICERS, AND EMPLOYEES OF THE ASSOCIATION.**

(a) IN GENERAL.—The Association shall not be deemed to be an insurer or insurance producer within the meaning of any State law, rule, regulation, or order regulating or taxing insurers, insurance producers, or other entities engaged in the business of insurance, including provisions imposing premium taxes, regulating insurer solvency or financial condition, establishing guaranty funds and levying assessments, or requiring claims settlement practices.

(b) LIABILITY OF THE ASSOCIATION, ITS DIRECTORS, OFFICERS, AND EMPLOYEES.—Neither the Association nor any of its directors, officers, or employees shall have any liability to any person for any action taken or omitted in good faith under or in connection with any matter subject to this subtitle.

¶ 1332

SEC. 332. **ELIMINATION OF NAIC OVERSIGHT.**

(a) IN GENERAL.—The Association shall be established without NAIC oversight and the provisions set forth in section 324, subsections (a), (b), (c), and (e) of section 328, and sections 329(b) and 330 of this subtitle shall cease to be effective if, at the end of the 2-year period beginning on the date on which the provisions of this subtitle take effect pursuant to section 321—

(1) at least a majority of the States representing at least 50 percent of the total United States commercial-lines insurance premiums have not satisfied the uniformity or reciprocity requirements of subsections (a), (b), and (c) of section 321; and

(2) the NAIC has not approved the Association's bylaws as required by section 328 or is unable to operate or supervise the Association, or the Association is not conducting its activities as required under this Act.

(b) BOARD APPOINTMENTS.—If the repeals required by subsection (a) are implemented, the following shall apply:

(1) GENERAL APPOINTMENT POWER.—The President, with the advice and consent of the Senate, shall appoint the members of the Association's Board established under section 326 from lists of candidates recommended to the President by the NAIC.

(2) PROCEDURES FOR OBTAINING NAIC APPOINTMENT RECOMMENDATIONS.—

(A) INITIAL DETERMINATION AND RECOMMENDATIONS.—After the date on which the provisions of subsection (a) take effect, the NAIC shall, not later than 60 days thereafter, provide a list of recommended candidates to the President. If the NAIC fails to provide a list by that date, or if any list that is provided does not include at least 14 recommended candidates or comply with the requirements of section 326(c), the President shall, with the advice and consent of the Senate, make the requisite appointments without considering the views of the NAIC.

(B) SUBSEQUENT APPOINTMENTS.—After the initial appointments, the NAIC shall provide a list of at least six recommended candidates for the Board to the President by January 15 of each subsequent year. If the NAIC fails to provide a list by that date, or if any list that is provided does not include at least six recommended candidates or comply with the requirements of section 326(c), the President, with the advice and consent of the Senate, shall make the requisite appointments without considering the views of the NAIC.

(C) PRESIDENTIAL OVERSIGHT.—

(i) REMOVAL.—If the President determines that the Association is not acting in the interests of the public, the President may remove the entire existing Board for the remainder of the term to which the members of the Board were appointed and appoint, with the advice and consent of the Senate, new members to fill the vacancies on the Board for the remainder of such terms.

(ii) SUSPENSION OF RULES OR ACTIONS.—The President, or a person designated by the President for such purpose, may suspend the effectiveness of any rule, or prohibit any action, of the Association which the President or the designee determines is contrary to the public interest.

(c) ANNUAL REPORT.—As soon as practicable after the close of each fiscal year, the Association shall submit to the President and to the Congress a written report relative to the conduct of its business, and the exercise of the other rights and powers granted by this subtitle, during such fiscal year. Such report shall include financial statements setting forth the financial position of the Association at the end of such fiscal year and the results of its operations (including the source and application of its funds) for such fiscal year.

¶ 1333

SEC. 333. RELATIONSHIP TO STATE LAW.

(a) PREEMPTION OF STATE LAWS.—State laws, regulations, provisions, or other actions purporting to regulate insurance producers shall be preempted as provided in subsection (b).

(b) PROHIBITED ACTIONS.—No State shall—

(1) impede the activities of, take any action against, or apply any provision of law or regulation to, any insurance producer because that insurance producer or any affiliate plans to become, has applied to become, or is a member of the Association;

(2) impose any requirement upon a member of the Association that it pay different fees to be licensed or otherwise qualified to do business in that State, including bonding requirements, based on its residency;

(3) impose any licensing, appointment, integrity, personal or corporate qualifications, education, training, experience, residency, or continuing education requirement upon a member of the Association that is different from the criteria for membership in the Association or renewal of such membership, except that counter-signature requirements imposed on nonresident producers shall not be deemed to have the effect of limiting or conditioning a producer's activities because of its residence or place of operations under this section; or

(4) implement the procedures of such State's system of licensing or renewing the licenses of insurance producers in a manner different from the authority of the Association under section 325.

(c) SAVINGS PROVISION.—Except as provided in subsections (a) and (b), no provision of this section shall be construed as altering or affecting the continuing effectiveness of any law, regulation, provision, or other action of any State which purports to regulate insurance producers, including any such law, regulation, provision, or action which purports to regulate unfair trade practices or establish consumer protections, including countersignature laws.

¶ 1334

SEC. 334. COORDINATION WITH OTHER REGULATORS.

(a) COORDINATION WITH STATE INSURANCE REGULATORS.—The Association shall have the authority to—

(1) issue uniform insurance producer applications and renewal applications that may be used to apply for the issuance or removal of State licenses, while preserving the ability of each State to impose such conditions on the issuance or renewal of a license as are consistent with section 333;

(2) establish a central clearinghouse through which members of the Association may apply for the issuance or renewal of licenses in multiple States; and

(3) establish or utilize a national database for the collection of regulatory information concerning the activities of insurance producers.

(b) COORDINATION WITH THE NATIONAL ASSOCIATION OF SECURITIES DEALERS.—The Association shall coordinate with the National Association of Securities Dealers in order to ease any administrative burdens that fall on persons that are members of both associations, consistent with the purposes of this subtitle and the Federal securities laws.

¶ 1335

SEC. 335. JUDICIAL REVIEW.

(a) JURISDICTION.—The appropriate United States district court shall have exclusive jurisdiction over litigation involving the Association, including disputes between the Association and its members that arise under this subtitle. Suits brought in State court involving the Association shall be deemed to have arisen under Federal law and therefore be subject to jurisdiction in the appropriate United States district court.

(b) EXHAUSTION OF REMEDIES.—An aggrieved person shall be required to exhaust all available administrative remedies before the Association and the NAIC before it may seek judicial review of an Association decision.

(c) STANDARDS OF REVIEW.—The standards set forth in section 553 of title 5, United States Code, shall be applied whenever a rule or bylaw of the Association is under judicial review, and the standards set forth in section 554 of title 5, United States Code, shall be applied whenever a disciplinary action of the Association is judicially reviewed.

¶ 1336

SEC. 336. DEFINITIONS.

For purposes of this subtitle, the following definitions shall apply:

(1) HOME STATE.—The term "home State" means the State in which the insurance producer maintains its principal place of residence and is licensed to act as an insurance producer.

(2) INSURANCE.—The term "insurance" means any product, other than title insurance, defined or regulated as insurance by the appropriate State insurance regulatory authority.

(3) INSURANCE PRODUCER.—The term "insurance producer" means any insurance agent or broker, surplus lines broker, insurance consultant, limited insurance representative, and any other person that solicits, negotiates, effects, procures, delivers, renews, continues or binds policies of insurance or offers advice, counsel, opinions or services related to insurance.

(4) STATE.—The term "State" includes any State, the District of Columbia, any territory of the United States, Puerto Rico, Guam, American Samoa, the Trust Territory of the Pacific Islands, the Virgin Islands, and the Northern Mariana Islands.

(5) STATE LAW.—The term "State law" includes all laws, decisions, rules, regulations, or other State action having the effect of law, of any State. A law of the United States applicable only to the District of Columbia shall be treated as a State law rather than a law of the United States.

Subtitle D—Rental Car Agency Insurance Activities

¶ 1341

SEC. 341. STANDARD OF REGULATION FOR MOTOR VEHICLE RENTALS.

(a) PROTECTION AGAINST RETROACTIVE APPLICATION OF REGULATORY AND LEGAL ACTION.—Except as provided in subsection (b), during the 3-year period beginning on the date of the enactment of this Act, it shall be a presumption that no State law imposes any licensing, appointment, or education requirements on any person who solicits the purchase of or sells insurance connected with, and incidental to, the lease or rental of a motor vehicle.

(b) PREEMINENCE OF STATE INSURANCE LAW.—No provision of this section shall be construed as altering the validity, interpretation, construction, or effect of—

(1) any State statute;

(2) the prospective application of any court judgment interpreting or applying any State statute; or

(3) the prospective application of any final State regulation, order, bulletin, or other statutorily authorized interpretation or action,

which, by its specific terms, expressly regulates or exempts from regulation any person who solicits the purchase of or sells insurance connected with, and incidental to, the short-term lease or rental of a motor vehicle.

(c) SCOPE OF APPLICATION.—This section shall apply with respect to—

(1) the lease or rental of a motor vehicle for a total period of 90 consecutive days or less; and

(2) insurance which is provided in connection with, and incidentally to, such lease or rental for a period of consecutive days not exceeding the lease or rental period.

(d) MOTOR VEHICLE DEFINED.—For purposes of this section, the term "motor vehicle" has the same meaning as in section 13102 of title 49, United States Code.

TITLE IV—UNITARY SAVINGS AND LOAN HOLDING COMPANIES

¶ 1401

SEC. 401. PREVENTION OF CREATION OF NEW S&L HOLDING COMPANIES WITH COMMERCIAL AFFILIATES.

(a) IN GENERAL.—Section 10(c) of the Home Owners' Loan Act (12 U.S.C. 1467a(c)) is amended by adding at the end the following new paragraph:

"(9) PREVENTION OF NEW AFFILIATIONS BETWEEN S&L HOLDING COMPANIES AND COMMERCIAL FIRMS.—

"(A) IN GENERAL.—Notwithstanding paragraph (3), no company may directly or indirectly, including through any merger, consolidation, or other type of business combination, acquire control of a savings association after May 4, 1999, unless the company is engaged, directly or indirectly (including through a subsidiary other than a savings association), only in activities that are permitted—

"(i) under paragraph (1)(C) or (2) of this subsection; or

"(ii) for financial holding companies under section 4(k) of the Bank Holding Company Act of 1956.

"(B) PREVENTION OF NEW COMMERCIAL AFFILIATIONS.—Notwithstanding paragraph (3), no savings and loan holding company may engage directly or indirectly (including through a subsidiary other than a savings association) in any activity other than as described in clauses (i) and (ii) of subparagraph (A).

"(C) PRESERVATION OF AUTHORITY OF EXISTING UNITARY S&L HOLDING COMPANIES.—Subparagraphs (A) and (B) do not apply with respect to any company that was a savings and loan holding company on May 4, 1999, or that becomes a savings and loan holding company pursuant to an application pending before the Office on or before that date, and that—

"(i) meets and continues to meet the requirements of paragraph (3); and

"(ii) continues to control not fewer than 1 savings association that it controlled on May 4, 1999, or that it acquired pursuant to an application pending before the Office on or before that date, or the successor to such savings association.

"(D) CORPORATE REORGANIZATIONS PERMITTED.—This paragraph does not prevent a transaction that—

"(i) involves solely a company under common control with a savings and loan holding company from acquiring, directly or indirectly, control of the savings and loan holding company or any savings association that is already a subsidiary of the savings and loan holding company; or

"(ii) involves solely a merger, consolidation, or other type of business combination as a result of which a company under common control with the savings and loan holding company acquires, directly or indirectly, control of the savings and loan holding company or any savings association that is already a subsidiary of the savings and loan holding company.

"(E) AUTHORITY TO PREVENT EVASIONS.—The Director may issue interpretations, regulations, or orders that the Director determines necessary to administer and carry out the purpose and prevent evasions of this paragraph, including a determination that, notwithstanding the form of a transaction, the transaction would in substance result in a company acquiring control of a savings association.

"(F) PRESERVATION OF AUTHORITY FOR FAMILY TRUSTS.—Subparagraphs (A) and (B) do not apply with respect to any trust that becomes a savings and loan holding company with respect to a savings association, if—

"(i) not less than 85 percent of the beneficial ownership interests in the trust are continuously owned, directly or indirectly, by or for the benefit of members of the same family, or their spouses, who are lineal descendants of common ancestors who controlled, directly or indirectly, such savings association on May 4, 1999, or a subsequent date, pursuant to an application pending before the Office on or before May 4, 1999; and

"(ii) at the time at which such trust becomes a savings and loan holding company, such ancestors or lineal descendants, or spouses of such descendants, have directly or indirectly controlled the savings association continuously since May 4, 1999, or a subsequent date, pursuant to an application pending before the Office on or before May 4, 1999.".

(b) CONFORMING AMENDMENT.—Section 10(o)(5)(E) of the Home Owners' Loan Act (12 U.S.C. 1467a(o)(5)(E)) is amended by striking ", except subparagraph (B)" and inserting "or (c)(9)(A)(ii)".

(c) RULE OF CONSTRUCTION FOR CERTAIN APPLICATIONS.—

(1) IN GENERAL.—In the case of a company that—

(A) submits an application with the Director of the Office of Thrift Supervision before the date of the enactment of this Act to convert a State-chartered trust company controlled by such company on May 4, 1999, to a savings association; and

(B) controlled a subsidiary on May 4, 1999, that had submitted an application to the Director on September 2, 1998;

the company (including any subsidiary controlled by such company as of such date of enactment) shall be treated as having filed such conversion application with the Director before May 4, 1999, for purposes of section 10(c)(9)(C) of the Home Owners' Loan Act (as added by subsection (a)).

(2) DEFINITIONS.—For purposes of paragraph (1), the terms "company", "control", "savings association", and "subsidiary" have the meanings given those terms in section 10 of the Home Owners' Loan Act.

TITLE V—PRIVACY

Subtitle A—Disclosure of Nonpublic Personal Information

¶ 1501

SEC. 501. **PROTECTION OF NONPUBLIC PERSONAL INFORMATION.**

(a) PRIVACY OBLIGATION POLICY.—It is the policy of the Congress that each financial institution has an affirmative and continuing obligation to respect the privacy of its customers and to protect the security and confidentiality of those customers' nonpublic personal information.

(b) FINANCIAL INSTITUTIONS SAFEGUARDS.—In furtherance of the policy in subsection (a), each agency or authority described in section 505(a) shall establish appropriate standards for the financial institutions subject to their jurisdiction relating to administrative, technical, and physical safeguards—

(1) to insure the security and confidentiality of customer records and information;

(2) to protect against any anticipated threats or hazards to the security or integrity of such records; and

(3) to protect against unauthorized access to or use of such records or information which could result in substantial harm or inconvenience to any customer.

¶ 1502

SEC. 502. **OBLIGATIONS WITH RESPECT TO DISCLOSURES OF PERSONAL INFORMATION.**

(a) NOTICE REQUIREMENTS.—Except as otherwise provided in this subtitle, a financial institution may not, directly or through any affiliate, disclose to a nonaffiliated third party any nonpublic personal information, unless such financial institution provides or has provided to the consumer a notice that complies with section 503.

(b) OPT OUT.—

(1) IN GENERAL.—A financial institution may not disclose nonpublic personal information to a nonaffiliated third party unless—

(A) such financial institution clearly and conspicuously discloses to the consumer, in writing or in electronic form or other form permitted by the regulations prescribed under section 504, that such information may be disclosed to such third party;

(B) the consumer is given the opportunity, before the time that such information is initially disclosed, to direct that such information not be disclosed to such third party; and

(C) the consumer is given an explanation of how the consumer can exercise that nondisclosure option.

(2) EXCEPTION.—This subsection shall not prevent a financial institution from providing nonpublic personal information to a nonaffiliated third party to perform services for or functions on behalf of the financial institution, including marketing of the financial institution's own products or services, or financial products or services offered pursuant to joint agreements between two or more financial institutions that comply with the requirements imposed by the regulations prescribed under section 504, if the financial institution fully discloses the providing of such information and enters into a contractual agreement with the third party that requires the third party to maintain the confidentiality of such information.

(c) LIMITS ON REUSE OF INFORMATION.—Except as otherwise provided in this subtitle, a nonaffiliated third party that receives from a financial institution nonpublic personal information under this section shall not, directly or through an affiliate of such receiving third party, disclose such information to any other person that is a nonaffiliated third party of both the financial institution and such receiving third party, unless such disclosure would be lawful if made directly to such other person by the financial institution.

(d) LIMITATIONS ON THE SHARING OF ACCOUNT NUMBER INFORMATION FOR MARKETING PURPOSES.—A financial institution shall not disclose, other than to a consumer reporting agency, an account number or similar form of access number or access code for a credit card account, deposit account, or transaction account of a consumer to any nonaffiliated third party for use in telemarketing, direct mail marketing, or other marketing through electronic mail to the consumer.

(e) GENERAL EXCEPTIONS.—Subsections (a) and (b) shall not prohibit the disclosure of nonpublic personal information—

(1) as necessary to effect, administer, or enforce a transaction requested or authorized by the consumer, or in connection with—

(A) servicing or processing a financial product or service requested or authorized by the consumer;

(B) maintaining or servicing the consumer's account with the financial institution, or with another entity as part of a private label credit card program or other extension of credit on behalf of such entity; or

(C) a proposed or actual securitization, secondary market sale (including sales of servicing rights), or similar transaction related to a transaction of the consumer;

(2) with the consent or at the direction of the consumer;

(3)(A) to protect the confidentiality or security of the financial institution's records pertaining to the consumer, the service or product, or the transaction therein; (B) to protect against or prevent actual or potential fraud, unauthorized transactions, claims, or other liability; (C) for required institutional risk control, or for resolving customer disputes or inquiries; (D) to persons holding a legal or beneficial interest relating to the consumer; or (E) to persons acting in a fiduciary or representative capacity on behalf of the consumer;

(4) to provide information to insurance rate advisory organizations, guaranty funds or agencies, applicable rating agencies of the financial institution, persons assessing the institution's compliance with industry standards, and the institution's attorneys, accountants, and auditors;

(5) to the extent specifically permitted or required under other provisions of law and in accordance with the Right to Financial Privacy Act of 1978, to law enforcement agencies (including a Federal functional regulator, the Secretary of the Treasury with respect to subchapter II of chapter 53 of title 31, United States Code, and chapter 2 of title I of Public Law 91-508 (12 U.S.C. 1951-1959), a State insurance authority, or the Federal Trade Commission), self-regulatory organizations, or for an investigation on a matter related to public safety;

(6)(A) to a consumer reporting agency in accordance with the Fair Credit Reporting Act, or (B) from a consumer report reported by a consumer reporting agency;

(7) in connection with a proposed or actual sale, merger, transfer, or exchange of all or a portion of a business or operating unit if the disclosure of nonpublic personal information concerns solely consumers of such business or unit; or

(8) to comply with Federal, State, or local laws, rules, and other applicable legal requirements; to comply with a properly authorized civil, criminal, or regulatory investigation or subpoena or summons by Federal, State, or local authorities; or to respond to judicial process or government regulatory authorities having jurisdiction over the financial institution for examination, compliance, or other purposes as authorized by law.

¶ 1503

SEC. 503. **DISCLOSURE OF INSTITUTION PRIVACY POLICY.**

(a) DISCLOSURE REQUIRED.—At the time of establishing a customer relationship with a consumer and not less than annually during the continuation of such relationship, a financial institution shall provide a clear and conspicuous disclosure to such consumer, in writing or in electronic form or other form permitted by the regulations prescribed under section 504, of such financial institution's policies and practices with respect to—

(1) disclosing nonpublic personal information to affiliates and nonaffiliated third parties, consistent with section 502, including the categories of information that may be disclosed;

(2) disclosing nonpublic personal information of persons who have ceased to be customers of the financial institution; and

(3) protecting the nonpublic personal information of consumers.

Such disclosures shall be made in accordance with the regulations prescribed under section 504.

(b) INFORMATION TO BE INCLUDED.—The disclosure required by subsection (a) shall include—

(1) the policies and practices of the institution with respect to disclosing nonpublic personal information to nonaffiliated third parties, other than agents of the institution, consistent with section 502 of this subtitle, and including—

(A) the categories of persons to whom the information is or may be disclosed, other than the persons to whom the information may be provided pursuant to section 502(e); and

(B) the policies and practices of the institution with respect to disclosing of nonpublic personal information of persons who have ceased to be customers of the financial institution;

(2) the categories of nonpublic personal information that are collected by the financial institution;

(3) the policies that the institution maintains to protect the confidentiality and security of nonpublic personal information in accordance with section 501; and

(4) the disclosures required, if any, under section 603(d)(2)(A)(iii) of the Fair Credit Reporting Act.

¶ 1504

SEC. 504. **RULEMAKING.**

(a) REGULATORY AUTHORITY.—

(1) RULEMAKING.—The Federal banking agencies, the National Credit Union Administration, the Secretary of the Treasury, the Securities and Exchange Commission, and the Federal Trade Commission shall each prescribe, after consultation as appropriate with representatives of State insurance authorities designated by the National Association of Insurance Commissioners, such regulations as may be necessary to carry out the purposes of this subtitle with respect to the financial institutions subject to their jurisdiction under section 505.

(2) COORDINATION, CONSISTENCY, AND COMPARABILITY.—Each of the agencies and authorities required under paragraph (1) to prescribe regulations shall consult and coordinate with the other such agencies and authorities for the purposes of assuring, to the extent possible, that the regulations prescribed by each such agency and authority are consistent and comparable with the regulations prescribed by the other such agencies and authorities.

(3) PROCEDURES AND DEADLINE.—Such regulations shall be prescribed in accordance with applicable requirements of title 5, United States Code, and shall be issued in final form not later than 6 months after the date of the enactment of this Act.

(b) AUTHORITY TO GRANT EXCEPTIONS.—The regulations prescribed under subsection (a) may include such additional exceptions to subsections (a) through (d) of section 502 as are deemed consistent with the purposes of this subtitle.

¶ 1505

SEC. 505. **ENFORCEMENT.**

(a) IN GENERAL.—This subtitle and the regulations prescribed thereunder shall be enforced by the Federal functional regulators, the State insurance authorities, and the Federal Trade Commission with respect to financial institutions and other persons subject to their jurisdiction under applicable law, as follows:

(1) Under section 8 of the Federal Deposit Insurance Act, in the case of—

(A) national banks, Federal branches and Federal agencies of foreign banks, and any subsidiaries of such entities (except brokers, dealers, persons providing insurance, investment companies, and investment advisers), by the Office of the Comptroller of the Currency;

(B) member banks of the Federal Reserve System (other than national banks), branches and agencies of foreign banks (other than Federal branches, Federal agencies, and insured State branches of foreign banks), commercial lending companies owned or controlled by foreign banks, organizations operating under section 25 or 25A of the Federal Reserve Act, and bank holding companies and their nonbank subsidiaries or affiliates (except brokers, dealers, persons providing insurance, investment companies, and investment advisers), by the Board of Governors of the Federal Reserve System;

(C) banks insured by the Federal Deposit Insurance Corporation (other than members of the Federal Reserve System), insured State branches of foreign banks, and any subsidiaries of such entities (except brokers, dealers, persons providing insurance, investment companies, and investment advisers), by the Board of Directors of the Federal Deposit Insurance Corporation; and

(D) savings associations the deposits of which are insured by the Federal Deposit Insurance Corporation, and any subsidiaries of such savings associations (except brokers, dealers, persons providing insurance, investment companies, and investment advisers), by the Director of the Office of Thrift Supervision.

(2) Under the Federal Credit Union Act, by the Board of the National Credit Union Administration with respect to any federally insured credit union, and any subsidiaries of such an entity.

(3) Under the Securities Exchange Act of 1934, by the Securities and Exchange Commission with respect to any broker or dealer.

(4) Under the Investment Company Act of 1940, by the Securities and Exchange Commission with respect to investment companies.

(5) Under the Investment Advisers Act of 1940, by the Securities and Exchange Commission with respect to investment advisers registered with the Commission under such Act.

(6) Under State insurance law, in the case of any person engaged in providing insurance, by the applicable State insurance authority of the State in which the person is domiciled, subject to section 104 of this Act.

(7) Under the Federal Trade Commission Act, by the Federal Trade Commission for any other financial institution or other person that is not subject to the jurisdiction of any agency or authority under paragraphs (1) through (6) of this subsection.

(b) ENFORCEMENT OF SECTION 501.—

(1) IN GENERAL.—Except as provided in paragraph (2), the agencies and authorities described in subsection (a) shall implement the standards prescribed under section 501(b) in the same manner, to the extent practicable, as standards prescribed pursuant to section 39(a) of the Federal Deposit Insurance Act are implemented pursuant to such section.

(2) EXCEPTION.—The agencies and authorities described in paragraphs (3), (4), (5), (6), and (7) of subsection (a) shall implement the standards prescribed under section 501(b) by rule with respect to the financial institutions and other persons subject to their respective jurisdictions under subsection (a).

(c) ABSENCE OF STATE ACTION.—If a State insurance authority fails to adopt regulations to carry out this subtitle, such State shall not be eligible to override, pursuant to section 45(g)(2)(B)(iii) of the Federal Deposit Insurance Act, the insurance customer protection regulations prescribed by a Federal banking agency under section 45(a) of such Act.

(d) DEFINITIONS.—The terms used in subsection (a)(1) that are not defined in this subtitle or otherwise defined in section 3(s) of the Federal Deposit Insurance Act shall have the same meaning as given in section 1(b) of the International Banking Act of 1978.

¶ 1506

SEC. 506. PROTECTION OF FAIR CREDIT REPORTING ACT.

(a) AMENDMENT.—Section 621 of the Fair Credit Reporting Act (15 U.S.C. 1681s) is amended—

(1) in subsection (d), by striking everything following the end of the second sentence; and

(2) by striking subsection (e) and inserting the following:

"Regulatory authority

"(e)(1) The Federal banking agencies referred to in paragraphs (1) and (2) of subsection (b) shall jointly prescribe such regulations as necessary to carry out the purposes of this Act with respect to any persons identified under paragraphs (1) and (2) of subsection (b), and the Board of Governors of the Federal Reserve System shall have authority to prescribe regulations consistent with such joint regulations with respect to bank holding companies and affiliates (other than depository institutions and consumer reporting agencies) of such holding companies.

"(2) The Board of the National Credit Union Administration shall prescribe such regulations as necessary to carry out the purposes of this Act with respect to any persons identified under paragraph (3) of subsection (b).".

(b) CONFORMING AMENDMENT.—Section 621(a) of the Fair Credit Reporting Act (15 U.S.C. 1681s(a)) is amended by striking paragraph (4).

(c) RELATION TO OTHER PROVISIONS.—Except for the amendments made by subsections (a) and (b), nothing in this title shall be construed to modify, limit, or supersede the operation of the Fair Credit Reporting Act, and no inference shall be drawn on the basis of the provisions of this title regarding whether information is transaction or experience information under section 603 of such Act.

¶ 1507

SEC. 507. RELATION TO STATE LAWS.

(a) IN GENERAL.—This subtitle and the amendments made by this subtitle shall not be construed as superseding, altering, or affecting any statute, regulation, order, or interpretation in effect in any State, except to the extent that such statute, regulation, order, or interpretation is inconsistent with the provisions of this subtitle, and then only to the extent of the inconsistency.

(b) GREATER PROTECTION UNDER STATE LAW.—For purposes of this section, a State statute, regulation, order, or interpretation is not inconsistent with the provisions of this subtitle if the protection such statute, regulation, order, or interpretation affords any person is greater than the protection provided under this subtitle and the amendments made by this subtitle, as determined by the Federal Trade Commission, after consultation with the agency or authority with jurisdiction under section 505(a) of either the person that initiated the complaint or that is the subject of the complaint, on its own motion or upon the petition of any interested party.

¶ 1508

SEC. 508. **STUDY OF INFORMATION SHARING AMONG FINANCIAL AFFILIATES.**

(a) IN GENERAL.—The Secretary of the Treasury, in conjunction with the Federal functional regulators and the Federal Trade Commission, shall conduct a study of information sharing practices among financial institutions and their affiliates. Such study shall include—

(1) the purposes for the sharing of confidential customer information with affiliates or with nonaffiliated third parties;

(2) the extent and adequacy of security protections for such information;

(3) the potential risks for customer privacy of such sharing of information;

(4) the potential benefits for financial institutions and affiliates of such sharing of information;

(5) the potential benefits for customers of such sharing of information;

(6) the adequacy of existing laws to protect customer privacy;

(7) the adequacy of financial institution privacy policy and privacy rights disclosure under existing law;

(8) the feasibility of different approaches, including opt-out and opt-in, to permit customers to direct that confidential information not be shared with affiliates and nonaffiliated third parties; and

(9) the feasibility of restricting sharing of information for specific uses or of permitting customers to direct the uses for which information may be shared.

(b) CONSULTATION.—The Secretary shall consult with representatives of State insurance authorities designated by the National Association of Insurance Commissioners, and also with financial services industry, consumer organizations and privacy groups, and other representatives of the general public, in formulating and conducting the study required by subsection (a).

(c) REPORT.—On or before January 1, 2002, the Secretary shall submit a report to the Congress containing the findings and conclusions of the study required under subsection (a), together with such recommendations for legislative or administrative action as may be appropriate.

¶ 1509

SEC. 509. **DEFINITIONS.**

As used in this subtitle:

(1) FEDERAL BANKING AGENCY.—The term "Federal banking agency" has the same meaning as given in section 3 of the Federal Deposit Insurance Act.

(2) FEDERAL FUNCTIONAL REGULATOR.—The term "Federal functional regulator" means—

(A) the Board of Governors of the Federal Reserve System;

(B) the Office of the Comptroller of the Currency;

(C) the Board of Directors of the Federal Deposit Insurance Corporation;

(D) the Director of the Office of Thrift Supervision;

(E) the National Credit Union Administration Board; and

(F) the Securities and Exchange Commission.

(3) FINANCIAL INSTITUTION.—

(A) IN GENERAL.—The term "financial institution" means any institution the business of which is engaging in financial activities as described in section 4(k) of the Bank Holding Company Act of 1956.

(B) PERSONS SUBJECT TO CFTC REGULATION.—Notwithstanding subparagraph (A), the term "financial institution" does not include any person or entity with respect to any financial activity that is subject to the jurisdiction of the Commodity Futures Trading Commission under the Commodity Exchange Act.

(C) FARM CREDIT INSTITUTIONS.—Notwithstanding subparagraph (A), the term "financial institution" does not include the Federal Agricultural Mortgage Corporation or any entity chartered and operating under the Farm Credit Act of 1971.

(D) OTHER SECONDARY MARKET INSTITUTIONS.—Notwithstanding subparagraph (A), the term "financial institution" does not include institutions chartered by Congress specifically to engage in transactions described in section 502(e)(1)(C), as long as such institutions do not sell or transfer nonpublic personal information to a nonaffiliated third party.

(4) NONPUBLIC PERSONAL INFORMATION.—

(A) The term "nonpublic personal information" means personally identifiable financial information—

(i) provided by a consumer to a financial institution;

(ii) resulting from any transaction with the consumer or any service performed for the consumer; or

(iii) otherwise obtained by the financial institution.

(B) Such term does not include publicly available information, as such term is defined by the regulations prescribed under section 504.

(C) Notwithstanding subparagraph (B), such term—

(i) shall include any list, description, or other grouping of consumers (and publicly available information pertaining to them) that is derived using any nonpublic personal information other than publicly available information; but

(ii) shall not include any list, description, or other grouping of consumers (and publicly available information pertaining to them) that is derived without using any nonpublic personal information.

(5) NONAFFILIATED THIRD PARTY.—The term "nonaffiliated third party" means any entity that is not an affiliate of, or related by common ownership or affiliated by corporate control with, the financial institution, but does not include a joint employee of such institution.

(6) AFFILIATE.—The term "affiliate" means any company that controls, is controlled by, or is under common control with another company.

(7) NECESSARY TO EFFECT, ADMINISTER, OR ENFORCE.—The term "as necessary to effect, administer, or enforce the transaction" means—

(A) the disclosure is required, or is a usual, appropriate, or acceptable method, to carry out the transaction or the product or service business of which the transaction is a part, and record or service or maintain the consumer's account in the ordinary course of providing the financial service or financial product, or to administer or service benefits or claims relating to the transaction or the product or service business of which it is a part, and includes—

(i) providing the consumer or the consumer's agent or broker with a confirmation, statement, or other record of the transaction, or information on the status or value of the financial service or financial product; and

(ii) the accrual or recognition of incentives or bonuses associated with the transaction that are provided by the financial institution or any other party;

(B) the disclosure is required, or is one of the lawful or appropriate methods, to enforce the rights of the financial institution or of other persons engaged in carrying out the financial transaction, or providing the product or service;

(C) the disclosure is required, or is a usual, appropriate, or acceptable method, for insurance underwriting at the consumer's request or for reinsurance purposes, or for any of the following purposes as they relate to a consumer's insurance: account administration, reporting, investigating, or preventing fraud or material misrepresentation, processing premium payments, processing insurance claims, administering insurance benefits (including utilization review activities), participating in research projects, or as otherwise required or specifically permitted by Federal or State law; or

(D) the disclosure is required, or is a usual, appropriate or acceptable method, in connection with—

(i) the authorization, settlement, billing, processing, clearing, transferring, reconciling, or collection of amounts charged, debited, or otherwise paid using a debit, credit or other payment card, check, or account number, or by other payment means;

(ii) the transfer of receivables, accounts or interests therein; or

(iii) the audit of debit, credit or other payment information.

(8) STATE INSURANCE AUTHORITY.—The term "State insurance authority" means, in the case of any person engaged in providing insurance, the State insurance authority of the State in which the person is domiciled.

(9) CONSUMER.—The term "consumer" means an individual who obtains, from a financial institution, financial products or services which are to be used primarily for personal, family, or household purposes, and also means the legal representative of such an individual.

(10) JOINT AGREEMENT.—The term "joint agreement" means a formal written contract pursuant to which two or more financial institutions jointly offer, endorse, or sponsor a financial product or service, and as may be further defined in the regulations prescribed under section 504.

(11) CUSTOMER RELATIONSHIP.—The term "time of establishing a customer relationship" shall be defined by the regulations prescribed under section 504, and shall, in the case of a financial institution engaged in extending credit directly to consumers to finance purchases of goods or services, mean the time of establishing the credit relationship with the consumer.

¶ 1510

SEC. 510. **EFFECTIVE DATE.**

This subtitle shall take effect 6 months after the date on which rules are required to be prescribed under section 504(a)(3), except—

(1) to the extent that a later date is specified in the rules prescribed under section 504; and

(2) that sections 504 and 506 shall be effective upon enactment.

Subtitle B—Fraudulent Access to Financial Information

¶ 1521

SEC. 521. **PRIVACY PROTECTION FOR CUSTOMER INFORMATION OF FINANCIAL INSTITUTIONS.**

(a) PROHIBITION ON OBTAINING CUSTOMER INFORMATION BY FALSE PRETENSES.—It shall be a violation of this subtitle for any person to obtain or attempt to obtain, or cause to be disclosed or attempt to cause to be disclosed to any person, customer information of a financial institution relating to another person—

(1) by making a false, fictitious, or fraudulent statement or representation to an officer, employee, or agent of a financial institution;

(2) by making a false, fictitious, or fraudulent statement or representation to a customer of a financial institution; or

(3) by providing any document to an officer, employee, or agent of a financial institution, knowing that the document is forged, counterfeit, lost, or stolen, was fraudulently obtained, or contains a false, fictitious, or fraudulent statement or representation.

(b) PROHIBITION ON SOLICITATION OF A PERSON TO OBTAIN CUSTOMER INFORMATION FROM FINANCIAL INSTITUTION UNDER FALSE PRETENSES.—It shall be a violation of this subtitle to request a person to obtain customer information of a financial institution, knowing that the person will obtain, or attempt to obtain, the information from the institution in any manner described in subsection (a).

(c) NONAPPLICABILITY TO LAW ENFORCEMENT AGENCIES.—No provision of this section shall be construed so as to prevent any action by a law enforcement agency, or any officer, employee, or agent of such agency, to obtain customer information of a financial institution in connection with the performance of the official duties of the agency.

(d) NONAPPLICABILITY TO FINANCIAL INSTITUTIONS IN CERTAIN CASES.—No provision of this section shall be construed so as to prevent any financial institution, or any officer, employee, or agent of a financial institution, from obtaining customer information of such financial institution in the course of—

(1) testing the security procedures or systems of such institution for maintaining the confidentiality of customer information;

(2) investigating allegations of misconduct or negligence on the part of any officer, employee, or agent of the financial institution; or

(3) recovering customer information of the financial institution which was obtained or received by another person in any manner described in subsection (a) or (b).

(e) NONAPPLICABILITY TO INSURANCE INSTITUTIONS FOR INVESTIGATION OF INSURANCE FRAUD.—No provision of this section shall be construed so as to prevent any insurance institution, or any officer, employee, or agency of an insurance institution, from obtaining information as part of an insurance investigation into criminal activity, fraud, material misrepresentation, or material nondisclosure that is authorized for such institution under State law, regulation, interpretation, or order.

(f) NONAPPLICABILITY TO CERTAIN TYPES OF CUSTOMER INFORMATION OF FINANCIAL INSTITUTIONS.—No provision of this section shall be construed so as to prevent any person from obtaining customer information of a financial institution that otherwise is available as a public record filed pursuant to the securities laws (as defined in section 3(a)(47) of the Securities Exchange Act of 1934).

(g) NONAPPLICABILITY TO COLLECTION OF CHILD SUPPORT JUDGMENTS.—No provision of this section shall be construed to prevent any State-licensed private investigator, or any officer, employee, or agent of such private investigator, from obtaining customer information of a financial institution, to the extent reasonably necessary to collect child support from a person adjudged to have been delinquent in his or her obligations by a Federal or State court, and to the extent that such action by a State-licensed private investigator is not unlawful under any other Federal or State law or regulation, and has been authorized by an order or judgment of a court of competent jurisdiction.

¶ 1522

SEC. 522. **ADMINISTRATIVE ENFORCEMENT.**

(a) ENFORCEMENT BY FEDERAL TRADE COMMISSION.—Except as provided in subsection (b), compliance with this subtitle shall be enforced by the Federal Trade Commission in the same manner and with the same power and authority as the Commission has under the Fair Debt Collection Practices Act to enforce compliance with such Act.

(b) ENFORCEMENT BY OTHER AGENCIES IN CERTAIN CASES.—

(1) IN GENERAL.—Compliance with this subtitle shall be enforced under—

(A) section 8 of the Federal Deposit Insurance Act, in the case of—

(i) national banks, and Federal branches and Federal agencies of foreign banks, by the Office of the Comptroller of the Currency;

(ii) member banks of the Federal Reserve System (other than national banks), branches and agencies of foreign banks (other than Federal branches, Federal agencies, and insured State branches of foreign banks), commercial lending companies owned or controlled by foreign banks, and organizations operating under section 25 or 25A of the Federal Reserve Act, by the Board;

(iii) banks insured by the Federal Deposit Insurance Corporation (other than members of the Federal Reserve System and national nonmember banks) and insured State branches of foreign banks, by the Board of Directors of the Federal Deposit Insurance Corporation; and

(iv) savings associations the deposits of which are insured by the Federal Deposit Insurance Corporation, by the Director of the Office of Thrift Supervision; and

(B) the Federal Credit Union Act, by the Administrator of the National Credit Union Administration with respect to any Federal credit union.

(2) VIOLATIONS OF THIS SUBTITLE TREATED AS VIOLATIONS OF OTHER LAWS.—For the purpose of the exercise by any agency referred to in paragraph (1) of its powers under any Act referred to in that paragraph, a violation of this subtitle shall be deemed to be a violation of a requirement imposed under that Act. In addition to its powers under any provision of law specifically referred to in paragraph (1), each of the agencies referred to in that paragraph may exercise, for the purpose of enforcing compliance with this subtitle, any other authority conferred on such agency by law.

¶ 1523

SEC. 523. **CRIMINAL PENALTY.**

(a) IN GENERAL.—Whoever knowingly and intentionally violates, or knowingly and intentionally attempts to violate, section 521 shall be fined in accordance with title 18, United States Code, or imprisoned for not more than 5 years, or both.

(b) ENHANCED PENALTY FOR AGGRAVATED CASES.—Whoever violates, or attempts to violate, section 521 while violating another law of the United States or as part of a pattern of any illegal activity involving more than $100,000 in a 12-month period shall be fined twice the amount provided in subsection (b)(3) or (c)(3) (as the case may be) of section 3571 of title 18, United States Code, imprisoned for not more than 10 years, or both.

¶ 1524

SEC. 524. **RELATION TO STATE LAWS.**

(a) IN GENERAL.—This subtitle shall not be construed as superseding, altering, or affecting the statutes, regulations, orders, or interpretations in effect in any State, except to the extent that such statutes, regulations, orders, or interpretations are inconsistent with the provisions of this subtitle, and then only to the extent of the inconsistency.

(b) GREATER PROTECTION UNDER STATE LAW.—For purposes of this section, a State statute, regulation, order, or interpretation is not inconsistent with the provisions of this subtitle if the protection such statute, regulation, order, or interpretation affords any person is greater than the protection provided under this subtitle as determined by the Federal Trade Commission, after consultation with the agency or authority with jurisdiction under section 522 of either the person that initiated the complaint or that is the subject of the complaint, on its own motion or upon the petition of any interested party.

¶ 1525

SEC. 525. AGENCY GUIDANCE.

In furtherance of the objectives of this subtitle, each Federal banking agency (as defined in section 3(z) of the Federal Deposit Insurance Act), the National Credit Union Administration, and the Securities and Exchange Commission or self-regulatory organizations, as appropriate, shall review regulations and guidelines applicable to financial institutions under their respective jurisdictions and shall prescribe such revisions to such regulations and guidelines as may be necessary to ensure that such financial institutions have policies, procedures, and controls in place to prevent the unauthorized disclosure of customer financial information and to deter and detect activities proscribed under section 521.

¶ 1526

SEC. 526. REPORTS.

(a) REPORT TO THE CONGRESS.—Before the end of the 18-month period beginning on the date of the enactment of this Act, the Comptroller General, in consultation with the Federal Trade Commission, Federal banking agencies, the National Credit Union Administration, the Securities and Exchange Commission, appropriate Federal law enforcement agencies, and appropriate State insurance regulators, shall submit to the Congress a report on the following:

(1) The efficacy and adequacy of the remedies provided in this subtitle in addressing attempts to obtain financial information by fraudulent means or by false pretenses.

(2) Any recommendations for additional legislative or regulatory action to address threats to the privacy of financial information created by attempts to obtain information by fraudulent means or false pretenses.

(b) ANNUAL REPORT BY ADMINISTERING AGENCIES.—The Federal Trade Commission and the Attorney General shall submit to Congress an annual report on number and disposition of all enforcement actions taken pursuant to this subtitle.

¶ 1527

SEC. 527. DEFINITIONS.

For purposes of this subtitle, the following definitions shall apply:

(1) CUSTOMER.—The term "customer" means, with respect to a financial institution, any person (or authorized representative of a person) to whom the financial institution provides a product or service, including that of acting as a fiduciary.

(2) CUSTOMER INFORMATION OF A FINANCIAL INSTITUTION.—The term "customer information of a financial institution" means any information maintained by or for a financial institution which is derived from the relationship between the financial institution and a customer of the financial institution and is identified with the customer.

(3) DOCUMENT.—The term "document" means any information in any form.

(4) FINANCIAL INSTITUTION.—

(A) IN GENERAL.—The term "financial institution" means any institution engaged in the business of providing financial services to customers who maintain a credit, deposit, trust, or other financial account or relationship with the institution.

(B) CERTAIN FINANCIAL INSTITUTIONS SPECIFICALLY INCLUDED.—The term "financial institution" includes any depository institution (as defined in section 19(b)(1)(A) of the Federal Reserve Act), any broker or dealer, any investment adviser or investment company, any insurance company, any loan or finance company, any credit card issuer or operator of a credit card system, and any consumer reporting agency that compiles and maintains files on consumers on a nationwide basis (as defined in section 603(p) of the Consumer Credit Protection Act).

(C) SECURITIES INSTITUTIONS.—For purposes of subparagraph (B)—

(i) the terms "broker" and "dealer" have the same meanings as given in section 3 of the Securities Exchange Act of 1934 (15 U.S.C. 78c);

(ii) the term "investment adviser" has the same meaning as given in section 202(a)(11) of the Investment Advisers Act of 1940 (15 U.S.C. 80b-2(a)); and

(iii) the term "investment company" has the same meaning as given in section 3 of the Investment Company Act of 1940 (15 U.S.C. 80a-3).

(D) CERTAIN PERSONS AND ENTITIES SPECIFICALLY EXCLUDED.—The term "financial institution" does not include any person or entity with respect to any financial activity that is subject to the jurisdiction of the Commodity Futures Trading Commission under the Commodity Exchange Act and does not include the Federal Agricultural Mortgage Corporation or any entity chartered and operating under the Farm Credit Act of 1971.

(E) FURTHER DEFINITION BY REGULATION.—The Federal Trade Commission, after consultation with Federal banking agencies and the Securities and Exchange Commission, may prescribe regulations clarifying or describing the types of institutions which shall be treated as financial institutions for purposes of this subtitle.

TITLE VI—FEDERAL HOME LOAN BANK SYSTEM MODERNIZATION

¶ 1601

SEC. 601. **SHORT TITLE.**

This title may be cited as the "Federal Home Loan Bank System Modernization Act of 1999".

¶ 1602

SEC. 602. **DEFINITIONS.**

Section 2 of the Federal Home Loan Bank Act (12 U.S.C. 1422) is amended—

(1) in paragraph (1), by striking "term 'Board' means" and inserting "terms 'Finance Board' and 'Board' mean";

(2) by striking paragraph (3) and inserting the following:

"(3) STATE.—The term 'State', in addition to the States of the United States, includes the District of Columbia, Guam, Puerto Rico, the United States Virgin Islands, American Samoa, and the Commonwealth of the Northern Mariana Islands."; and

(3) by adding at the end the following new paragraph:

"(13) COMMUNITY FINANCIAL INSTITUTION.—

"(A) IN GENERAL.—The term 'community financial institution' means a member—

"(i) the deposits of which are insured under the Federal Deposit Insurance Act; and

"(ii) that has, as of the date of the transaction at issue, less than $500,000,000 in average total assets, based on an average of total assets over the 3 years preceding that date.

"(B) ADJUSTMENTS.—The $500,000,000 limit referred to in subparagraph (A)(ii) shall be adjusted annually by the Finance Board, based on the annual percentage increase, if any, in the Consumer Price Index for all urban consumers, as published by the Department of Labor.".

¶ 1603

SEC. 603. SAVINGS ASSOCIATION MEMBERSHIP.

Section 5(f) of the Home Owners' Loan Act (12 U.S.C. 1464(f)) is amended to read as follows:

"Federal home loan bank membership

"(f) After the end of the 6-month period beginning on the date of the enactment of the Federal Home Loan Bank System Modernization Act of 1999, a Federal savings association may become a member of the Federal Home Loan Bank System, and shall qualify for such membership in the manner provided by the Federal Home Loan Bank Act.".

¶ 1604

SEC. 604. ADVANCES TO MEMBERS; COLLATERAL.

IN GENERAL.—Section 10(a) of the Federal Home Loan Bank Act (12 U.S.C. 1430(a)) is amended—

(1) by redesignating paragraphs (1) through (4) as subparagraphs (A) through (D), respectively, and indenting appropriately;

(2) by striking "(a) Each" and inserting the following:

"In general

"(a)(1) ALL ADVANCES.—Each";

(3) by striking the second sentence and inserting the following:

"(2) PURPOSES OF ADVANCES.—A long-term advance may only be made for the purposes of—

"(A) providing funds to any member for residential housing finance; and

"(B) providing funds to any community financial institution for small businesses, small farms, and small agri-businesses.";

(4) by striking "A Bank" and inserting the following:

"(3) COLLATERAL.—A Bank";

(5) in paragraph (3) (as so designated by paragraph (4) of this subsection)—

(A) in subparagraph (C) (as so redesignated by paragraph (1) of this subsection) by striking "Deposits" and inserting "Cash or deposits";

(B) in subparagraph (D) (as so redesignated by paragraph (1) of this subsection), by striking the second sentence; and

(C) by inserting after subparagraph (D) (as so redesignated by paragraph (1) of this subsection) the following new subparagraph:

"(E) Secured loans for small business, agriculture, or securities representing a whole interest in such secured loans, in the case of any community financial institution.";

(6) in paragraph (5)—

(A) in the second sentence, by striking "and the Board";

(B) in the third sentence, by striking "Board" and inserting "Federal home loan bank"; and

(C) by striking "(5) Paragraphs (1) through (4)" and inserting the following:

"(4) ADDITIONAL BANK AUTHORITY.—Subparagraphs (A) through (E) of paragraph (3)"; and

(7) by adding at the end the following:

"(5) REVIEW OF CERTAIN COLLATERAL STANDARDS.—The Board may review the collateral standards applicable to each Federal home loan bank for the classes of collateral described in subparagraphs (D) and (E) of paragraph (3), and may, if necessary for safety and soundness purposes, require an increase in the collateral standards for any or all of those classes of collateral.

"(6) DEFINITIONS.—For purposes of this subsection, the terms 'small business', 'agriculture', 'small farm', and 'small agri-business' shall have the meanings given those terms by regulation of the Finance Board.".

(b) CLERICAL AMENDMENT.—The section heading for section 10 of the Federal Home Loan Bank Act (12 U.S.C. 1430) is amended to read as follows:

"SEC. 10. ADVANCES TO MEMBERS.".

"(c) QUALIFIED THRIFT LENDER STATUS.—Section 10 of the Federal Home Loan Bank Act (12 U.S.C. 1430) is amended by striking the 1st of the 2 subsections designated as subsection (e).

(d) FEDERAL HOME LOAN BANK ACCESS.—Section 10(m)(3)(B) of the Home Owners' Loan Act (12 U.S.C. 1467a(m)(3)(B)) is amended—

(1) in clause (i), by striking subclause (III) and redesignating subclause (IV) as subclause (III); and

(2) by striking clause (ii) and inserting the following:

"(ii) ADDITIONAL RESTRICTIONS EFFECTIVE AFTER 3 YEARS.—Beginning 3 years after the date on which a savings association should have become a qualified thrift lender, or the date on which the savings association ceases to be a qualified thrift lender, as applicable, the savings association shall not retain any investment (including an investment in any subsidiary) or engage, directly or indirectly, in any activity, unless that investment or activity—

"(I) would be permissible for the savings association if it were a national bank; and

"(II) is permissible for the savings association as a savings association.".

¶ 1605

SEC. 605. **ELIGIBILITY CRITERIA.**

Section 4(a) of the Federal Home Loan Bank Act (12 U.S.C. 1424(a)) is amended—

(1) in paragraph (2)(A), by inserting, "(other than a community financial institution)" after "institution";

(2) in the matter immediately following paragraph (2)(C)—

(A) by striking "An insured" and inserting the following:

"(3) CERTAIN INSTITUTIONS.—An insured"; and

(B) by striking "preceding sentence" and inserting "paragraph (2)"; and

(3) by adding at the end the following new paragraph:

"(4) LIMITED EXEMPTION FOR COMMUNITY FINANCIAL INSTITUTIONS.—A community financial institution that otherwise meets the requirements of paragraph (2) may become a member without regard to the percentage of its total assets that is represented by residential mortgage loans, as described in subparagraph (A) of paragraph (2).".

¶ 1606

SEC. 606. **MANAGEMENT OF BANKS.**

(a) BOARD OF DIRECTORS.—Section 7 of the Federal Home Loan Bank Act (12 U.S.C. 1427(d)) is amended—

(1) in subsection (a), by striking "and bona fide residents of the district in which such bank is located" and inserting ", and each of whom shall be either a bona fide resident of the district in which such bank is located or an officer or director of a member of such bank located in that district";

(2) in subsection (d), by striking the 1st sentence and inserting the following: "The term of each director, whether elected or appointed, shall be 3 years. The board of directors of each Federal home loan bank and the Finance Board shall adjust the terms of members first elected or appointed after the date of the enactment of the Federal Home Loan Bank System Modernization Act of 1999 to ensure that the terms of the members of the board of directors are staggered with approximately 1/3 of the terms expiring each year."; and

(3) by striking subsection (g) and inserting the following:

"Chairperson and vice chairperson

"(g)(1) ELECTION.—The Chairperson and Vice Chairperson of the board of directors of each Federal home loan bank shall be elected by a majority of all the directors of such bank from among the directors of the bank.

"(2) TERMS.—The term of office of the Chairperson and the Vice Chairperson of the board of directors of a Federal home loan bank shall be 2 years.

"(3) ACTING CHAIRPERSON.—In the event of a vacancy in the position of Chairperson of the board of directors or during the absence or disability of the Chairperson, the Vice Chairperson shall act as Chairperson.

"(4) PROCEDURES.—The board of directors of each Federal home loan bank shall establish procedures, in the bylaws of such board, for designating an acting chairperson for any period during which the Chairperson and the Vice Chairperson are not available to carry out the requirements of that position for any reason and removing any person from any such position for good cause.".

(b) COMPENSATION.—Section 7(i) of the Federal Home Loan Bank Act (12 U.S.C. 1427(i)) is amended—

(1) by striking "(i) Each bank may pay its directors" and inserting "(i) DIRECTORS' COMPENSATION.—

"(1) IN GENERAL.—Subject to paragraph (2), each bank may pay its directors"; and

(2) by adding at the end the following new paragraph:

"(2) LIMITATION.—

"(A) IN GENERAL.—The annual salary of each of the following members of the board of directors of a Federal home loan bank may not exceed the amount specified:

"In the case of the—	**The annual compensation may not exceed—**
Chairperson	$25,000
Vice Chairperson	$20,000
All other members	$15,000

"(B) ADJUSTMENT.—Beginning January 1, 2001, each dollar amount referred to in the table in subparagraph (A) shall be adjusted annually by the Finance Board, based on the annual percentage increase, if any, in the Consumer Price Index for all urban consumers, as published by the Department of Labor.

"(C) EXPENSES.—Subparagraph (A) shall not be construed as prohibiting the reimbursement of expenses incurred by members of the board of directors of any Federal home loan bank in connection with service on the board of directors.".

(c) REPEAL OF SECTIONS 22A AND 27.—The Federal Home Loan Bank Act (12 U.S.C. 1421 et seq.) is amended by striking sections 22A (12 U.S.C. 1442a) and 27 (12 U.S.C. 1447).

(d) SECTION 12.—Section 12 of the Federal Home Loan Bank Act (12 U.S.C. 1432) is amended—

(1) in subsection (a)—

(A) by striking ", but, except" and all that follows through "ten years";

(B) by striking "subject to the approval of the Board" the first place that term appears;

(C) by striking "and, by its Board of directors," and all that follows through "agent of such bank," and inserting "and, by the board of directors of the bank, to prescribe, amend, and repeal by-laws governing the manner in which its affairs may be administered, consistent with applicable laws and regulations, as administered by the Finance Board. No officer, employee, attorney, or agent of a Federal home loan bank"; and

(D) by striking "Board of directors" where such term appears in the penultimate sentence and inserting "board of directors"; and

(2) in subsection (b), by striking "loans banks" and inserting "loan banks".

(e) POWERS AND DUTIES OF FEDERAL HOUSING FINANCE BOARD.—

(1) ISSUANCE OF NOTICES OF VIOLATIONS.—Section 2B(a) of the Federal Home Loan Bank Act (12 U.S.C. 1422b(a)) is amended by adding at the end the following new paragraphs:

"(5) To issue and serve a notice of charges upon a Federal home loan bank or upon any executive officer or director of a Federal home loan bank if, in the determination of the Finance Board, the Bank, executive officer, or director is engaging or has engaged in, or the Finance Board has reasonable cause to believe that the Bank, executive officer, or director is about to engage in an unsafe or unsound practice in conducting the business of the bank, or any conduct that violates any provision of this Act or any law, order, rule, or regulation or any condition imposed in writing by the Finance Board in connection with the granting of any application or other request by the Bank, or any written agreement entered into by the Bank with the agency, in accordance with the procedures provided in subsection (c) or (f) of section 1371 of the Federal Housing Enterprises Financial Safety and Soundness Act of 1992. Such authority includes the same authority to issue an order requiring a party to take affirmative action to correct conditions resulting from violations or practices or to limit activities of a Bank or any executive officer or director of a Bank as appropriate Federal banking agencies have to take with respect to insured depository institutions under paragraphs (6) and (7) of section 8(b) of the Federal Deposit Insurance Act, and to have all other powers, rights, and duties to enforce this Act with respect to the Federal home loan banks and their executive officers and directors as the Office of Federal Housing Enterprise Oversight has to enforce the Federal Housing Enterprises Financial Safety and Soundness Act of 1992, the Federal National Mortgage Association Charter Act, or the Federal Home Loan Mortgage Corporation Act with respect to the Federal housing enterprises under subtitle C (other than section 1371) of the Federal Housing Enterprises Financial Safety and Soundness Act of 1992.

"(6) To address any insufficiencies in capital levels resulting from the application of section 5(f) of the Home Owners' Loan Act.

"(7) To act in its own name and through its own attorneys—

"(A) in enforcing any provision of this Act or any regulation promulgated under this Act; or

"(B) in any action, suit, or proceeding to which the Finance Board is a party that involves the Board's regulation or supervision of any Federal home loan bank.".

(2) TECHNICAL AMENDMENT.—Section 111 of Public Law 93-495 (12 U.S.C. 250) is amended by striking "Federal Home Loan Bank Board," and inserting "Director of the Office of Thrift Supervision, the Federal Housing Finance Board,".

(f) ELIGIBILITY TO SECURE ADVANCES.—

(1) SECTION 9.—Section 9 of the Federal Home Loan Bank Act (12 U.S.C. 1429) is amended—

(A) in the second sentence, by striking "with the approval of the Board"; and

(B) in the third sentence, by striking ", subject to the approval of the Board,".

(2) SECTION 10.—Section 10 of the Federal Home Loan Bank Act (12 U.S.C. 1430) is amended—

(A) in subsection (c)—

(i) in the first sentence, by striking "Board" and inserting "Federal home loan bank"; and

(ii) by striking the second sentence; and

(B) in subsection (d)—

(i) in the first sentence, by striking "and the approval of the Board"; and

(ii) by striking "Subject to the approval of the Board, any" and inserting "Any".

(g) SECTION 16.—Section 16(a) of the Federal Home Loan Bank Act (12 U.S.C. 1436(a)) is amended—

(1) in the third sentence—

(A) by striking "net earnings" and inserting "previously retained earnings or current net earnings"; and

(B) by striking ", and then only with the approval of the Federal Housing Finance Board"; and

(2) by striking the fourth sentence.

(h) SECTION 18.—Section 18(b) of the Federal Home Loan Bank Act (12 U.S.C. 1438(b)) is amended by striking paragraph (4).

¶ 1607

SEC. 607. RESOLUTION FUNDING CORPORATION.

(a) IN GENERAL.—Section 21B(f)(2)(C) of the Federal Home Loan Bank Act (12 U.S.C. 1441b(f)(2)(C)) is amended to read as follows:

"(C) PAYMENTS BY FEDERAL HOME LOAN BANKS.—

"(i) IN GENERAL.—To the extent that the amounts available pursuant to subparagraphs (A) and (B) are insufficient to cover the amount of interest payments, each Federal home loan bank shall pay to the Funding Corporation in each calendar year, 20.0 percent of the net earnings of that Bank (after deducting expenses relating to section 10(j) and operating expenses).

"(ii) ANNUAL DETERMINATION.—The Board annually shall determine the extent to which the value of the aggregate amounts paid by the Federal home loan banks exceeds or falls short of the value of an annuity of $300,000,000 per year that commences on the issuance date and ends on the final scheduled maturity date of the obligations, and shall select appropriate present value factors for making such determinations, in consultation with the Secretary of the Treasury.

"(iii) PAYMENT TERM ALTERATIONS.—The Board shall extend or shorten the term of the payment obligations of a Federal home loan bank under this subparagraph as necessary to ensure that the value of all payments made by the Banks is equivalent to the value of an annuity referred to in clause (ii).

"(iv) TERM BEYOND MATURITY.—If the Board extends the term of payment obligations beyond the final scheduled maturity date for the obligations, each Federal home loan bank shall continue to pay 20.0 percent of its net earnings (after deducting expenses relating to section 10(j) and operating expenses) to the Treasury of the United States until the value of all such payments by the Federal home loan banks is equivalent to the value of an annuity referred to in clause (ii). In the final year in which the Federal home loan banks are required to make any payment to the Treasury under this subparagraph, if the dollar amount represented by 20.0 percent of the net earnings of the Federal home loan banks exceeds the remaining obligation of the Banks to the Treasury, the Finance Board shall reduce the percentage pro rata to a level sufficient to pay the remaining obligation.".

(b) EFFECTIVE DATE.—The amendment made by subsection (a) shall become effective on January 1, 2000. Payments made by a Federal home loan bank before that effective date shall be counted toward the total obligation of that Bank under section 21B(f)(2)(C) of the Federal Home Loan Bank Act, as amended by this section.

¶ 1608

SEC. 608. CAPITAL STRUCTURE OF FEDERAL HOME LOAN BANKS.

Section 6 of the Federal Home Loan Bank Act (12 U.S.C. 1426) is amended to read as follows:

"SEC. 6. CAPITAL STRUCTURE OF FEDERAL HOME LOAN BANKS.

"Regulations

"(a)(1) CAPITAL STANDARDS.—Not later than 1 year after the date of the enactment of the Federal Home Loan Bank System Modernization Act of 1999, the Finance Board shall issue regulations prescribing uniform capital standards applicable to each Federal home loan bank, which shall require each such bank to meet—

"(A) the leverage requirement specified in paragraph (2); and

"(B) the risk-based capital requirements, in accordance with paragraph (3).

"(2) LEVERAGE REQUIREMENT.—

"(A) IN GENERAL.—The leverage requirement shall require each Federal home loan bank to maintain a minimum amount of total capital based on the total assets of the bank and shall be 5 percent.

"(B) TREATMENT OF STOCK AND RETAINED EARNINGS.—In determining compliance with the minimum leverage ratio established under subparagraph (A), the paid-in value of the outstanding Class B stock and the amount of retained earnings shall be multiplied by 1.5, and such higher amounts shall be deemed to be capital for purposes of meeting the 5 percent minimum leverage ratio, except that a Federal home loan bank's total capital (determined without taking into account any such multiplier) shall not be less than 4 percent of the total assets of the bank.

"(3) RISK-BASED CAPITAL STANDARDS.—

"(A) IN GENERAL.—Each Federal home loan bank shall maintain permanent capital in an amount that is sufficient, as determined in accordance with the regulations of the Finance Board, to meet—

"(i) the credit risk to which the Federal home loan bank is subject; and

"(ii) the market risk, including interest rate risk, to which the Federal home loan bank is subject, based on a stress test established by the Finance Board that rigorously tests for changes in market variables, including changes in interest rates, rate volatility, and changes in the shape of the yield curve.

"(B) CONSIDERATION OF OTHER RISK-BASED STANDARDS.—In establishing the risk-based standard under subparagraph (A)(ii), the Finance Board shall take due consideration of any risk-based capital test established pursuant to section 1361 of the Federal Housing Enterprises Financial Safety and Soundness Act of 1992 (12 U.S.C. 4611) for the enterprises (as defined in that Act), with such modifications as the Finance Board determines to be appropriate to reflect differences in operations between the Federal home loan banks and those enterprises.

"(4) OTHER REGULATORY REQUIREMENTS.—The regulations issued by the Finance Board under paragraph (1) shall—

"(A) permit each Federal home loan bank to issue, with such rights, terms, and preferences, not inconsistent with this Act and the regulations issued hereunder, as the board of directors of that bank may approve, any 1 or more of—

"(i) Class A stock, which shall be redeemable in cash and at par 6 months following submission by a member of a written notice of its intent to redeem such shares; and

"(ii) Class B stock, which shall be redeemable in cash and at par 5 years following submission by a member of a written notice of its intent to redeem such shares;

"(B) provide that the stock of a Federal home loan bank may be issued to and held by only members of the bank, and that a bank may not issue any stock other than as provided in this section;

"(C) prescribe the manner in which stock of a Federal home loan bank may be sold, transferred, redeemed, or repurchased; and

"(D) provide the manner of disposition of outstanding stock held by, and the liquidation of any claims of the Federal home loan bank against, an institution that ceases to be a member of the bank, through merger or otherwise, or that provides notice of intention to withdraw from membership in the bank.

"(5) DEFINITIONS OF CAPITAL.—For purposes of determining compliance with the capital standards established under this subsection—

"(A) permanent capital of a Federal home loan bank shall include—

"(i) the amounts paid for the Class B stock; and

"(ii) the retained earnings of the bank (as determined in accordance with generally accepted accounting principles); and

"(B) total capital of a Federal home loan bank shall include—

"(i) permanent capital;

"(ii) the amounts paid for the Class A stock;

"(iii) consistent with generally accepted accounting principles, and subject to the regulation of the Finance Board, a general allowance for losses, which may not include any reserves or allowances made or held against specific assets; and

"(iv) any other amounts from sources available to absorb losses incurred by the bank that the Finance Board determines by regulation to be appropriate to include in determining total capital.

"(6) TRANSITION PERIOD.—Notwithstanding any other provision of this Act, the requirements relating to purchase and retention of capital stock of a Federal home loan bank by any member thereof in effect on the day before the date of the enactment of the Federal Home Loan Bank System Modernization Act of 1999, shall continue in effect with respect to each Federal home loan bank until the regulations required by this subsection have taken effect and the capital structure plan required by subsection (b) has been approved by the Finance Board and implemented by such bank.

"Capital structure plan

"(b)(1) APPROVAL OF PLANS.—Not later than 270 days after the date of publication by the Finance Board of final regulations in accordance with subsection (a), the board of directors of each Federal home loan bank shall submit for Finance Board approval a plan establishing and implementing a capital structure for such bank that—

"(A) the board of directors determines is best suited for the condition and operation of the bank and the interests of the members of the bank;

"(B) meets the requirements of subsection (c); and

"(C) meets the minimum capital standards and requirements established under subsection (a) and other regulations prescribed by the Finance Board.

"(2) APPROVAL OF MODIFICATIONS.—The board of directors of a Federal home loan bank shall submit to the Finance Board for approval any modifications that the bank proposes to make to an approved capital structure plan.

"Contents of plan

(c) The capital structure plan of each Federal home loan bank shall contain provisions addressing each of the following:

"(1) MINIMUM INVESTMENT.—

"(A) IN GENERAL.—Each capital structure plan of a Federal home loan bank shall require each member of the bank to maintain a minimum investment in the stock of the bank, the amount of which shall be determined in a manner to be prescribed by the board of directors of each bank and to be included as part of the plan.

"(B) INVESTMENT ALTERNATIVES.—

"(i) IN GENERAL.—In establishing the minimum investment required for each member under subparagraph (A), a Federal home loan bank may, in its discretion, include any 1 or more of the requirements referred to in clause (ii), or any other provisions approved by the Finance Board.

"(ii) AUTHORIZED REQUIREMENTS.—A requirement is referred to in this clause if it is a requirement for—

"(I) a stock purchase based on a percentage of the total assets of a member; or

"(II) a stock purchase based on a percentage of the outstanding advances from the bank to the member.

"(C) MINIMUM AMOUNT.—Each capital structure plan of a Federal home loan bank shall require that the minimum stock investment established for members shall be set at a level that is sufficient for the bank to meet the minimum capital requirements established by the Finance Board under subsection (a).

"(D) ADJUSTMENTS TO MINIMUM REQUIRED INVESTMENT.—The capital structure plan of each Federal home loan bank shall impose a continuing obligation on the board of directors of the bank to review and adjust the minimum investment required of each member of that bank, as necessary to ensure that the bank remains in compliance with applicable minimum capital levels established by the Finance Board, and shall require each member to comply promptly with any adjustments to the required minimum investment.

"(2) TRANSITION RULE.—

"(A) IN GENERAL.—The capital structure plan of each Federal home loan bank shall specify the date on which it shall take effect, and may provide for a transition period of not longer than 3 years to allow the bank to come into compliance with the capital requirements prescribed under subsection (a), and to allow any institution that was a member of the bank on the date of the enactment of the Federal Home Loan Bank System Modernization Act of 1999, to come into compliance with the minimum investment required pursuant to the plan.

"(B) INTERIM PURCHASE REQUIREMENTS.—The capital structure plan of a Federal home loan bank may allow any member referred to in subparagraph (A) that would be required by the terms of the capital structure plan to increase its investment in the stock of the bank to do so in periodic installments during the transition period.

"(3) DISPOSITION OF SHARES.—The capital structure plan of a Federal home loan bank shall provide for the manner of disposition of any stock held by a member of that bank that terminates its membership or that provides notice of its intention to withdraw from membership in that bank.

"(4) CLASSES OF STOCK.—

"(A) IN GENERAL.—The capital structure plan of a Federal home loan bank shall afford each member of that bank the option of maintaining its required investment in the bank through the purchase of any combination of classes of stock authorized by the board of directors of the bank and approved by the Finance Board in accordance with its regulations.

"(B) RIGHTS REQUIREMENT.—A Federal home loan bank shall include in its capital structure plan provisions establishing terms, rights, and preferences, including minimum investment, dividends, voting, and liquidation preferences of each class of stock issued by the bank, consistent with Finance Board regulations and market requirements.

"(C) REDUCED MINIMUM INVESTMENT.—The capital structure plan of a Federal home loan bank may provide for a reduced minimum stock investment for any member of that bank that elects to purchase Class B in a manner that is consistent with meeting the minimum capital requirements of the bank, as established by the Finance Board.

"(D) LIQUIDATION OF CLAIMS.—The capital structure plan of a Federal home loan bank shall provide for the liquidation in an orderly manner, as determined by the bank, of any claim of that bank against a member, including claims for any applicable prepayment fees or penalties resulting from prepayment of advances prior to stated maturity.

"(5) LIMITED TRANSFERABILITY OF STOCK.—The capital structure plan of a Federal home loan bank shall—

"(A) provide that any stock issued by that bank shall be available only to and held only by members of that bank and tradable only between that bank and its members; and

"(B) establish standards, criteria, and requirements for the issuance, purchase, transfer, retirement, and redemption of stock issued by that bank.

"(6) BANK REVIEW OF PLAN.—Before filing a capital structure plan with the Finance Board, each Federal home loan bank shall conduct a review of the plan by—

"(A) an independent certified public accountant, to ensure, to the extent possible, that implementation of the plan would not result in any write-down of the redeemable bank stock investment of its members; and

"(B) at least one major credit rating agency, to determine, to the extent possible, whether implementation of the plan would have any material effect on the credit ratings of the bank.

"Termination of membership

"(d)(1) VOLUNTARY WITHDRAWAL.—Any member may withdraw from a Federal home loan bank if the member provides written notice to the bank of its intent to do so and if, on the date of withdrawal, there is in effect a certification by the Finance Board that the withdrawal will not cause the Federal Home Loan Bank System to fail to meet its obligation under section 21B(f)(2)(C) to contribute to the debt service for the obligations issued by the Resolution Funding Corporation. The applicable stock redemption notice periods shall commence upon receipt of the notice by the bank. Upon the expiration of the applicable notice period for each class of redeemable stock, the member may surrender such stock to the bank, and shall be entitled to receive in cash the par value of the stock. During the applicable notice periods, the member shall be entitled to dividends and other membership rights commensurate with continuing stock ownership.

"(2) INVOLUNTARY WITHDRAWAL.—

"(A) IN GENERAL.—The board of directors of a Federal home loan bank may terminate the membership of any institution if, subject to Finance Board regulations, it determines that—

"(i) the member has failed to comply with a provision of this Act or any regulation prescribed under this Act; or

"(ii) the member has been determined to be insolvent, or otherwise subject to the appointment of a conservator, receiver, or other legal custodian, by a Federal or State authority with regulatory and supervisory responsibility for the member.

"(B) STOCK DISPOSITION.—An institution, the membership of which is terminated in accordance with subparagraph (A)—

"(i) shall surrender redeemable stock to the Federal home loan bank, and shall receive in cash the par value of the stock, upon the expiration of the applicable notice period under subsection (a)(4)(A);

"(ii) shall receive any dividends declared on its redeemable stock, during the applicable notice period under subsection (a)(4)(A); and

"(iii) shall not be entitled to any other rights or privileges accorded to members after the date of the termination.

"(C) COMMENCEMENT OF NOTICE PERIOD.—With respect to an institution, the membership of which is terminated in accordance with subparagraph (A), the applicable notice period under subsection (a)(4) for each class of redeemable stock shall commence on the earlier of—

"(i) the date of such termination; or

"(ii) the date on which the member has provided notice of its intent to redeem such stock.

"(3) LIQUIDATION OF INDEBTEDNESS.—Upon the termination of the membership of an institution for any reason, the outstanding indebtedness of the member to the bank shall be liquidated in an orderly manner, as determined by the bank and, upon the extinguishment of all such indebtedness, the bank shall return to the member all collateral pledged to secure the indebtedness.

"Redemption of excess stock

"(e)(1) IN GENERAL.—A Federal home loan bank, in its sole discretion, may redeem or repurchase, as appropriate, any shares of Class A or Class B stock issued by the bank and held by a member that are in excess of the minimum stock investment required of that member.

"(2) EXCESS STOCK.—Shares of stock held by a member shall not be deemed to be 'excess stock' for purposes of this subsection by virtue of a member's submission of a notice of intent to withdraw from membership or termination of its membership in any other manner.

"(3) PRIORITY.—A Federal home loan bank may not redeem any excess Class B stock prior to the end of the 5-year notice period, unless the member has no Class A stock outstanding that could be redeemed as excess.

"Impairment of capital

(f) If the Finance Board or the board of directors of a Federal home loan bank determines that the bank has incurred or is likely to incur losses that result in or are expected to result in charges against the capital of the bank, the bank shall not redeem or repurchase any stock of the bank without the prior approval of the Finance Board while such charges are continuing or are expected to continue. In no case may a bank redeem or repurchase any applicable capital stock if, following the redemption, the bank would fail to satisfy any minimum capital requirement.

"Rejoining after divestiture of all shares

"(g)(1) IN GENERAL.—Except as provided in paragraph (2), and notwithstanding any other provision of this Act, an institution that divests all shares of stock in a Federal home loan bank may not, after such divestiture, acquire shares of any Federal home loan bank before the end of the 5-year period beginning on the date of the completion of such divestiture, unless the divestiture is a consequence of a transfer of membership on an uninterrupted basis between banks.

"(2) EXCEPTION FOR WITHDRAWALS FROM MEMBERSHIP BEFORE 1998.—Any institution that withdrew from membership in any Federal home loan bank before December 31, 1997, may acquire shares of a Federal home loan bank at any time after that date, subject to the approval of the Finance Board and the requirements of this Act.

"Treatment of retained earnings

"(h)(1) IN GENERAL.—The holders of the Class B stock of a Federal home loan bank shall own the retained earnings, surplus, undivided profits, and equity reserves, if any, of the bank.

"(2) EXCEPTION.—Except as specifically provided in this section or through the declaration of a dividend or a capital distribution by a Federal home loan bank, or in the event of liquidation of the bank, a member shall have no right to withdraw or otherwise receive distribution of any portion of the retained earnings of the bank.

"(3) LIMITATION.—A Federal home loan bank may not make any distribution of its retained earnings unless, following such distribution, the bank would continue to meet all applicable capital requirements.".

TITLE VII—OTHER PROVISIONS

Subtitle A—ATM Fee Reform

¶ 1701

SEC. 701. **SHORT TITLE.**

This subtitle may be cited as the "ATM Fee Reform Act of 1999".

¶ 1702

SEC. 702. **ELECTRONIC FUND TRANSFER FEE DISCLOSURES AT ANY HOST ATM.**

Section 904(d) of the Electronic Fund Transfer Act (15 U.S.C. 1693b(d)) is amended by adding at the end the following new paragraph:

"(3) FEE DISCLOSURES AT AUTOMATED TELLER MACHINES.—

"(A) IN GENERAL.—The regulations prescribed under paragraph (1) shall require any automated teller machine operator who imposes a fee on any consumer for providing host transfer services to such consumer to provide notice in accordance with subparagraph (B) to the consumer (at the time the service is provided) of—

"(i) the fact that a fee is imposed by such operator for providing the service; and

"(ii) the amount of any such fee.

"(B) NOTICE REQUIREMENTS.—

"(i) ON THE MACHINE.—The notice required under clause (i) of subparagraph (A) with respect to any fee described in such subparagraph shall be posted in a prominent and conspicuous location on or at the automated teller machine at which the electronic fund transfer is initiated by the consumer.

"(ii) ON THE SCREEN.—The notice required under clauses (i) and (ii) of subparagraph (A) with respect to any fee described in such subparagraph shall appear on the screen of the automated teller machine, or on a paper notice issued from such machine, after the transaction is initiated and before the consumer is irrevocably committed to completing the transaction, except that during the period beginning on the date of the enactment of the Gramm-Leach-Bliley Act and ending on December 31, 2004, this clause shall not apply to any automated teller machine that lacks the technical capability to disclose the notice on the screen or to issue a paper notice after the transaction is initiated and before the consumer is irrevocably committed to completing the transaction.

"(C) PROHIBITION ON FEES NOT PROPERLY DISCLOSED AND EXPLICITLY ASSUMED BY CONSUMER.—No fee may be imposed by any automated teller machine operator in connection with any electronic fund transfer initiated by a consumer for which a notice is required under subparagraph (A), unless—

"(i) the consumer receives such notice in accordance with subparagraph (B); and

"(ii) the consumer elects to continue in the manner necessary to effect the transaction after receiving such notice.

"(D) DEFINITIONS.—For purposes of this paragraph, the following definitions shall apply:

"(i) AUTOMATED TELLER MACHINE OPERATOR.—The term 'automated teller machine operator' means any person who—

"(I) operates an automated teller machine at which consumers initiate electronic fund transfers; and

"(II) is not the financial institution that holds the account of such consumer from which the transfer is made.

"(ii) ELECTRONIC FUND TRANSFER.—The term 'electronic fund transfer' includes a transaction that involves a balance inquiry initiated by a consumer in the same manner as an electronic fund transfer, whether or not the consumer initiates a transfer of funds in the course of the transaction.

"(iii) HOST TRANSFER SERVICES.—The term 'host transfer services' means any electronic fund transfer made by an automated teller machine operator in connection with a transaction initiated by a consumer at an automated teller machine operated by such operator.".

¶ 1703

SEC. 703. **DISCLOSURE OF POSSIBLE FEES TO CONSUMERS WHEN ATM CARD IS ISSUED.**

Section 905(a) of the Electronic Fund Transfer Act (15 U.S.C. 1693c(a)) is amended—

(1) by striking "and" at the end of paragraph (8);

(2) by striking the period at the end of paragraph (9) and inserting "; and"; and

(3) by inserting after paragraph (9) the following new paragraph:

"(10) a notice to the consumer that a fee may be imposed by—

"(A) an automated teller machine operator (as defined in section 904(d)(3)(D)(i)) if the consumer initiates a transfer from an automated teller machine that is not operated by the person issuing the card or other means of access; and

"(B) any national, regional, or local network utilized to effect the transaction.".

¶ 1704

SEC. 704. **FEASIBILITY STUDY.**

(a) IN GENERAL.—The Comptroller General of the United States shall conduct a study of the feasibility of requiring, in connection with any electronic fund transfer initiated by a consumer through the use of an automated teller machine—

(1) a notice to be provided to the consumer before the consumer is irrevocably committed to completing the transaction, which clearly states the amount of any fee that will be imposed upon the consummation of the transaction by—

(A) any automated teller machine operator (as defined in section 904(d)(3)(D)(i) of the Electronic Fund Transfer Act) involved in the transaction;

(B) the financial institution holding the account of the consumer;

(C) any national, regional, or local network utilized to effect the transaction; and

(D) any other party involved in the transfer; and

(2) the consumer to elect to consummate the transaction after receiving the notice described in paragraph (1).

(b) FACTORS TO BE CONSIDERED.—In conducting the study required under subsection (a) with regard to the notice requirement described in such subsection, the Comptroller General shall consider the following factors:

(1) The availability of appropriate technology.

(2) Implementation and operating costs.

(3) The competitive impact any such notice requirement would have on various sizes and types of institutions, if implemented.

(4) The period of time that would be reasonable for implementing any such notice requirement.

(5) The extent to which consumers would benefit from any such notice requirement.

(6) Any other factor the Comptroller General determines to be appropriate in analyzing the feasibility of imposing any such notice requirement.

(c) REPORT TO THE CONGRESS.—Before the end of the 6-month period beginning on the date of the enactment of this Act, the Comptroller General shall submit a report to the Congress containing—

(1) the findings and conclusions of the Comptroller General in connection with the study required under subsection (a); and

(2) the recommendation of the Comptroller General with regard to the question of whether a notice requirement described in subsection (a) should be implemented and, if so, the manner in which such requirement should be implemented.

¶ 1705

SEC. 705. NO LIABILITY IF POSTED NOTICES ARE DAMAGED.

Section 910 of the Electronic Fund Transfer Act (15 U.S.C. 1693h) is amended by adding at the end the following new subsection:

"**Exception for damaged notices**

"(d) If the notice required to be posted pursuant to section 904(d)(3)(B)(i) by an automated teller machine operator has been posted by such operator in compliance with such section and the notice is subsequently removed, damaged, or altered by any person other than the operator of the automated teller machine, the operator shall have no liability under this section for failure to comply with section 904(d)(3)(B)(i).".

Subtitle B—Community Reinvestment

¶ 1711

SEC. 711. CRA SUNSHINE REQUIREMENTS.

The Federal Deposit Insurance Act (12 U.S.C. 1811 et seq.) is amended by inserting after section 47, as added by section 305 of this Act, the following new section:

"SEC. 48. CRA SUNSHINE REQUIREMENTS.

"**Public disclosure of agreements**

"(a) Any agreement (as defined in subsection (e)) entered into after the date of the enactment of the Gramm-Leach-Bliley Act by an insured depository institution or affiliate with a nongovernmental entity or person made pursuant to or in connection with the

Community Reinvestment Act of 1977 involving funds or other resources of such insured depository institution or affiliate—

"(1) shall be in its entirety fully disclosed, and the full text thereof made available to the appropriate Federal banking agency with supervisory responsibility over the insured depository institution and to the public by each party to the agreement; and

"(2) shall obligate each party to comply with this section.

"Annual report of activity by insured depository institution

"(b) Each insured depository institution or affiliate that is a party to an agreement described in subsection (a) shall report to the appropriate Federal banking agency with supervisory responsibility over the insured depository institution, not less frequently than once each year, such information as the Federal banking agency may by rule require relating to the following actions taken by the party pursuant to the agreement during the preceding 12-month period:

"(1) Payments, fees, or loans made to any party to the agreement or received from any party to the agreement and the terms and conditions of the same.

"(2) Aggregate data on loans, investments, and services provided by each party in its community or communities pursuant to the agreement.

"(3) Such other pertinent matters as determined by regulation by the appropriate Federal banking agency with supervisory responsibility over the insured depository institution.

"Annual report of activity by nongovernmental entities

"(c)(1) IN GENERAL.—Each nongovernmental entity or person that is not an affiliate of an insured depository institution and that is a party to an agreement described in subsection (a) shall report to the appropriate Federal banking agency with supervisory responsibility over the insured depository institution that is a party to such agreement, not less frequently than once each year, an accounting of the use of funds received pursuant to each such agreement during the preceding 12-month period.

"(2) SUBMISSION TO INSURED DEPOSITORY INSTITUTION.—A nongovernmental entity or person referred to in paragraph (1) may comply with the reporting requirement in such paragraph by transmitting the report to the insured depository institution that is a party to the agreement, and such insured depository institution shall promptly transmit such report to the appropriate Federal banking agency with supervisory authority over the insured depository institution.

"(3) INFORMATION TO BE INCLUDED.—The accounting referred to in paragraph (1) shall include a detailed, itemized list of the uses to which such funds have been made, including compensation, administrative expenses, travel, entertainment, consulting and professional fees paid, and such other categories, as determined by regulation by the appropriate Federal banking agency with supervisory responsibility over the insured depository institution.

"Applicability

"(d) Subsections (b) and (c) shall not apply with respect to any agreement entered into before the end of the 6-month period beginning on the date of the enactment of the Gramm-Leach-Bliley Act.

"Definitions

"(e)(1) AGREEMENT.—For purposes of this section, the term 'agreement'—

"(A) means—

"(i) any written contract, written arrangement, or other written understanding that provides for cash payments, grants, or other consideration with a value in excess of $10,000, or for loans the aggregate amount of principal of which exceeds $50,000, annually (or the sum of all such agreements during a 12-month period with an aggregate value of cash payments, grants, or other consideration in excess of $10,000, or with an aggregate amount of loan principal in excess of $50,000); or "(ii) a group of substantively related contracts with an aggregate value of cash payments, grants, or other consideration in excess of $10,000, or with an aggregate amount of loan principal in excess of $50,000, annually;

made pursuant to, or in connection with, the fulfillment of the Community Reinvestment Act of 1977, at least 1 party to which is an insured depository institution or affiliate thereof, whether organized on a profit or not-for-profit basis; and

"(B) does not include—

"(i) any individual mortgage loan;

"(ii) any specific contract or commitment for a loan or extension of credit to individuals, businesses, farms, or other entities, if the funds are loaned at rates not substantially below market rates and if the purpose of the loan or extension of credit does not include any re-lending of the borrowed funds to other parties; or

"(iii) any agreement entered into by an insured depository institution or affiliate with a nongovernmental entity or person who has not commented on, testified about, or discussed with the institution, or otherwise contacted the institution, concerning the Community Reinvestment Act of 1977.

"(2) FULFILLMENT OF CRA.—For purposes of subparagraph (A), the term 'fulfillment' means a list of factors that the appropriate Federal banking agency determines have a material impact on the agency's decision—

"(A) to approve or disapprove an application for a deposit facility (as defined in section 803 of the Community Reinvestment Act of 1977); or

"(B) to assign a rating to an insured depository institution under section 807 of the Community Reinvestment Act of 1977.

"Violations

"(f)(1) VIOLATIONS BY PERSONS OTHER THAN INSURED DEPOSITORY INSTITUTIONS OR THEIR AFFILIATES.—

"(A) MATERIAL FAILURE TO COMPLY.—If the party to an agreement described in subsection (a) that is not an insured depository institution or affiliate willfully fails to comply with this section in a material way, as determined by the appropriate Federal banking agency, the agreement shall be unenforceable after the offending party has been given notice and a reasonable period of time to perform or comply.

"(B) DIVERSION OF FUNDS OR RESOURCES.—If funds or resources received under an agreement described in subsection (a) have been diverted contrary to the purposes of the agreement for personal financial gain, the appropriate Federal banking agency with supervisory responsibility over the insured depository institution may impose either or both of the following penalties:

"(i) Disgorgement by the offending individual of funds received under the agreement.

"(ii) Prohibition of the offending individual from being a party to any agreement described in subsection (a) for a period of not to exceed 10 years.

"(2) DESIGNATION OF SUCCESSOR NONGOVERNMENTAL PARTY.—If an agreement described in subsection (a) is found to be unenforceable under this subsection, the appropriate Federal banking agency may assist the insured depository institution in identifying a successor nongovernmental party to assume the responsibilities of the agreement.

"(3) INADVERTENT OR DE MINIMIS REPORTING ERRORS.—An error in a report filed under subsection (c) that is inadvertent or de minimis shall not subject the filing party to any penalty.

"Rule of construction

"(g) No provision of this section shall be construed as authorizing any appropriate Federal banking agency to enforce the provisions of any agreement described in subsection (a).

"Regulations

"(h)(1) IN GENERAL.—Each appropriate Federal banking agency shall prescribe regulations, in accordance with paragraph (4), requiring procedures reasonably designed to ensure and monitor compliance with the requirements of this section.

"(2) PROTECTION OF PARTIES.—In carrying out paragraph (1), each appropriate Federal banking agency shall—

"(A) ensure that the regulations prescribed by the agency do not impose an undue burden on the parties and that proprietary and confidential information is protected; and

"(B) establish procedures to allow any nongovernmental entity or person who is a party to a large number of agreements described in subsection (a) to make a single or consolidated filing of a report under subsection (c) to an insured depository institution or an appropriate Federal banking agency.

"(3) PARTIES NOT SUBJECT TO REPORTING REQUIREMENTS.—The Board of Governors of the Federal Reserve System may prescribe regulations—

"(A) to prevent evasions of subsection (e)(1)(B)(iii); and

"(B) to provide further exemptions under such subsection, consistent with the purposes of this section.

"(4) COORDINATION, CONSISTENCY, AND COMPARABILITY.—In carrying out paragraph (1), each appropriate Federal banking agency shall consult and coordinate with the other such agencies for the purposes of assuring, to the extent possible, that the regulations prescribed by each such agency are consistent and comparable with the regulations prescribed by the other such agencies.".

¶ 1712

SEC. 712. **SMALL BANK REGULATORY RELIEF.**

The Community Reinvestment Act of 1977 (12 U.S.C. 2901 et seq.) is amended by adding at the end the following new section:

"SEC. 809. SMALL BANK REGULATORY RELIEF.

"In general

"(a) Except as provided in subsections (b) and (c), any regulated financial institution with aggregate assets of not more than $250,000,000 shall be subject to routine examination under this title—

"(1) not more than once every 60 months for an institution that has achieved a rating of 'outstanding record of meeting community credit needs' at its most recent examination under section 804;

"(2) not more than once every 48 months for an institution that has received a rating of 'satisfactory record of meeting community credit needs' at its most recent examination under section 804; and

"(3) as deemed necessary by the appropriate Federal financial supervisory agency, for an institution that has received a rating of less than 'satisfactory record of meeting community credit needs' at its most recent examination under section 804.

"No exception from CRA examinations in connection with applications for deposit facilities

"(b) A regulated financial institution described in subsection (a) shall remain subject to examination under this title in connection with an application for a deposit facility.

"Discretion

"(c) A regulated financial institution described in subsection (a) may be subject to more frequent or less frequent examinations for reasonable cause under such circumstances as may be determined by the appropriate Federal financial supervisory agency.".

¶ 1713

SEC. 713. FEDERAL RESERVE BOARD STUDY OF CRA LENDING.

The Board of Governors of the Federal Reserve System shall conduct a comprehensive study, in consultation with the Chairman and Ranking Member of the Committee on Banking and Financial Services of the House of Representatives and the Chairman and Ranking Member of the Committee on Banking, Housing, and Urban Affairs of the Senate, of the Community Reinvestment Act of 1977, which shall focus on—

(1) the default rates;

(2) the delinquency rates; and

(3) the profitability;

of loans made in conformity with such Act, and report on the study to such Committees not later than March 15, 2000. Such report and supporting data shall also be made available by the Board of Governors of the Federal Reserve System to the public.

¶ 1714

SEC. 714. PRESERVING THE COMMUNITY REINVESTMENT ACT OF 1977.

Nothing in this Act shall be construed to repeal any provision of the Community Reinvestment Act of 1977.

¶ 1715

SEC. 715. RESPONSIVENESS TO COMMUNITY NEEDS FOR FINANCIAL SERVICES.

(a) STUDY.—The Secretary of the Treasury, in consultation with the Federal banking agencies (as defined in section 3(z) of the Federal Deposit Insurance Act), shall conduct a study of the extent to which adequate services are being provided as intended by the Community Reinvestment Act of 1977, including services in low- and moderate-income neighborhoods and for persons of modest means, as a result of the enactment of this Act.

(b) REPORTS.—

(1) IN GENERAL.—The Secretary of the Treasury shall—

(A) before March 15, 2000, submit a baseline report to the Congress on the study conducted pursuant to subsection (a); and

(B) before the end of the 2-year period beginning on the date of the enactment of this Act, in consultation with the Federal banking agencies, submit a final report to the Congress on the study conducted pursuant to subsection (a).

(2) RECOMMENDATIONS.—The final report submitted under paragraph (1)(B) shall include such recommendations as the Secretary determines to be appropriate for administrative and legislative action with respect to institutions covered under the Community Reinvestment Act of 1977.

Subtitle C—Other Regulatory Improvements

¶ 1721

SEC. 721. **EXPANDED SMALL BANK ACCESS TO S CORPORATION TREATMENT.**

(a) STUDY.—The Comptroller General of the United States shall conduct a study of—

(1) possible revisions to the rules governing S corporations, including—

(A) increasing the permissible number of shareholders in such corporations;

(B) permitting shares of such corporations to be held in individual retirement accounts;

(C) clarifying that interest on investments held for safety, soundness, and liquidity purposes should not be considered to be passive income;

(D) discontinuation of the treatment of stock held by bank directors as a disqualifying personal class of stock for such corporations; and

(E) improving Federal tax treatment of bad debt and interest deductions; and

(2) what impact such revisions might have on community banks.

(b) REPORT TO THE CONGRESS.—Not later than 6 months after the date of the enactment of this Act, the Comptroller General of the United States shall submit a report to the Congress on the results of the study conducted under subsection (a).

(c) DEFINITION.—For purposes of this section, the term "S corporation" has the meaning given the term in section 1361(a)(1) of the Internal Revenue Code of 1986.

¶ 1722

SEC. 722. **"PLAIN LANGUAGE" REQUIREMENT FOR FEDERAL BANKING AGENCY RULES.**

(a) IN GENERAL.—Each Federal banking agency shall use plain language in all proposed and final rulemakings published by the agency in the Federal Register after January 1, 2000.

(b) REPORT.—Not later than March 1, 2001, each Federal banking agency shall submit to the Congress a report that describes how the agency has complied with subsection (a).

(c) DEFINITION.—For purposes of this section, the term "Federal banking agency" has the meaning given that term in section 3 of the Federal Deposit Insurance Act.

¶ 1723

SEC. 723. **RETENTION OF "FEDERAL" IN NAME OF CONVERTED FEDERAL SAVINGS ASSOCIATION.**

Section 2 of the Act entitled "An Act to enable national banking associations to increase their capital stock and to change their names or locations", approved May 1, 1886 (12 U.S.C. 30), is amended by adding at the end the following new subsection:

"Retention of 'federal' in name of converted federal savings association

"(d)(1) IN GENERAL.—Notwithstanding subsection (a) or any other provision of law, any depository institution, the charter of which is converted from that of a Federal savings association to a national bank or a State bank after the date of the enactment of the Gramm-Leach-Bliley Act may retain the term 'Federal' in the name of such institution if such institution remains an insured depository institution.

"(2) DEFINITIONS.—For purposes of this subsection, the terms 'depository institution', 'insured depository institution', 'national bank', and 'State bank' have the meanings given those terms in section 3 of the Federal Deposit Insurance Act.".

¶ 1724

SEC. 724. **CONTROL OF BANKERS' BANKS.**

Section 2(a)(5)(E)(i) of the Bank Holding Company Act of 1956 (12 U.S.C. 1841(a)(5)(E)(i)) is amended by inserting "1 or more" before "thrift institutions".

¶ 1725

SEC. 725. **PROVISION OF TECHNICAL ASSISTANCE TO MICROENTERPRISES.**

Title I of the Riegle Community Development and Regulatory Improvement Act of 1994 (12 U.S.C. 4701 et seq.) is amended by adding at the end the following new subtitle:

"Subtitle C—Microenterprise Technical Assistance and Capacity Building Program

"SEC. 171. SHORT TITLE.

"This subtitle may be cited as the 'Program for Investment in Microentrepreneurs Act of 1999', also referred to as the 'PRIME Act'.

"SEC. 172. DEFINITIONS.

"For purposes of this subtitle, the following definitions shall apply:

"(1) ADMINISTRATION.—The term 'Administration' means the Small Business Administration.

"(2) ADMINISTRATOR.—The term 'Administrator' means the Administrator of the Small Business Administration.

"(3) CAPACITY BUILDING SERVICES.—The term 'capacity building services' means services provided to an organization that is, or that is in the process of becoming, a microenterprise development organization or program, for the purpose of enhancing its ability to provide training and services to disadvantaged entrepreneurs.

"(4) COLLABORATIVE.—The term 'collaborative' means 2 or more nonprofit entities that agree to act jointly as a qualified organization under this subtitle.

"(5) DISADVANTAGED ENTREPRENEUR.—The term 'disadvantaged entrepreneur' means a microentrepreneur that is—

"(A) a low-income person;

"(B) a very low-income person; or

"(C) an entrepreneur that lacks adequate access to capital or other resources essential for business success, or is economically disadvantaged, as determined by the Administrator.

"(6) INDIAN TRIBE.—The term 'Indian tribe' has the meaning given the term in section 103.

"(7) INTERMEDIARY.—The term 'intermediary' means a private, nonprofit entity that seeks to serve microenterprise development organizations and programs as authorized under section 175.

"(8) LOW-INCOME PERSON.—The term 'low-income person' has the meaning given the term in section 103.

"(9) MICROENTREPRENEUR.—The term 'microentrepreneur' means the owner or developer of a microenterprise.

"(10) MICROENTERPRISE.—The term 'microenterprise' means a sole proprietorship, partnership, or corporation that—

"(A) has fewer than 5 employees; and

"(B) generally lacks access to conventional loans, equity, or other banking services.

"(11) MICROENTERPRISE DEVELOPMENT ORGANIZATION OR PROGRAM.—The term 'microenterprise development organization or program' means a nonprofit entity, or a program administered by such an entity, including community development corporations or other nonprofit development organizations and social service organizations, that provides services to disadvantaged entrepreneurs.

"(12) TRAINING AND TECHNICAL ASSISTANCE.—The term 'training and technical assistance' means services and support provided to disadvantaged entrepreneurs, such as assistance for the purpose of enhancing business planning, marketing, management, financial management skills, and assistance for the purpose of accessing financial services.

"(13) VERY LOW-INCOME PERSON.—The term 'very low-income person' means having an income, adjusted for family size, of not more than 150 percent of the poverty line (as defined in section 673(2) of the Community Services Block Grant Act (42 U.S.C. 9902(2)), including any revision required by that section).

"SEC. 173. ESTABLISHMENT OF PROGRAM.

"The Administrator shall establish a microenterprise technical assistance and capacity building grant program to provide assistance from the Administration in the form of grants to qualified organizations in accordance with this subtitle.

"SEC. 174. USES OF ASSISTANCE.

"A qualified organization shall use grants made under this subtitle—

"(1) to provide training and technical assistance to disadvantaged entrepreneurs;

"(2) to provide training and capacity building services to microenterprise development organizations and programs and groups of such organizations to assist such organizations and programs in developing microenterprise training and services;

"(3) to aid in researching and developing the best practices in the field of microenterprise and technical assistance programs for disadvantaged entrepreneurs; and

"(4) for such other activities as the Administrator determines are consistent with the purposes of this subtitle.

"SEC. 175. QUALIFIED ORGANIZATIONS.

"For purposes of eligibility for assistance under this subtitle, a qualified organization shall be—

"(1) a nonprofit microenterprise development organization or program (or a group or collaborative thereof) that has a demonstrated record of delivering microenterprise services to disadvantaged entrepreneurs;

"(2) an intermediary;

"(3) a microenterprise development organization or program that is accountable to a local community, working in conjunction with a State or local government or Indian tribe; or

"(4) an Indian tribe acting on its own, if the Indian tribe can certify that no private organization or program referred to in this paragraph exists within its jurisdiction.

"SEC. 176. ALLOCATION OF ASSISTANCE; SUBGRANTS.

"Allocation of assistance

"(a)(1) IN GENERAL.—The Administrator shall allocate assistance from the Administration under this subtitle to ensure that—

"(A) activities described in section 174(1) are funded using not less than 75 percent of amounts made available for such assistance; and

"(B) activities described in section 174(2) are funded using not less than 15 percent of amounts made available for such assistance.

"(2) LIMIT ON INDIVIDUAL ASSISTANCE.—No single person may receive more than 10 percent of the total funds appropriated under this subtitle in a single fiscal year.

"Targeted assistance

"(b) The Administrator shall ensure that not less than 50 percent of the grants made under this subtitle are used to benefit very low-income persons, including those residing on Indian reservations.

"Subgrants authorized

"(c)(1) IN GENERAL.—A qualified organization receiving assistance under this subtitle may provide grants using that assistance to qualified small and emerging microenterprise organizations and programs, subject to such rules and regulations as the Administrator determines to be appropriate.

"(2) LIMIT ON ADMINISTRATIVE EXPENSES.—Not more than 7.5 percent of assistance received by a qualified organization under this subtitle may be used for administrative expenses in connection with the making of subgrants under paragraph (1).

"Diversity

"(d) In making grants under this subtitle, the Administrator shall ensure that grant recipients include both large and small microenterprise organizations, serving urban, rural, and Indian tribal communities serving diverse populations.

"Prohibition on preferential consideration of certain SBA program participants

(e) In making grants under this subtitle, the Administrator shall ensure that any application made by a qualified organization that is a participant in the program established under section 7(m) of the Small Business Act does not receive preferential consideration over applications from other qualified organizations that are not participants in such program.

"SEC. 177. MATCHING REQUIREMENTS.

"In general

"(a) Financial assistance under this subtitle shall be matched with funds from sources other than the Federal Government on the basis of not less than 50 percent of each dollar provided by the Administration.

"Sources of matching funds

"(b) Fees, grants, gifts, funds from loan sources, and in-kind resources of a grant recipient from public or private sources may be used to comply with the matching requirement in subsection (a).

"Exception

"(c)(1) IN GENERAL.—In the case of an applicant for assistance under this subtitle with severe constraints on available sources of matching funds, the Administrator may reduce or eliminate the matching requirements of subsection (a).

"(2) LIMITATION.—Not more than 10 percent of the total funds made available from the Administration in any fiscal year to carry out this subtitle may be excepted from the matching requirements of subsection (a), as authorized by paragraph (1) of this subsection.

"SEC. 178. APPLICATIONS FOR ASSISTANCE.

"An application for assistance under this subtitle shall be submitted in such form and in accordance with such procedures as the Administrator shall establish.

"SEC. 179. RECORDKEEPING.

"The requirements of section 115 shall apply to a qualified organization receiving assistance from the Administration under this subtitle as if it were a community development financial institution receiving assistance from the Fund under subtitle A.

"SEC. 180. AUTHORIZATION.

"In addition to funds otherwise authorized to be appropriated to the Fund to carry out this title, there are authorized to be appropriated to the Administrator to carry out this subtitle—

"(1) $15,000,000 for fiscal year 2000;

"(2) $15,000,000 for fiscal year 2001;

"(3) $15,000,000 for fiscal year 2002; and

"(4) $15,000,000 for fiscal year 2003.

"SEC. 181. IMPLEMENTATION.

"The Administrator shall, by regulation, establish such requirements as may be necessary to carry out this subtitle.".

¶ 1726

SEC. 726. **FEDERAL RESERVE AUDITS.**

The Federal Reserve Act (12 U.S.C. 221 et seq.) is amended by inserting after section 11A the following new section:

"SEC. 11B. ANNUAL INDEPENDENT AUDITS OF FEDERAL RESERVE BANKS AND BOARD.

"The Board shall order an annual independent audit of the financial statements of each Federal reserve bank and the Board.".

¶ 1727

SEC. 727. **AUTHORIZATION TO RELEASE REPORTS.**

(a) FEDERAL RESERVE ACT.—The eighth undesignated paragraph of section 9 of the Federal Reserve Act (12 U.S.C. 326) is amended by striking the last sentence and inserting the following: "The Board of Governors of the Federal Reserve System, at its discretion, may furnish any report of examination or other confidential supervisory information concerning any State member bank or other entity examined under any other authority of the Board, to any Federal or State agency or authority with supervisory or regulatory authority over the examined entity, to any officer, director, or receiver of the examined entity, and to any other person that the Board determines to be proper.".

(b) COMMODITY FUTURES TRADING COMMISSION.—The Right to Financial Privacy Act of 1978 (12 U.S.C. 3401 et seq.) is amended—

(1) in section 1101(7)—

(A) by redesignating subparagraphs (G) and (H) as subparagraphs (H) and (I), respectively; and

(B) by inserting after subparagraph (F) the following new subparagraph:

"(G) the Commodity Futures Trading Commission;"; and

(2) in section 1112(e), by striking "and the Securities and Exchange Commission" and inserting ", the Securities and Exchange Commission, and the Commodity Futures Trading Commission".

¶ 1728

SEC. 728. GENERAL ACCOUNTING OFFICE STUDY OF CONFLICTS OF INTEREST.

(a) STUDY REQUIRED.—The Comptroller General of the United States shall conduct a study analyzing the conflict of interest faced by the Board of Governors of the Federal Reserve System between its role as a primary regulator of the banking industry and its role as a vendor of services to the banking and financial services industry.

(b) SPECIFIC CONFLICT REQUIRED TO BE ADDRESSED.—In the course of the study required under subsection (a), the Comptroller General shall address the conflict of interest faced by the Board of Governors of the Federal Reserve System between the role of the Board as a regulator of the payment system, generally, and its participation in the payment system as a competitor with private entities who are providing payment services.

(c) REPORT TO THE CONGRESS.—Before the end of the 1-year period beginning on the date of the enactment of this Act, the Comptroller General shall submit a report to the Congress containing the findings and conclusions of the Comptroller General in connection with the study required under this section, together with such recommendations for such legislative or administrative actions as the Comptroller General may determine to be appropriate, including recommendations for resolving any such conflict of interest.

¶ 1729

SEC. 729. STUDY AND REPORT ON ADAPTING EXISTING LEGISLATIVE REQUIREMENTS TO ONLINE BANKING AND LENDING.

(a) STUDY REQUIRED.—The Federal banking agencies shall conduct a study of banking regulations regarding the delivery of financial services, including those regulations that may assume that there will be person-to-person contact during the course of a financial services transaction, and report their recommendations on adapting those existing requirements to online banking and lending.

(b) REPORT REQUIRED.—Before the end of the 2-year period beginning on the date of the enactment of this Act, the Federal banking agencies shall submit a report to the Congress on the findings and conclusions of the agencies with respect to the study required under subsection (a), together with such recommendations for legislative or regulatory action as the agencies may determine to be appropriate.

(c) DEFINITION.—For purposes of this section, the term "Federal banking agencies" means each Federal banking agency (as defined in section 3(z) of the Federal Deposit Insurance Act).

¶ 1730

SEC. 730. CLARIFICATION OF SOURCE OF STRENGTH DOCTRINE.

Section 18 of the Federal Deposit Insurance Act (21 U.S.C. 1828) is amended by adding at the end the following new subsection:

"Limitation on claims

"(t)(1) IN GENERAL.—No person may bring a claim against any Federal banking agency (including in its capacity as conservator or receiver) for the return of assets of an affiliate or controlling shareholder of the insured depository institution transferred to, or for the benefit of, an insured depository institution by such affiliate or controlling shareholder of the insured depository institution, or a claim against such Federal banking agency for monetary damages or other legal or equitable relief in connection with such transfer, if at the time of the transfer—

"(A) the insured depository institution is subject to any direction issued in writing by a Federal banking agency to increase its capital;

"(B) the insured depository institution is undercapitalized (as defined in section 38 of this Act); and

"(C) for that portion of the transfer that is made by an entity covered by section 5(g) of the Bank Holding Company Act of 1956 or section 45 of this Act, the Federal banking agency has followed the procedure set forth in such section.

"(2) DEFINITION OF CLAIM.—For purposes of paragraph (1), the term 'claim'—

"(A) means a cause of action based on Federal or State law that—

"(i) provides for the avoidance of preferential or fraudulent transfers or conveyances; or

"(ii) provides similar remedies for preferential or fraudulent transfers or conveyances; and

"(B) does not include any claim based on actual intent to hinder, delay, or defraud pursuant to such a fraudulent transfer or conveyance law.".

¶ 1731

SEC. 731. INTEREST RATES AND OTHER CHARGES AT INTERSTATE BRANCHES.

Section 44 of the Federal Deposit Insurance Act (12 U.S.C. 1831u) is amended—

(1) by redesignating subsection (f) as subsection (g); and

(2) by inserting after subsection (e) the following new subsection:

"Applicable rate and other charge limitations

"(f)(1) IN GENERAL.—In the case of any State that has a constitutional provision that sets a maximum lawful annual percentage rate of interest on any contract at not more than 5 percent above the discount rate for 90-day commercial paper in effect at the Federal reserve bank for the Federal reserve district in which such State is located, except as provided in paragraph (2), upon the establishment in such State of a branch of any out-of-State insured depository institution in such State under this section, the maximum interest rate or amount of interest, discount points, finance charges, or other similar charges that may be charged, taken, received, or reserved from time to time in any loan or discount made or upon any note, bill of exchange, financing transaction, or other evidence of debt by any insured depository institution whose home State is such State shall be equal to not more than the greater of—

"(A) the maximum interest rate or amount of interest, discount points, finance charges, or other similar charges that may be charged, taken, received, or reserved in a similar transaction under the constitution, statutory, or other laws of the home State of the out-of-State insured depository institution establishing any such branch, without reference to this section, as such maximum interest rate or amount of interest may change from time to time; or

"(B) the maximum rate or amount of interest, discount points, finance charges, or other similar charges that may be charged, taken, received, or reserved in a similar transaction by a State insured depository institution chartered under the laws of such State or a national bank or Federal savings association whose main office is located in such State without reference to this section.

"(2) RULE OF CONSTRUCTION.—No provision of this subsection shall be construed as superseding or affecting—

"(A) the authority of any insured depository institution to take, receive, reserve, and charge interest on any loan made in any State other than the State referred to in paragraph (1); or

"(B) the applicability of section 501 of the Depository Institutions Deregulation and Monetary Control Act of 1980, section 5197 of the Revised Statutes of the United States, or section 27 of this Act.".

¶ 1732

SEC. 732. **INTERSTATE BRANCHES AND AGENCIES OF FOREIGN BANKS.**

Section 5(a)(7) of the International Banking Act of 1978 (12 U.S.C. 3103(a)(7)) is amended to read as follows:

"(7) ADDITIONAL AUTHORITY FOR INTERSTATE BRANCHES AND AGENCIES OF FOREIGN BANKS, UPGRADES OF CERTAIN FOREIGN BANK AGENCIES AND BRANCHES.—Notwithstanding paragraphs (1) and (2), a foreign bank may—

"(A) with the approval of the Board and the Comptroller of the Currency, establish and operate a Federal branch or Federal agency or, with the approval of the Board and the appropriate State bank supervisor, a State branch or State agency in any State outside the foreign bank's home State if—

"(i) the establishment and operation of such branch or agency is permitted by the State in which the branch or agency is to be established; and

"(ii) in the case of a Federal or State branch, the branch receives only such deposits as would be permitted for a corporation organized under section 25A of the Federal Reserve Act; or

"(B) with the approval of the Board and the relevant licensing authority (the Comptroller in the case of a Federal branch or the appropriate State supervisor in the case of a State branch), upgrade an agency, or a branch of the type referred to in subparagraph (A)(ii), located in a State outside the foreign bank's home State, into a Federal or State branch if—

"(i) the establishment and operation of such branch is permitted by such State; and

"(ii) such agency or branch—

"(I) was in operation in such State on the day before September 29, 1994; or

"(II) has been in operation in such State for a period of time that meets the State's minimum age requirement permitted under section 44(a)(5) of the Federal Deposit Insurance Act.".

¶ 1733

SEC. 733. **FAIR TREATMENT OF WOMEN BY FINANCIAL ADVISERS.**

It is the sense of the Congress that individuals offering financial advice and products should offer such services and products in a nondiscriminatory, nongender-specific manner.

¶ 1734

SEC. 734. **MEMBERSHIP OF LOAN GUARANTEE BOARDS.**

(a) EMERGENCY STEEL LOAN GUARANTEE BOARD.—Section 101(e) of the Emergency Steel Loan Guarantee Act of 1999 is amended—

(1) in paragraph (2), by inserting ", or a member of the Board of Governors of the Federal Reserve System designated by the Chairman" after "the Chairman of the Board of Governors of the Federal Reserve System"; and

(2) in paragraph (3), by inserting ", or a commissioner of the Securities and Exchange Commission designated by the Chairman" before the period.

(b) EMERGENCY OIL AND GAS LOAN GUARANTEE BOARD.—Section 201(d)(2) of the Emergency Oil and Gas Guarantee Loan Program Act is amended—

(1) in subparagraph (B), by inserting ", or a member of the Board of Governors of the Federal Reserve System designated by the Chairman" after "the Chairman of the Board of Governors of the Federal Reserve System"; and

(2) in subparagraph (C), by inserting ", or a commissioner of the Securities and Exchange Commission designated by the Chairman" before the period.

¶ 1735

SEC. 735. **REPEAL OF STOCK LOAN LIMIT IN FEDERAL RESERVE ACT.**

Section 11 of the Federal Reserve Act (12 U.S.C. 248) is amended by striking the paragraph designated as "(m)" and inserting "(m) [Repealed]".

¶ 1736

SEC. 736. **ELIMINATION OF SAIF AND DIF SPECIAL RESERVES.**

(a) SAIF SPECIAL RESERVE.—Section 11(a)(6) of the Federal Deposit Insurance Act (12 U.S.C. 1821(a)(6)) is amended by striking subparagraph (L).

(b) DIF SPECIAL RESERVE.—Section 2704 of the Deposit Insurance Funds Act of 1996 (12 U.S.C. 1821 note) is amended—

(1) by striking subsection (b); and

(2) in subsection (d)—

(A) by striking paragraph (4);

(B) in paragraph (6)(C)(i), by striking "(6) and (7)" and inserting "(5), (6), and (7)"; and

(C) in paragraph (6)(C), by striking clause (ii) and inserting the following:

"(ii) by redesignating paragraph (8) as paragraph (5)."

(c) EFFECTIVE DATE.—This section and the amendments made by this section shall become effective on the date of the enactment of this Act.

¶ 1737

SEC. 737. **BANK OFFICERS AND DIRECTORS AS OFFICERS AND DIRECTORS OF PUBLIC UTILITIES.**

Section 305(b) of the Federal Power Act (16 U.S.C. 825d(b)) is amended—

(1) by striking "(b) After six" and inserting the following:

"Interlocking directorates

"(b)(1) IN GENERAL.—After 6"; and (2) by adding at the end the following:

"(2) APPLICABILITY.—

"(A) IN GENERAL.—In the circumstances described in subparagraph (B), paragraph (1) shall not apply to a person that holds or proposes to hold the positions of—

"(i) officer or director of a public utility; and

"(ii) officer or director of a bank, trust company, banking association, or firm authorized by law to underwrite or participate in the marketing of securities of a public utility.

"(B) CIRCUMSTANCES.—The circumstances described in this subparagraph are that—

"(i) a person described in subparagraph (A) does not participate in any deliberations or decisions of the public utility regarding the selection of a bank, trust company, banking association, or firm to underwrite or participate in the marketing of securities of the public utility, if the person serves as an officer or director of a bank, trust company, banking association, or firm that is under consideration in the deliberation process;

"(ii) the bank, trust company, banking association, or firm of which the person is an officer or director does not engage in the underwriting of, or participate in the marketing of, securities of the public utility of which the person holds the position of officer or director;

"(iii) the public utility for which the person serves or proposes to serve as an officer or director selects underwriters by competitive procedures; or

"(iv) the issuance of securities the public utility for which the person serves or proposes to serve as an officer or director has been approved by all Federal and State regulatory agencies having jurisdiction over the issuance.".

¶ 1738

SEC. 738. APPROVAL FOR PURCHASES OF SECURITIES.

Section 23B(b)(2) of the Federal Reserve Act (12 U.S.C. 371c-1) is amended to read as follows:

"Subparagraph (B) of paragraph (1) shall not apply if the purchase or acquisition of such securities has been approved, before such securities are initially offered for sale to the public, by a majority of the directors of the bank based on a determination that the purchase is a sound investment for the bank irrespective of the fact that an affiliate of the bank is a principal underwriter of the securities.".

¶ 1739

SEC. 739. OPTIONAL CONVERSION OF FEDERAL SAVINGS ASSOCIATIONS.

Section 5(i) of the Home Owners' Loan Act (12 U.S.C. 1464(i)) is amended by adding at the end the following new paragraph:

"(5) CONVERSION TO NATIONAL OR STATE BANK.—

"(A) IN GENERAL.—Any Federal savings association chartered and in operation before the date of the enactment of the Gramm-Leach-Bliley Act, with branches in operation before such date of enactment in 1 or more States, may convert, at its option, with the approval of the Comptroller of the Currency or the appropriate State bank supervisor, into 1 or more national or State banks, each of which may encompass 1 or more of the branches of the Federal savings association in operation before such date of enactment in 1 or more States, but only if each resulting national or State bank will meet all financial, management, and capital requirements applicable to the resulting national or State bank.

"(B) DEFINITIONS.—For purposes of this paragraph, the terms 'State bank' and 'State bank supervisor' have the meanings given those terms in section 3 of the Federal Deposit Insurance Act.".

¶ 1740

SEC. 740. GRAND JURY PROCEEDINGS.

Section 3322(b) of title 18, United States Code, is amended—

(1) in paragraph (1), by inserting "Federal or State" before "financial institution"; and

(2) in paragraph (2), by inserting "at any time during or after the completion of the investigation of the grand jury," before "upon".

CONFERENCE REPORT—TABLE OF CONTENTS

CONFERENCE REPORT—S. 900/H.R. 10

Statement of Managers

Summary of Major Provisions

Monday—November 1, 1999

TITLE I [AFFILIATIONS]

¶ 5001 FACILITATING AFFILIATIONS AMONG BANKS, SECURITIES FIRMS, AND INSURANCE COMPANIES

The legislation approved by the Conference Managers eliminates many Federal and State law barriers to affiliations among banks and securities firms, insurance companies, and other financial service providers. The House and Senate bills established an identical statutory framework (except for minor drafting differences) pursuant to which full affiliations can occur between banks and securities firms, insurance companies, and other financial companies. The Conferees adopted this framework. Furthermore, the legislation provides financial organizations with flexibility in structuring these new financial affiliations through a holding company structure, or a financial subsidiary (with certain prudential limitations on activities and appropriate safeguards). Reflected in the legislation is the determination made by both Houses to preserve the role of the Board of Governors of the Federal Reserve System (the "Federal Reserve Board" or the "Board") as the umbrella supervisor for holding companies, but to incorporate a system of functional regulation designed to utilize the strengths of the various Federal and State financial supervisors. Incorporating provisions found in both the House and Senate bills, the legislation establishes a mechanism for coordination between the Federal Reserve Board and the Secretary of the Treasury ("the Secretary") regarding the approval of new financial activities for both holding companies and national bank financial subsidiaries. The legislation enhances safety and soundness and improves access to financial services by requiring that banks may not participate in the new financial affiliations unless the banks are well capitalized and well managed. The appropriate regulators are given clear authority to address any failure to maintain these safety and soundness standards in a prompt manner. The legislation also requires that Federal bank regulators prohibit banks from participating in the new financial affiliations if, at the time of certification, any bank affiliate had received a less than "satisfactory" Community Reinvestment Act of 1977 ("CRA") rating as of its most recent examination.

¶ 5002 SUBTITLE A—FINANCIAL AFFILIATIONS

Senate Position: The Senate bill contains provisions repealing restrictions in the Glass-Steagall Act and the Bank Holding Company Act of 1956 ("BHCA") on affiliations involving securities firms and insurance companies, respectively. The Senate bill establishes a new framework in section 4 of the BHCA for bank holding companies to engage in financial activities. It does not create a separate designation for bank holding companies engaged in the new financial activities but it does require that the subsidiary insured depository institutions of such holding companies be well capitalized and well managed in order to take advantage of the new activities. In the event that a bank holding company's subsidiary depository institutions fall out of compliance, a "cure" procedure is established. The Senate bill authorizes bank holding companies to engage in activities that the Federal Reserve Board has determined to be financial in nature and incidental to such financial activities. It also authorizes qualifying bank holding companies to engage in activities that the Federal Reserve Board determines are complementary to financial activities, or any other service that the Federal Reserve Board determines not to pose a substantial risk to the safety and soundness of depository institutions or the financial system generally. It contains a list of pre-approved activities that includes merchant banking and insurance company portfolio investment activities. There is also a grandfather provision for the commodities activities engaged in by a company as of September 30, 1997, if that company becomes a bank holding company after the date of enactment.

House Position: The House bill also repeals the restrictions contained in the Glass-Steagall Act on affiliations between banks and securities firms engaged in underwriting and in the BHCA on affiliations between banks and insurance companies and insurance agents. It creates a new section 6 of the BHCA which authorizes new financial activities for bank holding companies that qualify as "financial holding companies." In order for a bank holding company to qualify as a financial holding company ("FHC"), its subsidiary depository institutions must be well managed, well capitalized, and have received at least a "satisfactory" CRA rating as of their last examination. In the event that an FHC falls out of compliance, a "cure" procedure is established. It authorizes FHCs to engage in activities that the Federal Reserve Board has determined to be financial in nature, incidental to such financial activities or complementary to financial activities to the extent that the amount of such complementary activities remains small. It contains a list of pre-approved activities that includes investment banking and insurance company portfolio investment activities. The House bill also authorizes FHCs to engage in developing activities to a limited extent. A ten-year grandfather is included for the nonfinancial activities of companies that become bank holding companies after enactment of this legislation and are predominantly financial in nature at the time they become FHCs.

Conference Substitute: The Conferees acceded to the Senate by agreeing to amend section 4 of the BHCA to add a series of new subsections that contain the framework for engaging in new financial activities. The Conferees have acceded to the House in designating as FHCs those bank holding companies qualifying to engage in the new financial activities.

New section 4(k) permits bank holding companies that qualify as FHCs to engage in activities, and acquire companies engaged in activities, that are financial in nature or incidental to such financial activities. FHCs are also permitted to engage in activities that are complementary to financial activities if the Federal Reserve Board determines that the activity does not pose a substantial risk to the safety or soundness of depository institutions or the financial system in general.

Permitting banks to affiliate with firms engaged in financial activities represents a significant expansion from the current requirement that bank affiliates may only be engaged in activities that are closely related to banking. The Board has primary jurisdiction for determining what activities are financial in nature, incidental to financial in nature, or complementary. The Board may act by regulation or order. In determining what activities are financial in nature or incidental, the Federal Reserve Board must notify the Secretary of applications or requests to engage in new financial activities. The Federal Reserve Board may not determine that an activity is financial or incidental to a financial activity if the Secretary objects. The Secretary may also propose to the Federal Reserve Board that the Board find that a particular activity is financial in nature or incidental to a financial activity. A similar procedure is included in the legislation with regard to the determination of financial activities and activities that are incidental to financial activities for financial subsidiaries of national banks. The intent of the Conferees is that the Federal Reserve Board and the Secretary of the Treasury will establish a consultative process that will negate the need for either agency to veto a proposal of the other agency. Establishing such a process should bring balance to the determinations regarding the type of activities that are financial and limit regulatory arbitrage.

Section 4(k) contains a list of activities that are considered to be financial in nature. An FHC may engage in the activities on this list without obtaining prior approval from the Federal Reserve Board. Notice must be given to the Federal Reserve Board not later than 30 days after the activity is commenced or a company is acquired. The list includes securities underwriting, dealing, and market making without any revenue limitation such as sponsoring and distributing all types of mutual funds and investment companies. Other activities include insurance underwriting and agency activities, merchant banking, and insurance company portfolio investments. The reference to ". . .insuring, guaranteeing or indemnifying against. . .illness," is meant to include activities commonly thought of as health insurance, including such activities when provided by companies such as Blue Cross and Blue Shield organizations which are licensed under State laws to provide health insurance benefits in consideration of the payment of premiums or subscriber contributions. Such reference is not meant to include the activity of directly providing health care on a basis other than to the extent that it may be incidental to the business of insurance as defined in section 4(k)(4)(B) of the BHCA.

Merchant banking

The authorization of merchant banking activities as provided in new section 4(k)(4)(H) of the BHCA is designed to recognize the essential role that these activities play in modern finance and permits an FHC that has a securities affiliate or an affiliate of an insurance company engaged in underwriting life, accident and health, or property and casualty insurance, or providing and issuing annuities, to conduct such activities. Under this provision, the FHC may directly or indirectly acquire or control any kind of ownership interest (including debt and equity securities, partnership interests, trust certificates, or other instruments representing ownership) in an entity engaged in any kind of trade or business whatsoever. The FHC may make such acquisition whether acting as principal, on behalf of one or more entities (e.g., as adviser to a fund, regardless of whether the FHC is also an investor in the fund), including entities that the FHC controls (other than a depository institution or a subsidiary of a depository institution), or otherwise.

Section 122 provides that after a 5 year period from the date of enactment, the Board and the Secretary may jointly adopt rules permitting financial subsidiaries to engage in the activities under section 4(k)(4)(H) of the BHCA subject to the conditions that the agencies may jointly determine.

Insurance company portfolio investments

New section 4(k)(4)(I) of the BHCA recognizes that as part of the ordinary course of business, insurance companies frequently invest funds received from policyholders by acquiring most or all the shares of stock of a company that may not be engaged in a financial activity. These investments are made in the ordinary course of business pursuant to state insurance laws governing investments by insurance companies, and are subject to ongoing review and approval by the applicable state regulator. Section 4(k)(4)(I) permits an insurance company that is affiliated with a depository institution to continue to directly or indirectly acquire or control any kind of ownership interest in any company if certain requirements are met. The shares held by such a company: (i) must not be acquired or held by a depository institution or a subsidiary of a depository institution; (ii) must be acquired and held by an insurance company that is predominantly engaged in underwriting life, accident and health, or property and casualty (other than credit-related insurance) or in providing and issuing annuities; and (iii) must represent an investment made in the ordinary course of business of such insurance company in accordance with relevant state law governing such investments. In addition, during the period such ownership interests are held, the FHC must not routinely manage or operate the portfolio company except as may be necessary or required to obtain a reasonable return on the investment. To the extent an FHC participates in the management or operation of a portfolio company, such participation would ordinarily be for the purpose of safeguarding the investment of the insurance company in accordance with the applicable requirements of state insurance law. This is irrespective of any overlap between board members and officers of the FHC and the portfolio company.

CONDITIONS TO ENGAGE IN NEW ACTIVITIES

New section 4(l) of the BHCA establishes the requirements for permitting a bank holding company to engage in the new financial activities and affiliations. A bank holding company may elect to become a financial holding company if all of its subsidiary banks are well capitalized and well managed. A bank holding company that meets such requirements may file a certification to that effect with the Board and a declaration that the company chooses to be an FHC.

After the filing of such a declaration and certification, an FHC may engage either de novo, or through an acquisition, in any activity that has been determined by the Board to be financial in nature or incidental to such financial activity. FHCs may engage in activities on the preapproved list of financial activities contained in section 4(k) of the BHCA and any other financial activity approved by the Board without prior notice. Complementary activities, however, must be approved by the Board on a case-by-case basis under the notice procedures contained in section 4(j) of the BHCA.

The legislation also amends the CRA to provide that an election of a bank holding company to become an FHC shall not be effective if the Board finds that as of the date of the election not all of the subsidiary insured depository institutions of the holding company had received a "satisfactory" or better CRA rating at their most recent CRA examinations. In addition, the legislation amends the BHCA to require the appropriate Federal banking agency to prohibit an FHC, or a bank through a financial subsidiary, from commencing any new activities or acquiring any companies under sections 4(k) or (n) of the BHCA, section 5136A(a) of the Revised Statutes of the United States, or section 46(a) of the Federal Deposit Insurance Act, in the event that the bank or any of its insured depository institution affiliates or any insured depository institution affiliate of the FHC fails to have at least a "satisfactory" CRA rating at the time of its last examination. It is the most recent rating alone that shall be looked to by the regulator in connection with these provisions. This provision does not authorize any agency to require the divestiture of any company already owned by the FHC prior to the time that the prohibition becomes effective or to limit in any way any activity already engaged in by the FHC prior to that time. The prohibition ceases to apply once all of the insured depository institutions controlled by the FHC or the bank and all of its insured depository institution affiliates have restored their CRA performance rating to at least the "satisfactory" level.

This provision applies to the ownership and activities of financial subsidiaries of national banks to the same extent as it applies to FHCs. It also applies in the same way to subsidiaries held by insured State banks subject to newly added section 46(a) of the Federal Deposit Insurance Act.

OPERATION OF STATE LAW

Senate Position: The Senate bill establishes in section 104 the parameters for the appropriate balance between Federal and State regulation of the activities and affiliations allowed under this legislation.

House Position: The House provision is similar, with parallel provisions contained in sections 104, 301, and 302 of the House bill.

Conference Substitute: The House agreed to incorporate its sections 301 and 302 into section 104, and the Senate agreed to adopt the language of the House's section 302. The House discrimination standard was adopted with modifications, and the Conferees agreed to incorporate House provisions protecting the ability of the States to require restoration of an entity's capital, and restricting changes in stock ownership of demutualizing insurers, as modified. The House receded on its provision specifically addressing a North Carolina Blue-Cross Blue-Shield organization, as the State laws governing those types of entities would not be preempted so long as the State laws do not discriminate, as set forth in the legislation.

This section reaffirms the McCarran-Ferguson Act, recognizing the primacy and legal authority of the States to regulate insurance activities of all persons. No persons are permitted to engage in the business of insurance unless they are licensed by the States, as required under State law. States are not allowed to prevent certain affiliations or activities or discriminate against depository institutions in providing such insurance licenses.

In general, States are not allowed to prevent or restrict affiliations permitted under Federal law. With respect to an affiliation by an insurer, States may collect information, and the insurer's State of domicile may take action on the affiliation (including approval or disapproval), but only within 60 days of receiving notice of the affiliation, and only if the actions do not discriminate against the insurer based on an association with a depository institution. An affiliating insurer's State of domicile may require capital restoration to the level required under State law, so long as such request is made within 60 days of notice of the affiliation. Any State, as permitted under State law, may restrict changes in ownership of a demutualizing insurer so long as the restrictions are not discriminatory as set forth in the legislation. Section 104(c)(2)(C) means that State laws and State regulators shall not discriminate against depository institutions or their affiliates with respect to acquiring or otherwise changing the ownership of stock in newly demutualized insurance companies relative to other persons.

Except with respect to insurance, States may not prevent or restrict a depository institution or affiliate thereof from engaging in any activity set forth under the Gramm-Leach-Bliley Act. With respect to insurance sales, solicitations, and cross-marketing, States may not prevent or significantly interfere with the activities of depository institutions or their affiliates, as set forth in *Barnett Bank of Marion County N.A. v. Nelson*, 517 U.S. 25 (1996). However, State restrictions that are substantially the same as but no more burdensome than the thirteen general safe harbors provided are not subject to potential preemption. States are also allowed to continue the regulation of insurance activities other than sales, solicitation, and cross-marketing, and the preemption standard does not apply to such regulation if consistent with the standards set forth in the legislation.

State regulation other than of insurance or securities activities is not preempted even if it does prevent or restrict an activity so long as it does not discriminate. The Conferees adopted the House discrimination standard with respect to insurance activities. The discrimination standard does not apply to State regulations governing insurance sales, solicitations, or cross-marketing activities adopted before September 3, 1998, and does not apply to State regulations that are substantially the same as but no more burdensome than the safe harbors. State securities regulation is not preempted by the "prevent or restrict" standard with regard to a State securities commission's ability to investigate and enforce certain unlawful securities transactions or to require the licensure or registration of securities and securities brokers, dealers, and investment advisors and their associates. State actions of general corporate applicability applying to companies domiciled or incorporated in the State are also protected from the "prevent or restrict" preemption, as well as State laws similar to the antitrust laws, so long as the State actions are not inconsistent with the intent of this Act to permit affiliations. The term "depository institution" is defined as including foreign banks and their domestic affiliates and subsidiaries. The term "affiliate" is defined for section 104 to include any person under common control (including a subsidiary).

¶ 5003 SUBTITLE B—STREAMLINING SUPERVISION OF BANK HOLDING COMPANIES

Both the House and Senate bills generally adhere to the principle of functional regulation, which holds that similar activities should be regulated by the same regulator. Different regulators have expertise at supervising different activities. It is inefficient and impractical to expect a regulator to have or develop expertise in regulating all aspects of financial services. Accordingly, the legislation intends to ensure that banking activities are regulated by bank regulators, securities activities are regulated by securities regulators, and insurance activities are regulated by insurance regulators.

In keeping with the Board's role as an umbrella supervisor, the legislation provides that the Board may require any bank holding company or subsidiary thereof to submit reports regarding its financial condition, systems for monitoring and controlling financial and operating risks, transactions with depository institutions, and compliance with the BHCA or other Federal laws that the Board has specific jurisdiction to enforce. The Board is directed to use existing examination reports prepared by other regulators, publicly reported information, and reports filed with other agencies, to the fullest extent possible.

The Board is authorized to examine each holding company and its subsidiaries. It may examine functionally regulated subsidiaries only if: (1) the Board has reasonable cause to believe that such a subsidiary is engaged in activities that pose a material risk to an affiliate depository institution; (2) it reasonably believes after reviewing the relevant reports that examining the subsidiary is necessary to adequately inform the Board of the systems for monitoring risks; or, (3) based on reports and other available information, the Board has reasonable cause to believe that a subsidiary is not in compliance with the BHCA or other Federal law that the Board has specific jurisdiction to enforce and the Board cannot make such a determination through examination of an affiliated depository institution or the holding company. The Board is directed to use, to the fullest extent possible, examinations made by appropriate Federal and State regulators.

The Board is not authorized to prescribe capital requirements for any functionally regulated subsidiary that is in compliance with applicable capital requirements of another Federal regulatory authority, a State insurance authority, or is a registered investment adviser or licensed insurance agent. The legislation also makes it clear that securities and insurance activities conducted in regulated entities are subject to functional regulation by the relevant State securities authorities, the Securities and Exchange ("SEC"), or State insurance regulators.

The Board is prohibited from requiring a broker-dealer or insurance company that is a bank holding company to infuse funds into a depository institution if the company's functional regulator determines, in writing, such action would have a material adverse effect on the broker-dealer or insurance company. If the functional regulator makes such a determination, the Board may require the holding company to divest its depository institution. All the Federal banking agencies are subject to the same limits on reports, examinations and capital requirements for functionally regulated affiliates which apply to the Board. This ensures that the Office of the Comptroller of the Currency ("OCC"), the Office of Thrift Supervision ("OTS"), and the Federal Deposit Insurance Corporation ("FDIC") will not be able to assume and duplicate the function of being the general supervisor over functionally regulated subsidiaries. The legislation specifically preserves, however, the FDIC's authority to examine a functionally regulated affiliate. This authority, which should be used sparingly, is necessary to protect the deposit insurance funds.

The legislation also specifically addresses indirect action by the Board against functionally regulated affiliates. Consistent with functional regulation, the Board's authority to take indirect action against a functionally regulated affiliate is limited. The Board may not promulgate rules, adopt restrictions, safeguards or any other requirement affecting a functionally regulated affiliate unless the action is necessary to address a "material risk" to the safety and soundness of the depository institution or the domestic or international payments system *and* it is not possible to guard against such material risk through requirements imposed directly upon the depository institution.

The Federal banking regulators are empowered to adopt prudential safeguards governing transactions between depository institutions, their subsidiaries and affiliates so as to avoid, among other items, significant risk to the safety and soundness of the institution. The regulators are required to review these safeguards regularly and modify or eliminate those requirements which are no longer necessary.

Bank holding companies may elect to become FHCs by meeting the statutory requirements and filing a declaration and a certification with the Board. The legislation makes it clear that a duplicative registration statement under section 5 of the BHCA is not required. The integrity of the deposit insurance funds is preserved by prohibiting the use of deposit insurance funds to benefit any shareholder, subsidiary or nondepository affiliate of an FHC. This section ensures that the federal safety net is not extended to persons who are not entitled to Federal deposit insurance coverage.

The savings bank restrictions in the BHCA are repealed. This repeal is designed to conform the regulation of savings bank life insurance to other provisions of Federal banking law.

The Conferees intend that the Board be flexible in its application of holding company consolidated capital standards for the leverage requirement and the timing of the asset calculations to FHCs of which the predominant regulated subsidiary is a broker-dealer. The Conferees intend that, to the extent the Board deems feasible and consistent with the overall financial condition and activities of the holding company, the capital requirements for such holding companies be consistent with the capital standards applied by the SEC to the broker-dealer, which accounts for the predominant amount of assets and activities of the holding company.

¶ 5004 SUBTITLE C—SUBSIDIARIES OF NATIONAL BANKS

Senate Position: The Senate bill authorizes a national bank to control a subsidiary engaged in financial activities permissible for a bank holding company (but not permissible for a national bank directly) under section 4(k) if the bank has consolidated total assets not exceeding $1 billion, is not affiliated with a bank holding company, is well capitalized, and well managed. For the purpose of determining a parent national bank's regulatory capital, a deduction from assets and tangible equity is required for the amount of outstanding equity investments made in a financial subsidiary. In addition, the assets and liabilities of the financial subsidiary must not be consolidated with those of the parent bank. Equity investments in the operating subsidiary by a parent national bank must not exceed the amount the bank could pay as a dividend without obtaining prior regulatory approval. The Senate bill also clarifies that a national bank may conduct through a subsidiary any activity which the national bank may engage directly and any activity lawfully conducted as of the date of enactment of this legislation.

House Position: The House bill authorizes a national bank subsidiary to engage only in activities permissible for national banks to engage in directly, activities otherwise expressly authorized by statute, and activities that are financial in nature or incidental to financial activities. Financial activities are defined as those activities permissible for an FHC or activities that the Secretary of the Treasury determines to be financial in nature or incidental to financial activities in consultation and coordination with the Federal Reserve Board. Excluded from the list of permissible financial activities are insurance underwriting, insurance company portfolio investments, and real estate investment and development. National bank operating subsidiaries also may engage in developing activities. In order for a national bank operating subsidiary to engage in activities that are financial in nature, its parent bank and all its depository institution affiliates must be well capitalized, well managed, and have a satisfactory CRA rating. A cure procedure is established to address situations where there is a failure to comply with these conditions. It also requires that the aggregate amount of the national bank parent's equity investments in the bank be deducted from the bank's capital including the operating subsidiary's retained earnings. In addition, the assets and liabilities of the subsidiary must not be consolidated with those of its parent bank. Equity investments in the operating subsidiary by a parent national bank must not exceed the amount the bank could pay as a dividend without obtaining prior regulatory approval.

Conference Substitute: The Senate receded to the House with an amendment.

Under the amendment, national banks of any size are permitted to engage through a financial subsidiary only in financial activities (with exceptions) authorized by this Act. Section 121 specifically excludes four types of activities for financial subsidiaries: insurance or annuity underwriting, insurance company portfolio investments, real estate investment and development, and merchant banking (subject to section 122). These types of financial activities may only be done in FHC affiliates. The federal banking regulators are prohibited from interpreting these provisions to provide for any expansion of these activities contrary to the express language of this statute. It is the intent of the Conferees that these new statutory provisions - and the regulations to be adopted pursuant thereto - supercede and replace the OCC's Part 5 regulations on operating subsidiaries.

¶ 5005 SUBTITLE D—PRESERVATION OF FTC AUTHORITY

Section 131. Amendment to the Bank Holding Company Act of 1956 to modify notification and post-approval waiting period for section 3 transactions.

Senate Position: No provision.

House Position: Section 141 of the House amendment amends section 11(b)(1) of the BHCA (12 U.S.C. section 1849(b)(1)) to provide for notice to the Federal Trade Commission ("FTC") when the Board of Governors of the

Federal Reserve System approves a transaction under section 3 of the BHCA if that transaction also involves a transaction under section 4 or 6 of the BHCA.

Conference Substitute: The Senate receded to the House with an amendment.

Under section 131 of the Conference Report, the modification simply eliminated the reference to section 6 because the new activities for FHCs are now included within section 4 of the BHCA as amended by the Conference Report. The FTC currently has no role in reviewing pure section 3 transactions, and this amendment does not change that. However, the FTC does perform reviews of certain section 4 transactions. This amendment will simply allow the FTC to coordinate its review with the Board in those cases that also involve a section 3 transaction.

Section 132. Interagency data sharing.

Senate Position: No provision.

House Position: Section 142 of the House amendment provided that, except as otherwise prohibited by law, the banking regulators who review mergers or acquisitions (the OCC, the OTS, the FDIC, and Federal Reserve Board) shall make available to the antitrust agencies (the Department of Justice and the Federal Trade Commission ("FTC")) any information in the bank regulators' possession that the antitrust agencies deem necessary for their antitrust review under sections 3, 4, or 6 of the BHCA, section 18(c) of the Federal Deposit Insurance Act , the National Bank Consolidation and Merger Act, section 10 of the Home Owners' Loan Act, or the antitrust laws.

Conference Substitute: The Senate receded to the House with an amendment.

Under section 132 of the Conference Report, the modification eliminated the reference to section 6 of the BHCA because the new activities for FHCs are now included within section 4 of the BHCA as amended by the Conference Report. In addition, the modification added new sections 132(b) and 132(c). New section 132(b) requires that any information shared under this provision be kept confidential; that before any information shared under this provision is disclosed to a third party, the agency which shared it must be notified in writing and given a chance to oppose or limit the disclosure; that any sharing under this provision does not affect any claim of privilege with respect to such information; and that nothing in this section shall be construed to limit access to any information by the Congress or the Comptroller General. New section 132(c) simply applies the provisions of new section 132(b) to the sharing of information between Federal banking agencies and State regulators or any other party.

In the past, there have been difficulties with banking agencies sharing bank examination reports with the antitrust agencies because of doubts about whether they had sufficient authority to do so. The reports have generally been shared in the end. However, in cases of failing institutions in which review has been expedited or of institutions taken over by the government, delays in providing these reports have sometimes impeded antitrust review. This language simply allows all of the involved agencies to do their respective tasks in the most expeditious manner possible.

Section 133. Clarification of status of subsidiaries and affiliates.

Senate Position: No provision.

House Position: Section 143(a) of the House amendment provided that subsidiaries or affiliates of banks or savings associations which are not themselves banks or savings associations shall not be treated as banks or savings associations for purposes of the FTC Act or any other law enforced by the FTC. Section 143(b) clarified that nothing in this section shall be construed as restricting the authority of any Federal banking agency.

Section 143(c) amended the existing BHCA exceptions to the Hart-Scott-Rodino ("H-S-R") Act, 15 U.S.C. section 18a(c)(7) and 18a(c)(8). Under current law, transactions subject to approval under section 3 of the BHCA are exempt from H-S-R review. Likewise, assuming certain conditions are met, transactions subject to approval under section 4 are also exempt. The amendments in section 143(c) clarified that when FHCs acquire other FHCs and either of those companies was involved in new activities under section 6 of the BHCA as amended by the House amendment, the portion of the transaction involving those section 6 activities would be subject to H-S-R review. However, the remainder of the transaction will continue to be reviewed under the existing BHCA.

Conference Substitute: The Senate receded to the House with modifications.

Under section 133 of the conference report, the modification to section 133(a) clarified that the language applied to any provision of law applied by the FTC under the FTC Act. This clarification makes it clear that the section is limited to laws that the FTC currently enforces and is not intended to provide authority to enforce any new statutes. Under current law, section 5(a)(2) of the FTC Act prohibits the FTC from enforcing the Act against banks or savings associations. The conference report will, however, allow these entities to acquire other kinds of businesses, for example, securities firms, against which the FTC can currently enforce the Act. This provision simply makes it clear that these kinds of businesses do not fall within the bank or savings association exemption because they are owned by such an entity.

There was no modification to the savings provision contained in section 133(b).

The modification to section 133(c) replaced the reference to section 6 of the BHCA as amended by the House amendment with a reference to section 4(k) of the BHCA as amended by the conference report. Under the conference report, section 4(k) now contains the language allowing FHCs to engage in new activities. This amendment to the H-S-R exemptions will allow the antitrust agencies to continue to review mergers between insurance companies, securities firms, and other businesses newly allowed to FHCs as they are today, notwithstanding the ownership interest of the FHC. This clarification for the new FHC structure is consistent with, and does not disturb, existing law and precedents under which mergers involving complex corporate entities, some parts of which are in industries subject to merger review by specialized regulatory agencies and other parts of which are not, are considered according to agency jurisdiction over their respective parts, so that normal H-S-R Act requirements apply to those parts that do not fall within the specialized agency's specific authority. *See* 16 C.F.R. section 802.6.

Annual GAO report (section 144 of the House amendment).

Senate Position: No provision.

House Position: Section 144 of the House amendment provided for the General Accounting Office to submit an annual report to Congress on market concentration in the financial services industry for each of the next five years.

Conference Substitute: The House receded to the Senate.

¶ 5006 SUBTITLE E—NATIONAL TREATMENT

Section 141. Foreign Banks that are Financial Holding Companies.

Senate Position: The Senate bill, at section 151, permits termination of the financial grandfathering authority granted by the International Banking Act and other statutes to foreign banks to engage in certain financial activities. Foreign banks with grandfathered financial affiliates would be permitted to retain these grandfathered companies on the same terms that domestic banking organizations are permitted to establish them.

House Position: The House amendment, at section 151, is similar.

Conference Substitute: The Senate receded to the House.

Section 142. Representative offices.

Senate Position: The Senate bill, at section 152, requires prior approval by the Federal Reserve Board for the establishment of representative offices that are subsidiaries of a foreign bank.

House Position: The House bill, at section 153, contains the same provision.

Conference Substitute: The Senate receded to the House.

¶ 5007 SUBTITLE F—DIRECT ACTIVITIES OF BANKS

Senate Position: The Senate bill authorizes national banks to deal in, underwrite, and purchase municipal bonds for their own investment accounts.

House Position: The House amendment is identical.

Conference Substitute: The House receded to the Senate.

TITLE II [FUNCTIONAL REGULATION]

¶ 5008 SUBTITLE A—BROKERS AND DEALERS

Senate Position: The Senate bill repeals the exemptions from the definition of broker and dealer under the Federal securities laws that currently apply to banks, generally subjecting banks and their affiliates and subsidiaries to the same regulation as all other providers of securities products. However, the Senate bill replaces the general bank exemption with specific exemptions for certain bank activities.

House Position: The House amendment also repeals the general bank exemptions from the definition of broker and dealer under the Federal securities laws but provides more limited exemptions than does the Senate bill.

Conference Substitute: Subtitle A of title II of the Gramm-Leach-Bliley Act provides for functional regulation of bank securities activities. The Conferees retained certain limited exemptions to facilitate certain activities in which banks have traditionally engaged. These exceptions relate to third-party networking arrangements, trust activities, traditional banking transactions such as commercial paper and exempted securities, employee and shareholder benefit plans, sweep accounts, affiliate transactions, private placements, safekeeping and custody services, asset-backed securities, derivatives, and identified banking products.

The Conferees provided for an exception for networking arrangements between banks and brokers. Revisions to Rule 1060 recently approved by the National Association of Securities Dealers ("NASD") are in conflict with this provision. As a consequence, revisions to the rule should be made to exempt banks and their employees from the provisions' coverage.

The Conferees provided that banks that effect transactions in a trustee or fiduciary capacity under certain conditions will be exempt from registration under the Federal securities laws if the bank: (1) is chiefly compensated by means of administration and certain other fees, including a combination of such fees, and (2) does not publicly solicit brokerage business. The Conferees expect that the SEC will not disturb traditional bank trust activities under this provision.

The Conferees also provided that classification of a particular product as an identified banking product shall not be construed as a finding or implication that such product is or is not a security for purposes of the securities laws, or is or is not a transaction for any purpose under the Commodity Exchange Act. The Conferees do not intend in the Gramm-Leach-Bliley Act to express an opinion upon or to address the issue of legal certainty for swap agreements under the securities and commodity exchange laws.

The Conferees also provided that the Commodity Exchange Act is not amended by the Gramm-Leach-Bliley Act, and no transaction or person which is otherwise subject to the jurisdiction of the Commodity Futures Trading Commission pursuant to the Commodity Exchange Act is exempted from such jurisdiction because of the provisions of the Gramm-Leach-Bliley Act.

For new hybrid products, the Conferees codified in the securities laws a process that requires the SEC to act by rulemaking prior to seeking to regulate any bank sales of any such new product. This rulemaking process is designed to give notice to the banking industry in an area that could involve complex new products with many elements.

The process contemplated by the Conferees would work as follows. Prior to seeking to require a bank to register as a broker or dealer with respect to sales of any new hybrid product, the SEC would have to engage in a rulemaking. In its rulemaking, the SEC would need to find that the new product is a security. In addition, the SEC would have to determine that the product is a "new hybrid product."

A new hybrid product is not one of the products listed in the definition of "identified banking product". Including a product on the list of identified banking products shall not be construed as a finding or implication that such product is or is not a security, but it would not be a new hybrid product. The Conferees codified the definition of Identified Banking Products as a freestanding provision of law, neither in the securities laws nor in the banking laws.

In addition, during the rulemaking process, the SEC must also make a number of findings. When considering whether such an action is in the public interest, the SEC must also consider whether the action will promote efficiency, competition and capital formation, as set forth in section 3(f) of the Securities Exchange Act of 1934 ("Exchange Act"). The Conferees note that the SEC's record in implementing section 3(f) has failed to meet Congressional intent. The Conferees expect that the SEC will improve in this area.

Prior to commencing a rulemaking process, the SEC is required to consult with and seek the concurrence of the Federal Reserve Board concerning the imposition of broker or dealer registration requirements with respect to any new hybrid product. In developing and promulgating rules under this subsection, the SEC shall consider the views of the Board, including views with respect to the nature of the new hybrid product; the history, purpose, extent, and appropriateness of the regulation of the new product under the Federal banking laws; and the impact of the proposed rule on the banking industry.

If the Board seeks review of any final regulation under this section, such review will serve as a stay on the rulemaking until final adjudication of the matter between the SEC and the Board. In considering such an appeal, the United States Court of Appeals for the District of Columbia Circuit shall determine to affirm and enforce or set aside a regulation of the SEC under this subsection, based on the determination of the court as to whether: (1) the subject product is a new hybrid product; (2) the subject product is a security; (3) imposing a requirement to register as a broker or dealer for banks engaging in transactions in such product is appropriate in light of the history, purpose and extent of regulation under the Federal securities laws and under the Federal banking laws, giving deference neither to the views of the SEC nor to the Board.

¶ 5009 SUBTITLE B—BANK INVESTMENT COMPANY ACTIVITIES

Senate Position: No provision.

House Position: The House bill amends the Investment Advisers Act and the Investment

Company Act to subject banks that advise mutual funds to the same regulatory scheme as other advisers to mutual funds. It also requires banks to make additional disclosure when a fund is sold or advised by a bank.

Conference Substitute: The Senate recedes to the House provision with an amendment.

¶ 5010 SUBTITLE C—SECURITIES AND EXCHANGE COMMISSION SUPERVISION OF INVESTMENT BANK HOLDING COMPANIES

Senate Position: No provision.

House Position: The House amendment creates a new investment bank holding company structure under the Exchange Act. This subtitle is designed to implement a new concept of SEC supervision of broker/dealer holding companies (that do not control depository institutions with certain exceptions) that voluntarily elect SEC supervision. This provision is designed to assure that the supervision of an investment bank holding company by the SEC is a meaningful option. Non-U.S. financial institutions supervisors, when reviewing regulatory applications or notices submitted by a U.S. financial institution supervised in the United States as an investment bank holding company by the SEC under section 231, shall treat the SEC as the principal U.S. consolidated home country supervisor of such financial institution on the same basis and terms as if the Federal Reserve Board were the principal U.S. consolidated home country supervisor.

Conference Substitute: The Senate recedes with an amendment. The Conferees eliminated the authority of the SEC to regulate investment bank holding company capital.

¶ 5011 SUBTITLE D—BANKS AND BANK HOLDING COMPANIES

Senate Position: No provision.

House Position: The House amendment requires the SEC to consult and coordinate comments with the appropriate Federal banking regulators before any action or rendering any opinion with respect to the manner in which an insured depository institution or insured depository holding company reports loan loss reserves.

Conference Substitute: The Senate recedes to the House provision. The Conferees note that the SEC's actions with respect to the reporting of loan loss reserves by certain insured depository institutions did not reflect adequate consultation with the Federal banking agencies with respect to potential implications on the safety and soundness of the Federal deposit insurance fund. The Conferees expect that this provision will facilitate better coordination and decision-making by the SEC in this area.

TITLE III—INSURANCE

¶ 5012 SUBTITLE A—STATE REGULATION OF INSURANCE

Senate Position: The Senate bill contains a number of provisions intended to preserve State regulation of insurance.

House Position: The House amendment similarly contains a number of provisions intended to preserve and enhance State regulation of insurance.

Conference Substitute: The Senate receded to the House with an amendment.

In general, Subtitle A of Title III reaffirms that States are the regulators for the insurance activities for all persons, including acting as the functional regulator for the insurance activities of federally chartered banks. This functional regulatory power is subject to section 104 of Title I, however, which sets forth the appropriate balance of protections against discriminatory actions. Federally chartered banks and their subsidiaries are prohibited from underwriting insurance, except for authorized products. A rule of construction was added by the Conference Committee to prevent evasion of State insurance regulation by foreign reinsurance subsidiaries or offices of domestic banks, clarifying that providing insurance (including reinsurance) outside of the United States to indemnify an insurance product or company in a State shall be considered to be providing insurance as principal in that State.

Federally chartered banks are prohibited from engaging in any activity involving the underwriting or sale of title insurance, except that national banks may sell title insurance products in any State in which state-chartered banks are authorized to do so (other than through a "wild card provision"), so long as such sales are undertaken "in the same manner, to the same extent, and under the same restrictions" that apply to such state-chartered banks. Certain currently and lawfully conducted title insurance activities of banks are grandfathered, and existing State laws prohibiting all persons from providing title insurance are protected.

An expedited and equalized dispute resolution mechanism is established to guide the courts in deciding conflicts between Federal and State regulators regarding insurance issues. The "without unequal deference" standard of review does not apply to State regulation of insurance agency activities that were issued before September 3, 1998 (other than those protected by the scope of the safe harbor provision of section 104).

The Federal banking agencies are required to issue final consumer protection regulations within one year, to provide additional safeguards for the sale of insurance by any bank or other depository institution, or by any person at or on behalf of such institution.

State laws that prevent or significantly interfere with the ability of insurers to affiliate, become an FHC, or demutualize, are preempted, except as provided in section 104(c)(2), and with respect to demutualizing insurers for the State of domicile (and as set forth in the Redomestication Subtitle). State laws limiting the investment of an insurer's assets in a depository institution are also preempted, except that an insurer's State of domicile may limit such investment as provided.

The Federal banking agencies and the State insurance regulators are directed to coordinate efforts to supervise companies that control both depository institutions and persons engaged in the business of insurance, and to share, on a confidential basis, supervisory information including financial health and business unit transactions. The agencies are further directed to provide notice and to consult with the State regulators before taking actions which effect any affiliates engaging in insurance activities. A banking regulator is not required to provide confidential information to a State insurance regulator unless such State regulator agrees to keep the information in confidence and make all reasonable efforts to oppose disclosure of such information. Conversely, Federal banking regulators are directed to treat as confidential any information received from a State regulator which is entitled to confidential treatment under State law, and to make similar reasonable efforts to oppose disclosure of the information.

¶ 5013 SUBTITLE B—REDOMESTICATION OF MUTUAL INSURERS

Senate Position: No provision.

House Position: The House bill allows mutual insurance companies to redomesticate to another state and reorganize into a mutual holding company or stock company. It only applies to insurers in States which have not established reasonable terms and conditions for allowing mutual insurance companies to reorganize into a mutual holding company. All licenses of the insurer are preserved, and all outstanding policies, contracts, and forms remain in full force. A redomesticating company must provide notice to the state insurance regulators of each State for which the company is licensed. A mutual insurance company may only redomesticate under this Subtitle if the State insurance regulator of the new (transferee) domicile affirmatively determines that the company's reorganization plan meets certain reasonable terms and conditions: the reorganization is approved by a majority of the company's board of directors and voting policyholders, after notice and disclosure of the reorganization and its effects on policyholder contractual rights; the policyholders have equivalent voting rights in the new mutual holding company as compared to the original mutual insurer; any initial public offering of stock shall be in accordance with applicable securities laws and under the supervision of the State insurance regulator of the transferee domicile; the new mutual holding company may not award any stock options or grants to its elected officers or directors for six months; all contractual rights of the policyholders are preserved; and the reorganization is approved as fair and equitable to the policyholders by the insurance regulators of transferee domicile.

Conference Substitute: The Senate receded to the House with an amendment.

¶ 5014 SUBTITLE C—NATIONAL ASSOCIATION OF REGISTERED AGENTS AND BROKERS

Senate Position: The Senate bill contains a sense of the Congress statement that States should provide for a uniform insurance agent and broker licensing system.

House Position: The House bill encourages the States to establish uniform or reciprocal requirements for the licensing of insurance agents. If a majority of the States do not establish uniform or reciprocal licensing provisions within a three-year period (as determined by the National Association of Insurance Commissioners ["NAIC"]), then the National Association of Registered Agents and Brokers ("NARAB") would be established as a private, non-profit entity managed and supervised by the State insurance regulators. State insurance laws and regulations shall not be affected except to the extent that they are inconsistent with a specific requirement of the Subtitle. Membership in NARAB is voluntary and does not affect the rights of a producer under each individual state license. Any state-licensed insurance producer whose license has not been suspended or revoked is eligible to join NARAB. NARAB shall be base membership criteria on the highest levels insurance producer qualification set by the States on standards such as integrity, personal qualification, education, training, and experience. NARAB members shall continue to pay the appropriate fees required by each State in which they are licensed, and shall renew their membership annually. NARAB may inspect members records, and revoke a membership where appropriate. NARAB shall establish an Office of Consumer Complaints, which shall have a toll-free phone number (and Internet website) to receive and investigate consumer complaints and recommend disciplinary actions. The Office shall maintain records of such complaints, which shall be made available to the NAIC and individual State insurance regulators, and shall refer complaints where appropriate to such regulators.

If the NAIC determines that the States have not met the uniformity or reciprocity requirements, then the NAIC has two years to establish NARAB. The NAIC shall appoint NARAB's board of directors, some of whom must have significant experience with the regulation of commercial insurance lines in the 20 States with the most commercial lines business. If within the time period allotted for NARAB's creation, the NAIC has still not appointed the initial board of directors for NARAB, then the initial directors shall be the State insurance regulators of the seven States with the greatest amount of commercial lines insurance. NARAB's bylaws are required to be filed with the NAIC, taking effect 30 days after filing unless disapproves by the NAIC as being contrary to the public interest or requiring a public hearing. The NAIC may require NARAB to adopt or repeal additional bylaws or rules as it determines appropriate to the public interest. The NAIC is given the responsibility of overseeing NARAB, and is authorized to examine and inspect NARAB's records, and require NARAB to furnish it with any reports.

If at the end of two years after NARAB is required to be established, (1) a majority of the States representing at least 50% of the total commercial-lines insurance premiums in the United States have not established uniform or reciprocal licensing regulations, or (2) the NAIC has not approved NARAB's bylaws or is unable to operate or supervise NARAB (or if NARAB is not conducting its activities under this Act), then NARAB shall be created and supervised by the President, and shall exist without NAIC oversight. The President shall appoint NARAB's board, with the advice and consent of the Senate, from lists of candidates submitted by the NAIC. If the President determines that NARAB's board is not acting in the public interest, the President may replace the entire board with new members (subject to the advice and consent of the Senate). The President may also suspend the effectiveness of any rule or action by NARAB which the President determines is contrary to the public interest. NARAB shall report annually to the President and Congress on its activities.

State laws regulating insurance licensing that discriminate against NARAB members based on non-residency are preempted, as well as State laws and regulations which impose additional licensing requirements on non-resident NARAB members beyond those established by the NARAB board (pursuant to this Subtitle), except that State unfair trade practices and consumer protection laws are protected from preemption, including counter-signature requirements. NARAB is required to coordinate its multistate licensing with the various States. It is also required to coordinate with the States on establishing a central clearinghouse for license issuance and renewal, and for the collection of regulatory information on insurance producer activities. NARAB shall further coordinate with the NASD to facilitate joint membership. Any dispute involving NARAB shall be brought in the appropriate U.S. District Court under federal law, after all administrative remedies through NARAB and the NAIC have been exhausted.

Conference Substitute: The Senate receded to the House.

¶ 5015 SUBTITLE D—RENTAL CAR AGENCY INSURANCE ACTIVITIES

Senate Position: The Senate bill provides that the requirements under section 104 with respect to mandatory licensing do not apply to persons who offer insurance connected with a short term motor vehicle rental so long as the State does not require such licensing.

House Position: The House bill creates a Federal presumption for a three-year period that no State law imposes any licensing, appointment, or education requirements on persons who rent motor vehicles for a period of 90 days or less and sell insurance to customers in connection with the rental transaction. This presumption shall not apply to a State statute, the prospective application of a statutorily-authorized final State regulation or order interpreting a State statute, or the prospective application of a court judgment interpreting or applying a State statute, if such State statute or final State regulation or order specifically and expressly regulates (or exempts from regulation) persons who solicit or sell such short term vehicle rental insurance. This presumption shall apply to the retroactive application of a final State regulation or order interpreting a general State insurance licensing statute, or the retroactive application of a court judgment interpreting or applying a general

State insurance licensing statute, with respect to the regulation of persons who solicit or sell such short term vehicle rental insurance.

Conference Substitute: The Senate receded to the House.

¶ 5016 SUBTITLE E—CONFIDENTIALITY

Senate Position: No provision.

House Position: The House bill requires insurance companies and their affiliates to protect the confidentiality of individually identifiable customer health and medical and genetic information. Such companies may only disclose such information with the consent of the customer or for statutorily specified purposes.

Conference Substitute: The House receded to the Senate.

TITLE IV [UNITARY THRIFTS]

¶ 5017 UNITARY THRIFT HOLDING COMPANY PROVISIONS

Sec. 401. Prohibition on new unitary savings and loan holding companies.

Senate Position: The Senate bill, at section 601(a), amends the Home Owners' Loan Act to prohibit (except for corporate reorganizations) new unitary savings and loan holding companies from engaging in nonfinancial activities or affiliating with nonfinancial entities. The prohibition applies to a company that becomes a unitary savings and loan holding company pursuant to an application filed with the OTS after May 4, 1999. A grandfathered unitary thrift holding company (one in existence or applied for on or before May 4, 1999) retains its authority to engage in nonfinancial activities. The Senate bill, at section 601(b), allows mutual savings and loan holding companies to engage in new financial activities authorized under the Gramm-Leach-Bliley Act.

House Position: The House bill, at section 401(a), prohibits new unitary thrift holding companies after the grandfather date of March 4, 1999, from engaging in nonfinancial activities or from affiliating with a nonfinancial entity. The provision also allows a nonfinancial company to purchase a grandfathered unitary thrift holding company upon approval of an application filed with the OTS and approval or no objection to a notice filed with the Federal Reserve Board. The House bill, at section 401(b), permits a mutual holding company to engage in activities permissible for multiple stock holding companies and permits unitary mutual savings and loan holding companies to engage in the new financial activities authorized for FHCs.

Conference Substitute: The House receded to the Senate.

TITLE V—PRIVACY

¶ 5018 SUBTITLE A—DISCLOSURE OF NONPUBLIC PERSONAL INFORMATION

Senate Position: No provision.

House Position: The House bill contained important provisions providing consumers with new protections with respect to the transfer and use of their nonpublic personal information by financial institutions.

Among other things, the House bill directed relevant regulators to establish comprehensive standards for ensuring the security and confidentiality of consumers' personal information maintained by financial institutions; allowed customers of financial institutions to "opt out" of having their personal financial information shared with nonaffiliated third parties, subject to certain exceptions; barred financial institutions from disclosing customer account numbers or similar forms of access codes to nonaffiliated third parties for telemarketing or other direct marketing purposes; and mandated annual disclosure—in clear and conspicuous terms—of a financial institution's policies and procedures for protecting customers' nonpublic personal information.

Conference Substitute: The Senate receded to the House with an amendment.

The amendment modified the House position in the following ways:

1. The Federal functional regulators, the Secretary of the Treasury, and the FTC, in consultation with State insurance authorities, are directed to prescribe such regulations as may be necessary to carry out the purposes of the privacy subtitle. The House bill had called for a joint rulemaking. The relevant agencies are required to consult and coordinate with one another in order to assure to the maximum extent possible that the regulations each prescribes are consistent and comparable with those prescribed by the other agencies. It is the hope of the Conferees that State insurance authorities would implement regulations necessary to carry out the purposes of this title and enforce such regulations as provided in this title.

2. To address the concern that the House bill failed to provide a mechanism for enforcing

the subtitle's provisions against non-financial institutions, the Conferees agreed to clarify that the FTC's enforcement authority extends to such entities.

3. The Conferees agreed to clarify the relation between Title V's privacy provisions and other consumer protections already in law, by stating that nothing in the title shall be construed to modify, limit, or supersede the operation of the Fair Credit Reporting Act, and no inference shall be drawn on the basis of the provisions of the title regarding whether information is transaction or experience information under section 603 of that Act.

4. At the request of the Conferees from the Committee on Agriculture, the Conferees agreed to exclude from the scope of the privacy title any person or entity that is subject to the jurisdiction of the Commodity Futures Trading Commission under the Commodity Exchange Act, as well as the Federal Agricultural Mortgage Corporation or any entity chartered and operating under the Farm Credit Act of 1971. The Conferees also excluded from this subtitle institutions chartered by Congress specifically to engage in securitization or secondary market transactions, so long as such institutions do not sell or transfer nonpublic personal information to nonaffiliated third parties. The Conferees granted the exception based on the understanding that the covered entities do not market products directly to consumers.

5. The Conferees agreed to clarify that a financial institution's annual disclosure of its privacy policy to its customers must include a statement of the institution's policies and practices regarding the sharing of nonpublic personal information with affiliated entities, as well as with nonaffiliated third parties.

6. The Conferees agreed to provide that the disclosure of nonpublic personal information contained in a consumer report reported by a consumer reporting agency does not fall within section 502's notice and opt out requirements.

7. The Conferees agreed to modify the statutory definition of "nonpublic personal information" by clarifying that such term does not encompass any list, description, or other grouping of consumers (and publicly available information pertaining to them) that is derived without using any nonpublic personal information.

8. The Conferees agreed to exclude disclosures to consumer reporting agencies from section 502(d)'s limitations on the sharing of account number information.

9. The Conferees agreed to give the relevant regulatory agencies the authority to prescribe exceptions to subsections (a) through (d) of section 502, rather than just sections 502(a) and (b), as provided for in the House bill.

10. The Conferees inserted language stating that the privacy provisions in the subtitle do not supersede any State statutes, regulations, orders, or interpretations, except to the extent that such State provisions are inconsistent with the provisions of the subtitle, and then only to the extent of the inconsistency. The amendment provides that a State statute, regulation, order, or interpretation is not inconsistent with the provisions of this subtitle if the protection such statute, regulation, order, or interpretation affords any consumer is greater than the protection provided under this subtitle, as determined by the FTC in consultation with the agency or authority with jurisdiction under section 505(a) over either the person that initiated the complaint or that is the subject of the complaint, on its own motion or upon the petition of any interested party.

11. Section 506 authorizes the Federal banking agencies and the National Credit Union Administration to prescribe joint regulations governing the institutions under their jurisdiction with respect to the Fair Credit Reporting Act; the Conferees agreed to an amendment giving the Board of Governors of the Federal Reserve the authority to prescribe FCRA regulations governing bank holding companies and their affiliates.

12. The Conferees agreed to modify section 502(e)(5), to include the Secretary of the Treasury as a "law enforcement agency" for the purposes of the Bank Secrecy Act, to avoid unintended interference with the existing functions of the Treasury's anti-money laundering unit, the Financial Crimes Enforcement Network ("FinCEN").

The Conferees wish to ensure that smaller financial institutions are not placed at a competitive disadvantage by a statutory regime that permits certain information to be shared freely within an affiliate structure while limiting the ability to share that same information with nonaffiliated third parties. Accordingly, in prescribing regulations pursuant to this subtitle, the agencies and authorities described in section 504(a)(1) should take into consideration any adverse competitive effects upon small commercial banks, thrifts, and credit unions. In issuing regulations under section 503, the regulators should take into account the degree of consumer access to disclosure by electronic means.

In exercising their authority under section 504(b), the agencies and authorities described in section 504(a)(1) may consider it consistent with the purposes of this subtitle to permit the disclosure of customer account numbers or similar forms of access numbers or access codes in an encrypted, scrambled, or similarly coded form, where the disclosure is expressly authorized by the customer and is necessary to service or process a transaction expressly requested or authorized by the customer.

The Conferees recognize the need to foster technological innovation in the financial services and related industries. The Conferees believe that the development of new technologies that facilitate consumers' access to the broad range of products and services available through online media should be encouraged, provided that such technologies continue to incorporate safeguards for consumer privacy.

¶ 5019 SUBTITLE B—FRAUDULENT ACCESS TO FINANCIAL INFORMATION

Senate Position: The Senate bill contained provisions making it a Federal crime —punishable by up to five years in prison—to obtain or attempt to obtain, or cause to be disclosed or attempt to cause to be disclosed, customer information of a financial institution through fraudulent or deceptive means, such as by misrepresenting the identity of the person requesting the information or otherwise misleading an institution or customer into making unwitting disclosures of such information. In addition, it provided for a private right of action and enforcement by state attorneys general.

House Position: Similar provisions, with no private right of action or enforcement by State Attorneys General.

Conference Substitute: The Senate receded to the House with an amendment.

The amendment provided that authority for enforcing the subtitle would be placed in the FTC, the Federal banking agencies and the National Credit Union Administration (for enforcement of these provisions with respect to compliance by depository institutions within their jurisdiction).

TITLE VI [FHLB MODERNIZATION]

¶ 5020 FEDERAL HOME LOAN BANK SYSTEM MODERNIZATION

The Senate and House bills reforms the Federal Home Loan Bank ("FHLBank") System in several important ways. Mandatory FHLBank membership for Federal savings associations is eliminated, in order to provide completely voluntary membership. Small bank members are given expanded access to FHLBank advances. Governance of the FHLBanks is decentralized from the Federal Housing Finance Board ("FHFB") to the individual FHLBanks. The Resolution Funding Corporation ("REFCORP") obligation of the FHLBanks, stemming from the savings and loan crisis, is changed from a fixed dollar amount to a fixed percentage of annual net earnings. The Senate bill directs the General Accounting Office to study FHLBank capital and the House bill establishs a new capital structure for the FHLBanks. The conference committee addressed three of these major areas.

Sec. 604. Advances to members; collateral.

Senate Position: The Senate bill authorizes community financial institutions (FDIC-insured depository institutions with assets less than $500 million) to obtain long-term FHLBank advances for lending to small businesses, small farms, and small agri-businesses. Eligible collateral for community financial institutions receiving any FHLBank advances could include secured loans for small business, agriculture, or securities representing a whole interest in such loans.

House Position: The House bill authorizes community financial institutions to obtain long-term FHLBank advances for small business, agricultural, rural development, or low-income community development lending. Eligible collateral for community financial institutions receiving any FHLBank advances could include secured loans for small business, agriculture, rural development, or low-income community development, or securities representing a whole interest in such loans. Such advances-funded non-housing loans are treated as qualified thrift investments in determining required FHLBank stock purchases for community financial institutions that are not qualified thrift lenders ("QTLs").

Conference Substitute: The House receded to the Senate on the purposes and collateral for advances to community financial institutions. Greater stock purchases required of FHLBank members, that are not QTLs, when they receive advances are eliminated as is the requirement that such members only apply for advances for housing finance purposes. A priority for making advances to QTL members and a 30% limit on total advances to non-QTL members are also removed. Restrictions on obtaining new advances and having to repay advances after three years, applicable to savings associations that are not QTLs, are eliminated.

Sec. 606. Management of FHLBanks.

Senate Position: The Senate bill changed the term of elected FHLBank directors from two to four years to make the term the same as for appointed directors. It transferred from the FHFB to the individual FHLBanks authority over a number of operational areas. It also gave the FHFB the same enforcement authority over FHLBanks and their executive officers and directors as the Federal banking agencies and the Office of Federal Housing Enterprise Oversight have under their statutes.

House Position: The House bill contained the same provisions. It also empowered the FHFB to address any capital insufficiencies resulting from voluntary membership and eliminated the 20:1 advances to stock ratio limit for a FHLBank member.

Conference Substitute: The Conference set terms for both elected and appointed directors at 3 years (staggered with approximately one-third of the terms expiring each year). A FHLBank's board of directors is authorized to elect by majority vote the board's Chairperson and Vice Chairperson. The term of office for the Chairperson and Vice Chairperson is two years. The annual salaries of FHLBank directors may not exceed specified amounts plus reimbursement of expenses. The maximum amounts are: Chairperson—$25,000; Vice Chairperson—$20,000; and other directors—$15,000. FHLBank directors may reside outside the FHLBank district if they are an officer or director of a member institution located in the district. The Senate receded to the House regarding the provisions on capital insufficiencies and the advances to stock ratio limit.

Sec. 608. Capital structure of the FHLBanks.

Senate Position: The Senate bill directs the General Accounting Office to submit to Congress within one year of enactment a study on possible revisions to the FHLBanks' capital structure, including the need for more permanent capital, a statutory leverage ratio, and a risk-based capital structure. GAO would also study the impact such revisions might have on the FHLBanks' operations, including the REFCORP payment obligation.

House Position: The House bill establishes a new capital structure for the FHLBanks. The FHLBanks were authorized to issue three classes of stock: Class A (redeemable on 6-months notice), Class B (redeemable on 5-years notice), and Class C (nonredeemable). FHLBanks were required to meet a 5% leverage minimum tied to total capital and a risk- based requirement tied to permanent capital. Permanent capital included Class C stock, retained earnings, and up to 1% of a FHLBank's assets in Class B stock. Total capital included permanent capital plus Class A stock, Class B stock (other than what counted toward permanent capital), and a general allowance for losses. A FHLBank must at all times comply with both the leverage and risk-based capital requirements. In determining compliance with the 5% minimum leverage ratio, Class A stock was counted at paid-in value, Class B stock was weighted at 1.5 times paid-in value, and Class C stock and retained earnings at 2.0 times. The current capital structure of the FHLBanks must be maintained until the new capital requirements are fully implemented. Within one year of enactment, the FHFB must issue implementing regulations. The board of directors of each FHLBank must develop a capital plan, subject to FHFB approval. The FHLBanks have up to three years to carry out their plans.

Conference Substitute: The Senate receded to the House with an amendment regarding a new capital structure. Two classes of stock are authorized: Class A (redeemable on 6-months notice) and Class B (redeemable on 5-years notice). FHLBanks are required to meet a 5% leverage minimum tied to total capital and a risk-based requirement tied to permanent capital. Permanent capital includes Class B stock and retained earnings. Total capital includes permanent capital plus Class A stock, generally. In determining compliance with the 5% minimum leverage ratio, Class A stock is counted at paid-in value and Class B stock and retained earnings are weighted at 1.5 times; however, a FHLBank's total capital, determined without taking into account any multiplier, must not be less than 4% of total assets.

The weighting provision is included to encourage the FHLBanks to build more permanent, longer-term capital. Using the capital multiplier, the paid-in value of outstanding Class A stock plus 1.5 times the paid-in value of outstanding Class B stock and retained earnings must be at least 5% of total assets. Using no weighting factor, total capital must be at least 4% of total assets. For example, a FHLBank with $100 million in assets would comply with $5 million in Class A capital stock *or* $2 million in Class A capital stock and an unweighted $2 million in Class B capital stock and retained earnings (which would constitute $3 million on a weighted basis).

A FHLBank's permanent capital, used to measure its compliance with the risk-based capital requirement, consists of the amounts paid by members for Class B stock and the amount of the FHLBank's retained earnings. The amount of retained earnings that may be included in permanent capital must be determined in accordance with generally accepted accounting principles (GAAP), which precludes the use of non-GAAP regulatory accounting standards for measuring retained earnings. The amount of Class B stock that is to be included in permanent capital is the full amount paid by a member to the FHLBank for the purchase of Class B stock.

A FHLBank's total capital, used to measure its compliance with the statutory leverage ratio, consists of permanent capital, the amounts paid by members for Class A stock, any general allowance for losses (consistent with GAAP and subject to FHFB regulation), and any other amounts from sources determined by the FHFB to be available to absorb losses incurred by the FHLBank and appropriate for including as capital. Any loss reserve that is held or established against a specific asset of the FHLBank is expressly prohibited from being included in total capital, as such reserves are not capable of absorbing potential losses on other assets.

In recognition of Congressional concern regarding the Financial Management and Mission Achievement ("FMMA") rule recently proposed by the FHFB, the Chairman of the FHFB sent a letter on October 18, 1999 to the Senate and House Banking Committee Chairmen (inserted below) providing assurances that the proposal would be withdrawn, upon enactment of this legislation. It is the conference committee's understanding and expectation that the FMMA will be withdrawn and that the FHFB will take no action to promulgate proposed or final regulations limiting assets or advances beyond those currently in effect until the statutorily required FHLBank System capital rules are finalized and the statutory period for submission of capital plans by the FHLBanks has expired. If and when the FHFB develops a new FMMA, or similar rules, we expect that the FHFB will provide ample opportunity for public comment and hearings. It is the desire of the conference committee that the FHFB consult with the Banking Committees regarding both the capital regulations and any financial management and/or mission related rules prior to issuing them in proposed form.

TITLE VII—OTHER PROVISIONS

¶ 5021 SUBTITLE A—ATM FEE REFORM

Senate Position: The Senate bill at Title VII requires automated teller machine ("ATM") operators who impose a fee for use of an ATM by a noncustomer to post a notice on the machine and on the screen that a fee will be charged and the amount of the fee. This notice must be posted before the consumer is irrevocably committed to completing the transaction. A paper notice issued from the machine may be used in lieu of a posting to the screen. No surcharge may be imposed unless the notices are made and the consumer elects to proceed with the transaction. A notice is required when ATM cards are issued that surcharges may be imposed by other parties when transactions are initiated from ATMs not operated by the card issuer. ATM operators are exempt from liability if properly placed notices on the machines are subsequently removed, damaged, or altered by anyone other than the ATM operator.

House Position: Same.

Conference Substitute: The House receded to the Senate with an amendment.

The amendment grants a temporary exemption for those older machines that are unable to provide certain of the notices required.

¶ 5022 SUBTITLE B—COMMUNITY REINVESTMENT

Sec. 711. CRA sunshine requirements.

Senate Position: Section 312 of the Senate bill amends the Federal Deposit Insurance Act by creating a new Section 46, to require full disclosure of agreements entered into between insured depository institutions or their affiliates and nongovernmental entities or persons made pursuant to or in connection with the fulfillment of the CRA. The section does not confer any authority on the Federal banking agencies to enforce the provisions of these agreements.

House Position: No provision.

Conference Substitute: The House receded to the Senate, with an amendment.

As recommended by the Conferees, the provision requires full disclosure of agreements, as defined in this section, between an insured depository institution or affiliate and a nongovernmental entity or person where the agreement is made pursuant to or in connection with the CRA, involving funds or other resources of an insured depository institution or affiliate.

The provision is not intended to define as a CRA agreement an individual mortgage loan (although it could apply to agreements involving, for example, parties acting as mortgage intermediaries or facilitators), or other specific contract to an individual, business, farm, or other entity, where funds are loaned at rates not substantially below market rates and if the purpose of the loan or extension of credit does not include any re-lending of borrowed funds to other parties. In addition, the scope of the provision does not extend to an agreement entered into by an insured depository institution or affiliate with a nongovernmental entity or person who has not commented on, testified about, or discussed with the institution, or otherwise contacted the institution, concerning the CRA. This exception to the coverage could include, for example, service organizations such as civil rights groups, community groups providing housing or other services in low-income neighborhoods, the

American Legion, community theater groups, and so forth. The Federal Reserve Board may prescribe regulations to provide further exemptions consistent with the purposes of the provision.

In defining the agreements to which this provision would apply, the legislation assigns to the appropriate Federal banking agency the responsibility to identify a list of factors that the agency determines have a material impact on the agency's decision to approve or disapprove an application for a deposit facility or to assign a rating in an examination under the CRA. It is expected that the regulator will include in such list a full enumeration of the relevant factors that the agency reviews and considers in examining the performance of an insured financial institution in connection with the CRA, including any and all items a regulator would attach importance to in determining the evaluation under the act of the performance of a financial institution.

The Conferees note that while an agency may not give a great deal of weight to a mere agreement to perform certain CRA-related activities, *per se*, the agency does look carefully at the activities that the institution may have actually performed in fact pursuant to such an agreement. The disclosure and reporting requirements of this section apply to agreements defined in subsection (a) in either event.

As a general rule, the parties are required to disclose fully such agreements and make them available to the public and to the Federal banking agencies.

In addition, parties to each CRA agreement are required to report at least once each year on the use of resources provided pursuant to each agreement. A bank would file its report directly with its Federal regulator. A nongovernmental party is required to file its report with the appropriate Federal banking agency with supervisory responsibility over the insured depository institution that is a party to the agreement, either directly with the agency or via the insured depository institution, which would be required promptly to transmit the report to the Federal banking agency.

The Federal banking agencies are directed, in implementing regulations under this provision, to minimize the regulatory burden on reporting parties. One way in which to accomplish this goal would be wherever possible and appropriate with the purposes of this section, to make use of existing reporting and auditing requirements and practices of reporting parties, and thus avoid unnecessary duplication of effort. The Managers intend that, in issuing regulations under this section, the appropriate Federal supervisory agency may provide that the nongovernmental entity or person that is not an insured depository institution may, where appropriate and in keeping with the provisions of this section, fulfill the requirements of subsection (c) by the submission of its annual audited financial statement or its Federal income tax return.

Sec. 712. Small bank regulatory relief.

Senate Position: The Senate provision amended the CRA to exempt from the provisions of that Act banks and savings and loan associations with total assets less than $100 million and that are located in nonmetropolitan areas.

House Position: No provision.

Conference Substitute: The House receded to the Senate provision with an amendment.

The provision directs that "regulated financial institutions" with aggregate assets not exceeding $250 million will be subject to routine examinations under the CRA as follows: (i) not more than once every 60 months if the institution received a rating of 'outstanding record of meeting community credit needs' at its most recent examination; (ii) not more than once every 48 months if the institution received a rating of 'satisfactory record of meeting community credit needs' at its most recent examination; and (iii) as deemed necessary by the appropriate Federal banking agency if the institution received a rating of less than 'satisfactory record of meeting community credit needs' at its most recent examination. The provision also states that the Federal banking agencies may subject an institution to more frequent or less frequent examinations for reasonable cause. A regulated financial institution shall remain subject to examination under this title in connection with an application for a deposit facility.

Sec. 713 -715. Federal Reserve Board and Treasury studies, Impact on CRA.

Senate Position: No provision.

House Position: The House bill at Section 110 requires a study by the Secretary of the Treasury, in consultation with the Federal banking agencies, of the extent to which adequate services are being provided as intended by the CRA, including services in lowand moderate-income neighborhoods and for persons of modest means, as a result of the enactment of the Gramm-Leach-Bliley Act. The report must be submitted to the Congress within two years.

Conference Substitute: The Senate receded to the House with an amendment directing, in addition, that the Federal Reserve Board conduct a comprehensive study of the CRA, in consultation with the Chairman and Ranking Member of the House Banking and Financial Services Committee and the Chairman and Ranking Member of the Senate Banking, Housing, and Urban Affairs Committee. The study is to focus on default rates, delinquency rates, and the profitability of loans made in conformity with that Act. The report must be submitted to the House and Senate Banking Committees no later than March 15, 2000. The provision also directs that the report and all of the supporting data be made available at the same time to the public by the Federal Reserve Board, to the extent that the data are not confidential.

The Conferees recommended further amending the House study with an amendment permitting the Secretary of the Treasury to submit to the Congress by March 15, 2000, a baseline report in addition to the final report as required in the House provision. The purpose of the baseline report is to give a set of data against which the Secretary will be able to measure change by the end of the two-year reporting period.

The Conferees also recommended an amendment to the House language to state that nothing in the Gramm-Leach-Bliley Act shall be construed to repeal any provision of the CRA.

¶ 5023 SUBTITLE C—OTHER REGULATORY IMPROVEMENTS

Sec. 721. Expanded small bank access to S corporation treatment.

Senate Position: The Senate bill at section 302 requires the GAO to study and report to Congress within six months of the date of enactment on certain revisions to S corporation rules permitting greater access by community banks to S corporation treatment.

House Position: No provision.

Conference Substitute: The House receded to the Senate.

Sec. 722. "Plain Language" requirement for Federal banking agency rules.

Senate Position: The Senate bill at section 306 directs the Federal banking agencies to use plain language in all proposed and final rule-makings published by the agency in the Federal Register after January 1, 2000, and to report to Congress by no later than March 1, 2001 on how they have complied with the plain language requirement.

House Position: No provision.

Conference Substitute: The House receded to the Senate.

Sec. 723. Retention of "Federal " in name of converted Federal savings associations.

Senate Position: The Senate bill at section 307 would permit Federal savings associations that convert to national or state bank charters to keep the word "Federal" in their names.

House Position: Same.

Conference Substitute: The Senate receded to the House.

Sec. 724. Control of Bankers Banks.

Senate Position: The Senate bill at section 310 allows one or more thrift institutions to own a state-chartered bank or trust company, whose business is restricted to accepting deposits from thrift institutions or savings banks, deposits arising from the corporate business of the thrift institutions or savings banks that own the bank or trust company, or deposits of public funds.

House Position: No provision.

Conference Substitute: The House receded to the Senate.

Sec. 725. Provision of technical assistance to microenterprises.

Senate Position: The Senate bill at section 316 establishes a grant program to fund nonprofit microenterprise development organizations, programs, collaboratives, or intermediaries engaged in (1) providing training and technical assistance to low-income and disadvantaged entrepreneurs interested in starting or expanding their own businesses; (2) building the capacity of organizations that serve low-income and disadvantaged entrepreneurs; and (3) supporting research and development aimed at identifying and promoting training and technical assistance programs that effectively serve low-income and disadvantaged entrepreneurs.

House Position: No provision.

Conference Substitute: The House receded to the Senate with an amendment.

While the Senate bill made the new microenterprise program a part of the Treasury Department's Community Development Financial Institutions program, the Conferees chose to have the new program administered by the Small Business Administration.

Sec. 726. Federal Reserve audits.

Senate Position: The Senate bill at section 317 requires annual outside independent accounting firm audits of the Federal Reserve Banks and the Federal Reserve Board. In addition, the bill changes the definitions and rules that apply to the pricing of Federal Reserve System services under the Monetary Control Act.

House Position: No provision.

Conference Substitute: The House receded to the Senate with an amendment in the nature of a substitute. The substitute provision requires the Federal Reserve Board to order an annual independent audit of the financial statements of each Federal Reserve Bank and of the Board.

Sec. 727. Authorization to release reports.

Senate Position: No provision.

House Position: The House bill at section 132 permits the Federal Reserve Board, at its discretion, to furnish exam reports and other confidential supervisory information concerning State member banks or other entities it examines to any Federal or State authorities with supervisory authority over an examined entity, to officers, directors, or receivers of the entity, or any other person that the Federal Reserve Board determines is proper. In addition, the House bill includes the Commodity Futures Trading Commission under definitions in the Right to Financial Privacy Act.

Conference Substitute: The Senate receded to the House with an amendment.

The amendment adds to the provision allowing the disclosure of reports and information by applying certain confidentiality requirements and procedures for disclosure.

Sec. 728. General Accounting Office study of conflicts of interest.

Senate Position: No provision.

House Position: The House bill at section 193 requires the Comptroller General of the GAO to study the conflict of interest faced by the Federal Reserve Board between its role as a primary regulator of the banking industry and its role as a vendor of services. Specifically, the GAO should address the conflict between the Board's role as a regulator of the payment system and its role as a competitor with private sector providers of payment services, and how best to resolve that conflict. The study is due one year after enactment of the legislation.

Conference Substitute: The Senate receded to the House.

Sec. 729. Study and report on adapting existing legislative requirements to online banking and lending.

Senate Position: No provision.

House Position: The House bill at section 195 requires the Federal banking agencies to conduct a study of banking regulations regarding the delivery of financial services, including those regulations that may assume that there will be face-to-face contact, and report their recommendations on adapting those existing requirements to online banking and lending. The report, with any recommended legislative or regulatory action, is due one year after the date of enactment of the legislation.

Conference Substitute: The Senate receded to the House with an amendment changing the due date of the study to two years after date of enactment.

Sec. 730. Clarification of source of strength doctrine.

Senate Position: No provision.

House Position: The House bill at section 197 enhances the source of strength doctrine by, in certain circumstances, protecting the Federal banking agencies and the deposit insurance funds from claims brought by the bankruptcy trustee of a depository institution holding company or other person for the return of capital infusions.

Conference Substitute: The Senate receded to the House with an amendment in the nature of a substitute.

The substitute narrows and clarifies the circumstances under which a Federal banking agency would be protected from a claim. First, it clarifies that the transferred assets must be those of an affiliate or a controlling shareholder of an insured depository institution. The House amendment did not so specify. Second, section 730 provides that the transfer must be to or for the benefit of an insured depository institution and that it must be made by an affiliate or controlling shareholder of such insured depository institution. The House amendment did not include such clarifying language. Third, section 730 specifies that no person may bring a claim against a Federal banking agency for monetary damages, return of assets, or for other legal or equitable relief in connection with such transfer, consistent with certain limitations. The House amendment only referred to claims for monetary damages or for the return of assets or other property. Fourth, section 730 adds a definition of the term "claim." For purposes of this provision, a claim is defined as a cause of action based on Federal or State law providing for the avoidance of preferential or fraudulent transfers or conveyances, or providing for similar remedies. The definition, however, explicitly excepts any claim based on actual intent to hinder, delay or defraud pursuant to such fraudulent transfer or conveyance law.

This section does not limit the right of a depository institution, a controlling stockholder, or a depository institution holding company to seek direct review of an order or directive of a Federal banking agency under the Administrative Procedure Act in accordance with various banking statutes. In addition, the provision does not limit the rights of a claimant to bring suit against the United States for a breach of contract or a taking under the 5th Amendment to the Constitution.

Sec. 731. Interest rates and other charges at interstate branches.

Senate Position: No provision.

House Position: The House bill at section 198 provides loan pricing parity among interstate banks. Specifically, if an interstate bank can charge a particular interest rate, then a local bank in the State into which the interstate bank has branched, may charge a comparable rate.

Conference Substitute: The Senate receded to the House.

Sec. 732. Interstate branches and agencies of foreign banks.

Senate Position: The Senate bill at section 313 allows a Federal or State agency of a foreign bank to upgrade to a branch with the approval of the appropriate chartering authority and the Federal Reserve Board.

House Position: Same.

Conference Substitute: The House receded to the Senate.

Sec. 733. Fair treatment of women by financial advisers.

Senate Position: No provision.

House Position: The House bill at section 198B establishes the sense of the Congress that estate planners, trust officers, investment advisers, and other financial planners and advisors should eliminate examples in their training materials which portray women as incapable and foolish, and develop fairer and more balanced presentations that eliminate outmoded and stereotypical examples which lead clients to take actions that are financially detrimental to their wives and daughters.

Conference Substitute: The Senate receded to the House with an amendment in the nature of a substitute.

The substitute establishes the sense of the Congress that individuals offering financial advice and products should do so in a nondiscriminatory, nongender-specific manner.

Sec. 734. Membership of loan guarantee boards.

Senate Position: No provision.

House Position: No provision.

Conference Substitute: The Conferees adopted a provision that would modify the membership of the Emergency Steel Loan Guarantee Board and the Emergency Oil and Gas Loan Guarantee Board. Where under existing law the Chairmen of the Federal Reserve Board and SEC were designated as members, the provision permits both to designate another Member of the Board or another Commissioner as appropriate.

Sec. 735. Repeal of stock loan limit in Federal Reserve Act.

Senate Position: No provision.

House Position: The House bill at section 124 repeals the restrictions in section 11(m) of the Federal Reserve Act on loans by Federal Reserve member banks secured by stock or bond collateral. Limitations on loans to one borrower imposed pursuant to other statutory authority are not affected.

Conference Substitute: The Senate receded to the House.

Sec. 736. Elimination of SAIF and DIF Special Reserves.

Senate Position: The Senate bill at section 301 eliminates the need for the establishment of a SAIF "special reserve" which the FDIC was required to establish beginning in 1999. This revision becomes effective on the date of enactment.

House Position: Same other than the effective date.

Conference Substitute: The House receded to the Senate.

Sec. 737. Bank officers and directors as officers and directors of public utilities.

Senate Position: The Senate bill at section 309 amends the Federal Power Act to permit officers or directors of public utilities to serve as officers or directors of banks, trust companies, or securities firms, if certain safeguards against conflicts of interest are complied with.

House Position: No provision.

Conference Substitute: The House receded to the Senate.

Sec. 738. Approval for purchases of securities.

Senate Position: The Senate bill at section 315 authorizes a majority of the entire board of directors of a bank to vote on the purchase of securities from an affiliate, based on a determination that the purchase is a sound investment for the bank. Such a standard does not exist under current law, which simply requires the vote to be taken by a majority of independent directors.

House Position: No provision.

Conference Substitute: The House receded to the Senate.

Sec. 739. Optional conversion of Federal savings associations.

Senate Position: The Senate bill at section 602 allows a Federal savings association chartered prior to the date of enactment to convert into one or more national banks, subject to the approval of the OCC, each of which may encompass one or more of the branches of the Federal savings association in one or more States.

House Position: No provision.

Conference Substitute: The House recedes to the Senate with an amendment.

The amendment would allow the conversion to State as well as national banks.

Sec. 740. Grand jury proceedings.

Senate Position: No provision.

House Position: No provision.

Conference Substitute: The Conferees adopted a provision that would permit U.S. Attorneys offices to seek a court order to provide financial institution regulatory agencies with access to grand jury material, giving State regulatory agencies parity with Federal regulatory agencies.

TOPICAL INDEX

References are to paragraph numbers.